RACE, CLASS, AND POWER IN SCHOOL RESTRUCTURING

SUNY Series, Restructuring and School Change

H. Dickson Corbett and Betty Lou Whitford, Editors

RACE, CLASS, AND POWER IN SCHOOL RESTRUCTURING

※

PAULINE LIPMAN

FOREWORD BY GLORIA LADSON-BILLINGS

STATE UNIVERSITY OF NEW YORK PRESS

Published by
State University of New York Press, Albany

For information, address the State University of New York Press,
90 State Street, Suite 700, Albany, NY 12207

Production by M. R. Mulholland
Marketing by Patrick Durocher

Library of Congress Cataloging-in-Publication Data

Lipman, Pauline, 1944–
     Race, class, and power in school restructuring / Pauline Lipman ;
  foreword by Gloria Ladson-Billings.
        p.   cm. — (SUNY series, restructuring and school change)
     Includes bibliographical references and index.
     ISBN 0-7914-3769-8 (hardcover : alk. paper). — ISBN 0-7914-3770-1
  (pbk. : alk. paper)
     1. School management and organization—Social aspects—United
  States—Case studies.   2. Afro-Americans—Education—Case studies.
  3. Educational change—United States—Case studies.   I. Title.
  II. Series.
  LB2806.L54   1998
  371.2'00973—DC21   97-26328
                                                                              CIP

10 9 8 7 6 5 4 3

To Rico, Jesse, Sandi, Cristina, and Malaya
and to the children of Riverton

❖

CONTENTS

FOREWORD

Restructuring became the buzzword of the late 1980s and 1990s. Corporate America used it interchangeably with terms such as "quality reinvestment," "downsizing," and "outsourcing." Restructuring became another way to reduce the workforce in an effort to become "lean and mean" in competitive global markets. However, when restructuring became a part of the educational reform discourse, it came to signify a variety of organizational and structural changes not necessarily tied to reducing personnel. More typically, school restructuring involves redesigning and streamlining curriculum, untracking courses, developing what are seen as authentic assessment methods, and localizing and delegating administrative responsibilities (or site-based management).

Restructuring offered great promise for schools that are failing. Instead of focusing on the micro-analytic environment of the classroom, restructuring pointed educators toward the importance of systemic change (Smith & O'Day, 1991). By understanding the way the entire school (or system) works, administrators, teachers, students, parents, and community members believe that changes can be implemented that ensure improvement for the entire school.

One of the elements of systemic reform is the development of a schoolwide professional community. Louis, Marks, and Kruse (1996) suggest that when schools attempt to develop professional communities they move toward five elements of practice: shared values, focus on student learning, collaboration, deprivatized practice, and reflective dialogue. Further, Kruse and Louis (1993) identify two interrelated factors necessary to support the creation of strong professional communities—structural conditions and human and social resources. In this Foreword I focus on the elements of practice.

However, what has been missing from the restructuring discourse is a careful and critical look at the ways teachers' beliefs and status are either incorporated in the restructuring activity or dismissed and marginalized from it. In *Race, Class, and Power in School Restructuring* Pauline Lipman addresses these very issues. By grappling with the complex issue of race—that of both the teachers and the students— Lipman forces the reader to reconsider the ways conventional

approaches to school reform and restructuring may reinforce and reproduce patterns of school failure for African American students. If
we examine the Louis, Marks, and Kruse elements of schoolwide professional community, we can see how Lipman's powerful questions
challenge a notion of seamless transition from school failure to school
success.

Shared norms and values are fundamental to any sense of community. About what does the community care? In what direction is the
community headed? What are the underlying assumptions about teaching and the learners? These are important questions to be addressed.
But what if members of the community are not in an equal status
relationship? Are certain teachers more respected and influential or,
more pointedly, are certain teachers routinely ignored and dismissed?
What if African American teachers are a numerical minority on a faculty and express a different set of norms and values about the educability of African American students? For example, if most of the teachers
believe there is some value to creating "honors" or "gifted" classes
while African American teachers see these classes as contributing to
the disparity between White and Black students, the community clearly
is not engaged in shared norms and values. However, if Black teachers
constitute a small fraction of the faculty, their dissent can very easily
be overlooked and minimized. The faculty may believe and act as if
they have consensus. They may assert that there are shared norms and
values, but the missing voices of the African American teachers belie
that assertion.

Collective focus on student learning seems like an obvious element of schooling. However, many of the reports that identified the
need to reform the nation's public schools suggested that much of the
instructional day was eaten up by noninstructional tasks such as discipline, organization, and management. Seemingly, teachers would
welcome the opportunity to focus on that for which they were prepared, but once again, we can see how this focus might be racially
differentiated. Far too often, teachers demonstrate a belief that it is
more important to control and manage African American learners
(particularly males) rather than teach them.

Research (see Irvine, 1990) indicates that African American male
students are much more likely to be suspended and expelled from
school than their White counterparts. And those suspensions often are
for what Majors and Billson (1992) term noncontact violations, that is,
wearing a hat in the school building, wearing other banned clothing,
or saying the "wrong" thing. In 1996, one school district located outside a major urban center declared female students would be sus-

pended for wearing their hair in braids, waves, or a French roll—styles popular primarily among African American girls. Where is the focus on learning in these situations?

Collaboration is another feature of professional communities. This requires that members of the community share expertise and clarify expectations and practices. But if teachers, because of their differential status, are unequally valued in the community, what opportunities are available for collaboration? Also, consider some of the demographics concerning teaching. First off, the percentage of African American teachers is about 5% (down from about 8% in the early 1980s), thus, there are fewer African American teachers available to participate in collaboration with other teachers. Secondly, the distribution of African American teachers across subject areas is uneven. In many of the high-status subject areas (mathematics, science, technology) African American teachers are poorly represented. How, then, do they enter into collaborations about improving mathematics and science teaching and learning? While the literature focuses on the way collaboration occurs within the school, much of the work of an organization can occur outside of the organization. Teachers who socialize beyond the school have opportunities to build professional friendships and share ideas for improvement. How and whether African American teachers gain access to these collaborative relationships is not clear. Foster (1996) documents clearly the isolation and estrangement of Black teachers.

Deprivatized practice refers to a movement away from the typical closed classroom door toward an open and public demonstration of expertise. This requires a high level of confidence and safety. The role of teacher as workers has contributed to an atmosphere where teachers must protect themselves from public scrutiny. Administrators participate in contractually agreed upon observations and evaluations. These bifurcated roles—teacher and administrator—often are adversarial and members of neither group are willing to perform the role of the other. However, restructuring efforts have supported opportunities for teachers to demonstrate their practice and witness that of others. This openness must take place in an environment where teachers are assured that their teaching practices will not be used to evaluate them negatively. But, more specifically, in the case of successful teachers of African American students (and also among many African American teachers), what counts as good practice may be in dispute.

Recent efforts toward teacher assessment have indicated that few teachers of color have been judged to be exemplary teachers (National Commission on Teaching & America's Future, 1996). As a part of its attempt to understand this phenomenon, the National Board for Professional Teaching Standards (NBPTS) has created an adverse impact panel to examine the test protocol, trainers, training, and scorers. How could it be that so few African American (or Latino) teachers have passed the NBPTS assessment? To be sure, relatively few teachers have even presented their credentials for board certification. However, the proportion of African American teachers who have passed the assessment is far below that of White teachers. Is the problem the practice of African American teachers or might it be the differential criteria used to determine what counts as good practice.

In work with successful teachers of African American children (Ladson-Billings, 1994) I learned that such teachers employ a variety of strategies, both conventional and unorthodox, to ensure the academic success of their students. A trip to an assessment center could easily dismiss most of the teachers in the study because the complexity of teaching cannot be captured merely by demonstration. Why teachers do what they do must be unearthed and understood in context. One of the teachers used a basal text and phonics approach to the teaching of reading. Another employed the more current practice termed, "whole-language" or "literature-based" reading instruction. Videotapes of both teachers viewed in an assessment center would likely endorse the latter. However, over the course of the semester students in both teachers' classrooms became confident, fluent readers, even those students who previously had been designated as "poor readers" or "nonreaders."

In this book, Pauline Lipman examines the ways that teachers' ideologies or belief systems about African American students interfere with the goals and aims of school restructuring. Thus, like putting new wine in old wine skins, teachers who do not believe in the educability of African American students are unlikely to be persuaded otherwise by a change in scheduling, detracking, or other school-based changes.

Professional communities also are characterized by reflective dialogue. Teachers must be able to "engage in in-depth conversations about teaching and learning" (Louis, Marks, & Kruse, 1996, p. 761). Restructuring certainly can support the conditions that make reflective dialogue possible. Schedules can be organized to allow teachers to meet and talk about the substantive issues of "academic, curricular, and instructional concerns of schooling as well as [about] issues of student development and progress" (ibid.). But, as I asked earlier, how do teachers whose opinions, perspectives, and practices are either undervalued or not valued gain access to the reflective dialogue?

Consider this. In many urban schools there exist a few adults who are noted for their ability "to handle" African American students with whom other adults have been unsuccessful. These adults may or may not be classroom teachers. Sometimes they are administrators or counselors, but increasingly they are instructional aides and other paraprofessionals with a minimum of formal preparation for teaching. However, despite their apparent success with those students thought to be unsalvageable, their ideas, opinions, strategies, or techniques are not incorporated into the classroom practices of others. Rather, they become the "outlet" or "holding cell" for "problem students." Interestingly, in some settings a paraprofessional is hired solely to discipline "difficult" (read, African American) students, and faculty become upset when this one, minimum-wage, usually untrained individual does not prove to be the solution to all of their concerns. I remember working with a group of teachers in a school where there was a growing concern about the escalating discipline problems among African American students, particularly males. Although we talked at length about some of the things teachers might try to handle these issues in the classroom, one teacher finally said with an exasperated voice, "Well, after all we hired 'Mr. So and So' as an educational assistant, why isn't he taking care of this?" The teacher only valued the educational assistant for what he could do to alleviate her problems. He was not a part of the "reflective dialogue" for improving teaching and learning in the school.

This volume takes a hard look at the rush to restructure. It moves us inside the experiences of teachers and students in restructured schools. Lipman's description of Riverton as a city in the forefront of the state's restructuring effort helps us to see that even when there is wide support for change, without confronting the underlying beliefs of teachers about the educability of particular groups of students, that change is likely to be subverted.

Lipman develops a rich portrait of each school that underscores the specificity of school reform at each site. At one school, Gates, the White, upper-middle-class parents continue to wield an inordinate amount of power that impacts student placement and course offerings. At the other, Franklin, an entrenched attitude toward African American students (and their culture) as deficient made it virtually impossible for externally generated changes to create real change in the academic lives of its students. However, the particularities of the school sites do not take away from the possibilities for broader theorizing about the ways that cultural, political, and structural factors influence restructuring efforts.

Finally, this book ends with a description of exemplary teachers, a subject about which I know a little bit. In the midst of situations where schools fail to educate African American students, there are some teachers who succeed in spite of the structure (or restructure). Lipman shares well-drawn portraits of three teachers—Paulette, Samuel, and Helen—who exist on the fringes of their middle schools, but are central to the educational lives of the students. This chapter reminds us of what we are quick to forget in the push toward systemic change. At the heart of the educative process there still remains the teacher.

The centrality of the teacher does not mean that we can dismiss the importance of systemic change. In the best of all worlds we want high-quality teachers working in well-organized, well-administered schools. Unfortunately, we do not live in the best of all worlds. Systemic change and pedagogical improvement do not always go hand in hand in public education. In our eagerness to "fix" the whole system, we often overlook the most obvious. In this case, the most obvious is the teacher who stands before the students in a classroom. His or her responsibility remains the same regardless of the changes in scheduling, grouping, or curriculum. This book challenges us to see both the forest and the trees—to care about superstructure, infrastructure, and core. It is destined to help us think differently about a word we have taken for granted—restructuring.

—*Gloria Ladson-Billings*

References

Jordan, J. J. (1990). *Black students and school failure.* Westport, CT: Greenwood Press.

Kruse, S. & Louis, K. S. (1994, April). *Teaching teaming in middle schools: Dilemmas for school-wide community.* Paper presented at the annual meeting of the American Educational Research Association, San Francisco.

Ladson-Billings, G. (1994). *The Dreamkeepers: Successful teachers of African American children.* San Francisco: Jossey-Bass.

Louis, K. S., Marks, H., & Kruse, S. (1996). Teachers' community in restructuring schools. *American Educational Research Journal, 33,* 757–798.

Majors R. & Billson, J. (1992). *Cool pose: The dilemmas of black manhood in America.* New York: Lexington Books.

National Commission on Teaching & America's future (1996). *What matters most: Teaching for America's Future*. Report. New York: Teachers' College, Columbia University.

Smith, M. & O'Day, J. (1991). Systemic school reform. In S. Furhman & B. Mahlen (Eds.), *The politics of curriculum and testing* (pp. 233–267). New York: Falmer.

ACKNOWLEDGMENTS

Protecting the anonymity of the people and places in this book prevents me from naming the many educators, students, and community members in Riverton who generously spent many hours talking with me, sharing their perspectives, and allowing me to sit in on their lives in school. I want to thank them all for their help and patience and all I learned. I also owe a debt of gratitude to my collaborators, the Riverton field researchers, particularly for the insights they provided into their community and schools.

Many people read and provided invaluable critiques of various parts and versions of this book. Mike Olneck, Mary Metz, and Gloria Ladson-Billings spent many hours meticulously reading drafts of the initial manuscript. Their thorough and penetrating critiques helped me think more carefully about my data and analysis and its theoretical implications. I deeply appreciate their intellectual support, encouragement, and our ongoing friendship. Dick Corbett, Sandra Jackson, Stacy Lee, Donna Muncey, Barabara Sizemore, Gary Wehlage, and Belinda Williams read and provided helpful comments on various versions and parts of the book. Gloria Ladson-Billings has done me an honor by writing the Foreword. Her work and her example as a scholar-activist are a source of inspiration to me and a model to strive for.

I thank Gary Wehlage and Fred Newmann for the opportunity to be part of the Wisconsin Center for Educational Research and for the material support to carry out my research. I owe Gary Wehlage special appreciation for his confidence in my capacity to lead the research for the evaluation study in Riverton and for his spirit of collaboration. A generous dissertation fellowship from the Graduate School of the University of Wisconsin-Madison provided support to write the intitial manuscript. From our first discussions about publication, Dick Corbett has offered me the encouragement and unqualified backing to make the book a reality. Andrea Kaminsky helped me reduce a six-hundred page manuscript to something reasonable. Priscilla Ross at SUNY Press has been extremely helpful throughout, providing the guidance, encouragement, and flexibility I have needed to see this project through to completion. I also want to thank Barbara Sizemore, my dean at

De Paul University, who has respected and defended my work every step of the way, even when we have disagreed.

Most of all, Eric Gutstein (Rico) has been my chief reader, editor, friend, colleague, comrade, and my partner. I simply could not have written this book without his unselfish support on every single front, not least of which was his meticulous reading and thoughtful critique of all the chapters, many times. This book has benefited immeasurably from his intellect and perspective. He relentlessly pointed out my "fuzzy thinking" and pushed me to write more clearly, to work for political clarity, to believe in myself, to have a sense of humor, and to finish. Of course, in the end, all the shortcomings of the book are my own. I also was sustained by my daughter, Sandi, whose interest in my work, love, playfulness, sharp thinking, and willingness to put off everything until "the book" was done made this project possible.

Finally, I need to speak about the people who inspire me through their lives of social justice and whose shoulders I stand on: my father, Hymn Melcher, a Jew who taught me to hate injustice; Sandi Smith, Jim Waller, Mike Nathan, Cesar Cauce, and Bill Sampson who gave their lives in the struggle for racial justice and economic and social transformation; Signe Waller, Marty Nathan, Joyce Johnson, Nelson Johnson, Dale Sampson, Floris Cauce, Paul Bermanzohn and the rest of the Greensboro Justice Fund who refuse to let up against racial and economic injustice; and my family—Eric (Rico), Sandi, Jesse, and Cristina who live their lives with determination to make a humane world for all of us. Thank you.

1

Introduction

The reason that kids fail is that there is not a lot of home support. Education is not important.

—Teacher, Franklin Junior High School

They [teachers] only see the Black kids as "deprived." They don't see kids' strengths . . . Teachers need to understand Black kids better. . . . These are issues we would be dealing with if we were serious about [racial] disparities. We deal so much with discipline that we don't get on with the real restructuring. We need time in the team for the larger issues but we don't think about our strengths. If you look at the agenda it's always about so and so student. Each teacher is doing their own thing. They've just taken the path of least resistance and each one is just going back to his or her own style or philosophy

—Teacher, Gates Junior High School

They [teachers] spent a lot of time training, worked night and day to put the program together. They did everything but tap dance. We've done our level best. Teachers gave up their time during the summer, but as soon as we go out on a limb, they [the school district] cut it off. It's racial. That's what the whole thing is about. They try to cover it over by talking about the quality of the program but the real issue is heterogeneous grouping. It's going to take generations, lifetimes, for things to change.

—Administrator, Franklin Junior High School

Some [upper-middle-class White] parents think that when their kids get to junior high school they will be able to say that they are supporters of the public schools, and they'll put their children into the public schools, but that their kids can be isolated and tracked. The real bottom line is that they don't want their kids going to school with Black kids. That's what we're fighting. . . . They try to discredit and destroy what you're trying to do. The problem in this community is that it's a very difficult context in which to make reforms. No matter what, you always have to deal with this opposition and they try to wear you down.

—District administrator, Riverton Public Schools

The issues and contradictions resonating here are ones I heard and saw played out over 3 years as I followed the progress of school restructuring in one city and its implications for African American students. Race, social class, and power. Isolation and division as well as collaboration. Cultural models of African American students as deprived and deficient counterposed against appreciation of strength and possibility. These were the themes echoing in voices of teachers and administrators, manifest in decisions on educational practice and policy, and salient in the responses of various members of the community. They reflect a web of cultural and political contradictions in the schools and in the broader contexts in which schools are embedded.

The Education of African American Students and School Restructuring

In this book I examine how these contradictions shaped educational change. On one level, the book is a story about two schools in a medium-sized Southern city with a limited vision of school restructuring. On another, it is a story with broader implications because life in U.S. schools generally is shot through with these same issues of power rooted in race, class, gender, and ethnicity, in teachers' ideologies and school culture, and in broader social structures. It is the specific questions this book takes up that make it relevant in the current educational and social context. At the heart of the book is the intersection of two central issues in American education today: the failure of schools to educate students of color and school restructuring.

The overwhelming failure of schools to develop the talents and potential of students of color is a national crisis. The character and depth of this crisis are only dimly depicted by low achievement scores and high rates of school failure and dropping-out. More profoundly, these outcomes are indicators of deeply alienating and unjust educational experiences. These experiences, in turn, point to a wider set of oppressive social and economic conditions, cultural marginality, racism, and disempowerment that is daily reality for millions of children of color in the United States today.

At the same time, the demands of a postindustrial age, the explosion of knowledge in all fields, and a flourishing of curricula aimed at higher forms of literacy are creating a mandate from inside and outside the educational establishment for sweeping educational change. Proponents from a wide range of social positions argue that even students who are successful on conventional measures of achievement are failing to develop the skills and dispositions needed for the 21st century. Since the early 1980s, much of the impetus for education re-forms has come from corporate interests that have tied the global decline in U.S. business competitiveness to a decline in academic "ex-cellence" (Business Higher Education Forum, 1983; National Commis-sion on Excellence in Education, 1983). But educational researchers and advocacy groups have also argued that serious inequalities in educational experiences and outcomes (Firestone & Rosenblum, 1988; Quality Education for Minorities Project, 1990) and the failure of schools to produce "thoughtful" students (Sizer, 1984) demand fundamental changes in the content and structure of schooling. Moreover, the chang-ing demographics of the school-age population (and demands of marginalized groups) have pushed educators and concerned policy-makers, to reshape schools in ways that are more responsive to racial, ethnic, cultural, and linguistic diversity.

The compelling idea that schools must be fundamentally re-structured has given birth to countless local and national efforts. As changes in organization, governance, the role of teachers, curricu-lum, instruction, and assessment have begun to unfold, the central question is: Will they make a qualitative difference in students' edu-cational experiences? In particular, in this book I ask, will these changes make a difference in the education of those children whom schools are most failing—especially low-income working-class chil-dren of color?[1] Will reforms challenge educational inequalities and move beyond narrow definitions of individual achievement toward preparing children for participation in democratic public life? Un-derlying these questions is a broader vision of education that works against inequality, honors multiple perspectives—particularly the knowledge and experiences of marginalized groups, and helps stu-dents become active participants in shaping a more just and demo-cratic future for themselves and society as a whole. It is this vision that motivated me to write this book.

The book challenges common assumptions about the potential for organizational change and teacher empowerment to engender change in educational practice and policy. In particular, it questions the relationship between these reforms and change in the stance edu-cators take toward educational experiences of African American stu-dents. The book brings to the foreground the relationship between school restructuring and the constellation of social forces that shape its direction—teachers' ideologies; the culture of the school; how reforms are framed; and the historical and present socioeconomic context, particularly structural inequalities and relations of power in schools, school districts, communities, and the broader society.

I take up these issues through a case study of two urban, junior high schools, which I call Gates and Franklin, located in a Southern city I call Riverton. (All proper names and places throughout the book are pseudonyms.) I describe and compare the process of educational change in these two schools. My interest is in the relationship of the changes in school organization, teacher collaboration, and teacher-led initiatives brought about by restructuring and the intellectual and social experiences of students. In particular, I focus on the role restructuring played in teachers' beliefs about and practices with African American students who, as a group, were intellectually, culturally, and politically marginalized and who were in greatest danger of school failure, alienation, and dropping out.

This study encompassed a short span in the life of an educational reform. Both schools were in the beginning stages of restructuring during the period of my research, and the book is limited to educators' ideologies and practices as I understood them in this initial phase. Because it was premature to analyze the effect on students, I concentrated on the impact on educators. Nevertheless, by tracking the evolution of educators' practices and beliefs, as well as changes in school policy, I infer consequences for students. On the basis of studies of race, class, and education, I go on to surmise what some of the implications of these consequences might be for low-income working-class African American students.

The educators in this study brought to their daily work with students and with each other their social identities and complex ideologies and their normalized ways of viewing students who were often very different from themselves. I describe ways in which teachers' and administrators' educational and social beliefs and commonsense understandings, their racial and class identities, and their relative positions of power within the school influenced their attitudes toward students, their educational practice, and their response to reforms. I was especially interested in studying dialogue and collaboration among teachers of different backgrounds and perspectives. More broadly, I examined the ways in which teachers' and administrators' actions were mediated by the cultural, social, economic, and political contexts within which they operated. In Riverton, parents, community members, and teachers viewed restructuring through the long lens of historical struggles over race and class, and the dynamics of reform were played out within present-day relations of power and privilege.

Race and class interests were so intertwined in Riverton that it was difficult to separate them and to say which had a greater impact on the schools and the events I describe in this study. The influence of upper-middle-class White parents surely accrued from their social class positions as a local ruling elite of corporate lawyers and businesspeople with connections to city and state political leaders. They not only secured privileged positions for their children within Riverton's public schools but were perhaps the dominant force on the school board. Maintaining political stabilty was certainly in their class interest, and representatives of this group were quite explicit about the need to improve the quality of the schools to attract investment to the city. Yet, the salience of race and the dominance of White interests was also clear. Prominent influential parents and local elites belonged to the all-White country club and all-white social clubs, and some African American students from professional families experienced what they described to me as racist treatment, particularly in unfair discipline actions. Riverton was a city seared by legendary resistance to desegregation. Race—racial divisions, power, and privilege—was the leitmotif that seemed to run through both the talk and the silences of nearly everyone I encountered over 3 years in Riverton. How race and class relations and the schools' and community's cultural norms affected the actions of educators and the potential of educational change became a central issue.

Although this book is a critique, it also illustrates the possibility of transforming schools. In the Riverton context, there were teachers who embodied in their educational philosophy and practice and their beliefs about African American students the seeds of a more culturally responsive and enabling educational experience. This book is about them also—their role in school change and the consequences of their role for a dialogue about the purposes of restructuring. It is part of my argument that educators, such as these teachers, represent potentially transformational leadership for school change.

My overarching concern is how educational reform may prompt educators to transform beliefs, practices, and policies in ways that nurture, intellectually challenge, and promote the agency of all students, but especially those whom schooling, as it is presently constituted, has most failed. Hopefully, what I have learned through this case study can inform projects that will lead toward more transformational change elsewhere. Finally, by examining restructuring in a specific social context, which is embedded in wider national contexts, I wish to focus attention on the necessary connection between educational and social change.

Education Reform and Social Transformation

There may be little teachers can do to alleviate the social and personal crises many children face. The litany of problems—unemployment, growing impoverishment, lack of adequate health care and housing, violence—is familiar. These are symptoms of profound economic and social dislocations which require far-reaching economic and social transformation. Schools alone cannot ameliorate these conditions. In fact, contrary to the rhetoric of influential national reports of the 1980s that blamed schools for the nation's economic difficulties (Business Higher Education Forum, 1983; National Commission on Excellence in Education, 1983), the current state of American education is itself in many ways the product of economic and political policies and actions of U.S. monopoly capitalism. The political and economic system—not the schools—should be held accountable for the current economic and social crisis.

However, schools are not neutral. Critical studies in the sociology of education (Apple, 1995; Giroux, 1983) hold that schools are "contested terrains," crucial arenas in which the struggle over ideas, values, and power in society are acted out. In the politics of everyday life in schools, in the ideology and practice of curriculum and social interaction, dominant social relations are both reproduced and contested, influencing curricular and policy decisions and institutional norms and values (Apple & Weis, 1983). For example, schools are key institutions in which the knowledge of those who hold economic and social power is transmitted and legitimated (Apple, 1979). And the knowledge and dispositions, or cultural capital (Bourdieu, 1977), of dominant groups is rewarded while that of subordinated groups is negated (Keddie, 1971). Through differential distribution of knowledge and skills, schools socialize and sort students for unequal positions within the social division of labor, thus helping to reproduce social inequality (Oakes, 1985). And schools legitimate inequality along lines of class, race, ethnicity, and gender. But in the sense students and teachers make of what goes on in schools, they may resist and disrupt these processes (Apple, 1995). There is always a struggle. Teachers and students may acknowledge diverse lives, histories, cultures, and multiple sources of knowledge and redefine curriculum to bring the experiences of women and marginalized racial and ethnic groups to the center (McCarthy, 1993). Teachers may quite consciously support education as transformative social practice by helping students critically examine dominant culture and power relations and by taking a critical stance toward knowledge (Freire, 1993; McLaren, 1989). Thus, the contest over what knowledge is legitimate and how student identities are constructed, as well as which groups of students have access to what knowledge, is central to what goes on in schools.

Schools are also neither neutral nor passive in the face of social crises affecting youth from marginalized communities. Through miseducation and institutionalized failure, schools contribute to students' alienation, dropping out of school, and lack of a sense of power to act on the world (Fine, 1991), thus reproducing social inequality and disempowerment. Alternatively, schools can be centers of democracy and community coherence, building students' intellectual and cultural resources for social change in partnership with parents (Giroux, 1988; Gutstein, Lipman, & Hernandez, 1997; MacLeod, 1991). Education can be a tool to strengthen the efficacy of persons of color on behalf of their communities (King & Wilson, 1990, Ladson-Billings & Henry, 1990). In this light, educational reforms that benefit working-class students and students of color and that promote their sense of personal and social efficacy may also contribute to community renewal and collective empowerment.

The issues I take up in this book—race and social class, teachers' ideologies and the culture of schools, the influence of power relations on individuals' actions and on institutional reform—transcend education policy and practice. They reflect broader social issues. Although education is just one arena where they are played out—it is a significant one. It is because of the importance of schools as sorting and socializing institutions and as sites where knowledge is constructed and student identities are formed that fundamental change in schools has wider implications. Accordingly, the potential significance of school restructuring is both its impact on individual students, teachers, and schools, and its broader social consequences. Schools that "prefigure the [democratic, multicultural] society we want rather than reinforce existing social and political arrangements" (Perry and Fraser, 1993, p. 17) are a step toward creating that society. An education that supports personal and social action is also essential to the development of leadership within disempowered communities and for the broader society. Thus, transforming the educational experiences and promoting the intellectual, social, and cultural excellence of marginalized groups is both an educational goal and an aspect of economic, political, and social empowerment. The possibility that educators and schools can play an active role in the process of emancipatory social transformation is a starting point for this study.

The Social and Economic Context of Educational Reform

School restructuring has specific meanings in relation to local settings—particular teachers and students, schools, and communities. But these meanings are also embedded in a wider social context, particularly an historical moment of profound economic and social transformation, crisis and opportunity. Indeed, the challenges facing U.S. schools today are shaped by three powerful inter-related societal trends: (a) the transition to postindustrialism and the decline of U.S. global economic hegemony; (b) growing economic and social polarization along lines of race, class, and ethnicity; and (c) an increasingly diverse, multiracial, multicultural population.

It is hardly necessary to point out that low achievement, disproportionate assignment to low academic tracks and special education classes, high drop-out rates, and academic disengagement and alienation of students of color continue to be critical issues. Many of the compensatory and entitlement programs of the 1960s and 1970s were directed to reducing inequalities and improving achievement of students of color. Despite these efforts, and allowing for improvement in achievement and school completion rates of minorities since the early 1960s (Jaynes & Williams, 1989; Smith & O'Day, 1990), if current trends hold, many students of color will continue to face these problems (Joint Center for Political Studies, 1989; Quality Education for Minorities, 1990). In fact, according to the Education Trust, despite a 50% decline in the achievement gap between African Americans and Whites during the 1970s and 1980s, the gap increased between 1990 and 1994. In 1996, African Americans had the lowest average composite ACT and SAT scores of any nationality group (ACT, 1996; College Board, 1996). In 1994 only 40% of African American recent high school graduates not in college were employed as compared with 72% of Whites (U.S. Dept. of Education, 1996).

However, there is a qualitative difference in the current challenge to provide an equitable and empowering education to low-income children of color. Both the obstacles and the educational needs faced by people of color are being reshaped by profound macro-economic and social changes caused by the transition to postindustrialism and the decline of U.S. economic hegemony. A host of ruinous corporate and government policies over the past 45 years,[2] compounded by the revolution in information-based technology and new international centers of economic power, have engendered profound economic and social dislocations. These dislocations are reflected in the dramatic deterioration of industrial regions and urban infrastructures, a two-tiered economy, growing impoverishment, and crises of direction and values in social institutions, including schools. As a whole, these phenomena are, in general, severely undermining the standard of living and sense of future of working-class people (Rubin, 1994).

Growing economic and social polarization, by race and class, is manifested in trends in wealth and income distribution. While the top

20% of the population gained just under 99% of the growth in market-able wealth between 1983 and 1989, the remaining 80% of the popu-lation gained only a little over 1% (Wolf, 1995, pp. 12–13). Income also became more concentrated with the top 1% of households receiving most of the gain in income and the bottom 80% sustaining almost all the loss in income (Wolf, 1995, pp. 11–12). The effects of these trends are manifested in the growing impoverishment of children. Poverty is particularly acute for African American and Latino children who in 1994 had poverty rates near 42% (U.S. Dept. Of Education, 1996). In 1990 the poverty rate for African American children under three was 52% as compared with 42% for Hispanic children and 15% for White children (National Center for Children in Poverty, 1992). Low educa-tional outcomes are one component of this acute economic and social crisis gripping poor students of color (Haynes & Comer, 1990).

For African Americans, ongoing racial discrimination is com-pounded by the economic and social transitions underway (Wilson, 1987). The revolution in technology places higher educational demands on workers, posing serious problems for unskilled and undereducated workers who no longer have access to high-paying, entry-level manu-facturing jobs. At the same time, high-tech jobs have moved to subur-ban areas or other regions less accessible to inner-city residents. While some African Americans benefited in the 1970s and 1980s from affirmative action and enhanced opportunities for higher education, and went on to become professionals or win solid working-class jobs, today many working-class African Americans have experienced down-ward mobility, plunging into the ranks of the unemployed or under-employed (Rubin, 1994). Meanwhile, urban tax bases have eroded and with them physical infrastructures and access to decent schooling and health care (Kozol, 1991). Inner-city residents—overwhelmingly people of color—experience increased social isolation and threats to their communities from gentrification, marginalization from the mainstream, and political and social disempowerment. Despite the gains of the civil rights movement, current economic hardships and uncertainties have also begotten intensified racism, as reflected, for example in anti-immigrant legislation, African American church burnings and racial incidents on campuses, and efforts to roll back affirmative action. The implications of these trends for the entire society are a deep and grow-ing polarization between haves and have-nots that is both interracial and intraracial.

Moreover, the nation as a whole is becoming increasingly multicultural and multilingual, with a growing proportion of the popu-lation composed of people of color and people whose first language is

not English. By the year 2010, 38% of K–12 enrollment will be "minorities," and by 2020, 48% will be children of color (Carnegie Council on
Adolescent Development, 1989). African Americans and Latinos already are a majority of the students in most large city school systems
(Quality Education for Minorities, 1990, p. 15), and people of color are
a majority in many urban areas. In the future, Euro-Americans will be
a numerical minority in the United States, and the proportion of those
who speak English as a first language will also decline. Clearly, the
education of students of color and language minorities has serious
implications for the society as a whole.

While students are becoming more racially, ethnically, and culturally diverse, the teaching force is overwhelmingly White. In 1996,
89% of teachers identified themselves as White (Feistritzer, 1996), and
many teachers say they prefer not to teach in low-income, urban schools
(Zeichner, 1992). Nevertheless, there are also many dedicated teachers
who choose these settings because they "want to make a difference."
However, given the racial, ethnic, and class segregation in the United
States. and the parochialism of many teachers' own educational experiences, most teachers are unprepared to teach children whose racial,
ethnic, linguistic, and cultural background is different from their own
(Zeichner, 1992).

But greater diversity presents fresh opportunities as well as challenges. A multicultural, multilingual population is a rich source of
knowledge and talent for the society as a whole. Diverse cultures and
social experiences enrich a nation's aesthetic, political, and ethical
dialogue and its approach to social questions. Exclusion impoverishes
us all. The African American experience and liberation struggle, for
example, has deepened and expanded the moral and political vision
of our society as a whole (Harding, 1990). In this context, schools must
find ways to capitalize on the knowledge and culture of all children
and to develop them to their full potential. Moreover, in a democratic
society, equality and inclusion are moral imperatives. Justice requires
not only equal opportunity but equality of social, economic, political,
and cultural resources and participation. Beginning with the strengths
of students' backgrounds, educators need to help students develop
the knowledge, competencies, and sense of agency to participate fully
in shaping our collective future (Trueba, 1989).

A measure of the relevance of educational reforms is the extent
to which new initiatives address the challenges posed by structural
change and growing inequality and by the extent to which they confront central issues of race and class inequality, racism, and the need
to teach to racial and ethnic diversity. Whether educational initiatives

address these issues head-on, or whether educators and policy makers choose to side-step them, their impact on students' educational experiences and life chances is inescapable. Although these issues are central to our collective future, in the lives of working class students and students of color they are immediate and urgent. Their immediacy and their relevance to school restructuring is born out by this study.

The Social Construction of Public Problems and Public Policy

The public discourse about social problems and public policy is also part of the context of educational change. Public policy itself may be understood as a set of discursive practices that shape our thinking about public problems and define the universe of possible actions and practical choices. From this perspective, policy shapes how we define complex social issues and the range of solutions that appear rational. The essence of debate in public life, then, is over the construction of social problems and the broader cultural meanings various constructions evoke (Edelman, 1964; Reich, 1987). Although local discourses, policies, and interpretations owe something to a community's particular history and social relations, they can only be fully understood in relation to the broader, national discourse about public issues. Indeed, this national discourse, elaborated in popular media and policy analyses, is a potent cultural force shaping how we understand local problems and our response to them. In this way, it is part of the cultural context of educational reform in Riverton. Here I focus on the way desegregation has been framed and the national discourse about African American and "at-risk" students. The construction of these issues had an important effect on both the Riverton community and school district and on the direction of the restructuring project itself.

Analyzing the history of school desegregation since *Brown v. Board of Education*, scholars have argued that desegregation policy has been framed by what is in the interest of whites, has abstracted equity from excellence in education, and has been constructed as racial integration, thus avoiding the central problem of institutional racism.[3] For example, Bell (1980) argues that the history of school desegregation policy has not been formulated to ensure equal educational outcomes for African Americans and other "minority" groups. Instead, the remedies that have been devised are those that satisfy Whites. This "interest convergence principle" (Bell) (Whites support desegregation when it converges with their interests) resulted in magnet schools that provide quality education for Whites within contexts of racial integration and busing plans in which African American students bore the burden of relocation to White schools. Levine and Eubanks (1986), in their discussion of magnet schools for desegregation, conclude that generally Whites have not enrolled voluntarily in magnet schools they associated with a minority community, and upper-SES (socioeconomic status) Whites have refused to attend magnets located in lower-SES neighborhoods. Orfield (1978) notes that many excellent schools have been under-enrolled by Whites for this reason. Magnets have only been successful in attracting large numbers of White students when minority enrollment is less than 30% (Rossell, 1979). Metz (1986) argues that in the context she studied the magnet school strategy was successful in meeting the short-term goal of preventing White opposition by directing attention away from the goal of desegregation and focusing instead on educational alternatives that would attract Whites. The history is significant here because projects for educational change cannot escape the concrete realities of school districts shaped by desegregation policies and the ways in which these policies have ensconced the interests of Whites over African Americans and other people of color.

Moreover, desegregation policy has been constructed as racial balance, rather than equal access to quality education. Reviewing the history since *Brown*, Judge Robert L. Carter, who was the NAACP general counsel and leading attorney in the *Brown* case, said, "While we fashioned Brown on the theory that equal education and integrated education were one and the same, the goal was not integration but equal educational opportunity" (Carter, 1980 p. 27). Framing desegregation this way substituted formal equality for universal access to educational excellence.

Kohl (1996/97) also argues that by constructing the issue as racial integration, we have ignored the main problem—institutional racism. Integrated schools remained White-dominated institutions (Scherer & Slawski, 1979)—a characteristic of the schools in this study. Integration in the United States has been a one-way street. "African Americans have been asked to go into schools with a dominant white culture and power structure. That racism did not disappear when the schools were integrated" (Kohl, 1996/97, p. 26), and it is one reason desegregation, to the extent it occurred, did not lead to equal and quality education for African Americans and other people of color.

A second contextual feature is the national discourse about African Americans as problems, or "problem people" (Height quoted in West, 1993, p. 2). Scrutinized on TV and in public policy analysis, African Americans are discussed, analyzed, counted, and displayed. In popular culture, African American inner-city neighborhoods are demonized as pathological, dysfunctional, and violent. The media is saturated with images of young African American males, as amoral menaces to (White, middle-class) society (Haymes, 1995). These images magnify deeply ingrained racist stereotypes and obscure the real strengths of supportive African American communities, families, and institutions. They also deepen the wedge between low-income African American communities and the rest of U.S. society, further fracturing a sense of public, collective responsibility for the socioeconomic conditions these communities are battling (Wallis, 1994). Missing from much of the public discourse about African Americans is recognition of the strength of solidarity, rooted in survival, that has characterized African American social life (Stack, 1974). This cultural onslaught against Black identity in the popular media negates the historical resistance, vitality, collectivity, and dynamic resilience of African American communities—strengths that have nurtured African American children and which are the core of continuing struggle (Haymes, 1995).

A related issue is the way in which public policy has constructed low-income and children of color as "at-risk." The "at risk" label operates as if it were a scientifically determined trait of youth who embody a diffuse set of supposedly perverse personal and social characteristics (teen pregnancy, drug use, resistance to school, school failure, dropping out, etc.). In popular use, "at risk" has become a signifier for race and class and a badge of deviance to be pinned on urban youth. Marking African American and other youth in this way provides two popular explanations for low school achievement: The students themselves lack ability, motivation, and character, and their families' social pathologies and deficiencies prevent them from succeeding (Cuban, 1989).[4] Thus, naming children "at-risk" directs attention away from institutional practices, policies, and ideologies and implies that widespread school failure is a rather natural consequence of these students' characteristics.

Education policies devoid of social justice, the demonization of African American youth as social problems, and the construction of equity as relevant to Whites only to the extent their interests are served—all are part of the fracturing of U.S. society. By portraying the economic and social crises, unjust education, and racism experienced by African American youth as African American problems, we reject our collective responsibility for each other and deny our interconnectedness (Wallis, 1994). One challenge of educational reform, at all levels, is to reframe these issues and to propose policies that generate a discourse of community and commitment to social justice.

Themes of Restructuring

Restructuring is ubiquitous in the current rhetoric of school-based educational reform. Under this slogan emerged national reform projects, the overhaul of some of the country's largest school districts, and thousands of local efforts. Organizations as diverse as the American Federation of Teachers and the National Education Association, on the one hand, and IBM and the Business Roundtable, on the other, have produced their own blueprints.

The term *restructuring* implies a fundamental redefinition of the means and ends of education (Schlecty, 1990). However, in practice, restructuring carries a variety of meanings. Site-based management, steering committees of teachers and parents, collaborative management by principals and staff, instructional teams, reorganization of schools into houses or clusters, coordination of schools and social services, scaled-down bureaucracies—all have become common organizational features of schools that claim to be restructuring (Clune & White, 1988; Elmore & Assoc., 1990). Restructuring may also include national and local curriculum projects which redefine teaching and learning to emphasize problem solving and students constructing their own knowledge, interdisciplinary studies, and performance-based assessments of students' knowledge (David, Purkey, & White, 1989; Elmore & Assoc., 1990; Newmann, 1990). It also generally involves teacher participation in educational change and in the overall direction of the school as well as increased collaboration among educators.

Beginning in the mid-1980s, national commissions, policy groups, and teachers' organizations called for expanding the professional competence and authority of educators at the school site (Holmes Group, 1986; Shanker, 1990; Task Force on Teaching as a Profession, 1986). This enhanced role for teachers or "teacher empowerment" has become a major theme of school restructuring, creating new forms of organization for professional collaboration, teacher leadership, and expanded professional development (David, Purkey & White, 1989; Lieberman & Miller, 1990). In contrast with mandated, top-down reforms of past decades (Berman & McLaughlin, 1978), educators at the school level are encouraged to collaboratively plan and develop innovations in teaching and learning and other aspects of life in schools (Sirotnik, 1987). The goal is to give those who work directly with students the authority and flexibility to exercise judgment and creativity and to generate change from the bottom up.

Proponents of teacher-centered change (Holmes, 1986; Task Force on Teaching as a Profession, 1986) and of decentralizing schools and school systems (Schlecty, 1990) argue teacher-centered reforms will facilitate innovation and result in improvements in teaching and learning. Although these reforms might be expected to revitalize teachers' work life, implications for students are not yet understood. and it is the consequences for students that are most critical. Certainly, restructuring must be evaluated by its enhancement of students' personal, social, and educational life in school and by the extent to which it increases their intellectual and social efficacy (Newmann, 1990). In my view, it must also be judged by its ability to address entrenched inequalities, ideologies, and practices that marginalize and alienate those students schools are most failing.

The schools I studied were just beginning to restructure. For these schools, restructuring meant reorganizing students and teachers into teams, teacher-led initiatives and greater teacher participation in school-level decisions, and teacher collaboration. Although there was discussion about redesigning instruction and curriculum, and organizational changes were meant in part to facilitate this, a framework for transforming teaching and learning was not at the center of their work, as is more typical of some national projects such as the Accelerated Schools (Levin, 1988) or the Coalition of Essential Schools (Coalition of Essential Schools, 1989). Consequently, this book does not focus on some of the issues and possibilities posed in those contexts. Rather, it addresses the kinds of organizational changes and teacher collaboration that the literature suggests are common in many restructuring schools. Although the particularities are specific to Riverton, I believe the representativeness of restructuring there makes this study relevant for similar efforts elsewhere (Schoffield, 1990). Moreover, as I have said, the dynamics of race, class, and power, so central to educational change in Riverton, are at the core of what happens in schools throughout the United States.

Methodology

I began fieldwork in Riverton in the summer of 1988 and continued through the summer 1991. During this time, I was also conducting a parallel and overlapping evaluation study of school reform in Riverton on behalf of a community collaborative and a national foundation that sponsored the reform. (See Methodological Appendix for a discussion of the evaluation study and implications of my dual role.) Although my fieldwork during the first 2 years gave me insight into restructuring at its inception, I collected the bulk of the data for this book during the 1990–1991 school year. As part of the evaluation study,

I was assisted, in all 3 years, by two local researchers who each spent about 2 days a week in the schools and occasionally attended district meetings. Because I was interested in school culture, social relations, and teachers' meanings—public and explicit, tacit and unrecognized— I used ethnographic methods (Erickson, 1986). Local researchers and I attended team and schoolwide faculty meetings, school board meetings, school steering committee meetings, various school functions and assemblies. We observed classes and informal interactions between teachers and students and among teachers and administrators, and simply spent time in the schools. We collected meeting agendas and minutes, descriptions of staff development activities and curricula, school and district policy statements, guidelines for restructuring, school schedules, and classroom handouts. Throughout the year, I conducted semistructured interviews (Spradley, 1979) and talked informally with teachers, nonteaching staff, students, school and district administrators, the teachers' union president, a few parents, community leaders, and social service workers. I interviewed the superintendent, restructuring director, and principals repeatedly during the year. All these people generously shared their insights, perceptions, and frustrations as well as documents related to restructuring. I also talked with several educational and community activists, African Americans and Whites, about restructuring and the politics and history of education in Riverton.[5]

I took notes during and after observations and interviews, and these were subsequently written up as field notes. Some student interviews were audiotaped and transcribed verbatim. Local researchers' field notes, oral and written reports, and notes from our monthly meetings are also part of the data. I iteratively coded the data by topic (Hammersley & Atkinson, 1983). Starting with a broad theoretical framework, I used a grounded theory approach (Glaser & Strauss, 1967) to generate descriptive and analytical themes from these codes. These themes became the backbone of my analysis.

In order to observe the relationship of organizational reforms and ideological processes in some depth over time, I focused more intensively on two teams of five teachers at each of the schools. (See Methodological Appendix for a discussion of how I selected these teams.) Together, the four focus teams included all three grade levels and had somewhat different student and teacher compositions. Thus, they offered a range within which to study dialogue and change. I also concentrated on other contexts that offered new opportunities for teacher collaboration, exchange of ideas, and participation in classroom and school-level decision-making, for example, school steering committees and teacher-initiated collaborative projects.

All of these contexts provided an opportunity to explore the relationship of restructuring to educators' responses to African American students. Race and class were intertwined in these contexts. At Gates, it was difficult to disentangle race and class in teachers' perceptions about African American students and their practices with them because most were low-income. In retrospect, at Franklin, it was possible to sort out race and class because the vast majority of students, African American and White, were working-class, but I did not frame the study to disentangle race and class, and my data are insufficient to elaborate this issue. This, frankly, is a limitation.

The Study from My Point of View

The researcher is the principle medium of ethnographic research, and research decisions and interpretations are filtered through her subjectivity. As with any methodology, the ideological dispositions, identity, and perspectives of the researcher influence what she sees and how she sees it (Peshkin, 1985). The key is to triangulate data and to be conscious of ideological, cultural, and personal assumptions and how they influence selectivity in observations, as well as one's interpretations. In addition, the researcher needs to be conscious of how her participation influences events, discourse, stated beliefs, behaviors, and other factors and to take advantage of this participation to gain additional insights (Metz, 1983).

I began this project with a strong point of view. I believed that the negative educational experiences of children of color are rooted in their oppression in society and that daily life in schools can reproduce, disrupt, or transform dominant relations of power. I believed that academic failure and student alienation must be analyzed through an examination of educational policy and practice. My goal throughout was to understand how schools can be changed to support the efforts of marginalized students and communities to transform their lives.

This point of view motivated my research questions, as well as my scrutiny of educators' practices and beliefs, school district policies, and the change process itself. It led me to probe educators' definitions of school success and to investigate the social context of educational reform. And it led me to examine the place of White and African American students, staff, and parents within the schools in this study. It also led me to look for ways in which reforms might create opportunities to support the empowerment of African American students. This stance also shaped the writing of this book. Thus, the book advocates for moving the condition of students of color and other marginalized groups to the center of discussions about school restructuring. I am also conscious that the power of advocacy within academic scholarship is premised on the honest and systematic gathering, presentation, and analysis of data, as well as openness to unexpected interpretations. Throughout, I tried to be reflective about my own perspectives, to look for countervailing evidence, and to triangulate data.

Over the course of 3 years, five people worked on the two-person local research teams. The data they gathered complimented my study of Franklin and Gates. Although there were different individuals in these teams over 3 years, each team was composed of an African American female and a white male. The teams included a former principal, a teacher, a journalist, an education researcher, and a cultural worker—all long-time residents of Riverton. Two had children who attended public schools. Several had been active in school and community affairs, and they introduced me to people with a history of involvement in educational issues and desegregation in Riverton. In addition to being colleagues, these local researchers were significant and diverse sources of information about the school district and community. Their intimate knowledge of the schools, the city, and the state supplied a context within which to situate, triangulate, and interpret my observations and interviews. Our dialogue was a significant means of checking and elaborating my perceptions and of interpreting data. My conversations with Rivertonians from a wide range of social locations, experiences, and connections with education and the community also informed my interpretations.

A White Northerner in a Southern Setting

Interpretations of racial dynamics are inevitably filtered through one's own racially specific experiences and consciousness. For Whites, there is the danger of normalizing Whiteness—assuming that one's experiences reflect the norm and seeing those who are different as *other*. As a White female, my consciousness is obviously not shaped by the historical experience of racial oppression or by the solidarity that has evolved out of a common struggle against racial oppression. These are significant limitations in a context in which issues of racism are central.

These limitations were perhaps somewhat mitigated by my previous years of teaching in a predominantly African American school that stressed African American cultural-centeredness, an awareness of racism and racial dynamics, and my history of social activism in which persons of color were the majority and racism was a central concern. It also helped to compare my own perceptions with other members of an interracial research team in which we made racial issues a consistent topic.

Being White can be a barrier to winning the trust of people of color in the research setting, but, because I frankly initiated discussions about race and racism, African Americans and Whites concerned about these issues became quite open with me about their views. Some considered me a potential ally because I was associated with a project, or at least a foundation, that some educators saw as an advocate of African American students. As a result, the majority of my closest informants were African American teachers who consistently shared their opinions and concerns with me. Still, my interpretations of African American perspectives are clearly those of the outsider.

Frank questions about racial disparities had the opposite effect with some White educators. Their discomfort at broaching the topic of race was an indication of the sensitivity of racial issues. On the other hand, I was occasionally the recipient of unsolicited confidences from some White teachers and counselors who initially assumed I would be sympathetic to their complaints against African American teachers and students because I was White. These confidences broke through the veneer of color blindness that pervaded much of the public discourse in both schools. As a whole, the variety of reactions I encountered from African American and White teachers indicated the existence of multiple racial perspectives behind a public facade of racelessness. Ultimately, my interpretations of meanings about race will be measured against my informants' own voices—White and African American—in this book.

A second issue was regional differences. I can hardly overstate the cultural dissonance I experienced as a Northerner conducting research in a Southern school district. It became apparent early on when I found my words and behavior frequently being misunderstood and discovered that I was all too often confused by the behavior of others. Although I became more familiar with life in the two schools and in the city over time, I continued to feel very much an outsider. This cultural distance from many of the people I was observing and talking with has to be acknowledged in my interpretations. Nevertheless, I strove to understand events and ideas from the viewpoint of the Riverton teachers and administrators themselves and in the context of their history. Checking interpretations and perceptions with local researchers helped me develop a feel for the encoded meanings of what I was seeing and hearing. Although I was an outsider, I saw the Riverton schools and community in a way that perhaps natives of the area did not see it.

Regionalism had an effect similar to race, in that some teachers and administrators mistrusted me because I was a Northerner. They were quick to point out that non-Southerners could not understand the unique history and culture of the South and that educational solutions devised elsewhere were inappropriate for them. Conversely, some African American and White teachers perceived that my Northern origins distanced me from traditional Southern race relations and the particular history and culture of Riverton. Consequently, they considered me a potentially sympathetic outsider. In our conversations, they were quite openly critical of the racial dynamics in their schools and shared their perspectives on Riverton's history of school desegregation.

Plan of the Book

In the following chapters, I discuss and compare restructuring at Gates and Franklin. I analyze the implications of the reforms for teachers' beliefs about and practices with African American students, the effects on school policies, and the ways in which reforms were mediated by ideological, cultural, and structural factors. I pay special attention to the role of several exemplary teachers of African American students and the implications of their participation for the direction of restructuring. In chapter 2, I situate my research questions in explanations for the school performance and educational experiences of students of color, assumptions about school restructuring and teacher-centered educational change, and the role of cultural change in transforming schools. In chapter 3, I describe the historical and social context of the study, the city of Riverton, the Riverton School District, the two junior high schools, and the restructuring process there. Chapter 4 launches the case studies with a typology of teachers' ideologies regarding African American students and the configuration of these ideologies in each of the schools.

The next four chapters describe and analyze the process of restructuring in the two schools. In chapters 5 and 6, I describe and analyze how teachers interpreted restructuring at Gates Junior High School and the implications for African American students there. In chapter 5, I focus specifically on two ninth-grade teams and the actions and dialogue of these teachers as they began using new opportunities for collaboration and collective decision-making. Chapter 6 examines restructuring schoolwide at Gates. It discusses the principal's perspective and the influence of the school's culture and of ideological and political forces beyond the school on the direction of restructuring there. Chapters 7 and 8 develop a comparative analysis at Franklin Junior High School. In chapter 7, I describe and analyze the activities of a seventh- and an eighth-grade focus team and compare them with the focus teams at Gates. In chapter 8, I discuss the ways in which school culture, competing ideologies, and the school's and principal's position within a hierarchy of power in the district influenced how restructuring unfolded, drawing comparisons with Gates. In chapter 9, I describe three exemplary teachers and their roles in the restructuring process. I examine the implications of their role for the nature of dialogue and change at both schools. In the concluding chapter, I return to the assumptions underlying restructuring and examine them in relation to the process of change at Franklin and Gates. The chapter also discusses the relationship between restructuring and ideological, political, and structural factors in schools and the broader social context. It examines the relationship of educational change, social change, and power and the role of exemplary teachers and advocates of marginalized students in promoting transformative change.

It is my hope that this book will contribute to understanding the relationship of school restructuring to students' experiences in school. My analysis highlights the importance of ideology and relations of power in educational change. Although my conclusions are constructed from what I have learned from the efforts of a group of educators in a specific context, I expect that the ideological and political processes I uncover reflect wider patterns. My aim in writing this book is to spur dialogue about the fundamental premises of educational change, its focus and direction in relation to social justice. I hope the insights gleaned from this project will be of value to teachers, administrators, and others who conceive and implement educational reforms, to parents and community members concerned with educational equality and justice, to those who make educational and social policies, and to those who study educational change. In writing this book I have tried to follow bell hooks's (1989) reminder that to speak in a language accessible to all of us is a political choice about whom we are speaking to, whom we want to hear us, and whom we want to motivate with our words.

2

THE EDUCATION OF AFRICAN AMERICANS AND SCHOOL RESTRUCTURING

Undeniably, the nexus of poverty, racial discrimination, social inequality, and the erosion of the African American community's economic and social infrastructure has a profound influence on students' educational experiences (Haynes & Comer, 1990). Fundamentally, these conditions are rooted in the social organization of U.S. society, its class, race, and gender relations. However, this construction of the problem situates it wholly outside of schools, diminishing the structural inequalities and cultural processes in schools and the significance of what individual educators do to support or alienate African American students and to foster or thwart meaningful educational experiences. A more powerful analysis considers the complex interrelationship of social structures and cultural processes in schools and society.

I take this to be the thrust of Cummins's (1986) theoretical framework for educational reform. Cummins attributes the educational difficulties of "minority" students to three interconnected relationships: (a) classroom interactions between students and teachers; (b) relationships between schools and minority communities; (c) intergroup power relationships in society as a whole. Cummins argues that the social organization of the school and its bureaucratic constraints "reflect not only broader policy and societal factors but also the extent to which *individual educators* [emphasis original] accept or challenge the social organization of the school in relation to minority students and their communities" (p. 10). It is within this framework that I examine, at the local level, the process of school restructuring.

This book is about the relationship between school restructuring and the education of African American students. In the first part of this chapter, I discuss three broad influences on African American students' educational experiences. These influences provide a framework from which to consider restructuring in Riverton. In the second part of the chapter, I outline some key assumptions in the literature about school restructuring. These are assumptions that I question throughout this study.

Influences on the Educational Experiences
of African American Students

Research in sociology and anthropology of education over the past 20 years has advanced numerous explanations for the low achievement and alienation of students of color and of African Americans in particular. These explanations are far-ranging in their emphases, focusing on various cultural and structural aspects of the relationship between students and schools and between schools and society. For example, research points to cultural mismatches between minority students and schools (Au & Jordan, 1981), lack of cultural synchronization between African American students specifically and the culture and norms of schools (Irvine, 1991), cultural differences as part of the broader struggle for power in society (Villegas, 1988), unequal school resources (Kozol, 1991), academic tracking as a form of structural inequality (Oakes, 1985), teachers' ideologies (Grant, 1984, 1985; King, 1992), student resistance as a response to lack of opportunity in the labor market (Ogbu, 1974, 1978), and student responses to racial subordination (Fordham & Ogbu, 1986) and cultural marginalization (Fordham, 1988).

Clearly, the reasons for African American students' academic difficulties, alienation, and marginality in schools are complex and a comprehensive analysis accounts for the interrelationship of multiple factors. In the following sections I discuss three broad, school-related influences on the educational experiences of African American students: teachers' ideologies, cultural differences and power, and institutional norms and policies that structure inequality. Although I discuss them separately, they are interrelated. Ideologies influence and legitimate structures, and structures influence ideologies and limit individuals' actions. Throughout the book I consider student-teacher-administrator interactions in light of these three influences and the broader social, cultural, and political contexts within which they occur.

Teachers' Ideologies

One focus of this study is teachers' ideologies and ideologically informed pedagogical practices, social interactions, and educational discourse. I use the term *ideology* broadly to include: (a) formal belief systems, social theories, and elaborated worldviews; (b) commonsense understandings, cultural models, and everyday explanations through which people make sense of their world; and (c) ideologies-in-use—social practices of individuals and institutions. In my research, I drew on all three to gather information about teachers' ideologies. I understand ideological makeup to be complex, contradictory, and dynamic (Therborn, 1980), a product of individuals' multifaceted identities, social experiences, and cultural influences.

Formal belief systems may be drawn from educational theories and philosophies, social science theories, political doctrines, ethical and religious worldviews, and so on. These formal theories and belief systems may help explain teachers' assessment of students' potential, their pedagogical and curricular choices, their perspective of their own role and responsibilities as educators—in short, how they view students, teaching, and the role of schools in society. A number of qualitative studies have examined the influence of teachers' formal ideologies on their practice (e.g., Ball, 1981; Metz, 1978; Weiler, 1988).

However, the beliefs, values, and normative behaviors of teachers may be drawn less from formal ideologies (systems of ideas) than from a more elusive, shared cultural framework. *Culture* in this sense refers to broadly shared understandings of social phenomena (Williams in Gusfield, 1986, p. 207). These understandings draw on concrete experiences that, when interpreted through a shared framework, create everyday explanations through which people make sense of their world (Therborn, 1980). As Gramsci (1971) argued, these widely shared, commonsense understandings are the basis of cultural hegemony through which elites legitimate the existing social order and maintain their power.

These understandings are often constructed as stories or *cultural models*—"taken-for-granted models of the world which are widely shared by the members of a society," and which they draw upon to make sense of social phenomena (Quinn & Holland, n.d.). Anthropological studies of the motivational effect, or *directive force,* of cultural models suggest that they are lived out in social practice, in the decisions people make, and in the way they respond to events (D'Andrade, 1986; Strauss, 1986). Like more formal ideologies, cultural models frame teachers' educational decisions and their response to students. Identifying and tracking the influence of these cultural models is a way of understanding ideological processes.

The meritocratic theory of academic success is an example of a commonly held cultural model that has significant implications for all students and for commonly held assumptions about social inequality. The notion of meritocracy is rooted in classical liberalism and the rise of capitalism with its emphasis on competition, individualism, individual virtue, and the possibility of class mobility. It continues to justify social selection by class, race, and gender and to legitimate inequality and the inevitability of winners and losers (Conforti, 1992). Its credibility rests on a set of implicit assumptions about equal opportunity, the rewards of hard work, and variation in human ability. But its explanatory power for the differential school success of students also rests with popularized stories and national myth about individuals who succeeded through hard work and superior talent. This myth resonates with personal stories of self-made success, which in turn confirm and nourish the myth. Its concrete social power lies in its resonance with individuals who draw upon it to make sense of individual failure and success in school and to rationalize the failure of large numbers of students. Belief in meritocracy intersects with other cultural models and ideologies which assign more or less value to particular social groups, that is, races/ethnicities, genders, social classes, thus rationalizing an unequal social structure. For example, racism (as well as sexism and class bias) intersects with the ideology of meritocracy to elevate attributes and characteristics that favor White, middle-class males over African Americans and then to rationalize the latter's failure to succeed as the outcome of a fair and necessary contest.

Ideology (whether formal theories or cultural models) comes to life in the implementation of school policies, interactions between adults and children, curricular choices, and so on (Apple & Weis, 1983). Teachers' ideological dispositions (a) influence how they define and label students and (b) affect their pedagogical choices. Everyday educational decisions reflect ideologies-in-use: placement of students in "slow" or "fast" tracks validation or denigration of students' knowledge, perceptions of student strengths and weaknesses, and expectations for student performance and behavior (Keddie, 1971; Page, 1991; Wilcox, 1982). For African American students, the constellation of factors that influence these decisions include teachers' beliefs about and attitudes toward African Americans. For example, Grant, in her study of desegregated elementary school classrooms, found that White teachers saw Black females as the least academically competent but the most socially mature and thus used them as helpers in the classroom but gave them less attention than White females (Grant, 1984). The teachers generally saw Black males (first graders) as threatening, and except for one or two "superstars" whom they singled out for their academic competence, Black males were the least connected with their teachers (Grant, 1985). In both instances, definitions of student competencies and students' opportunities to learn were mediated by teachers' ideologies of race and gender.

Thus, teachers' ideologies influence how they construct student identities and this in turn influences the reproduction or disruption of social inequalities, for example, what knoweldge students have accesss to or which track they are assigned to. In this study, I was interested in how teachers' formal theories, cultural models, and educational practices might be influenced by restructuring and might also influence it. I attempted to interpret teachers' ideological processes in the context of restructuring by tracking their educational practices and their talk about students. This was one way of inferring potential consequences of the reforms for African American students. Focusing on teachers' ideologies emphasizes the role that individuals play in students' educational experiences. However, individuals operate within and are constrained by wider cultural processes and structures.

Cultural Differences, Power, and African American
Students' Subordination

Some anthropologists locate the educational problems of African American, Latino, Native American, and some Asian students in the cultural discontinuities these students experience in mainstream U.S. schools. *Culture* in this more anthropological sense denotes ways in which a group of people, out of their shared experiences and history, makes meaning of their world. Shared meanings are manifested in such factors as common language, values, beliefs, material artifacts, and behavioral and communicative norms (Goodenough, 1971). Well-meaning teachers may be unaware of ways in which they act out of their own cultural frame of reference and interpret the actions of others who are different from themselves. A host of sociolinguistic and microsocial classroom studies demonstrate these discontinuities between teachers' cultural orientation and the behavior, language, and competencies of children who differ from them in race, ethnicity, or social class and show the ways in which these discontinuities disrupt learning (e.g., Au & Jordan, 1981; Erickson & Mohatt, 1982; Heath, 1983; McDermott & Gospodinoff, 1979).

However, many microsocial studies fail to examine cultural differences in relation to social inequality and unequal relations of power (Villegas, 1988). How cultural differences are defined by those with power is a means of maintaining that power. In a social context in which race, class, and gender oppression are pervasive and historic, the imposition of the dominant group's language, behavioral norms, and values is a way of maintaining dominance. Throughout U.S. history, the languages, experiences, knowledge, and values of racial and ethnic minorities have been suppressed, degraded, and marginalized, and schools have been integral to the process of cultural assimilation and marginalization of those defined as "other" (e.g., Spring, 1994; Takaki, 1993). The values, behaviors, language, and knowledge of White, middle-class students is often the standard in schools, and those whose identities do not reflect this standard are marginalized and/or pressured to change and conform (Fordham, 1988). Thus, although behavioral competence may be defined differently by various cultural groups, many educators tend to see the culture of the dominant group as "normal" and the culture of subordinate groups as "deviant."

This cultural subordination has concrete manifestations for students' educational experiences and their future positions in society and the economy. For example, it determines whose knowledge gets into the curriculum, as clearly demonstrated by the Eurocentrism of curriculum in U. S. schools. On the classroom level, how teachers interpret African American students' language, interactional styles, and competencies influences their assessments of these students' abilities and decisions about their placement in slow or fast tracks (Michaels, 1981; Rist, 1970). Teachers' culturally inscribed interpretations of African American students' behaviors and interactional styles also influence their assessment of student behavior. This helps explain the disproportionate disciplining of African American students and their disproportionate assignment to Behavior Disordered and Special Education classes (Irvine, 1991; Majors & Billson, 1992). As a whole, these decisions have concrete consequences for students' educational opportunities and their future role in society.

Student success or failure is constructed in the politics of everyday life in schools, in the dynamic interactions between teachers, students, and the social organization of schools (McDermott, 1974). In situations where cultural differences are politicized and students' sense of personal and cultural identity is negated, the trust between adults and children that is essential to learning is broken (Erickson, 1987). Student resistance to the marginalization of their identities may lead to affirmation and strength (Kohl, 1994), but it may also result in denial of educational opportunities, for example, when schooling is constructed in such a way that African American students define academic success as "acting white" (Fordham, 1988). McDermott (1974) argues that school failure for some students of color becomes something to be "achieved," a way to protect their personal integrity and dignity in the face of degrading policies, practices, and beliefs of educators. Imposition of the dominant culture and the resistance of dominated groups to cultural subordination make up one facet of a larger struggle, and cultural differences in schools are a terrain on which battles over unequal power relations are fought (Darder, 1995; Delpit, 1988).

This analysis of cultural differences and power is a lens through which I interpret discourse about, and responses to, African American students and the evolution of beliefs, practices, and policies. I am mindful that because of the complexity of identity shaped by the interrelation of social class, gender, racial, and other differences, social groups cannot be characterized by an *essential* cultural identity (McCarthy, 1995). Nevertheless, in this study, I recognized a basis for shared cultural meanings forged out of African roots and shaped by the common historical experiences of oppression and resistance of African American people to racism in the United States[1] Within a framework of complex, multifaceted identities, I was concerned with social interactions and perspectives of African American students in Riverton as meaningful expressions of shared experiences and history and with the ways in which race and class, in particular, shaped educators' responses to students.

Moving beyond studies of school failure, emerging theoretical and empirical studies point to educational practices that not only bridge cultural differences and foster academic success (Ernst, Statzner, Trueba, 1994), but uphold the identities of diverse students, work against unequal relations of power, and help marginalized students develop tools of critical literacy and a sense of personal and social agency (Bartolome, 1994; Darder, 1995; Sleeter, 1991). Studies that attempt to capture the culturally relevant practices, knowledge, and relationships that typify empowering educational experiences for African American students (Foster, 1991; King, 1991; Ladson-Billings, 1994) are particularly relevant to my research. Articulating the connection of culture and power, proponents of *culturally relevant* pedagogy argue that, beyond cultural congruence or responsiveness, schooling must be relevant to the empowerment of African American people. According to Ladson-Billings and Henry (1990), unlike assimilationist teaching, culturally relevant teaching " . . . uses the students' culture to empower students to be able to critically examine educational content and process and ask what role they have in creating a truly democratic and multicultural society. It uses students' culture to help students create meaning and understand the world" (p. 82). The theory of culturally relevant teaching is a lens through which to interpret the perspectives and practices of teachers at Gates and Franklin and the collaborative decisions they made regarding African American students. As my research progressed, I also became interested in individual teachers whom I roughly characterized as culturally relevant. I investigated their perspectives and practices and followed their influence on restructuring.

Institutional Norms and Policies

Institutional norms such as testing, tracking, and discipline policies are the taken-for-granted regularities that govern everyday life in schools and school districts (Sarason, 1982). These regularities are both ideological and structural. They organize, sort, and regulate students. They also convey messages about student identities—notions about their intelligence, behavior, and value. The decision to adopt one policy or another, to support or reject a particular organizational feature is itself ideological (Fine, 1991). Although all students are affected by them, the meaning of these norms and the consequences of policies vary in relation to students' race, social class, and gender differences.

Academic tracking, which originated in the demands of developing industry for a hierarchically differentiated labor force and in the assumption that students with different "abilities" and "interests" should have different curricula and educational futures (Oakes, 1985), has taken on a life of its own as a "normal" feature of schooling. Tracking is a means of producing and normalizing markedly different and unequal educational experiences (Wheelock, 1992). Students assigned to low tracks and remedial classes have fewer opportunities to acquire higher-level academic competencies; they spend less time on academic tasks and more time on remediation and low-level, repetitive activities; and teachers in these tracks have lower expectations for students' academic success (Levin, 1988; Oakes, 1985). Lower-track students also have less access to a core curriculum for college, limiting their potential to pursue higher education and increasing the likelihood that they will be relegated to lower-paid jobs within the segmented labor market. Because African American, Latino, and working-class students are disproportionately assigned to lower tracks (Oakes, 1985), tracking is a powerful selection process through which educational and social inequality are reproduced.

Selecting and sorting students by ability and achievement is legitimated by the measurement and quantification of intelligence, knowledge, personality traits, and aptitudes through "objective" procedures. Yet the processes of selection and the criteria by which excellence is defined are socially constructed.[2] What knowledge is valued, how students represent their knowledge, what attitudes and dispositions are prized, how individual educators perceive abilities, and so on, all represent a decision. These decisions—codified in tests, labels assigned to students, and academic tracks—are all ideological, although cloaked in the rationality of scientific measurement (Karier, 1972). Selection for higher or lower tracks or "ability" groups is also mediated by individual teachers' judgments about students' abilities and their cultural norms.

The reliance on punishment to resolve student-teacher and student-student conflicts is another norm with significant consequences for African American students. The punitive, authoritarian culture and plethora of punishments that dominate many schools infantilizes students, leads to perceptions of unfairness and persecution, and alienates students, eventually driving them out of school (Wehlage & Rutter, 1986). In a snowball effect, student resistance to a pervasively punitive climate results in suspensions and other forms of removal from classes that undercut students' academic progress, lead to course failure, and contribute to further disaffection from school and dropping out (Wehlage, Rutter, Smith, Lesko, & Fernandez, 1989).

Although discipline policies and a punitive climate affect all students, the onus of these policies falls most heavily on working-class students and students of color (Irvine, 1991). For African American students, especially males, punitive policies intersect with racist ideologies and the stigmatization of African American students' cultural identities. In Grant's study (1985), White treachers perceived even first-grade African American males as threatening. One result is that African American students, especially males, are disproportionately suspended and assigned to behavior disordered classes and otherwise excluded from school and from the core curriculum. Not only does this contribute to low achievement and resistance to schooling (Irvine, 1991), but it further stigmatizes and criminalizes African American students, legitimating the need to control their behavior.

Despite research demonstrating negative consequences of these and other institutional norms and policies, for the most part they remain taken-for-granted elements of the institutional culture of many schools and make sense to many educators. Moreover, despite some rhetoric at the national level, and a few reform projects that directly confront issues of equity (Comer, 1988; Levin, 1988), overrepresentation of African Americans in suspension rooms, low-track and remedial classes, and the lower quartiles of academic achievement have become rationalized institutional outcomes. Failure, low achievement, and dropping out have come to be seen as inevitable. Drop-out rates of 50% and more in some cities among African Americans, Latinos, and Native Americans are routine (Fine, 1991). Normalizing these outcomes absolves educators as well as the general public from the responsibility to change them. Making problematic the institutional regularities that make up the texture of day-to-day life in schools and the ideologies that are embedded in them is crucial to beginning a process of reconceptualizing them (Sarason, 1982). Thus, beginning to question the meanings of institutional norms in relation to African American students is an important step in transforming these students' experiences in school and in challenging the ways schools structure inequality. Therefore, I investigated which institutional norms and policies reinforced African American students' inequality and marginality. And I examined teachers' interpretations of these norms and the steps, if any, they took to change them.

Summary

Three broad influences on the educational experiences of African American students frame my study. These are teachers' ideologies, cultural differences and power, and institutional norms and policies. Ideological, cultural, and structural factors are interrelated and influence each other. For example, structural aspects of schools and institutional norms such as tracking, testing, and discipline policies, sort and set limits on students' educational opportunities. At the same time, these taken-for-granted institutional regularities normalize the differentiation of students and reinforce notions of varied, measurable abilities. Tracking is then perpetuated because it "makes sense," that is, fits a particular set of assumptions. Teachers' ideas and their practices are influenced by school norms, but educators and the public operating from a different set of assumptions, may also influence these norms and change them, as in recent efforts to untrack schools (Wheelock, 1992).

In this study, I was interested in the ways in which restructuring influenced various aspects of African American students' school experiences. First, I focused on teachers' cultural models of African American students, expectations for their academic performance, and judgments about their abilities. I followed how teachers constructed racial and educational issues and their collective discussion and response to these issues. Second, I explored how educators perceived cultural differences and the centrality or marginality of African American cultural identities in the schools. Third, district data showed a pattern of overrepresentation of African Americans in lower-track classes and significantly higher rates of suspension compared to Whites. Therefore, I paid particular attention to tracking, suspension and discipline practices and policies, and the discussions surrounding them. I also attended to changes in these and other institutional policies as a result of teachers' collaboration and participation in decision making. Finally, I followed educators' discussions about, and practical responses to, school and district-level discrepancies between African American and White students' educational outcomes.

Assumptions Underlying Restructuring

Bottom-up change—decentralization of school bureaucracies and increased roles for teachers, collaboration among teachers and with administrators, and reorganizing schools into smaller units such as houses or teams—is fundamental to many restructuring projects. Underpinning these changes is an assumed connection between their implementation and the goal of improving teaching, learning, and social relations in schools. Teachers and administrators in Riverton echoed this assumed connection, and the theories underlying it shaped their efforts.

Teacher Participation

Since the mid-1980s there has been a call to increase the professional roles, responsibilities, and expertise of teachers (Holmes, 1986; Task Force on Teaching as a Profession, 1986). Proponents contend that giving teachers more authority and professional opportunities is central to regenerating teaching and learning. They argue that the bureaucracy of most schools blocks innovation and stifles initiative by denying those closest to students the authority to make essential educational decisions. Moreover, the narrow roles to which teachers are generally confined restrict their opportunities to grow professionally and to take leadership in curriculum and instruction. At the same time, the knowledge base of the most effective teachers is not tapped to promote the development of new teachers and the growth of those with experience. The assumption then is that giving educators greater professional responsibility will help breathe new life into classrooms and schools.

This argument dovetails with contemporary, efficiency-oriented organizational theories calling for decentralization, visionary and inspirational leadership, improving human relations within organizations, and worker participation and collaboration in decisions regarding their work (Deal & Kennedy, 1982; Peters & Waterman, 1982). The idea is that these changes in organizational structures and culture will lead to more effective organizations and will promote innovation throughout the system. Applied to schools, these theories argue for school-based management, teacher collaboration, and participatory decision making at the school level, as well as reorganization of schools into smaller groupings of students and teachers to foster more personalized, familylike relationships (Schlechty, Ingwerson, & Brooks, 1988; Sizer, 1984). A central assumption underlying these proposals is that the people closest to the problems—teachers and principals—need both the authority and the accountability to solve them (National Committee for Citizens in Education, 1988). Moreover, the transformation of schools is such a monumental and complex task that it will require unprecedented commitment, innovation, and initiative at all levels of the system. By replacing hierarchical organizations with democratic forms such as school-based management, school improvement councils, and steering committees, school change will benefit from the input of a broad range of actors (Marburger, 1985).

From a more critical perspective, others argue that educators who have no meaningful role in determining school policies and curriculum, and who are neither nurtured nor respected themselves, are unlikely to engage students as active and critical learners (Giroux, 1985). On the other hand, working in a vigorously democratic and reflective system may give teachers a renewed sense of purpose and opportunity to work for change. This assumption is supported by evidence that when teachers' work is valued, and they have a significant voice in the operation of their school, they demonstrate more commitment to pedagogy and a more caring attitude and higher expectations for their students (McNeil, 1986).

Collaboration, the Enhancement of Teaching, and Dialogues of Change

It is widely acknowledged that the individualized, semi-autonomous nature of teachers' work and a bureaucratic, hierarchical structure impede professional collaboration and exchange among educators (Rosenholtz, 1989; Sizer, 1984). Daily professional isolation is debilitating for individual teachers, and it stifles constructive dialogue among faculty and between teachers and administrators (Freedman, Jackson, & Boles, 1983). On the other hand, collaborative arrangements such as common planning periods, teaching teams or clusters of teachers, school steering committees and task forces, and shared governance councils can facilitate cooperation and discussion of substantive educational issues (Hopfenberg, 1991; Sizer, 1984). Proponents reason that these organizational changes will foster a climate that will contribute to teachers exchanging ideas, questioning basic assumptions, and considering new professional knowledge (Sirotnik, 1987). Collaborative work might also be expected to nourish risk-taking and collective innovation.

Suppression of controversy is often the norm in schools. This is especially the case with the issues we as a society are unwilling to talk about together, such as race and other forms of difference and competing beliefs about diverse students' abilities. As a result, school policies, practices, and ideologies that undermine students of color are unlikely to be considered candidly by school faculties. For example, several studies of desegregated schools show teachers publicly failed to acknowledge the patently unequal status of African American students; a color blind philosophy perpetuated racial inequalities despite the salience of these inequalities in the schools (Clement, Eisenhart, & Harding, 1979; Scherer & Slawski, 1979; Schofield, 1982).

Schools with enriched opportunities for teachers to work together and exercise initiative may be environments more conducive to reflection and dialogue on controversial issues. Especially in schools where interracial teams of teachers are charged with improving the education of students of color, it is perhaps more likely that teachers will examine the implications of practices and policies for these students. It seems plausible then that collaborative environments may be conducive to dialogue and change in the interest of marginalized students.

Collective, Familylike Structures and Student Experiences

Proponents of restructuring also suggest that reconfiguring large schools into smaller units will enhance students' educational experiences. They argue that the anonymity of large impersonal schools contributes significantly to students' sense of academic disengagement (Wehlage et al., 1989). There is evidence that students' commitment to educational experiences in school is strengthened when they are part of a community of learners with shared goals and sustained personal contact (Ratzki & Fisher, 1989/90). In particular, research in middle schools suggests that smaller, familylike groupings, such as clusters, teams, houses, and "schools within schools," create a more supportive environment for young adolescents' social and intellectual development and create stronger bonds between adults and students (Lipsitz, 1984; Massachusetts Advocacy Center, 1988). This point is potentially relevant to the two junior high schools in this book.

It is also possible that nurturing environments with sustained interaction between teachers and students will facilitate empathy and trust across cultural, racial, and class differences. In this regard, it is plausible that teachers, through sustained interactions with students, will develop a greater understanding of, and appreciation for, the strengths of students culturally different from themselves. Students also may have more commitment to institutions led by concerned, mentoring adults. Caring environments may help break the spiral of cultural misunderstandings, subordination of minority students, student resistance, and censure that contributes to the failure and alienation of students of color. However, change on the part of adults responsible for the development of students must be central to this process.

Finally, it is possible that the call to restructure will generate a kind of *perestroika* in schools. Potentially, the restructuring process itself will spawn a climate for critical reappraisal of the school failure of students of color. Reshaping seemingly inviolable organizational features may be a mood-creating factor provoking broad-based reflection on other supposedly immutable regularities of curriculum, instruction, and social relations. Policies accepted as conventional wisdom, such as tracking, might be subjected to fresh scrutiny. This climate may also strengthen the hand of those teachers, parents, and others whose views have been dismissed as too radical or who are advocates for students generally bypassed by the school and/or district.

Summary

Three underlying assumptions of restructuring are: (1) decentralized organizations that strengthen teachers' participation and initiative foster innovation; (2) collaboration may promote critical inquiry and dialogues of change; (3) smaller, collective settings will nurture students, strengthen their commitment to school, and build trust between students and teachers.

For teachers of African American students, there are several plausible implications of these assumptions. One is that teachers who experience a new sense of efficacy and professional responsibility may be more likely to tackle tough issues such as racism and entrenched inequality. Their potential to influence the educational experience of these students might counter the impotence and the inertia fostered by the bureaucratic, formal authority typical of conventional schools and districts. Another is that new opportunities for collegial learning and dialogue may foster a critical reexamination of beliefs about and practices with marginalized students and create an arena for advocates of African American students to challenge existing regularities. Yet another is that the interchange generated by closer relationships with students may prompt teachers to question some of their taken-for-granted notions about African American students.

Problematic Assumptions and the Need for Research

Despite their logic, the assumptions guiding restructuring are problematic. The rhetoric of empowerment and collaboration may be a way to gain teachers' assent to decisions made elsewhere, to legitimate these decisions, and to blur contradictions between competing interests (Apple, 1995). Hargreaves (1991), for example, distinguishes between collaborative working relationships that are voluntary and spontaneous and "contrived collaboration" that is mandated and administratively regulated. Moreover, even if collaboration and participation enhance teachers' influence and worklife, it is the educational consequences for students (particularly those whom schools have most failed, for example, poor and working-class children and children of color) that are most crucial. Organizational reforms and teacher empowerment may encourage participation, collaboration, and professional development, but there is no necessary link between these processes and the transformation of teaching, learning, and social relations within schools. For example, conditions can favor dialogue and reflection, but they do not guarantee that it will occur, or what its content will be. Empowered educators also may not use their newly acquired authority and improved working conditions to create qualitatively better intellectual and social experiences for students (Moore & Davenport, 1989). The relationship between teacher empowerment and the invigoration of student learning may be particularly problematic when educators differ from their students in race, class, culture, or home values (Fine, 1991). There is no necessary relationship between expanded roles and responsibilities for teachers and greater commitment to students schools have most failed. One of the tenets of the involvement of parents and community members in, for example, Chicago's school reform, is that educators need their input to restructure schools in ways that acknowledge students' home values, strengths, and culture and that give voice to those who have an unequivocal stake in students' future, their families and communities. Parent advocacy is seen as necessary to hold educators accountable for a genuine commitment to the education of all children.

Researchers have begun to publish studies that systematically examine contemporary school reform projects (Muncy & McQuillan, 1996; Wasley, 1991) and the process of restructuring in various contexts (Lieberman, 1995; Murphy & Hallinger, 1993). The results of initial empirical studies that examine the connections between changes in governance, organization, and educators' professional roles, on the one hand, and educational performance on the other suggest that re-structuring can contribute to improvements in teaching and learning (e.g., Lee & Smith, 1992; Newmann & Wehlage, 1995). Still, this wave of school reform is still young, and it may be too soon to specify consequences for students.

We do not know that restructuring will support reforms that will lead to more empowering educational experiences for students. For example, we do not know how, why, or under what conditions orga-nizational reforms and teacher empowerment will influence teachers' conception of school knowledge, of teaching and learning, and of the needs and capacities of diverse students. We do not know how these reforms may influence relationships with heretofore marginalized stu-dents. Nor do we know that these reforms will lead to expanded opportunities and competencies of students, particularly those cur-rently most at risk of school failure—and if they do, under what cir-cumstances. In short, studies do not yet capture the implications of restructuring for educational equality and for the cultural and political marginalization of workingclass students and students of color.

Sarason (1982) argues that the essential problem of school reform is the transformation of the culture of the school—the purposes and values that are reflected in the "behavioral and programmatic regu-larities" of daily life in school. The culture of the school influences the ways in which goals and problems are understood and addressed and the conceptions of "what is right, natural, and proper" (Sarason, p. 28). Unless educators challenge existing values, practices, and policies that are taken for granted, meaningful and lasting change is unlikely. A related point is that the meaning and direction of reforms are shaped by teachers' ideologies and beliefs about students (Ball, 1981; Keddie, 1971; Sharp & Green, 1975). The values of faculties or faculty subcul-tures are also consequential for how a reform is understood, adopted, ignored, or transformed (Metz, 1986; Popkewitz, Tabachnick & Wehlage, 1982). Thus, a recurring theme in recent literature on educational change is the need for the school community to develop new shared mean-ings, values, and assumptions (Fullan, 1982; Wehlage, Smith, & Lipman, 1992). The issue is under what conditions might the organizational, teacher-centered changes associated with restructuring spur reflection on, and change in, those taken-for-granted beliefs, practices, and power relations that work against African American students. To address this question, more investigation is needed of actual contexts in which restructuring unfolds.

Building on Sarason's theme, in the schools I studied, I assumed that the potential for new shared meanings depended on critical inquiry about beliefs, values, routine practices, and procedures (cf. Hopfenberg, 1991; Sirotnik, 1987) and on the participation of advocates for African American students. Accordingly, I looked for evidence that educators were using collaborative contexts to begin to scrutinize and reevaluate the daily regularities of life in their schools, especially pertaining to the experiences and educational outcomes of African American students. I also focused on how teachers used their expanded decision making to take concrete steps to improve the education of low-achieving African American students.

However, the possibility and pace of educational change depend not only on the will and dispositions of educators and the culture of schools, but also on the relative political power, influence, and resources of various social groups in the school and in the community. Whether marginalized social groups are able to change aspects of power in schools—such as the distribution of resources, access to academic curricula, and what knowledge is legitimated in the curriculum—depends on their ability to mobilize political power and resources (McCarthy, 1993). In addition, educational change is influenced by wider political and cultural trends in society and is shaped by the balance of cultural, political, and economic forces beyond the school. For instance, multicultural education grew out of social movements for ethnic and women's studies in the 1960s and 1970s (Banks, 1995). And the demands of U.S. corporate interests that schools prepare students to work in a globally competitive, information-based economy have been a significant force driving current educational reforms (National Commission on Excellence, 1983).

Therefore, not only do the values, practices, and beliefs of individual teachers influence the direction of restructuring, but reforms are shaped by social/structural factors such as current and historical patterns of economic, political, and social inequality; racial exploitation; the capitalist economy; relations between schools and communities of color; unequal resources and structures of inequality in schools; and the relative political power of social groups. The ideological influence of dominant constructions of race and the importance of educational ideologies, the framing of public policies, and the national as well as local political climates within which educators work—all shape educational reform. The challenge of a more comprehensive analysis is to reveal the relationship of classroom and school dynamics and these wider social and cultural contexts. My intent is to consider the actions of individuals and the contexts within which they work as they are knitted together in the process of restructuring (cf. Mehan, Hertweck, & Meihls, 1986). Through analyses of these interrelationships, we may understand better the possibilities and limitations of what teachers and schools can do to challenge the present realities faced by African American students.

Finally, I want to reiterate that the debilitating educational experiences of students of color cannot be transformed without uprooting broader social inequality and oppression. Transformative educational change is one aspect of a larger project of social transformation. The implications of my research should be viewed within this framework of interactive school and societal factors. I turn now to Riverton and its schools, the immediate contexts within which restructuring occurred.

3

RIVERTON, ITS SCHOOLS, AND RESTRUCTURING

Race is the great divide of all Southern politics and power.

—Report on race relations in Riverton, 1989

The first [Riverton] public school crisis opened wounds in the community and though the wounds have healed, the scars remain tender for those who advocated a particular position. One consequence of this three decades later . . . is that some of those who entered the fray in 1957 were emotionally drained by the experience and now are reluctant to become involved again. This has left a gap in leadership and has deprived the community of a valuable resource for devising practical solutions to current school problems and race relations.

—Riverton report on desegregation, 1988

The City of Riverton

Riverton is a mid-sized Southern city of about 200,000, part of a larger metropolitan area of nearly 500,000. In 1990, the city itself was about two-thirds White and one-third African American, with around 3 percent Southeast Asians and other people of color. Built on a large river at the foot of a mountain range, from its fashionable neighborhoods in the "Hills" there is a panoramic view of the wide, meandering river, the bluffs that rise up from its far banks, and the hills beyond.

As in many other Southern states, African Americans and Whites have been separated not only by a history of slavery and White supremacy but by geography and distinct economic and regional traditions. In 1990, racial segregation still prevailed in many aspects of daily life, by dint of economics, location, and tradition, if not by law. Despite the elimination of many legal barriers to education and job opportunities for African Americans, several recently published local studies pointed to the continued existence of separate cultures, segregated by race and class. Although African Americans were a majority in some parts of the state, their population concentration had not translated into political power at state or congressional levels.

The state's regions and cultures converged in Riverton. They were reflected in the city's varied population—its hill-country, agricultural, professional, and cosmopolitan residents. On a typical working day in downtown Riverton, it was common to see White men striding along in cowboy boots and hats, long lines of African American women domestic workers waiting for buses to take them to work in affluent neighborhoods, African American and White professionals on their way to the city's offices, and well-heeled couples of both races headed for one of the city's chic restaurants. As a whole, this mélange of race and class reflected the city's mixed, and changing, economy.

Riverton is in one of the fastest-growing regions of the country. Like many other U.S. cities, it has been affected by the structural transformation of the economy. Agriculture, mining, and manufacturing are being replaced by medical research and financial and other services. These structural changes have brought about increasing economic polarization and greater impoverishment, particularly for African Americans and low-income Whites. In 1986, the year before I began this study, official unemployment was 6.3%, slightly lower than elsewhere in the nation, with Black unemployment rates almost double those of Whites. One reason Riverton and the state may have been experiencing lower unemployment is that, with wages below the national average, it is an attractive area for businesses to relocate. In 1987, more than one quarter of Riverton's youth lived in poverty, and the school district reported that nearly half of the school-age population was "economically disadvantaged" (School District Data, 1988).

Residential Neighborhoods Served by Gates and Franklin

In 1990, Riverton had fairly distinct residential areas, which were generally quite segregated by race and class. Gates Junior High School drew about one third of its students from the northeast section, largely made up of two predominantly White, affluent neighborhoods: the "Hills" and the "Palisades." These neighborhoods stretched out over the high bluffs and rolling hills that dominated the city and provided a commanding view of the river below.

The Hills is where Riverton's families of old wealth have lived for generations. Here, ancestral, colonial-style homes, some of them listed in the state historical register, are nestled together along shady, tree-lined streets, with occasional clusters of expensive shops and small restaurants. In the upper Hills are the sequestered mansions of families with enormous fortunes, including some of the wealthiest in the United States. Below them are the elegant homes of the local ruling elite of corporate lawyers, heads of the major businesses and local corporations, and political leaders. In the lower Hills are the smaller homes of the strivers. The Riverton Country Club, located in the Hills, is the oldest country club in the city. In 1990, there were no African American or Jewish members.

Farther east, the mansions with their columns and shutters give way to sprawling, modern split-level houses of brick and natural wood, flanked by swimming pools, private greenhouses, tennis courts, and expanses of lawn and garden with panoramic vistas. In this area, known as the Palisades, are the homes of the *nouveau riche*—bankers, medical professionals, government officials, and business people, also members of the Riverton elite. In 1990, a sprinkling of African American professionals and Jews lived in the Palisades. The Palisades Country Club, which was newer than the Riverton, had some Jewish and African American members.

African American students from the Old West Side, southwest of downtown, were also bused to Gates Junior High School. In stark contrast with the Hills and Palisades, the Old West Side was one of the poorest African American communities in the city and the first to flood when the river periodically overflowed its banks. The area seemed at once industrial and rural, with small, ramshackle houses sandwiched between factories and truck routes and spread out along streets that seemed more like country roads with their absence of sidewalks and curbs. Warehouses and factories were scattered throughout. The city sewage plant occupied one corner, its stench detectable for blocks, and there was a steady roar of planes overhead from the nearby airport.

Most Old West Side houses were one-story, constructed of crumbling clapboard. Some had sunken or even fallen-in roofs and broken windows. A series of one-story, red brick, barracks-like housing projects occupied the center of the community. The business district consisted of a storefront grocery, three taverns, the Kitty Cat restaurant with barred windows, and a small church. The local African American radio station was also headquartered here. The only modern structures were a large, new, city-funded community center, with playing fields and basketball courts; a former elementary school that now housed Riverton's alternative school for "violent and problem" students; and a magnet elementary school.

Franklin Junior High School drew its students from the Expressway Corridor, or "the Corridor," a predominantly working-class and poor African American section of town. Apart from a few gentrified sections near the city center, the most prosperous neighborhoods in the Corridor were composed of one-story, ranch-style brick houses where Franklin's most well-off students lived—African American and White middle-class children. Surrounding the school was a racially integrated neighborhood of small, somewhat worn, ranch-style homes and frame bungalows with neat yards, the homes of African American and White working-class families. But the majority of Franklin students lived in neighborhoods of dilapidated frame and concrete houses east of the school. Or they lived in tracts of rusting trailer parks and unpainted, battered frame houses located across from a huge junkyard in an area that flooded after heavy rains, filling with pools of standing water. These tracts were primarily African American but included low-income Whites as well. Some Franklin students of both races from these neighborhoods were so impoverished that they lacked clothes, shoes, and basic necessities like pencils. It was not uncommon for teachers to buy students clothing and school supplies, and the nurse kept a supply of soap and toothbrushes for students who did not have them at home. Although there were differences in the socioeconomic status of students, they were not as extreme as at Gates, nor were they so clearly associated with race.

City Politics

Most of Riverton's elected political leaders were White males. The city was not highly organized politically through coalitions or power blocks, or political party machines. Rather, political leaders and powerful public figures seemed to operate through spheres of personal influence. As a recent, foundation-authored report on politics in the state put it, "power and politics are highly personalized." This was also true of the business community, where a few extremely wealthy individuals wielded a great deal of power. Until 1991, when key business leaders supported a school millage increase, business interests were widely acknowledged to have given up on the public schools.

There was little evidence of an organized African American political structure with real clout and little in the way of African American grassroots organization outside the churches. The most outspoken African American leaders were clergy and lawyers. The most public racial issue during my years in Riverton was ongoing monitoring by several African American lawyers of Riverton's school desegregation settlement won on behalf of a group of African American parents. Over the 3 years of my study, African American students, parents, and teachers also demanded a Black history celebration at a high school and African American history in the curriculum. They challenged the disproportionate suspension of Black students, significant under-prepresentation of African Americans in honors classes, and the district's 2.0 grade point average requirement to participate in extra-curricular activities. However, none of these issues galvanized much visible public involvement, although the two African American School Board members were supportive. Meanwhile old-line civil rights organizations played a minimal role in city politics, although the local NAACP took public stands on various issues. Divisions among leaders in the African American community were apparent in their stands on desegregation—some continued to fight within the framework of desegregation while others argued for improving African American schools, and some called for a separate African American district. The leaders were also split on supporting the millage referendum, with some seeing it as accommodation to a racist school system. In any case, Africa American leaders seemed to operate more as individuals than as spokespersons of organized constituencies.

Indeed, there was little grassroots organization of any type in Riverton. The state was an anti-union stronghold, a right-to-work state, and in 1991 a local labor union leader told me that the labor movement, which was historically weak, was on the decline. During my 3 years in the city I saw only a few examples of teacher union activity, and none at Franklin or Gates.

Social History

Some of Riverton's most significant social history could be discerned from the architecture of the central city. The colonial facade of the carefully maintained Old Court House stood as a testament to the city's Confederate heritage. The wealth of that era was displayed in the sumptuous, newly restored Riverview Hotel and the rejuvenated antebellum houses of the central district. So too, the artifacts of slavery on exhibit in the Court House Museum gave evidence of generations of African American oppression and of the great racial divisions—often focused in battles over education—that shaped the city's culture and politics.

A prominent historically Black college occupied a large block on the edge of the central district. Its small campus stood as evidence of the persistent struggle for education waged by Riverton's African American citizens. Just a few blocks away was one of the first college-preparatory Black high schools of the South. In the late 1920s, African Americans thwarted the attempts of powerful local Whites and Northern foundations to make the new school a training center for industrial occupations. Instead, Frederick Douglas High School, established to provide a solid foundation for a college education for Black students, opened with great ceremony in 1929. With its classical liberal arts curriculum, the school was once recognized as a model for African American academic high schools throughout the South, as well as the pride of the local African American community.

By 1990, Douglas had become a junior high school, somewhat in disrepair with a parking lot badly in need of paving. Located in the heart of an historically Black neighborhood, the school grounds were ringed by the modest homes of low-income African American families. However, despite its apparent neglect, the expansive three-story, red brick structure, with its wide hallways and spacious grounds, was a reminder of the generations of youth trained there, their accomplishments nurtured, their characters molded, and their aspirations stretched by a corps of committed and exacting Black teachers working against the obstacles of Jim Crow (former Douglas student, personal communication, December 1989) (cf. Siddle Walker, 1996).

About a mile away, historically all-White Hamilton High School, built around the same time, dwarfed Douglas by comparison. Hamilton's elaborate colonial facade with two-story columns and massive front stairway was the site, in the late 1950s, of violent clashes over school desegregation. Scenes of angry segregationist Whites, raging against a score of young Black teenagers determined to enroll at Hamilton, were played out across the South, dramatizing Southern White resistance to racial integration.

When I began my research, the student population of Hamilton was about 55% Black, 43% White, 2% Asian and other. Nevertheless, the shadow of the conflict begun 35 years ago still hung over the city, touching nearly every important school board decision, and was still played out in ongoing court cases. Its legacy was also very much alive in the collective memory of Riverton's inhabitants, African American and White alike. Frustration with interminable legal battles over desegregation surfaced in even casual conversations with ordinary people of both races. There was a deeply felt sense of ignominy communicated by some White community leaders when they talked about "the trouble at Hamilton High." Other Whites, who supported civil rights organizations and continued to work for racial justice, expressed frustration at the seemingly unyielding White opposition in Riverton. For them, the bitter fight over school integration exemplified the general intractability of racial attitudes and conservatism in the city and the state. During my 3 years of research, racial tensions continued to surface at Hamilton in fights between students and charges of discrimination by African American teachers and parents.

Desegregation of the Riverton Public Schools

In the 35 years since the first confrontation at Hamilton High School, Riverton had been attempting to desegregate its schools in a series of reassignment plans involving busing, school choice, and magnet schools. In an attempt to block efforts to desegregate Hamilton High School, the Riverton schools were actually closed for a time in the 1950's. When they reopened, many White parents avoided racial integration by enrolling their children in all-White Christian academies. In 1990, these schools continued to draw White students away from the public schools, particularly at the elementary level. Since the struggle at Hamilton High, the school district had been in litigation almost constantly, either as plaintiff or defendant in desegregation suits. In the last decade, the district remained under the direct supervision of a federal district court judge for desegregation.

A Riverton School District report in the early 1980s projected that the district would be 100% African American by the year 2000 if the existing trend of White flight continued. The various desegregation plans that were fashioned in the 1980s outlined measures aimed at reversing this trend, including redrawing district boundaries to encompass outlying White areas, but a failed choice plan begun in the mid-1980s accelerated White flight. Almost three fourths of the nonmagnet schools lost White students between 1986 and 1988. In these 2 years, the district lost 17% of Whites assigned to elementary schools. With the apparent lack of success of the choice strategy, the district submitted yet another plan in 1989 to address the reality of persistent racial segregation and unequal education. The introduction to the 1989 plan warned that this might be the city's "last opportunity" to achieve "quality desegregated education." A district official commented that the desegregation plan would either "make us or break us." And the superintendent asserted quite bluntly that three and a half decades after *Brown v. Board of Education* the issue of school desegregation "remained an elusive goal."

Meanwhile, African American leaders in Riverton continued to voice demands for quality education for African American children. While some appeared regularly at school board meetings and in public forums to press for policies that, in their view, would promote equity, others publicly expressed an unwillingness to persist. Toward the end of the 1980s, some African American church leaders concluded that African American children, especially at the elementary level, would do better in the nurturing environment of Black schools with Black principals and teachers. As a result, a fledgling Africentric educational movement began to emerge among some African American teachers and clergy.

It is important to recall that desegregation, in addition to being incomplete and conflictual, was a fairly recent development in cities like Riverton. Black and White teaching and administrative staffs were merged just 15 to 20 years ago, and racially separate schools were a living memory for many parents, teachers, and administrators in my study. Many African American teachers attended all-Black schools, and most veteran African American teachers taught in them, even after segregation was legally struck down. Several of the most experienced White teachers at Gates had taught at Gates, or at Magnolia Ridge, a neighboring school, when both were all-White. Many teachers and at least half of the district's central administrators also were products of the segregated system. (Many African American teachers and administrators charged that they were given positions in the desegregated system that were inferior to those they held in African American schools.) Thus, the culture and practice of segregated schools was very much a part of the consciousness of many of the educators in Riverton. It was not uncommon for teachers and administrators of both races to hark back, for different reasons, to the merits of Black or White schools in their advocacy of specific curricula, discipline practices, or social support networks for students.

The Riverton School District

In 1990–91, Riverton public schools enrolled about 25,000 students. Based on school district data, in 1987–88, 43% of all students attending Riverton public schools were "economically disadvantaged," and in 1990–91, 33% were eligible for free or subsidized lunch—an indicator of family income near or below the poverty level.

As in most U.S. urban school districts, children of color were a growing proportion of Riverton's school age population. According to district data, by 1990–91 Black enrollment had risen to about 64%. While Black enrollment was increasing, total enrollment for the district steadily decreased since 1987, reflecting a rapid decline in White enrollment. This trend was explained in part by the steady in-migration of African Americans from rural areas and an out-migration of Whites to nearby suburbs and by a steady increase in private school population.

The year 1987 was one of substantial change in the Riverton School District. There was the annexation of portions of the county school districts and the incorporation of staff from those districts in an attempt to increase the percentage of Whites. The state also began to implement statewide minimum achievement standards for promotion and required competency tests at the third, sixth, and eighth grades. On grounds of racial discrimination, African American parents successfully sued for the elimination of a remedial "basic" track consisting overwhelmingly of African American students.

Schools and Administration

In 1990, the Riverton district was an amalgam of the newly annexed county schools and Riverton schools. Teaching faculties, administrators and students reflected this mix. The district had 37 elementary schools, 8 junior high schools, and 5 high schools. Most were "area" schools whose enrollment was based on attendance zones. Five elementary schools, two junior highs, and two high schools were magnet specialty schools, designed to offer curricular options that would entice White parents to remain in the district and send their children to schools in African American neighborhoods.

Of the eight junior high schools, Crestwood, a math/science and arts magnet, generally scored at the top of the junior high schools on standardized achievement tests—just above Gates. Among the area schools there was a hierarchy of reputation, with Gates at the top. Schools acquired their informal reputations by dint of the socioeconomic and racial composition of their neighborhood and student body, their test scores, and perhaps most important, their traditional place in the history and culture of Riverton. For example, schools like Hamilton High School, that historically trained the college-bound and the Riverton elite, continued to rank as premier schools although desegregation and population migrations had somewhat altered their demographic composition and student culture. Conversely, Franklin, although it had had a more solidly working-class and middle-class White student population in the late 1970s to early 1980s, had never had the reputation of Hamilton or Gates. Known in 1990 as a low-income African American school, its past history did not help it attract teachers or support from district officials.

The district had a rather conventional top-down bureaucratic organization. Despite its stated intent in 1987 to move to site-based management, no steps were taken toward local school decision making until the advent of "whole school restructuring" in 1990. From 1978 to 1990 the Riverton district had four superintendents, three from 1982 to 1990. This turnover in leadership contributed to the district's instability.

The district was divided into seven geographical sectors, each with a representative elected to the Riverton School Board, and board members came to the table representing particular constituencies with their own agendas. At the time of this study, the board was composed of two African Americans (a lawyer and an administrator at an histori- cally Black college) who represented primarily low-income African American working-class areas. The other five were White. There were two representatives of the areas that included the Hills and Palisades. One was a partner in one of Riverton's top corporate law firms and an unofficial adviser to the governor of the state. The other was a wife of a local business leader. Two of the remaining three members repre- sented conservative White working-class neighborhoods, the third a racially mixed but primarily White middle-class area. (One was a former teacher; another had a small business; the third was a lawyer with a small firm.) In general, the African American members supported restructuring as did the Heights and Palisades members until, as I discuss in later chapters, it posed what they saw as a threat to the honors track. The other three members were less consistent, but two were quite conservative on social issues such as school-based clinics that were part of high school reform. During the years of my research in Riverton, nearly every board decision was contentious and subject to political bargaining, and the superintendent described the board's narrow, constituency politics as a major obstacle to educational re- form. Because of the board's divisions, district administrators chose not to consult with the board on particulars of school restructuring. In fact, the introduction of an untracked class came as a surprise to the board in mid-year. These competing interests on the board came to play an important role in restructuring.

Racial Inequality

The introduction to the 1989 Desegregation Plan stated that the Riverton School District had not only been unable to achieve racial balance, it had also been unsuccessful in educating many of its African American students. Standardized test results were just one indication of the district's failure. Despite Riverton's relatively high average scores on standardized measures of achievement as compared with national norms, the tests reflected striking discrepancies between African Americans and Whites. For example, the district reported an average 25 percentile point difference in the achievement of Black and White students in 1988, the first year of my research in Riverton (Project Data, 1989). According to the 1989 Desegregation Plan, these dispari- ties persisted despite "thousands of hours of student remediation and technical assistance for teachers."

Moreover, inequalities extended to other aspects of African American school experience such as grade retention, course failure, and disciplinary actions. Three-year longitudinal data (1988–89 to 1990–91) for grades 7 through 12 revealed a pattern of inequality. While 16.2% of White students were suspended at least once, 33.7% of Black students were suspended at least once; 7.8% of White students were retained at least one year compared with 16.1% of Black students; and 37.6% of Whites failed at least one course compared with 61.1% of Blacks (Project Data, 1991). When the district began planning restructuring in 1987, although African American youth comprised 54% of the 7th through 10th-graders, they were nearly 75% of the dropouts and 98% of the district's expelled students (Project Documents, 1988).

A 1990 audit of the district's curriculum also pointed out marked racial discrepancies in educational opportunity. For example, the audit found tracking was resulting in resegregation; racial bias was evident in the distribution of teachers and resources; and honors classes were racially identifiable [White]. According to a survey of seniors in 1988, African American students were more likely than White students to be enrolled in vocational education, and White students were more likely to be enrolled in college preparatory programs (Project Documents, 1988). Racial disparities were a significant educational issue in the Riverton community. An indication of the political significance of this issue was that, under pressure from Court desegregation mandates, the state made forgiveness of a large loan to the district contingent upon raising the test scores of African American children to 90% of those of White children by the year 2000.

Lack of Public Confidence in the Schools

Any picture of the Riverton School District must be painted against a background of repeated desegregation-related crises, controversies, and disruptions for students, families, and school personnel. At all levels of the community, there was a residue of pessimism about the permanence of any decision of the courts or the central administration. When I began this study in 1988, I found teachers to be generally cynical and worn out by the instability in their own professional lives and in the lives of their schools. People were uniformly frustrated and embittered, but from opposite sides of the issue, as they framed it. Put simplistically, on one side, some (African American and White alike) blamed influential White parents and an intractable White power structure that seemed bent on pulling everything down with it rather than yield to educational equality. On the other side, some (mainly Whites) voiced their annoyance at what they perceived as the district's exaggerated preoccupation with race at the expense of "getting on with the job of educating the children."

In 1988 the community was also widely acknowledged to have little confidence in the quality of its schools. Riverton voters had refused to pass a millage increase for school financing for more than 10 years, and the local press regularly printed columns, editorials, and letters to the editor berating the schools, which were often blamed for the city's inability to attract investment. Meanwhile, in my interviews with school leaders, many expressed frustration at their own impotence in the face of court supervision of all administrative and policy decisions.

The lack of public confidence, coupled with ongoing court regulation, helped explain why school leaders seemed preoccupied with test scores and with maintaining stability at all costs. The district's success in reducing the gap between White and Black standardized achievement scores had become a public touchstone for measuring its success in alleviating inequality. Public disclosure of these scores every May seemed to have become an annual spring ritual, a time to decry the dismal state of education in Riverton and to search for culpability. The local newspapers raked school administrators over the coals. School board members, school administrators, and teachers all blamed each other, and were in turn blamed in the media. As a result, school leaders were defensive and without much apparent initiative. An outside curriculum auditor in 1990 noted that the administration and the board of education seemed always to be reacting to crises. Principals reported that they were continually under pressure to maintain stability and stifle conflict in their schools.

This environment of crisis and defensiveness significantly influenced the course of restructuring and teachers' willingness to confront controversial issues related to the marginalization of African American students. Meanwhile, teachers complained that the district's leadership structure was capricious and authoritarian. "They treat us like children," was a repeated refrain during my first year of interviewing teachers. They claimed they were not consulted by district leaders, not supported by the community, and not considered in board decisions. These grievances were exacerbated by extremely low salaries (the state was among the 10 lowest nationally). In spring 1988, I found few educators who would take seriously the possibility of effecting significant educational change.

However, during the next 2 years, there was some evidence that conditions in the Riverton district were improving. In the spring of 1990 the desegregation suit was finally settled, and voters passed a millage increase for school financing for the first time in 10 years. With the largest voter turnout in the city's history, the referendum represented a vote of public confidence in the schools. Moreover, the increase was actively lobbied for by a coalition of some of the city's leading business interests, traditionally outspoken critics of the schools.

Still, African American leaders appeared divided, some favoring the referendum, others refusing to support what they viewed as a racist school system. This was the context in which Riverton began restructuring its junior high schools.

Gates Junior High School

Gates Junior High School was the flagship junior high in Riverton, the traditional choice for those at the top of Riverton's social ladder who did not opt for a local private school or a boarding school. (However, in recent years it faced competition from the new magnet junior high school.) Located on the southern edge of the affluent Hills district, the sons and daughters of Riverton's business and civic leaders could walk to the school.

Gates was an older, well-kept, three-story, squarish red brick building, emblematic of American education in a past era of stability. A newer, one-story addition was connected to the main building by a covered walkway and housed classrooms and the gym. Sunlight streamed into the school's main entrance through large, clean windows onto pots of red geraniums—a gift from the PTO. Plaques on the wall in the front hallway registered the school's honors in debate and Quiz Bowl. A laminated sign proclaimed "All Children Can Learn," and hand-drawn charts recorded the results of team contests for the fewest fights and suspensions—both products of the new restructuring project. Off the main hallway were the school offices, a spacious, well-stocked library, a large auditorium, a few classrooms, and the faculty lounge.

The lounge was a large, pleasant, carpeted room, well equipped and tastefully decorated in soft grays. Anyone familiar with faculty lounges in other Riverton junior high schools would have been struck by their contrast with Gates. Typically, they were one-half to one-third the size, poorly equipped, cramped and dark, with a clutter of hodge-podge furniture in varying states of disrepair. The superiority of Gates's faculty lounge was due to the efforts of the PTO, which raised the money to have the room refurbished in the mid-1980s.

From the ground floor hallway, one narrow flight of stairs led down to basement-level classrooms, the school cafeteria, and special education classrooms in the far rear of the building. Another, wider stairway, led up to second- and third-floor classrooms. Some were spacious and sunny, but others had been subdivided to accommodate the school's burgeoning enrollment. In 1989, a group of parents of students with classes on the third floor, where the honors classes were located, took the initiative to have doors installed to reduce the noise filtering between classrooms. The parents discussed the problem at the school open house in the fall and wrote checks on the spot to hire carpenters and purchase materials. Second-floor teachers related that the construction did not include their classrooms, where predominantly regular track classes were held. (In the interim, the principal did provide curtains for both floors to help reduce noise.)

The third-floor doors and renovation of the faculty lounge were two examples of the active role that White Hills and Palisades parents played at Gates. The Parent Teacher Organization (PTO) raised thousands of dollars for the school annually. The annual PTO sock hop, held at a fashionable hotel ballroom, was important enough in Riverton's social calendar to be written up, complete with pictures, in the society pages of the local newspapers. It was common to see well-dressed White parents visiting the principal or working on a PTO project in the faculty lounge. Through their involvement, these parents not only provided resources that enhanced their children's education and teachers' work life, but they also gained leverage over decisions about school policies, curriculum, student assignments, and faculty. Gates was what Connell, Ashenden, Kessler, and Dowsett (1982) refer to as a school that functioned as a "class organizer." As one administrator put it, "They're a bunch of bourgeois parents, but they have a lot of power in this town and in this school, and we have to coddle 'em." As I will demonstrate, the influence of these parents became a significant factor in school restructuring at Gates.

Gates's wide hallways were well lit and immaculate. In my frequent visits, custodians with brooms, floor polishers, and window-washing equipment seemed nearly ubiquitous. The hallways were also generally quiet and orderly with only an occasional student on some errand, oversized hall pass prominently displayed. The school's two mandatory security guards were visible but unobtrusive as they patrolled the halls and the campus. Only at arrival, departure, and lunch time were the assistant principals and some teachers with walkie-talkies conspicuously on watch.

In substance and image, Gates was what Metz (1990) has called "real school." The school posted the highest test scores for Whites (with the exception of the magnet school), and Gates's students continued to compete well in citywide debates and essay contests. Its curriculum was the standard series of academic core subjects and a good selection of college preparatory and vocational electives. Except for a self-contained group of special education students, all students were tracked into regular track or gifted classes, known as honors classes, for math, English, science, and social studies. A little less than half of each grade was in honors classes at Gates. In the view of teachers, administrators, and most students, a student's placement in either of these two tracks was central to the construction of her/his identity and place in the school.

Honors classes were implicitly the standard for Gates's academic reputation. It was the image and tradition of rigorous academic preparation that drew the children of affluent families to the school. At the end of the school day, they gathered noisily on the corners or stayed for afterschool activities. In their preppie clothes, they were easily identified as neighborhood kids as they hiked up the hill toward home. They were all White. Another group of White students, and a few African Americans, were bused in from the Palisades. However, many of the other students who traveled by bus to Gates were a different crowd altogether. They also congregated noisily in the school parking lot, waiting to get on buses that would transport them back to their homes in the Old West Side, one of Riverton's poorest communities. They were all African American. At Gates, class and race corresponded. The tension between a de facto White, affluent academic culture and tradition and the new realities of a multiracial, multiclass student body was at the very center of what went on there (cf. Schofield, 1982).

In 1990–91 there were about 750 students enrolled at Gates, with about 65% African American, 34% White, and 1% "other"—Asians and Native Americans. For children from the Hills and Palisades, Gates was an extension of their world (cf. Connell et al., 1982). Their families were in the same social and professional circles. Many attended the same summer camps, went to the same parties, and belonged to the same churches. To these students, Gates's strong academic tradition, with its sequence of honors-track classes and academically oriented competitions, was perhaps challenging, but expected and familiar. As I will elaborate in the following chapters, Gates's cultural norms were compatible with those of their own families. When they got into trouble it was within the context of their own behavioral framework.

The experiences of low-income African American students revealed another side of Gates. These students who were bused in traveled not only across town, but across chasms of class and race. At Gates they entered the foreign terrain of the wealthy and powerful. The same traditions and unspoken cultural rules that made life comfortable for well-off White students could be a formidable barrier to outsiders. Indeed, African American students did not do well at the school, where standardized measures of achievement and grade-point averages were the quintessence of school success. According to district data, in 1989–90, they scored, on average, about 39 percentile points lower than White students on standardized tests of reading and math across all three grades (Blacks averaged in the 44th percentile, Whites in the 83rd; see table 3.1). The largest differential was a 52-point difference in the reading scores of Black and White females in the seventh grade. In fact, racial disparities at Gates were the largest in the district. African American students were also disproportionately concentrated in regular track classes and overrepresented in special education, and had significantly higher suspension and failure rates than Whites.

Veteran teachers at Gates said the enrollment had been reshuffled four or five times over the past 16 years for desegregation. In 1970 the entire faculties of Magnolia Ridge and Gates were traded because of "racial problems" (an event no one wanted to discuss with me in detail). Ten of the teachers from the group traded in 1970, all White, were still teaching at Gates in 1990. Along with a number of others who had been there for 10 or 15 years, these teachers identified very strongly with Gates's traditional academic culture. For years an important aspect of their mission had been to prepare students for matriculation to Hamilton High School's college preparatory program. Many had taught the older brothers and sisters of current students and knew their parents. They were known as "good" teachers in a conventional sense: They knew their disciplines, were thorough, serious, held high academic standards, stuck to their texts and lectures, and ran traditional, teacher-centered classes.

TABLE 3.1

Achievement Comparisons in Reading and Math (Percentile Scores) Across Grade by Race, 1989–90, for Gates and Franklin.

Gates

| | Reading | | | Math | | |
	7	8	9	7	8	9
Black	36.9	42.4	50.0	42.4	36.9	53.7
White	84.1	82.9	87.3	84.1	76.2	85.2

Franklin

| | Reading | | | Math | | |
	7	8	9	7	8	9
Black	36.9	35.2	48.1	38.7	31.7	53.7
White	63.0	80.3	74.7	53.7	66.5	64.8

Source: Project Data.

The marginality of African American students at Gates was replicated and reinforced by the subordinate position of African American staff. In 1990–91, Gates had 41 White teachers and 8 African American teachers. With 16% of the faculty African American, Gates had the lowest percentage of any junior high school in the district. Furthermore, all but two of the African American teachers were concentrated in low-status remedial or nonacademic areas such as physical education, special education, and reading. One assistant administrator, one counselor, and a few teacher aids were also African American. As a whole, the African American staff had little prestige and little power within the faculty. This proved to be a significant factor influencing the nature of dialogue among teachers and their responses to restructuring at Gates.

The principal, Ron Walters, a White male in his forties, returned to the school in 1988 after a 3-year stint as an administrator at the central office. His job at Gates was highly political. He faced continual pressure from neighborhood parents, school board members from the Hills and Palisades, and some district leaders to maintain the traditional college preparatory curriculum and cultural norms for which Gates was known. At the same time, he was pressed by district leaders under court mandate to reduce racial disparities. A considerable part of his job was balancing what he construed as competing demands. Nevertheless, he seemed to thrive under the pressure, sometimes comparing it favorably with his days in the army. As one district administrator commented, "Ron is the only one who can hold that school together."

Franklin Junior High School

A low brick wall marking the corner of the school grounds announced "Franklin Junior High School—Home of the Tigers." Beneath the inscription was an image of a tiger, poised to strike. The school itself was a single-story, flat-roofed, yellowish brick and concrete structure built in the shape of an "H" with a central hallway and four wings. Each of the three grades and the related arts classes occupied a wing. Unlike Gates, special education classrooms were prominently located in the very center of the building, and these students were a regular and visible part of the action in the central hallway. A single row of small, high, rectangular windows ran across the outside of the building, much like a horizontal line of garage door windows. Many of the interior walls were painted concrete block, adding to the garage-like feel of the building.

There were two faculty lounges. One, a lunchroom adjacent to the cafeteria, was just large enough for two round formica tables that seated three or four, a longer table with eight folding chairs, a microwave oven, a refrigerator, and a sink. A dysfunctional juke box still displaying songs from the 1970s partially blocked a sign admonishing teachers to "have a positive attitude." There was little else—no coffee or soda machine, no carpet, couch, or phone. Unlike the bustling lounge at Gates, this room was often unoccupied. Some teachers did not frequent it at all, preferring to hang out in the custodians' storeroom during breaks or to sit in empty classrooms. Others—a group of White women—spent their time in the smoking lounge, a dingy room with a forlorn couch, several chairs, and a table sandwiched into a narrow, smoke-choked space adjacent to the women's bathroom.

Near the east end of the building were three double trailers, each with two classrooms, which were brought in in 1985 to accommodate increased enrollment. These classrooms were windowless and cramped, just large enough for a teacher's desk and four tightly packed rows of student desks, with inadequate shelf space and tiny blackboards. The trailers were hot in the spring and fall and cold in the winter. Teachers complained that any innovation such as cooperative learning groups was precluded by the physical limitations of these classrooms.

Although Franklin was only about 40 years old, its newer, but inferior construction contrasted sharply with the traditional solidity of Gates, and the building seemed to have been poorly maintained. Prefabricated ceiling tiles were often discolored and askew; metal window frames needed paint; streaks of rust discolored the outside of the building. Hallways were not dirty, but always seemed to be littered with small scraps of paper that adults were endlessly picking up. Although Franklin's custodians were often sweeping and mopping, unlike the intensity with which Gates's custodial staff maintained the building, their work seemed almost casual. Franklin's parking lot was unpaved and pocked with deep potholes. When it rained, the lot flooded, and teachers could not get to their cars without being splashed with mud. Despite 2 years of requests and a thick stack of work orders, as of summer 1991, the principal could not get the central office to allocate funds to pave the parking lot. She could not even get gravel. For faculty and administrators, the lot had become emblematic of the district's neglect of the school.

Indeed, deficiency of resources of all kinds was a major issue at Franklin. In 1991, counselors did not have a decent typewriter, much less a computer; by the end of the year teachers had run out of paper;

math teachers did not have a set of calculators; there was no science equipment. The trailers did not alleviate the severe overcrowding. In 1990 the library reference room was converted to classroom space, and the librarian was forced to store reference materials on carts in a closet. Several offices were also converted to classrooms, and a former storage closet served as the office of the school caseworker.

Throughout most of its existence, Franklin had a stable administration and student population and a decent academic reputation. However, there were three principals in the period from 1986 to 1990, and the series of student reassignment plans, coupled with the city's shifting demographics, caused a rapid turnover in students and staff. As African Americans migrated eastward from downtown Riverton and Whites moved beyond the city limits, the area served by Franklin became increasingly African American. In 1988 Franklin was 68% African American. In 1990, it was 80% African American and 20% White, the highest percentage of African Americans of any junior high in the district. It was also during these years that its academic standing declined. In 1990 Franklin students posted some of the lowest achievement scores in the district, averaging in the 56th percentile nationally (see Table 3.1). By comparison, Gates averaged in the 65th even with its significantly lower scores for African Americans. According to data provided by the school district, racial disparities in achievement and socioeconomic status (SES) were less than at Gates, averaging about 12 percentile points in each of the years 1987–88 through 1990–91.

By 1990–91, Franklin had an enrollment of 780 and was rapidly becoming known as a "Black school." Many Franklin staff members also believed that the school had become the district's unofficial destination for problem students from other schools. In 1990–91 the central office transferred a record number of students to Franklin, many of whom had been expelled from other schools or had been attending the district's alternative school for "disruptive" students. During that year several well-publicized, isolated incidents of weapons and fighting on school grounds reinforced Franklin's image as an "inner city" or "tough" school. (Although sometimes more boisterous than Gates, Franklin never seemed tense or intimidating to us as observers over 3 years.)

Franklin had fewer honors classes than at some other junior highs. For example, the single ninth-grade Algebra II class had only eight students as compared with two full sections of over 20 students at Gates. At Franklin, only math and English were tracked as compared with all core subjects at Gates. Franklin also offered fewer college preparatory electives and had none of the traditional college-prep extracurricular activities such as the debate club or quiz bowl that were popular at Gates. While Gates's reputation was built on its college preparatory honors-track classes, Franklin was known as a general studies, average-track school.

Despite its reputed problems, Franklin's families were obviously concerned about their children's education. More than 450 family members attended a Franklin orientation meeting in the fall of 1990— more than triple the number who had attended in previous years and far more than attended open houses at Gates. This huge turnout was the result of phone calls made by teachers as well as advertising in the community. But school staff were unable to create ways to translate this interest into ongoing relationships with parents. A few parents were active in the PTO, which had African American and White co-chairs, but the PTO also had little presence in the school. When parents did come to school, it was usually in response to a problem with their child.

At Gates, I found that a sense of order and adult control predominated. At Franklin the ambiance was much more lively. Class changes were often somewhat raucous, filled with the singing, shouting, jostling, and occasional verbal altercations of large numbers of energetic young adolescents all jamming the corridors at once. Their commotion was punctuated by the yelling of security guards and teachers. During classes there were a few clumps of students wandering the building, some with passes, others without. Confrontations between these latter offenders and security guards were a routine part of life at Franklin. On the other hand, there were rich interactions between some teachers and students. For example, it was common to see groups of students crowded around a teacher who was alternately proffering stern admonitions, solemn advice, hugs, and spirited teasing.

In 1990–91, half of Franklin's teachers were African American, the largest percentage of any junior high in the district. The school's teaching and support staff was sharply divided along lines of race, years of tenure, subject area, and views about students. Schisms were so deep that some teachers simply never spoke to each other. The various sets of teachers congregated in different lounges or classrooms, rode in separate car pools, segregated themselves at faculty meetings, and led separate existences within the same building. Unlike Gates's dominant faculty culture, Franklin was a mélange of philosophies and values that coexisted and contended.

There were five, somewhat overlapping, groupings that I could identify. Perhaps the largest was a tightly knit group of about 12 White teachers, many of whom congregated in the smoking lounge and had little apparent interaction with the rest of the staff. Predominantly noncore subject teachers and Franklin veterans, they were publicly outspoken about what they perceived as the school's degeneration and privately critical of the present administration and of African American teachers who they said "coddled" disruptive students. This group found recruits among some of the school's young White teachers with similar attitudes.

A second distinct group was composed of African American teachers who defined themselves as advocates and mentors of Franklin's many students designated "at risk." Several were also vocal critics of racism among the staff and in the curriculum. They included about seven African American women whom I call the *Othermothers*, borrowing Hill Collins's (1991) term to capture the essence of teachers who behaved as community mothers to "their kids" at Franklin. Their parallel was a small circle (five or six) of African American men teachers who saw themselves as role models for Franklin's young African American males. Much of their free time was spent in the hallways where they monitored students in a manner similar to the Othermothers.

A third, looser grouping of four or five mainly African American teachers, including several Othermothers and Mentors were the school's academic leaders. They led the honors society, tutored, directed student projects, and talked enthusiastically about their curriculum and various student accomplishments. There was also a small group of primarily young innovators, African American and White, who were the source of energy for creative projects and curricular experiments. Finally, there was a not-inconsequential collection of teachers, African American and White, who seemingly were just there, as one teacher put it, "for a paycheck." Others remained aloof from these groups or exhibited shifting alliances. These groups sometimes overlapped, and associations changed with issues and events. The complex divisions among the faculty were central to the ways teachers interpreted restructuring and to how it evolved at Franklin.

In 1990–91, the principal, Delisa Johnson, an African American woman in her early forties, was in her second year at Franklin. She confided that when she saw the building for the first time she cried. However, Johnson was not one to be overwhelmed by adversity. She immediately recruited teachers to join her in raking and cleaning up the school grounds and scrubbing the building. She set an example for the faculty by personally monitoring the halls at every class change, frequently visiting classrooms, and intervening in student conflicts. It was common for her to take students shopping when they needed clothes and other necessities, to make home visits in crisis situations, even to tutor failing students after school.

Transforming Franklin became Johnson's personal crusade; she worked nights and weekends and vacations, lobbied the central office, and politicked with the restructuring office and the media. Nevertheless, she had relatively little power in the district. She was untenured and the lowest-paid junior high school principal, with few connections to veteran African American administrators. Unlike the Gates principal, she had little influence with the central administration and school board and no organized powerful parent group. She also had not yet acquired a clear-cut power base within Franklin's fractious faculty. The character of Johnson's leadership and her new position in the district and the school had important ramifications for the course of restructuring at Franklin.

Restructuring in Riverton

School restructuring in Riverton, with its explicit goal of reducing racial disparities in achievement and discipline actions and addressing the needs of "at-risk"students, was partially a response to desegregation mandates and litigation by African American families for equal education. School reform was part of a broader, foundation-funded effort to improve youth-serving institutions for students identified as "at-risk." The foundation grant was secured by a community collaborative made up of leaders of youth-related social services and schools, political leaders, the president of the teacher's union, and representatives of community agencies, business interests, and a Black church federation. Apart from school personnel, most collaborative members were not actively involved in restructuring. The president of the teacher's union said little in collaborative meetings we observed, and the union was invisible in restructuring activities and planning throughout the year. In an interview, the union president contended that early on the district administration had rejected a proposed union oversight committee for restructuring. Although he contended that restructuring would be used to undermine the union, the union took no visible initiative and did not put forward its own vision or independent agenda for educational reform. Notably absent from the board were outspoken African American community activists and several Whites known for their history of supporting racial equality (several of whom were used as consultants during the planning phase but excluded from the collaborative) and strong, democratically chosen parent and teacher representation.

Restructuring was an evolutionary process, beginning in 1988 from a narrow set of school reforms involving a few teachers in three junior high schools (Franklin, Magnolia Ridge, and Douglas). In addition to some remedial, tutoring, and mentoring programs, and the addition of caseworkers, in 1988 three junior high schools were reorganized into teams at one grade level. In the second year, an additional school was added. This was the precursor to "whole school restructuring." In the third year, the faculties of Gates, Franklin, and two other schools agreed by majority vote to become "restructured schools." There did not seem to be consistent criteria guiding the selection of these schools. According to the restructuring director, Gates was chosen because it was the most prestigious junior high with an experienced and competent staff. The Gates principal also lobbied aggressively to be included. Franklin had been a participant since the inception of reform and had been identified by district administrators as having a low-achieving population relevant to a project focused on "at-risk" students.

The "At-risk" Label

In the district's restructuring proposal, the classification "at risk" was applied to youth experiencing academic, attendance, or discipline problems; to youth seemingly alienated from school and its academic goals; and to students assumed to be facing serious family and social problems. The foundation and school district documents defined "risk factors" as pregnancy, poverty, single-parent families, drug abuse, course failure, poor attendance, low achievement, and suspension from school. In practice, the criteria teachers used to identify these students were highly subjective. For example, teachers often included students who were resistant or appeared tough, and a youth's reputation or peer group might be enough to qualify him or her as "at-risk."

Although many students, White and Black, might fit the descriptors, it was predominantly low-income African Americans who were identified as "at risk," especially at Gates. One Gates teacher commented that some of her Hills students were out until midnight every night. "Their parents are never at home. . . . I know some of them drink a lot, get in trouble. They have no supervision. Really they're at risk too. But we never consider them." In fact, at Gates, many teachers *assumed* that low-income African American youth were "at risk," and the label was applied almost generically to them. Indeed, labeling African Americans this way seemed to be a way to declare them deficient and different from the norm without naming race. But, since most African American students were also from low-income working-class families, it was difficult to disentangle race and class in these perceptions. At Franklin, faculty and administrators expressed the belief that the majority of their students faced serious social and family problems, and many educators there referred generically to White as well as African American students as "at risk."

Features of Restructured Schools

The district's stated goals for school restructuring were to: (a) create a more supportive environment for young adolescents; (b) develop innovations in teaching and instruction; (c) reduce out-of-school suspension and school exclusion; (d) increase attendance and academic achievement of low-achieving, "at-risk" students; and (e) reduce racial disparities in discipline and academic outcomes. In practice, restructuring altered many organizational and governance features of the four schools, affecting almost 3,000 students and nearly 250 teaching and nonteaching staff in the four junior highs. For the first time, special education students were integrated into regular classes, and their teachers became resource people within these classes.

Most important, in 1990, all students, teachers, counselors, and administrators were divided into 11 teams at each of the four restructuring schools, each with a designated leader who also sat on the school steering committee. The grade-level "core teams" consisted of five core subject teachers (English, math, social studies, science, Study and Research Methods) and about 120 students. There were two core teams at each of the three grade levels. The three school counselors, each assigned to a grade, also worked closely with the core teams at their grade level. Because students shared a common set of teachers and many of the same classes, they were expected to "bond' during the year. These core teams were the centerpiece of restructuring. Each school also had two related subjects teams composed of music, art, physical education, computer science, foreign languages, home economics, technology, and health teachers. There was also a support team made up of the schools' counseling staff, nurse, special education and reading teachers, and librarian. Custodians, office staff, security, and cafeteria workers were in a separate support team. Finally, the administrative team included the principal and her/his assistants.

Core teams were really small schools-within-a-school with a common set of classes and teachers. One purpose was to create a more nurturing environment for students; by fostering more personalized relationships students were expected to "buy-in" to school. Another purpose was to encourage teachers to work cooperatively, to innovate, and to solve collaboratively many issues that had been the province of administrators. Collectively, teachers were encouraged to develop in-

terdisciplinary curricula and student activities and to devise solutions
to educational and behavioral problems. Flexible schedules and the
elimination of bells allowed teams to experiment with the length of
classes, class schedules, and combined classes. The number of class
periods was increased from six to seven to allow all teachers two
planning periods a day. Each team of teachers had the same planning
periods, giving them 100 minutes a day to meet and to work together.
An additional class, Study and Research Methods (SRM), was added
to accommodate the extra planning time. It also fulfilled one of the
stated goals of restructuring, to "actively involve students in the learning process and emphasize the development of students' higher order
thinking skills." SRM was described as a class that would work intensively on writing, help students develop analytic and research skills,
help them identify their own learning styles, and lay a stronger foundation for other classes.

The restructuring director and the principals said they configured
the teams to create a balance of perspectives, teaching styles, experience, and race on each team. The formal criteria they established for
team leaders were: commitment to restructuring, ability to work well
with others, and leadership. However, several principals said certain
teachers who might have met these criteria were rejected because they
were "too outspoken" or had their own agendas. It was pretty much
common knowledge that the selection of team leaders had been a
political process of balancing the interests of factions among the faculties as well as achieving a visible racial balance, and there was a
good deal of behind-the-scenes grumbling about these assignments,
especially at Franklin where the staff was most divided.

One problem with the design of the teams was that related
subjects teachers and support staff (with the exception of counselors)
were not structurally integrated into the core teams, and therefore
not connected with a common set of students. The related subjects
teams brought together teachers from two worlds: High-status li-
brarians and teachers of foreign languages, art, and music were joined
with physical education teachers, coaches, and industrial arts teachers who had lower status, especially at Gates. There were few natural bonds and little common activity among this hodgepodge of
professionals. If anything, reorganization into teams distanced them
from the center of restructuring. Indeed, these teams met less and
less frequently as the school year wore on, and by mid-1990 they
were questioning what purpose they fulfilled. This increased professional marginality of related arts and support staff, in conjunction
with their racial composition, was to have substantial consequences

for their role in restructuring and for the direction of restructuring at both schools.

Although the official rhetoric was for "teacher empowerment," from the beginning restructuring was devised by a few central school administrators and foundation staff. There was no significant input from teachers, parents, students, the teachers' union, or building administrators. The district restructuring director, Louis Dixon, was a driving force behind restructuring at the district level. This was his project. It was his initiative, energy, and personal involvement with teachers and principals that propelled it forward, at least in the first 2 years. He seemed expert at maneuvering through the minefield of central office and school board politics. Dixon was the chief liaison between the central office and the four schools and between the foundation and the school district. Much of the political pressure on Gates and Franklin and their teachers was transmitted through his decisions and actions.

Although in 1991 the school district did receive an award from a national center for education reform for its accomplishments in restructuring, and the participating schools receivied intensive, ongoing technical assistance from another national center for educational reform, the schools could not be called model restructuring schools, as defined, for example, by the selection criteria of the National Center on Organization and Restructuring (Newmann, 1991). Changes were mainly organizational and focussed on increasing the roles, responsibilities, and knowledge base of teachers with less systematic attention to teaching, learning, and assessment. It is probably safe to assume that Gates and Franklin were typical of modest, incremental approaches to school restructuring around the country (see, for example, David, Purkey, & White, 1989). I chose to study them not as advanced lessons but as examples of schools engaged in rather typical forms of restructuring addressing a very pervasive set of problems.

Ideologies Underpinning Staff Development and the Restructuring Institute

Citing the centrality of teachers in reform, the restructuring director concentrated the foundation's considerable resources and technical assistance on professional development. Since the initiation of the grant in 1988, many teachers visited restructuring schools in other states and nearby districts and attended local and national conferences and workshops on school restructuring, curriculum reform, and more specific topics such as multicultural education, cooperative learning, and early adolescent development. In fact, at both Gates and Franklin by the spring of 1990 probably one third of the teachers had participated in at least one conference or delegation of this sort.

This preparation was augmented in August 1990 by an intensive 5-day Restructuring Institute for all teachers, support staff, and administrators in the restructuring schools. The Institute agenda illustrated the district's orientation to preparing teachers for what Dixon described as "a paradigm shift" in schools. Despite several substantive presentations and a hefty collection of readings on topics such as teachers as facilitators, organizational change, professional collaboration, changing school cultures, and "minority achievement," we observed little concrete talk about curriculum and instruction or specific educational goals. There was a script for the workshop sessions that all consultants were admonished to follow to ensure that each workshop covered predetermined topics. The agenda provided little opportunity to discuss either the presentations or the readings and left little room for issues outside the predetermined plan. There was virtually no debate or controversy. Most sessions centered on the technical issues and the process of team building, not the issues/problems teams could or should address. The emphasis was on organizational and process aspects of collaboration and on specific team activities rather than the values and philosophy guiding the teams' work.

Although "participation" was probably the dominant theme of presentations and suggested readings during the week, the hidden message was limits and controls. Teacher empowerment looked much like "contrived collaboration," mandated to get teachers' assent to decisions made elsewhere, to legitimate these decisions, and to blur contradictions between competing interests (Hargreaves, 1991). Though no explicit boundaries were set for the actions and decisions of teams and steering committees (the question of boundaries did not come up), the institute set a tone that foregrounded technical/operational issues, rather than reflection on assumptions, educational theories, or curricula. Each team left with guidelines for team planning and roles and behaviors of team members, a team name and logo, and intensive training in group dynamics and running meetings.

What was not discussed was also illuminating. For example, the dearth of talk about the underachievement of African American students and their high rates of failure and discipline actions—in the context of a project specifically addressed to "at-risk students"—was remarkable. Equally remarkable—in the context of a purported "paradigm shift" in education—was the absence of substantive disagreement and the failure to critically examine prevailing practices. The character of this institute and the ongoing leadership of restructuring

set a tone consistent with Riverton School District's culture of control
and were part of the ideological background influencing the direction
of restructuring.

Possibilities of Collaboration and Empowerment

Nevertheless, in Riverton's highly conservative and bureaucratic
educational context, restructuring was unprecedented. For the first
time, teachers had time for, and were expected to, work collaboratively
with their colleagues. "Participatory management," "shared decision
making," and "teacher empowerment" became cardinal slogans. The
restructured schools were to be governed collaboratively by teachers
and administrators through a building steering committee composed
of team leaders and building administrators. All four schools established in-school suspension programs, giving teachers and building
administrators greater flexibility and authority in handling disciplinary infractions and a means of reducing out-of-school suspensions.
Restructuring guidelines also gave teachers permission to experiment
with curriculum, plan student activities, make decisions about the
placement of students in regular or honors tracks, work with parents,
and handle discipline problems directly.

Restructuring also opened up new opportunities for professional
growth. Teachers flew across the country to attend conferences and
traveled together to visit models of restructuring in other cities and
states. For some, these were their first plane rides or trips out of state.
In the fall of 1990, there was a flurry of team activities, meetings, and
faculty study groups to solve policy issues. Teachers joined together to
write grants and plan projects. Everyone attested to being busy, although not all were enthusiastic. Regular visits by national consultants on new instructional practices and learning styles, group process,
grant writing, and leadership training became routine in the four
schools. Evaluators, foundation representatives, and even community
leaders wandered the halls, observed classes, and interviewed everyone. The jargon of restructuring became common currency, and there
was a sense that Riverton was part of a national educational movement, albeit with its own local flavor and determination to "move
slowly" and do things in a way "appropriate to Riverton."

Conclusion

Riverton was a city marked by a history of protracted struggle
over the place of Whites and African Americans within every sphere
of social life. The schools had been, and, as I began this study, contin-

ued to be, a critical arena within which these struggles were played out. After over 30 years of desegregation suits and a variety of plans, African American students still fared significantly worse than Whites on every educational indicator. Although dramatically different in many ways, both Franklin and Gates typified this entrenched subordination of African Americans—especially those who were low-income and working-class.

Although meant to improve the education of all students, restructuring was explicitly directed to reducing these racial disparities and creating a more supportive and engaging environment for "at-risk" students. At Gates, students labeled "at risk" were overwhelmingly African American; at Franklin, most were African American because they were the large majority of the school population. As I began research in August 1990, the official rhetoric emanating from district leaders and the restructuring director, and echoed by principals and some teachers, was that all the changes associated with restructuring would enable educators to make a substantive, positive difference in the educational experiences of these students.

It was this assumed connection between restructuring, educators' practices, and student experiences that was my starting point. I looked for evidence that new forms of teacher collaboration and decision making were beginning to prompt reflection and dialogues of change, greater understanding and respect between adults and children across race and class, and reevaluation of common practices and policies, especially as related to the students who were the focus of the reforms. As I listened and exchanged ideas, observed, and questioned, I wanted to know: How did educators construct the school failure and alienation of African American students? And what were the consequences of restructuring for how teachers thought about and interacted with African American students? In what ways were Gates and Franklin changing? And for whom? What were the political, structural, and cultural influences on teachers and administrators and the decisions they made and how did they respond? It is to these questions that I now turn.

4

Teachers' Beliefs About African American Students

The most important aspect of political discourse is not the appraisal of alternative solutions to our problems, but the definition of the problems themselves.

—Robert Reich, *Tales of a New America*

Reich and others (e.g., Gusfield, 1986) contend that how a problem is defined frames the universe of reasonable public actions. Further, the power of a certain formulation of a public problem is drawn from its resonance with specific cultural subtexts. As I suggested in chapter 1, the essence of debate in public life, then, is over the construction of social problems and the broader cultural meanings various constructions evoke (Edelman, 1964, 1971). It follows that the strength of a particular definition of a problem within a school (or school system, state, or nation) limits policy choices and alternative programs and actions. How the educational experiences and the disproportionately low academic performance of children of color are framed implies particular educational practices, solutions, and policy directions. Depending on whether the roots of the problem are seen to lie with families and communities, social relations in schools, curriculum and instruction, a system of racial and class domination in school and society, or some relationship of these, the weight of responsibility lies more or less heavily on the shoulders of teachers and schools. The tasks set for educators and the changes they work for are likely to be quite different depending on how they understand the roots of the problem. Indeed, the very parameters of the conversation about the education of children of color are defined by the issues included within a given framework. It is with this perspective that I examined how educators at Gates and Franklin framed the educational experiences of African American students.

Explanatory Models for African American Students'
Lack of School Success

Because cultural change—changing beliefs, values, and norms in schools—is central to educational change, it is important to understand the prevailing mix of ideas and values and their relative standing in a school if one is to trace the process of educational change there. Thus, I attempted to construct a picture of teachers' beliefs and values related to African American students at the outset of, restructuring. Establishing these viewpoints at the outset is important to subsequent discussions of dialogue and collaboration and the evolution of beliefs.

Despite Riverton's 30-year history of desegregation, state competency tests meant to set uniform educational standards, remedial programs, and the abolition of a racially identifiable remedial track, dramatic disparities remained in the educational outcomes of African American and White students. Somehow, teachers had to make sense of this fact. And if they chose to reflect on it, they had to find a way to deal with the frustration it engendered.

"Why do so many Black students do poorly at this school?" Teachers' answers to this question reflected a range of beliefs and various pedagogical practices, adult/student interactions, and curricular choices. In this chapter, I describe teachers' ideological constructs regarding this question at the beginning of restructuring. Focusing on a representative sample of teachers, I characterize the various perspectives among the faculties at Gates and Franklin. I also analyze the place of each perspective within the dominant culture of each school. My purpose is to provide enough detail to give the reader a picture of teachers' ideas about African American students and about their practices with them. I have selected comments representative of a particular viewpoint shared by others. Some of the teachers I quote were members of the teams I focus on in later chapters.

As discussed in chapter 2, I use the term *ideology* to include formal belief systems (rational systems of argument, social theories, and elaborated worldviews); commonsense notions and cultural models through which people make sense of their world; and ideologies-in-use—social practices of individuals and institutions. Often, in interviews and casual conversation, educators articulated formal belief systems and theories or they related cultural models to explain the social processes taking place in their schools and community. And they called up concrete experiences with specific students to serve as examples of these theories and models. Teachers' ideologies also were embodied in their pedagogical decisions, curricular choices, interactions with children and other adults, and in interpretations of school policies.

I do not attempt to characterize teachers' educational ideologies in all their complexity (that is obviously not possible). Specifically, I am interested in teachers' (a) characterizations of low-achieving African American students and their backgrounds, as well as their perceptions of high-achieving African American students; (b) explanations for the lack of school success of so many African American students; (c) concepts of "at-risk students." The discussion in this chapter is based on interviews and observations of teachers prior to restructuring and at the beginning of the 1990–91 school year. It focuses on individual teachers. In later chapters, I look at their dialogue with each other and their cooperative efforts.

Teachers at Gates and Franklin approached low-achieving African American students with a variety of perspectives. Their analyses of why many were academically unsuccessful and frequently in trouble in school were diverse, as were their professed pedagogical and disciplinary strategies. Teachers had differing social and academic expectations for African American students who were considered to be at risk, and they had various conceptions of what constituted appropriate social relations with them.

From conversations and observations, I identified four, non–mutually exclusive explanations for African American students' low academic achievement. The four explanations were:

1. A *deficit model* that attributed school failure to deficiencies in students' social and economic condition, their families and culture (cf. Flores, Cousin, & Diaz, 1991) and which was captured by the label "at risk";
2. A *social relations model* that assumed that students did not do well because of an absence of support from school adults and because of a lack of a sense of school membership;
3. A *critique of racism* that emphasized the role of racial inequality, racism, and marginalization and powerlessness in the low achievement and alienation of African American students;
4. An *educational critique* of curriculum, instruction, and school policies.

These categories are clearly abstractions of complex and dynamic ideological processes. Certainly, the unique personalities and experiences of the many teachers I interacted with and the nuances of their beliefs and practices are not captured by these idealized models. In reality, few teachers held dogmatically to monocausal explanations. Most, if pressed, tended to believe that the problem was multifaceted, even contradictory. Also teachers' stated beliefs and their practice were sometimes at odds. Despite this complexity, these four explanatory frameworks recurred with enough frequency to serve as an analytic tool. They resonated in the discourse of the teachers with whom I talked and served as frameworks for their analysis of African American students' experiences in school. They were also manifested in pedagogical practices and interactions with African American students and in school policies and procedures.

The Deficit Model and "At-Risk" Students

The parents could care less about education. Half of them are on drugs. The kids come from broken homes. You wouldn't believe the stuff I see here. I mean we're dealing with kids who are raped by their fathers and step-fathers, their mothers' boyfriends. The kids live day to day. They don't see the importance of education. Their values are not in order.

—A Franklin administrator

At both schools, the deficit model was the most common explanation for African American students' low achievement. Its essence was the connection between a supposedly deprived family, culture, and social environment on the one hand, and academic failure on the other. The deficit model situated the problem outside of schools and beyond the purview of traditional teacher responsibilities. It is reflected in these comments:

Marie (White Gates teacher): The kids I have now have more family problems and are harder to teach. They have more behavior problems. I think the cause of the disparities is societal. Parents need parenting skills. A lot of the kids we have are actually emancipated minors. And the things they have to deal with are absolutely shocking. You just wouldn't believe it.

Perhaps some teachers were eager to shirk the responsibility of educating children they found difficult. For them, the deficit explanation may have provided a convenient rationale for their own indifference. However, most teachers were dedicated, but also frustrated. Convinced they were doing all they were able to do, they were discouraged by students' apparent lack of motivation, their inadequate academic skills, and the inordinate amount of time they felt they must spend controlling student behavior. At the same time, they shared cultural models of youth, primarily African Americans, engulfed in poverty, drugs, gangs, violence, family crises—problems beyond the reach of schools. These social conditions, both assumed and real, were a compelling explanation for educators' own failure to teach them effectively. (See Fine, 1991, for a similar analysis.) Certainly, students living in Riverton's poorest neighborhoods faced real economic and social pressures that affected their lives in school, and some teachers worried and did what they could to help students deal with them. But what distinguished educators with a deficit explanation was that economic and social conditions were grounds for low expectations and for not considering how to improve students' educational experiences and academic performance, and these conditions were linked in educators' cultural models with social and moral pathologies. The power of the deficit model was so great at both schools and its ramifications proved to be so complex that it deserves considerable discussion here.

Construction of "At-Risk" Students

One manifestation of the deficit explanation was labeling students "at-risk" and attributing school failure to being a member of this category. The at-risk label covered a range of social conditions and school problems, and teachers' talk about students they placed in this category resonated with the national at-risk discourse. Although some factors, such as course failure, objectively pushed children to drop out, judgments about who was "at risk" were more frequently subjective. Indeed, the concept of being "at risk" was so global and intuitive that it might encompass any behavior or situation that did not fit a particular teacher's version of mainstream, middle-class norms[1] (Cuban, 1989). In particular, cultural misunderstandings and racial stereotyping (with potentially grave consequences for students) occurred when teachers, proceeding from their own norms, equated typically African American interactional styles, dress, looks, and language with behaviors such as gang membership, drug use, and belligerence. For example, one teacher commented that one of his classes was "all at-risk kids." "I probably have a quorum of the West Side Kings" (a local gang). He concluded this based on the students' neighborhoods, their aggressive posturing (cf. Majors & Billson, 1992; Irvine, 1991), and their affinity for black and gray clothes (supposedly gang colors) in a year when these were fashionable colors among African American students in general.

Assumed social and cultural deprivation was seldom explicitly ascribed to students' race. Although a few teachers used terms like "at-risk" or "deprived" interchangeably with "Black," the connection was generally tacit, but nonetheless pervasive. Especially at Gates, to be "at-risk" was to be from the "inner city," virtually ensuring that the majority of low-income African American students might be considered in this category. At Franklin, a school with fewer social class differences, where White youth might be as poor, or poorer, than their African American peers, race and class were entangled in notions about at-risk students, and White students might also be considered at risk. However, in 1990–91, Franklin was 80% African American, and nearly all discussions about at-risk students that I observed were, in fact, about African American students. At both schools, African American teachers were perhaps more likely to interpret distinctive African American behaviors from a sympathetic cultural perspective and more likely to investigate before calling a student "at risk." Nevertheless, the perspective that African American students were "at risk" was shared by teachers of both races.

Sources of Deficit Assumptions About African American Students

In part, assumptions about the environment of "at-risk" students were based on hearsay or reports in the local media. White teachers, in particular, acknowledged that their generalizations about African American students and parents were often conjectural. The fabric of everyday life in Riverton did not offer many opportunities for substantive cross-racial or cross-class experiences outside the workplace. White teachers generally did not live or shop in the same communities, nor did they attend the same churches or social clubs as the families of their African American students, or their African American colleagues. About half of the White teachers at Franklin lived in neighboring towns, and many had never lived in Riverton.

There were also social distances between many African American teachers and students, and some of these teachers were also ready to ascribe school failure to cultural and social deprivation, although they were more selective in choosing students to whom to attribute these problems. Perhaps this reflected class differences between themselves and their students (Rist, 1970). Not only were these teachers middle-class professionals, but their own children were generally successful in school. In many cases, there were also generational differences between the teachers and the young parents of their students. Most of the teachers were in their early forties. They had grown up in close, racially segregated communities. And they were educated in generally supportive African American schools in a period of emerging opportunity and rising expectations.

Nevertheless, African American teachers were much more likely to be connected with African American students through churches and community institutions, social networks, history, culture, and common experience than were White teachers. Some routinely called on students at home, and several, who ran after-school tutoring programs or led extracurricular activities, also drove students home. At Gates, as far as I could learn, nearly all of these "connected" teachers were African American. Since there were few African American teachers at Gates, the majority of teachers there had little personal contact with the daily reality of their African American students and little opportunity to come to appreciate both the strengths of communities and families as well as the actual difficulties.

Consequently, especially for White teachers, most information about students' homes and communities was based on conversations with other teachers, the media, reports provided to the school by social service or juvenile justice agencies, or student talk. Generalizations about children based on the reputations of their neighborhoods were quite common. Despite being superficial and unconfirmed, a lot of what teachers heard figured prominently in diagnoses of individual students. As a whole, disparate sources of information coalesced into taken-for-granted models of African American students' out-of-school lives.

For White teachers, in particular, speculative judgments about African American students' personal lives influenced expectations about their capabilities and potential and justified deficit explanations for academic failure. Interviews with teachers suggested a widely shared cultural model of defective home environments, negligent parents, and deficient students:

PL: Why is such a large percentage of Black kids failing?
Elaine: (White Franklin teacher) Low economic status. Poor home
         environment—what they get when they leave here. Is there
         anyone at home? And is there anyone at home who cares?
         Education is not valued and reinforced in these kids' homes.
PL: What do you base that on?
Elaine: Well, I don't know for a fact, but I assume that's the case.

PL: How do you explain the low achievement of so many Black
         students?

Mark: (White Franklin teacher) Well, the high achiever has had break-
          fast. His parent was there when he got home. He had a hot
          meal for dinner. These kids haven't seen their parents for a
          week. They haven't eaten. They have other things on their
          minds . . . they have short-term goals, or no goals at all.
PL: How do you know this?
Mark: You hang around some of these kids long enough and you
          know.

Deficit assumptions were nurtured by stories told about individual students. Teachers were quick to recall cases of physical and
sexual abuse, drug use, gang membership, prostitution, and family
upheaval. Often vivid accounts of the traumas of individuals became
emblematic of a whole group. As with cultural models generally, individual cases were exemplars that lent a persistent authenticity to a
familiar story, in this case the belief that students' lives were so crisis-
ridden and street-oriented that they could not, or would not, concentrate on school. When pressed, most teachers and administrators were
able to cite counterexamples, but these success stories were often attributed to "something inside the student." The "horror stories" were
salient in the explanations many teachers offered for students' low
achievement and academic disengagement.

Although I cannot demonstrate a connection with the national
discourse about African American youth as amoral and a threat to
society, teachers' characterizations of these students clearly echoed this
construction of African American youth identity.

Parents' Assumed Disregard for Education

There was an assumed connection between social crises, poverty,
and the devaluation of education. Teachers who held to notions of the
pathology of the Black family expressed that many African American
parents had low academic expectations and goals for their children
and little commitment to education (cf. Lightfoot, 1978). They thought
that without this necessary parental support, children lacked the
motivation to excel in school. By extension, students designated "at
risk" were said to have "at-risk parents."

Elaine (White Franklin teacher): The reason kids fail is that there
is not a lot of home support. Education is not important. . . .
They're not achieving because *they don't care* [emphasis original].
And they don't care because someone at home doesn't care. That's
still the problem.

At Gates, the principle evidence for this theory was the lack of African American parent participation at the school. Teachers complained that they had "no parent support for what we're trying to do with the at-risk kids."

> Connie (White Gates teacher): When we had the open house, no parents of my pre-algebra kids [predominantly African American] came. But my room was filled with Algebra I parents. Kids don't do as well when their parents are not involved. The reason some of these kids fail is there is no one at home showing interest. They don't care, the kids aren't responsible, and then the kids don't do as well. When we have parent days, my parents from my regular classes don't come.

The sparse attendance of African American parents at school openhouse and orientation meetings, and their infrequent contacts with teachers seemed to verify that they had little commitment to their children's education. This analysis was uncritically repeated by most of the teachers I talked with. (See Lareau, 1989, for similar findings related to parents' social class.)

In fact, few African American parents visited Gates except when summoned by the principal or a teacher. Prior to the fall of 1990, they usually came to the school for a disciplinary problem or a mandatory parent conference preceding an out-of-school suspension. African American family members could frequently be observed waiting in the school office to see the principal or one of his assistants for such conferences. However, in the 2 years that my colleagues and I conducted research in the school, we never observed an African American parent participating in a school activity or volunteering in the school. When the AfroNotions student club presented a play and musical program for Black History Month in February 1990, only one African American family attended, although many African American students performed. (The principal did make a special point of welcoming that family.)

On the other hand, Hills and Palisades families maintained consistent contact with their children's teachers and with the principal. Teachers usually knew them and spoke with them during the school year. Affluent parents also made their presence felt in the school through the PTO and fund-raising projects. They were physically present in the building, working on projects in the faculty lounge or volunteering in the school library. Their active involvement made the nonparticipation of African American parents all the more glaring and seemingly derelict.

Most Gates and Franklin teachers were familiar with research on the correlation of parent involvement and student achievement (Henderson, 1987). Some referred to educational articles to bolster their argument that lack of parent involvement was at the root of low achievement. Here, conventional educational theory intersected with the deficit model to reinforce the belief that deficiencies in family values were the root of school failure. On the other hand, most had little formal knowledge or awareness of the limitations of conventional, middle-class forms of parent participation or the ways in which Gates aliented African Americans. As I note below, some teachers believed Gates was an unwelcoming place for African American families, but, significantly, I found no evidence that most teachers recognized the ways in which the school marginalized low-income parents and families of color (Epstein, 1986; Irvine, 1991). Not surprisingly, they were also unfamiliar with the idea that direct parent involvement in school is culturally specific and that in some communities it is neither traditional nor appropriate for parents to participate in their children's schools in the ways Hills parents did, despite their strong support for their children's education (Lareau, 1989; Siddle Walker, 1993; Valdés, 1996). Thus, teachers took the lack of parental presence in the school building as evidence that families did not care about education. As a result, the lack of African American families' involvement reinforced teachers' notions of their deficiency, seemingly manifested in an absence of concern for education. (This is an issue I return to in my discussion of Gates.)

Practical Implications of the Deficit Model

One perspective that grew out of the deficit explanation was that counseling should be a school priority. In interviews, responses to the question, "What support do you and other teachers need with restructuring?" were frequently, "more counselors," "case workers," "more help with teen pregnancy," "drug counseling" and so forth.

Marissa: (White Franklin staff) These type of students have to have some help. . . . For a school like this. . . .
PL: What do you mean by "a school like this"?
Marissa: You know, kids who come from the lower social economic base, who are culturally deprived. Kids who are going to be abused. Some of these kids' parents need help as much as they do. These kids need counseling.

But other Franklin teachers contended that since parents were apathetic and students' social problems undermined whatever efforts teachers might make, there was really very little they could do. They believed that student deficiencies, rooted in social conditions beyond the school, posed an insurmountable obstacle. This was especially the view of White teachers of non–core subjects. "The parents don't care. What can *we* do?" they asked. At Gates, there were few teachers engaged in the intensive counseling that took place at Franklin. Some also believed that low-achieving African American students were so deficient as to be beyond their help. As Christine, a White, non–core subject teacher described it, "How can these kids succeed when their parents can't even use good grammar?" Her solution was academic counseling to steer them away from challenging college preparatory classes.

Low academic and behavioral expectations for African American students were a logical extension of the deficit model (Irvine, 1991). Some, like Christine, frankly advocated lower standards. Others, simply lowered requirements for performance, explaining that they could not do projects, analytical work, or extended writing assignments with "at-risk" students because they "have shorter attention spans," "too many behavior problems," or "need to work on the basics."

Jim Meier, a team leader at Gates, was representative. A 15-year veteran teacher, Jim was still enthusiastic about teaching. He seemed to spend every available minute working on lesson plans, designing projects for his classes, and discussing them with other teachers. His two honors classes followed a rather conventional regimen of ninth-grade civics. They adhered closely to the text. Sometimes he lectured and they took notes. The students wrote research reports and gave oral presentations. Jim often arranged the students in teams that competed with each other for the right answers to questions about the history and structure of U.S. government. Students also did projects that involved their families or community members.

He ran his three regular-track classes somewhat differently. Although students used the same text, and did some of the same projects as honors students, the reading assignments were shorter. He rarely lectured and students wrote fewer reports. But the distinguishing feature of his regular-track classes was the coupons he awarded to the first to produce the correct answer to a factual question. The class was run much like a TV game show. (See Page, 1991, for a similar account of lower-track classes.) All the students competed with each other for these coupons, which could be redeemed for trinkets and candy or for a night's reprieve from homework. In a catalogue of discrete facts, Jim shifted from one topic to the next, one question to the next, with virtually no discussion or conceptual framework (cf. Oakes, 1985).

Jim's limited expectations for this class were conveyed by his pedagogical approaches and curricular choices. He explained that he used coupons to motivate unmotivated students, "to keep their interest . . . otherwise they don't want to learn." He said that he "gets into these issues a lot deeper with my honors classes. You can't with the at-risk kids." After one class, pleased with the enthusiastic participation, Jim commented, "Don't you think that was good for an at-risk class?"

Deficit models also led to an emphasis on controlling student behavior. Many teachers at both schools assumed that some African American students did not know how to behave because it was thought they came from chaotic environments with behavioral norms and values sharply at odds with those of the school. The correlation between misbehavior and low socioeconomic status (which implied to many educators deficient families and neighborhoods) was one of the most salient ideas in teachers' conversations about students:

> Irene Curran (White Franklin staff member): Discipline has really gone down at this school [gestures thumbs down]. I'm very concerned about gang activity. It's a dangerous situation. . . . The kids are worse, which is a reflection of society. And the demographics have changed as we have annexed certain areas.

In some instances, educators were quite candid about their belief that African Americans posed greater behavioral problems. The Gates principal reported at a faculty meeting that a visitor from another district had praised the student behavior at Gates. "She said our students are better behaved than the kids in her restructured schools. And we have a higher percentage of Blacks."

Summary

The deficit explanation was rooted in a negative and degrading cultural model of low-income African American families—uneducated, uncaring, and unable to provide their children with the skills, values, and social support they needed in school. This model was confirmed by dramatic stories about individual students in crisis. These individuals became emblematic for "at-risk" students in general. Some teachers who held this model wanted counseling to be the priority of restructuring. Others had simply given up. In general, the deficit model was reflected in lower expectations for academic performance, a watered-down curriculum, more rote learning, and an emphasis on controlling behavior.

The Social Relations Model

If the kids have more social support, the academic problems will take care of themselves. If they are at ease socially, they can learn.

—A Franklin teacher

The four junior highs slated to begin restructuring in 1990–91 conducted a school assessment in the spring of 1990. At Franklin, one outcome of the assessment was a decision to strengthen relationships between students and adults. Teachers frequently cited "better student-teacher relations" and "making school more like a family" as objectives. At Gates, an assessment team member concluded that the faculty should concentrate on building students' self-esteem and on strengthening social interactions. Interviews prior to restructuring suggest that perhaps half the teachers at Gates believed that detachment from the school's values and teachers was a significant reason so many students did poorly. It is important to note that this detachment was seen as a problem of individual students.

This view, which I call the *social relations model*, was a psychological approach to low achievement. It was rooted in a story of academically unsuccessful students who do not feel a part of their school. The logic was that because these students had little attachment to the adults or the institutional ethos, they have little commitment to academic goals and requirements. Thus, breaking through this alienation and helping students feel a sense of belonging, or school membership, was seen as central to academic success. (See Wehlage et al., 1989, for an elaboration of this theory.) Teachers espousing this philosophy stressed personal relationships with students, team spirit, and symbolic activities that theoretically would build a sense of group identification with the school. Their role was to "nurture" students in order to improve behavior and academic achievement. Apart from the anonymity of a large school and the need for more caring adults, this analysis did not extend to the culture of the school as a whole, curriculum, discipline policies, academic expectations, the role of tracking, or other structural and cultural aspects that could potentially contribute to students' alienation.

Among teachers at Franklin and Gates, the social relations model was the second most common explanation for low academic achievement of African American students. The social relations perspective was particularly influential at Gates, where most teachers were optimistic that restructuring, with its emphasis on school and team membership, would improve the attendance and achievement of the students they considered at risk and who were quite obviously estranged from the core values of the school. Team activities (parties, contests, field trips, etc.) and the creation of a team identity complete with names, T-shirts, logos, and a common hallway or area of the building were designed to cultivate team spirit.

The extent to which this view was generated by the ideology of the restructuring project itself is unclear, but whatever the preexisting beliefs in the efficacy of strengthening school membership, they were reinforced by the district's plan for restructuring and by the framework of the foundation grant. District leaders and foundation advisors identified "students' limited involvement in school" as a central problem and argued, in language common to recent middle school reforms, that young adolescents do better in schools that are divided into smaller units and that foster close ties with caring adults (Carnegie Council on Adolescent Development, 1989).

Early Experiences With Teams and the Mentoring and Counseling Program

The first teams, which were piloted at two junior highs (Franklin and one other) in 1988–1989 and at one grade level at four junior highs (Franklin, Gates, and two others) in 1989–90, validated the social relations approach. The testimonies of the eight teachers who were part of these initial teams at Gates confirmed for their colleagues the value of strengthening teacher-student and student-student bonds. Margaret, an African American teacher who was a member of a seventh-grade team at Gates in 1989–90, described the team structure as "like a house, a family—that feeling of belonging to something. It's as if they leave something in the living room, they can just go and get it. Go from room to room, from teacher to teacher. Like a family."

The team teachers said they were unsure whether it was this particular group of kids or their special efforts to build stronger bonds with them, but they were convinced they had been more successful with "at-risk" students in these teams than with any others in recent years. Ellen, a team leader in 1989–90, believed that the teams had made a real difference for students, bonding them to the school and to school goals: "The students feel that the teachers care, and last year they felt like the teachers didn't have time for them. More kids made the honor role this year, and I attribute that to their feeling of belonging [at Gates]."

Another highly touted program, the Mentoring and Counseling Program (MCP), begun in 1988, paired a teacher with 8 to 10 "at-risk" students. The five or six teachers who participated in each junior high school gave personal and academic guidance to their MCP students throughout the year. The reputed success of MCP was frequently cited as another example of the efficacy of student support. MCP, together with the first teams, provided concrete experience to bolster those who believed that strengthening social relations would improve the achievement and, what were perceived as, behavior problems of students defined as at risk.

A visit by teachers and administrators to restructured schools in another state solidified the social relations model for many of those who participated. Anticipating the coming school year, a number of teachers at Gates and Franklin described restructuring as more social than academic. This corresponded with the belief that teams and closer relations between students and teachers should lead to a drop in discipline problems and absenteeism. Anticipated outcomes of teams were quite far-reaching. Expectations ran the gamut from better behavior and attendance to higher academic achievement and enjoyment of school. One Franklin teacher said he wanted to believe that

> the kids will be more motivated. They'll have a better attitude toward the facility... better discipline, less noise, lower drop outs, higher test scores, better Black/White relations. All because the school will be more like a family.

Intersection With the Deficit Model

For some teachers, the emphasis on social relations fit well with the notion that schools had to somehow compensate for the social and affective deficiencies of families. Because they assumed families failed to provide children with emotional or social support, they believed students had never experienced a close affiliation with a social group. The teacher's role, then, was to create that affiliation within school, particularly through teams.

> Adele (White Franklin teacher, at the beginning of the year): We [the team] have the same rules. We're consistent. It gives kids a sense of belonging. Kids don't have that sense of belonging anywhere as a person because their home situations are so bad. The team gives them the opportunity to be part of a positive group.

Indeed, a number of teachers simultaneously offered deficit explanations and were proponents of improving social relations. In this sense, the two models were complementary, allowing teachers to act within the sphere of social relations without challenging existing racial configurations or conventional curriculum and instruction. However, unlike teachers who saw the solution mainly outside the school through fixing deficient children, families, and communities, social relations proponents wanted to change the school's affective and social climate, especially relations between teachers and students. As I go on to discuss, others saw racism as an underlying issue and adopted a variant of the social relations approach. In particular, a number of African American teachers developed supportive relationships with African American students and worked to provide a sense of African American identity within the context of their schools.

Critique of Racism

They don't relate what they're teaching to what the [African American] kids already know. They don't understand their culture. They don't start with what the kids are equipped with. We're supposed to be intelligent enough to know what they know and work with that. . . . They don't see kids' strengths.

—African American Gates teacher

Some faculty members attributed the educational problems of African American students to racism. This view was voiced by four to six mainly African American teachers at each school. Unlike others who placed the blame for students' educational problems on students, those with a critique of racism cast their eyes on inequalities within school and society. One thing that distinguished this group of teachers was that they rarely referred to alienated or academically failing students as "at risk." The heart of their analysis was that many African American students, particularly those from low-income families, were estranged from an institution whose culture, curriculum, pedagogical and interactional styles, structures, goals, and values excluded them, *as African Americans,* and even punished them for *being* African American. They contended that students responded by withdrawing their commitment from an institution they perceived as hostile (Erickson, 1987; King, 1991). Although a minority opinion, this analysis was a potentially powerful perspective at both schools. It was the only explanation that directly addressed the racial implications of African American school failure, low achievement, and punishment.

African American Disempowerment and Cultural Alienation

At Gates, most African American teachers were assigned to remedial and special education classes or lower-status noncore subjects. The effect of having a small number of African American faculty was exacerbated by the schools' location in a White, upper-class neighborhood and the disproportionate influence of White parents. In the eyes of some teachers, White and African American, one manifestation of this problem was that African American students had few positive adult African American role models in the school. However, the lack of role models was understood by those who shared a racial critique as simply one aspect of a larger problem. Larissa, an African American teacher, agreed on the need for more African American teachers. But her analysis suggested that the small cadre at Gates was reflective of the general marginalization of African American parents, students, and teachers at the school. Consequently, students tended to dismiss an institution in which they, as a people, were not included:

> Black kids are not connected to school as White kids are. They see school as relevant, but not as Black people important in it. School is important to life because they need it to get the skills for a job or whatever. But they don't see Black people as being vital in schools. There's no real representation and no valued parent involvement. Black parents are not seen as valuable within the school, and kids just don't see Black adults as a part of this school. What kind of representation is it when there are seven or eight Black teachers with a student population that's 67% Black?

Cultural differences and disempowerment were strong themes among a few African American teachers at Gates. They believed the school's behavioral norms and subtext of valued cultural knowledge were alien and debilitating to African American students. In addition, they described the curriculum as Eurocentric. In other words, it felt like a White school. This point of view was echoed in Larissa's comment that African American students might see the utilitarian value of education but that it had little intrinsic meaning for students generally, and for African Americans in particular, and in that sense it was not relevant. Further, she and others contended that many teachers did not understand the students. In what was essentially a critique of the deficit model, she argued that as a result they were unable to recognize and capitalize on African American students' strengths. Instead, teachers saw cultural differences as defects. Several teachers at Gates, in particular, made this point.

Even at Franklin, a school that was 80% African American and had a faculty that was half African American, some African American teachers had a similar critique of colleagues of both races. Without romanticizing Jim Crow, one of their themes was that with school desegregation they lost the supportive culture and encouragement that they believed had been central to the success of Black children in Black schools (hooks, 1994; Siddle Walker, 1993). Desegregation ruptured the ties between schools and the Black community and undermined community within schools. The negative consequences of this rupture were seen as a fundamental cause of the resistance of so many African American students. Like those who advocated strengthening social relations, this group of African American–centered teachers also stressed building support systems. However, their concern was that African American students experience a sense of community that reaffirmed their identity as African American people. They defined issues of trust, of social bonds, of reconstructing community within schools for African American students in African American-centered terms (Foster, 1991). At both schools, these teachers developed formal and informal African American–identified clubs, discussion groups, performances, and projects to support African American identity within White-dominated institutions.

Accordingly, their critique centered on the present marginalization of African American students within their school. Several White teachers also talked about African American students' alienation. This perspective is reflected in the comments of three teachers in separate interviews:

Juanita: (Black Franklin teacher) Black kids are in school, but they're not a part of it. . . . We lost something when we went to integration because Black schools were a community and we don't have that anymore.

Chris: (White Franklin teacher) This is not their world and they don't know how to be teacher pleasers.

Jonetta: (Black Franklin staff member) No matter what they may be able to achieve, we have to build a sense of self-worth into the curriculum. . . . We need a more positive stance toward ourselves [African Americans] and really toward all children . . . Schools cannot undo what has already occurred in a child's life, but they do need to identify, to work with

> each child's talents and gifts and establish within them that
> sense of "Yes, you can."

In interviews, these Franklin staff members portrayed youth who
were essentially strangers in their schools, trying to function in a context that systematically denied their potential, their history, and their
value. Aware that they could not "undo what has already occurred in
a child's life," they continued to believe in the power of education to
make a difference in the lives of African American children. Their
mission, then, was to build on students' strengths and to inculcate a
sense of "yes, you can," in Jonetta's words. This was a powerful theme
in their talk about teaching African American students and in their
practice. (I elaborate this in chapter 9.)

These teachers did not agree with their colleagues who faulted
African American parents for their disinterest in education. To Larissa,
the lack of African American parent involvement at Gates was an
indication of race and class barriers, rather than a sign that parents did
not value education or care about their children. Her view was shared
by several others, both African American and White, who identified a
number of barriers to the meaningful participation of parents of color
and low-income families (cf. Hollins & Spencer, 1990; Lightfoot, 1978).
They pointed to African American parents' obvious discomfort with
the school's upper-middle-class White neighborhood and the fact that
most authority figures in the school (teachers, administrators, and
counselors) were White. They reasoned that parents' own negative
experiences in school reinforced a general sense, as Larissa put it, that
"they don't really belong here." Indeed, they felt Gates, a "White institution," had done little to make low-income African American parents feel welcome or to find meaningful forms for their involvement.

> Kevin (White Gates teacher): It's all doctors' wives and school
> board members. The low-income parents don't feel welcome. They
> are usually only at school when there's a problem. They have to
> go through a negative experience to get here.

Practices of Teachers With a Critique of Racism

Some, not all, teachers who identified racism as a significant
problem were also critical of the low expectations of African Americans held by many of their colleagues. This was a small set (about six)
of the African American teachers and a few Whites (one to three) at
each school. Some, like Jonetta, believed that this was a conscious act

of racism in which "there's selective teaching going on. Some teachers choose to teach more to some kids than to other kids." On their part, this group of teachers tended to have high expectations for all students. Based on my observations, although their classes varied from quite traditional to highly innovative, and although their interactional styles ranged from strict to relaxed and sociable, they consistently seemed to challenge their students, maintaining a fairly high intellectual content, even in remedial classes such as reading.

They also held high expectations for behavior. In fact, the respect commanded by this group of teachers was one of the most salient differences between them and other teachers, both White and African American. Their discipline methods combined high standards of conduct with caring and high academic expectations. Helen was legend at Franklin in this regard. She presided with quiet authority over classrooms of attentive and respectful students. (Her perspective and role in restructuring is discussed in chapter 9.)

Teachers who voiced a critique of racism also believed that African American students were treated unfairly in disciplinary actions, and most were outspokenly opposed to academic tracking, which they believed limited the educational opportunities of the majority of African American students. At Gates, most of the eight African American teachers and one White teacher were especially concerned that interpretations of student behavior favored privileged White students, and that this bias was reflected in the disproportionate disciplining and suspensions of African American students. Paulette, another Gates teacher, claimed that the disrespect displayed by some White students was seen as "no problem" while "Black kids' behavior is 'bad,' and they are the ones who get punished."

Educational Critiques

> The problems are bigger than schools. But one thing schools could do is use the magnet school concept. Get kids into an interesting environment. These kids just aren't interested in school as it is now.
>
> —A Franklin teacher

Teachers in Riverton were aware of the educational reform movement sweeping the United States. The state was affiliated with a national educational initiative that had brought several well-known advocates of school restructuring to Riverton to speak. Even before whole school restructuring began at Franklin and Gates in the fall of 1990, at least a few teachers at each school were critical of the education in their schools and in the Riverton school system. At least five teachers from each of the four restructuring schools had participated in workshops on educational reforms, which further kindled interest in alternatives to the conventional practices that characterized their schools. Some teachers tied their interest in educational change with an analysis of the problems African American students had in school. Essentially, those with an *educational critique* described the low achievement of African American students as the mark of a failing educational system. Chris, a White teacher at Franklin, reflected this view: "The schools are fighting against so many things—gangs, lack of resources. . . . Kids need to do experiments in science. They need active learning."

The educational perspective of this group of teachers was partly rooted in their own experience. Facing classrooms of bored and resistant students day after day convinced them that the standard pedagogical approaches and curricular content simply were not working. However, most could offer no clear alternative, repeatedly expressing the need for "more training" in "new techniques." A major theme was relevance—making classroom knowledge and learning experiences more meaningful to students. The comments of Patricia, a young White teacher at Franklin, were typical of this group:

> The kids just aren't interested. When I was in school I loved to read. I read all the time. I want these kids to love reading too, but they don't read. Something has to be done differently. I don't know. This is something I wanted to do all my life. But I never thought it would be like this.

A few were influenced by educational literature, university classes, and broader discussions of educational change as well as summations of their own experience. They were proponents of specific curricular and pedagogical innovations, for instance, cooperative learning, heterogeneous grouping, whole language approaches to reading and writing, story theater projects, use of manipulatives and calculators in mathematics, multicultural curricula, and experiential learning. Included in this group were some teachers who were also critical of Eurocentric biases and racism in the schools. But there were really just a few teachers at each school who possessed enough knowledge of educational innovations to make specific proposals and to try them out in their classrooms.

Some teachers assumed that conventional pedagogy was appropriate for most students, but different methods were needed with "at-risk" students. As William, an African American teacher at Gates, put it, "They are using traditional methods with nontraditional students, and they are not working." Others questioned the value of a traditional Riverton education for anyone. Those with a sharper educational critique tended to see the school problems of "at-risk" students as but the tip of the iceberg of an educational system in need of overhauling. Their talk about low-achieving students frequently shifted to the need to make fundamental changes for all students. However, the district's control over curriculum was seen as a formidable obstacle.

> Larissa (Black teacher at Gates): The content of schooling is not relevant to kids and as a result they dismiss it. The content of schooling has relevance to only a few. The problem is how to change the content when all the curriculum requirements are in place.

Tracking was an issue on which Riverton educators were sharply split, but there was a committed core of opponents at both schools. They argued that the separation of regular and honors students exacerbated low achievement. Reasons varied. Some argued that students were held back by the watered-down curriculum and "drill and kill" of regular-track classes, and this institutionalized achievement gaps. Others believed regular-track students needed the example of high-achieving peers. Still others contended tracking was an explicitly racist policy that assured that African American students would be concentrated in regular classes.

At each school there were a few teachers who put their critique of tracking into practice by circumventing official policy, informally transferring students from regular to honors classes or "using honors methods with my regular kids." For example, Mr. Whitney, a veteran White teacher at Franklin, offered what he considered an honors curriculum to all his classes. He also temporarily transferred failing regular-track students into his honors classes to boost their "self-esteem" and facilitate peer tutoring. Then he quietly propagated his success stories. Anecdotes of this kind were salient in teachers' arguments against tracking.

A claim of a different sort was that low achievement began in elementary school where weaknesses in basic skills that "could have been caught sooner . . . put some kids so far behind by junior high school that there is almost no way they can catch up" (Franklin teacher). (The district had a very low retention rate of 3–5%).[2] Another target was the school system's hierarchical and bureaucratic organization. On one level, teachers (and building administrators) were angry at what they perceived to be the district's profound lack of respect for them as educational professionals. But others interested in educational change also argued that the district's authoritarianism stifled innovation and teacher initiatives that might increase the achievement of low-achieving students.

Although there was plenty of criticism from this group, there was little consensus about how schooling should be changed. In particular, at the outset of restructuring there was little agreement about remedies for the low achievement and academic disengagement of low-income African American students. Among critics there were educational progressives, advocates of culturally centered curricula, and traditionalists who harked back to the days of all-Black schools. Indeed, some teachers fit all of these categories, depending on the issue.

The School Cultures of Gates and Franklin

Some have argued that organizational culture—the meaning, values, and symbols of an institutionalized group—is central to the function and cohesion of organizations, including schools, and shapes their daily regularities (Bolman & Deal, 1988). Both Gates and Franklin embodied multiple and contradictory cultures, competing values and ideologies (cf. Metz, 1978). There were subtexts subordinate to the dominant culture at Gates and perspectives that were marginalized in both schools. Indeed, each of these schools was a context in which meanings, values, and beliefs, as well as their ability to shape the institutional culture and practice, were contested. As I go on to demonstrate, the relationship between ideology, culture, and power became a central aspect of what occurred at Gates and Franklin during the first year of restructuring.

Structures, practices, and policies may be prescribed and concretely delineated, but the web of beliefs, norms, values, and meanings, which are often tacit and assumed, is more elusive. As proposed earlier, to change the regularities of educational practice and the character of life in schools, educators must reflect upon that which is unstated and taken-for-granted, ultimately challenging assumptions and beliefs (Sarason, 1982) and questioning the relations of power embodied in these beliefs. And they must do so in an environment in which some individuals and their views carry more weight than others and in which the larger society, as well as the local community, sanctions some values and norms and suppresses or even vilifies others and concretizes dominant ideas in policies and structures.

Gates's Faculty Culture

Overtly, Gates had a clearly identifiable faculty culture defined by its college preparatory honors curriculum and the academic success of its upper-middle-class, mainly White students. Most of the staff—experienced and competent—were proud that Gates was the quintessential academic junior high school—well-run, disciplined, and conventionally successful. Yet two thirds of the students were low-income children of color who, on average, scored dramatically below their White peers on standardized measures of achievement.

In reality, the two worlds at Gates—one successful, congruent with the dominant ethos, overwhelmingly White, and visible within its valued academic domains; the other incongruent, marginalized, overwhelmingly Black, and largely invisible within these domains—coexisted within the same building. The chasm between them was reflected in the standard explanations teachers gave for low achievement by African American students. The mostly White staff often interpreted cultural, class, and racial characteristics of African American students as shortcomings, particularly in comparison with upper-middle-class White students. A narrow definition of parental support for education, coupled with students' seeming resistance to instruction, fueled arguments that these children and their families had little regard for education and little motivation to achieve. The social relations model also resonated with the Gates faculty because they were mainly a self-confident group of veteran teachers, comfortable with the efficacy of their educational practices, which were regularly reconfirmed by the achievements of their affluent White students. Unlike some of the more demoralized Franklin faculty, they were convinced there was something that could be done to address the problems of the "at-risk" students. Emphasizing social relations allowed them to take concrete measures without questioning educational and racial norms.

With its powerful academic culture, its predominantly White faculty, and the dominating influence of upper-middle-class White parents, racial critiques at Gates were subterranean. Educational critiques also had little credence among the teachers. It was mainly African American teachers with a racial analysis of student failure who advocated sweeping educational changes, but despite the educational vision of several of these teachers, they were generally marginal within the faculty. Their familiarity with current educational theories and their notions of curricular and pedagogical reform had no apparent currency in the professional culture at Gates.

A faculty-directed school assessment in May 1990 indicated the staff was sharply divided on issues related to the school's vision, the role of teachers in decision making, and opportunities for successful experiences for all students. A teacher leading the assessment said it showed "we are not as together as we think we are." However, at the outset of restructuring, dissident voices were submerged beneath a united front of stability and self-confidence.

Franklin's Faculty Culture

In contrast, Franklin was, in one sense, an African American school. That is, its students were overwhelmingly African American; its faculty was 50% African American, and it had an African American principal. Yet the content of the curriculum and the pictures and slogans that adorned halls and classrooms were not much different from Gates. There was no dominant ethos and the behavior of the faculty toward the students was so varied, that one could not generalize about it. Nor could one generalize about the faculty except to say that it was deeply fragmented, a collage of subgroups, each with their own turf within the school, most with their own ax to grind and their own framework for analyzing why so many students did poorly at Franklin. White teachers who congregated in the smoking lounge and a group of faculty who seemed to have given up had a deficit analysis of the low achievement of African American students.

Among Franklin teachers with intimate knowledge of African American students' family situations, there was more talk about ameliorating social problems than about strengthening their sense of belonging to the school. This interpretation of student support may have caught on at Franklin because the culture and ethos of this school was more fragmented than at Gates, and it was less clear what students were to gain membership in. Perhaps because Franklin's African American and White student body did not clearly break down into insiders and outsiders as it did at Gates, building a sense of belonging was less salient. But because school membership was a formal goal of restructuring, it was a topic at Franklin as well.

The educational critique was more common at Franklin than at Gates. Franklin teachers were more frustrated by widespread student failure, and they did not have high-achieving students to validate conventional curriculum and instruction. So, nearly all teachers, except for those who had become cynical, thought that "we have to do something different." While some believed that building stronger social bonds would help, they also doubted the efficacy of existing educational practice. More so than at Gates, however, there was a void of curricular and pedagogical knowledge upon which to base discussions of reform. As a result, their educational critiques lacked the potency of an alternative educational vision.

The Principals' Perspectives

The principals of Franklin and Gates differed in how they explained low achievement by African American students. Delisa Johnson, the African American principal at Franklin, voiced a very strong social relations explanation. An articulate proponent of creating a nurturing environment to foster achievement, she propagated her views in faculty meetings, in discussions with teachers, and by modeling them through her own actions. An advocate of mentoring, family counseling, and establishing caring personal relationships with students, she spent considerable time doing these things herself. Prior to the fall of 1990, it was not apparent that her approach had much influence in the school. As a new African American principal walking a fine line between a contentious and racially divided faculty, her influence seemed limited. For the same reasons (from my observations and comments of teachers), prior to fall 1990, Johnson kept her views on racial issues to herself and did not publicly advance a racial critique as an explanation for African American students' difficulties at Franklin or in the Riverton schools generally. Johnson also was not overtly critical of conventional educational practices.

Ron Walters, at Gates, was more enigmatic. Publicly, he was a vocal critic of traditional education. "What we've been doing for 100 years just doesn't work" was his recurring theme. In his speeches to teachers, civic organizations, and restructuring institutes he championed organizational restructuring—site-based management, participatory leadership, collaboration—but he did not offer any specific curricular or pedagogical vision or critique of the substance of teaching and learning. The strongest theme in Walters's philosophy of educational change was captured by the slogan, "Success for All." It seemed that he saw improving students' sense of school membership, that is, the social relations approach, as well as his faith in organizational change per se, as the path to this goal. Yet, in private conversations I participated in, he blamed African American principals, teachers, parents, and the African American community for setting low standards, lacking educational expertise, and not caring about their children's education. To what extent he conveyed this deficit model to others I do not know. In practice, prior to and during restructuring, his overarching concern was with the discipline of African American students. He insisted, "We have to get discipline in order first before we can do anything else." Again, he had faith in the teams to foster school membership, which, he averred, would "get behavior under control." It is plausible that his punitive orientation and preoccupation with controlling African American students fueled teachers' deficit explanations; it certainly did not counter them.

Conclusion

Beneath the schema of explanatory models described in this chapter, the reality was far less neat. Explanations for the alienation and low achievement of African American students tended to overlap and intertwine at Franklin and Gates. The social relations approach was in part a perceived panacea for student deficiencies and in part a response by some empathetic teachers to the alienation of African American students. Racial critiques were often educational critiques as well. Furthermore, educators' own views were often more mixed and conditional, and definitions of the problem were often multifaceted and variable. For example, the Othermothers, an empathetic group of African American women teachers at Franklin, described students as culturally deprived, victims of racist institutions, lacking in school membership, or all three. These and other examples, repeatedly illustrated to me, as Therborn (1980) argues, the complexity, contradictoriness, and fluidity of ideological makeup. Thus, I do not want to reify these ideologies or label people with them. What is important is that the four models outlined here were salient within the faculty discourse and culture of both Gates and Franklin. They framed how educators, at different times, saw their students and how they interpreted the potential of restructuring, and these models rang out clearly in teachers' language and practice.

Explanations for the lack of school success of students in general carry cultural meanings linked to beliefs about race, class, opportunity and success in the United States and the role of schools and teachers. Teachers operate from these cultural subtexts and from their own race, class, gender, and other social identities. To change educational practice, teachers with different understandings, coming from different social locations, need dialogue and interaction. Among other things, they need collectively to explore the implications of various definitions of educational problems and of alternative solutions. In the following chapters, I examine the nature of dialogue and interaction among teachers as they attempted to influence the educational experiences of African American students.

5

FOCUS TEAMS AT GATES: CONCENTRATING ON INDIVIDUALS*

In the [team] meeting, I found out the other teachers had the same problems with [student]. Then I realized it wasn't anything I was doing. It was [the student].

—Team teacher

To study the development of teams at Gates Junior High School, I focused on two ninth-grade teams. In this chapter, I describe the dialogue, interactions, and activities of these two teams over the course of the 1990–91 school year, the first year that they participated in school restructuring. My analysis focuses on the interplay of teachers' beliefs and practices, the mandate to improve the success of "at-risk" students, and new structures of collaboration and teacher "empowerment." Four themes defined the character of the ninth-grade teams' work: (a) focus on individuals and the personalization of social problems, (b) competitions and incentives, (c) dichotomy of social support and academic success, (d) perspectives on tracking and differentiated curriculum. My discussion of these themes points to the absence of substantive dialogue about cultural, structural, and curricular regularities at Gates and to the persistence of deficit models of low-achieving African American students.

The Ninth-Grade Focus Teams

As described in chapter 3, the division between affluent White and low-income African American students at Gates was manifested in their social segregation, in disparities in academic success and disciplinary actions, and in their separation into honors- and regular-

---

*Portions of this chapter appeared in Lipman, P. (1997). Restructuring in context: A case study of the dynamics of ideology, power, and teacher participation. *American Educational Research Journal, 34*(1), 3–37.

track classes. One result of tracking was that regular-track students tended to be concentrated in one team and honors students in the other. According to the school registrar, who worked out the assignments in consultation with the principal, this was necessary to keep a common group of students together with their five core-subject teachers. The correlation of teams and academic tracks was especially strong in the ninth grade, where the majority of African Americans were in regular-track classes and the majority of Whites in honors-track classes.

School administrators were reluctant to provide exact numbers of regular and honors students in each team, and most teachers did not want to discuss the correlation between tracking and race. (We had raised this issue in 1989 flowing from our observations of eighth-grade teams, and it created quite a political storm. Alluding to this incident, in the fall of 1990 the principal told teachers they did not have to answer "sensitive questions" about the teams.) Consequently, we could not corroborate teachers' reports of the distribution of students by race in each track with official school data. (Teachers' reports also conflicted with each other.) However, that each ninth-grade team was substantially weighted toward one of the tracks was apparent. The ninth-grade A Team was quickly identified by students and teachers alike as the "regular team" and the B team as the "honors team." (Team names are pseudonyms.) At the end of the first 9 weeks, the leader of the A Team said 17 of a total of 122 students (14%) on his team were honors track. On the B Team, 46 of a total of 98 students (47%) took all honors classes with an additional 10 to 15 students in some honors classes. In addition, there were two full sections of advanced math classes in the B Team, and more B Team students took high-status foreign language classes than did A Team students. The B Team had most of the ninth grade's academic superstars, and both sections of advanced math were taught by the B Team math teacher. Students reported that the B Team faculty were "harder teachers." The B Team also had more White students. The racial breakdown in B Team classes at the end of the first 9 weeks is shown in table 5.1.

TABLE 5.1

Team B Classes by Race and Track

| | Regular | | Honors | |
	White	Black	White	Black
Math	14	48	30	4
History	5	37	34	16
Science	7	46	27	17
English	7	51	32	14

Each teacher had roughly the same numberes of honors classes. To accommodate this, a number of students were "crossover" students; they took some of their classes from teachers not in their team. Thus, students were not simply grouped with their teachers. Some other logic had been used to assign a disproportionate number of honors and regular students to the B and A Teams respectively. The principal's explanation for the ninth-grade teams' sharper divisions along lines of race and academic track was that because the advanced math classes were taught by one teacher, and because most honors students also took advanced foreign languages and other academic electives, it was difficult to mix honors and regular students. He contended that there simply was not enough flexibility in the schedule to make the two teams more heterogeneous. He suggested that this stratification was more acceptable in ninth grade, the last year of junior high school in Riverton, since high school students were openly sorted into academic tracks.

In fact, the link between students' race and their academic track was particularly significant in ninth grade. This was the transition year to high school, the year in which tracking could be expected to have the most dramatic consequences. A student's academic success in ninth grade greatly influenced which high school she/he would be encouraged to attend and which high school track she/he would be placed in. In addition, course taking in mathematics, which was differentiated by track in the ninth grade, determined how much math a student would be able to take in high school. Research indicates that access to advanced mathematics course work at earlier stages (algebra in eighth grade) is the "gatekeeper keeping students out of college preparatory programs and technology related careers" and that tracking blocks students' opportunity to learn advanced mathematics (Robinson, 1996: 389). In short, a student's educational trajectory in large measure jelled in ninth grade. It was therefore an interesting context in which to study the influences of restructuring on the racial and academic divisions in the school and on African American students' educational opportunities.

The A Team Teachers

The A Team leader, Jim Meier, a White male in his forties, was a respected 20-year veteran teacher. Jim lived in one of the surrounding county suburbs and expressed some shock at the living conditions of his "at-risk" students, which he pictured as dramatically at odds with his own conservative, lower-middle-class, semirural environment. Jim speculated that "the inner city lifestyle," with its reputed violence, drugs, gangs, and disincentive for academic achievement, was at the root of the widespread failure of African Americans at Gates.

His A Team colleagues were all White—Marie and Geraldine, each with more than 30 years seniority, and two younger teachers, Connie, with a 5-year tenure at Gates, and Doris, a new teacher who taught the new Study and Research Methods (SRM) class. Marie and Gerrie were two of eight teachers remaining at Gates who had been part of the Magnolia Ridge faculty that was exchanged en masse with the Gates faculty in the early 1970s. They had both lived through several changes in student body and administration at Gates. Although still proud of their affiliation with the school, they were also nostalgic about past years when, as Gerrie said, "Honors students were really gifted," and African American students were from less impoverished, middle- and working-class families.

Marie said she was doing pretty much what she had been doing in her classroom for 30 years—leading teacher-centered discussions of assigned material, having students write reports and answer questions at the end of each chapter of the text. In interviews in the spring of 1990 and again in the following fall, she attributed African American students' achievement and behavior problems to family crises and poor parenting.

Gerrie was a similarly conventional teacher who had devised a system of competitions that governed many class activities. In the past she had assigned creative projects, some of which she still kept in a large storage closet in her room and brought out to show visitors as mementos of a time when she taught "really talented kids." Gerrie often talked about her affection for her "sweet at-risk kids," yet she allowed their playing around and inattention to go unchecked, and demanded relatively little from her regular classes. When asked directly about African American students' poor academic performance, she averred that she had no ready explanation, but her talk was peppered with comments about students' "abilities," about who was "resource" (special education) or who was "probably retarded," how little she could expect from her "low students" and how much she expected from "the really bright ones."

Connie, a dynamic young teacher, conducted classes that were less teacher-centered and more varied and informal than those taught by her team colleagues. She also seemed to have more personal interactions with students, particularly young African Americans, who often clustered outside her classroom door during breaks. She was one of six teachers at the school who participated in the Mentoring and Counseling Program (MCP)—a mentorship program for "at-risk" students. In her classes students often worked in groups, and she moved energetically around the room from one group to another, good-naturedly glaring at an occasional student who was off-task. Students described her as "nice" and "more interesting" than many of their other teachers. She also seemed to consistently challenge regular as well as honors students to reason and justify their mathematical answers. She described low-achieving African American students as "great kids" victimized by cultural deficits and incompetent parents.

Doris, the fifth member of the team, was new to Riverton and the only A Team teacher with children in district schools. She had a lot of trouble keeping students' attention and seemed uncertain of the material in the new Study and Research Methods course (SRM). She described herself as an advocate for low-achieving African American students. In contrast to her colleagues, Doris thought White students "got away with murder" at Gates and that some teachers there "don't care about Black students." She also believed that the standard approaches to curriculum and pedagogy "weren't working" for these students but said she didn't know what to do differently.

The B Team Teachers

Elaine Ross, the B Team leader, was a 15-year Gates veteran. She was one of the insiders who had the principal's ear and was in charge of prestigious academic activities such as the debate team and the Academic Challenge Bowl team, which competed statewide. In part, her status accrued from her close ties with prestigious families of Gates students—she lived in the Hills and belonged to the same social circles and country club. Elaine was active in the Restructuring Institute in August 1990, had attended various district meetings in preparation, and was excited about restructuring. She pointed to the success of several middle-class African American students to support her theory that socioeconomic conditions and personal problems, not race, explained lack of academic success. She was the team's strongest proponent of strengthening social relations, adult support, and counseling. Nevertheless, in interviews she insisted on a meritocratic model of academic success, arguing, "Face it, the best students are the ones who are the smartest and the ones who are really motivated, who really work hard." A Northerner, Elaine prided herself on not being swept up in the "racism" of Riverton and in being able to relate well to "all kinds of students." Her classes were lively and interactive, punctuated with jokes and friendly repartee with students.

The other B Team teachers were: Colleen, a White woman; two White males, Stanley and Robert, and Paulette, the only African

American on either team. Colleen lived in a middle-class neighborhood adjacent to the Hills and seemed to know many Hills students personally. She was charged with the responsibility of preparing Gates's college-bound and academically talented math students for Riverton's best high schools. She came in early and spent nearly every lunch hour and one to two hours after school every day tutoring these students. Like Elaine, she believed that the "lower-level kids" needed more personal support to succeed. They were unmotivated because "they have failed too much and the effort is too great to do well."

Robert was a first-year teacher in his early thirties who began a teaching career at a considerable cut in pay from his previous "boring" job. He commuted from a nearby community. Although Robert started off the year enthusiastically, he gradually began to burn out from all the extra duties he took on to boost his paycheck and from discouragement over his students' lack of motivation. Robert stated unequivocally that social conditions and cultural and family deficiencies, particularly parents' lack of education and concern for their children, and "behavior problems," were at the root of school failure.

A fourth member of the team, Stanley, had transferred 2 years ago to Gates from one of the county schools. He commuted from his home in the county where his children attended a White Christian Academy school. Stanley was an experienced high school teacher, confident of his subject matter and of his conventional lecture-and-recitation teaching style. He was a strict disciplinarian with stringent academic standards. He was blunt in his attribution of African American students' failure to their families, their personal attitudes and deficiencies, and mainly, what he saw as "laziness." Stanley strongly disagreed with wasting time on affective (social relations) solutions to academic problems.

Paulette, one of eight African American faculty, was an experienced teacher who had been at the school 6 years. As a remedial reading teacher prior to 1990–91, when she was assigned to teach Study and Research Methods, she had been outside the core academic faculty so pivotal at Gates. Paulette initiated the school's fledgling African American cultural club, AfroNotions, and was a Mentoring and Counseling Program teacher in 1989–90. According to her White colleagues, she won the cooperation and respect of students other teachers said they "could not handle." Paulette was critical of racism at Gates and also elaborated a broader analysis of the need to transform curriculum and instruction overall. Her perspectives were frequently sharply at odds with those of other members of her team, and in interviews she often illustrated her analysis by comparing her colleagues' practices and beliefs about students with her own. At mid-year, the principal moved her from SRM back to remedial reading. Although she still attended some team meetings, this move, coupled with her own disillusionment with the team, distanced her from it. (Paulette's role in restructuring is a focus of chapter 9.)

The Team Agendas

Building on their new opportunities for collaboration and initiative, in the beginning of the school year, both teams set a rather broad agenda for themselves. For example, in its initial meetings, the B Team agreed on a plan that focused on academic development and team/school membership:

Academic Development
Goal: Challenge each student to perform to his or her fullest potential in all academics and to demonstrate this performance by improving scores by at least one year on the [standardized achievement] test.

Strategies:
1. Incentives
2. Challenging and stimulating assignments
3. Cooperative learning
4. Interdisciplinary approach
5. Increase parental involvement and support
6. Independent research
7. Team support and encouragement

Team/School Climate
Goals:
1. Involve parents of all SES levels in the school community
2. Develop school and team spirit, tradition, respect toward academic achievement and fellowship with others from all backgrounds

Strategies:
1. Team events and competition with other teams
2. Incentive awards
3. School/team service projects
4. Teacher and parent attendance at school/athletic events
5. Incentives for teams with low attendance
6. More frequent parent meetings

Both teams discussed several innovative projects: interdisciplinary units, a team newspaper written by students, and student advisory committees that would be a channel for student input. However, their actual practice was more limited. Few interdisciplinary units materialized. The two developed by each team mainly reorganized existing curricula to address a common topic (such as "the Law"). The role of student advisory groups was reduced to making suggestions about extracurricular activities, such as what movie to show for a team party. There was only one issue of the student newspaper—produced not by students but by A Team teachers as an example. It generated so little enthusiasm that no students volunteered to work on subsequent issues, and it was dropped. What the teams actually focused on is the subject of the remainder of this chapter.

In practice, both teams developed three main strategies for low-achieving students: (a) an individualized plan for each "problem student," (b) a system of extrinsic rewards for achievement, and (c) team activities to create a sense of collective identity and belonging. Other pedagogical and curricular strategies to increase achievement and academic engagement that had been discussed at the Restructuring Institute, such as active and experiential learning, interdisciplinary units, independent research projects, and teaching to multiple learning styles, received diminishing attention at meetings and were increasingly less the focus of team activities as the year progressed. At the same time, the concentration on individual students, incentives, and nonacademic team activities became more central.

Focus on Individual Students

From the beginning of the school year, team planning sessions included identifying "problem" students and figuring out how to meet their particular needs, compensate for their weaknesses, and modify their behavior. Any teacher on the team could identify a student, and the members of the team would compare notes on the student's behavior, academic performance, and whatever they knew of the student's personal circumstances. If the teachers felt they had enough information, they settled on an intervention plan such as counseling, a parent conference, a collective scolding, tutoring, or a contract for improved behavior, academic performance, or attendance. Often they sought additional information from the school counselor as well. These notes of a meeting of the B Team are representative of these discussions:

They begin by naming students they want discussed. [They briefly discuss other team business, including such details as schedule changes, cafeteria behavior, and team T-shirts.]

Elaine: OK, lets get into the students. There's a long list here, as usual. Marcus.

[This is a student who has had a lot of behavior infractions, and this is the second time the team has discussed him.] Several teachers say he is developing a different attitude.

Elaine: He's doing his work and he's passing in my class. And, he's even paying attention (laugh). That call we made to his grandmother seemed to do a lot of good.
Robert: We need to do that with all of 'em, especially the ones that are just out there running wild. We need to get on 'em and let their parents know—if any of them care.

[They discuss Darnell, another student who has been hostile recently.]

Elaine: Carlton. What are we going to do about him? I talked to Myra [eighth grade counselor] who knows the family. His stepfather is an alcoholic and he beat his [Carlton's] mother up and she ran away from home. I don't know where he's staying. His whole world has fallen apart.
Stanley: Friends he's staying with say he's OK.
Elaine: How could he be, Stan?
Robert: They don't know. They're not highly educated. They don't get beyond the surface things. We've got to get him some counseling.
Elaine: OK, what do you think, Coretta [counselor]? [There is an extended discussion about what sort of counseling would be useful and the counselor agrees to follow up.]
Elaine: Latania. Now there's a real challenge. Is she passing anything? [She looks around the table, all the teachers check their grade books and shake their heads.] (To the counselor:) What do you know about her home situation? . . .

Typically, as in this discussion, profiles of students meshed academic and social characteristics. The conversation flowed from failing grades or poor attendance to questions about a student's family situation or out-of-school behaviors. In my observations of team meetings throughout the year, I found all of the individuals discussed in this way were students whom the teachers had identified as "at-risk," usually on the basis of behavioral or social characteristics. For example, negatively defined behaviors (such as acting up in class), known personal or family problems, or "at-risk activities" (such as suspected gang affiliation) qualified a student for being "at-risk," just as surely as demonstrable academic problems. As the weeks progressed, discussions of individual students became a regular agenda item and eventually dominated the teams' work.

Early in the second semester, caseworkers were installed to work with students teachers identified as "at-risk" and to broker social services for them. Many team meetings were taken up with discussing individual students with the caseworkers and essentially passing them off to the latter. Turning over students with identified school problems (achievement, attendance, discipline) in this way both practically and symbolically solidified the causal connection between school problems and social conditions or family "deficiencies." Concretely, it made the deficit model the basis of action.

Collaboration Reinforces the Deficit Model

As individual needs became the centerpiece of team meetings, restructuring was adapted to the prevailing ideology. The language of "needs," as contrasted with potential or resilience (Winfield, 1991), itself implied deficiencies. In fact, the intervention that the teams arrived at after reviewing a child's personal or family problems was much like the Individual Education Plan (IEP) usually developed for students labeled "learning disabled" or "emotionally handicapped"— that is, wanting.

Moreover, the team structure itself reinforced the deficit model. It provided a new arena for teachers to collaborate in psychological and social profiles of students. In the discussions I observed, almost invariably, some teacher or counselor was cognizant of a personal situation to which school problems could be ascribed—a "family problem" or undesirable behavior could usually be found in the background of every student they discussed. When none was apparent, the matter was delegated to a counselor or teacher to investigate "the home situation." Teachers traded stories about student deficiencies and family pathologies. Each story became a variation on a cultural model of deprivation, the aggregate reaffirming and embellishing that model.

In addition, when teachers shared information about a "problem" student, they generally found that other teachers also had difficulties with that student, confirming that the problem was with the student her/himself, rather than with educational practice. In this way, in the absence of conflicting views, collaboration created a new context within which teachers could be reassured that their own practice was not at fault. In fact, some teachers reported they had actually become less critical of their own teaching since the creation of the teams. (This was not the case with adult/student relations as discussed below.) In March, Connie (A Team) described this process:

> We meet as a team and identify problems with kids. It's helpful because you see that it's not just you, not just the teacher but the kids. That has been the most important thing for me. It makes you aware. I used to think maybe it was something in my own teaching. Or a lot of times you think you just can't relate to the kid. Then in the team you see it's not just you. You see it's something in the kid.

In my observation, the only dissenting voices were Paulette and Stanley, both on the B Team. Throughout the year, Stanley stubbornly insisted that students be held accountable for their own failures. He disagreed with focussing discussions on family problems and refused to be lenient on account of students' personal circumstances. His position became a major point of contention in the team. (This debate is described below.)

Paulette's assessment was also at odds with the rest of the team. However, rather than dwell on students' weaknesses, she tended to talk about strengths that teachers could build on. She also frequently brought to the discussion personal knowledge about a student's interests and learning and described ways she had been successful with that student. For example, in a fall team meeting about an apparently unmotivated student, after several teachers had speculated about his family situation, this dialogue ensued:

Paulette: Darnel knows a lot about machines. He can fix almost anything. If you can relate to him on that and give him a chance to show what he knows, he'll get involved. He's writing a good report in my class on [topic].
Elaine: I'd like to see him write something, anything.
Colleen: (shaking her head) He's failing in [subject]. [Pause]
Elaine: Well, I'll talk to the counselor. Next is Marcus.

This exchange was quite typical of the conversations I observed. Although team members acknowledged that Paulette "had a way" with some of the most "difficult" students, her perspective did not substantively alter the team's bent toward family and social problems, nor did it appear to encourage others to reflect on their own attitudes. Deficit explanations seemed to be so powerful that they prevailed despite her counter views. The response to Paulette was complicated. In conversations, other teachers described her success with African American students as unique, perhaps because she was African American. This assessment of Paulette, allowed them to dismiss the pedagogical stance underlying her practice. Thus, although Paulette was a counterexample, her practice did not seem to generate much rethinking. (I revisit this issue in chapter 9.) The point here is that underlying assumptions regarding low-achieving African American students were not discussed, even though conflicting views existed within the team. Like the suppressed differences that exist in many faculty cultures (Metz, 1978), it was as if they had tacitly agreed to disagree and work within that framework.

Success Stories Validate Reforms: The Example of Cory

To illustrate that "teaming is working," teachers touted individual students who had dramatically transformed their behavior and/or academic standing. These exemplary students were often cited as evidence of the value of giving attention to individual students. The A Team repeatedly referred to the example of Cory, an African American male, to verify the efficacy of restructuring. During the first semester, Cory had gone from being a "D" student who had been sullen and bored to an "A" student in line for promotion to honors classes. The team attributed Cory's metamorphosis to their collaborative effort.

Jim: [Cory] is a high-risk student, one of the most likely to fail. Last year he slapped a teacher. He's the kind of student who will grow up to be a pimp or a gangster. He's most anything you'd expect from inner-city poverty. He said he couldn't stand it here because there were all White teachers and he was going to transfer to _____. But now this year because of restructuring, he is excited. He's getting an A in my class. He's our team's best success.

PL: What's the reason for the change?

Jim: The team's attitude toward him. We're never hateful. We had a team meeting with him and his aunt. When we had the conference, he was real scared because he thought he had done something wrong. But we told his aunt that we want him to be successful, that we're very human with him.

And he promised that he would stop talking and pay attention. At the beginning of the year he was very hostile. Sometimes he sat in class and pulled his head up inside his sweatshirt. . . . But then I called his aunt to brag on him, and I said, "Be sure to give him a message on behalf of the whole team. Tell him I called to brag on him." The next day I asked him, "Did you know I called?" And he was really excited about it. He's an example of a very bright kid who's always been in trouble. He's the biggest success our team has had.

Connie: Our most positive example is Cory Hicks. He went from 3 Fs, a D, and a C to 4 As. I taught eighth grade last year so we know each other. Now he's going into honors. He's one of my MCP students too. He changed because the team decided they weren't putting up with anything from him. . . . So we met with his aunt. He likes to test people but we know him as a group—and he knows it. We all watch him. He is very receptive to rewards. He and I have a special relationship—I have great respect for him and him for me.

In several ways, then, Cory was distinguished from his peers. Having identified Cory as "very bright," his teachers demonstrated high expectations for his academic performance. They called his aunt to "brag on him," and both Jim and Connie assigned him to the seat they reserved for their "top student." Others mentioned collectively monitoring his behavior. Indeed, in conversations throughout the year, teachers referred to Cory and several others as students they were concentrating on because these were the ones they thought they could "save," separating them from a broader group they had no overall strategy for, or perhaps had largely given up on (cf. Fordham, 1991). The teams' practice of "working with those we can save" was very similar to Fine's (1991) description of teachers who narrow their responsibility to "working with the survivors."

Perhaps, as the example of Cory suggests, the focus on individuals was salutary for selected students because teachers expected more from them and monitored them more closely, providing additional personal and academic support. In any case, it seemed to pay off in some instances, and these success stories provided validation for the strategy. Indeed, in assessing restructuring as a whole, most team members talked about a few students, all African Americans, who had "turned around" during the year, ostensibly because the team zeroed in on them. They measured their success by the progress of these students who validated their efforts. Perhaps as Fine (1991) suggests, teachers working in an institution that consistently produces failure "generate belief systems that explain their efforts as anything but futile, their dreams as anything but illusory, and their work as anything but wasteful" (p. 154).

The Colorblind Perspective and the Salience of Race

Conversations in team meetings were shaped by a culture that tacitly prohibited discussion of race and racism and educational consequences for African Americans *as a group*. As far as I could determine, all of the students brought up for discussion in the ninth-grade team meetings, and all of the students identified by teachers as "problems," were African American. However, the teachers assiduously avoided discussions of race and racial identification. Instead, designations such as "inner-city," "low-income," "low-SES," "deprived," "regulars," or "at-risk" were a mutually understood code for African American students; "our neighborhood kids" signified Whites and perhaps upper-middle-class African Americans. In the team meetings I observed, there were no discussions of the educational experiences of African American students—as African Americans—or of teachers' practices with African American students per se. One exception was when a White teacher on the B Team blurted out his frustration at what he felt was a challenge to his authority by African American males. "This big Black kid threatened me and I sent him to Mr. Wilson [an administrator]. Threatened me! Wilson did nothing. If they're Black, he bends over backwards." (This incident occurred after Paulette, the only African American member, was removed from the team.)

Silence about race also pervaded classrooms. Although segregation and racism were occasional topics, they were generally treated as abstract social issues, unrelated to students' life experiences. With the exception of Paulette, most teachers held racial issues at arm's length, limiting the class to obligatory and redundant accounts of Dr. King and the Civil Rights Bill, which were treated as historical events divorced from present realities,

Periodically, particularly after each grading period, there was some discussion of the district mandate to reduce racial disparities in achievement. Solutions proposed included tutoring failing students, enrolling them in the afterschool homework center, or getting them to sign a contract to complete their work. At the end of the first 9 weeks, each team spent many extra hours meeting with the parent/guardian of every student in danger of failing one or more subjects. Yet, in the midst of all this effort, there was no visible attention to the fact that all of the students in question were African American or to the implications of this fact for either policy or practice. The consequence of this "colorblind perspective" (Schofield, 1982) was that the particular experiences of African Americans, and the institutional ideologies and practices that shaped their lives as a group at Gates, were not examined.

Why the Concentration on Individuals?

Why was the pull to focus on individuals so strong? In part, it fit assumptions that students were the problem. In part, teachers were simply continuing what they had been doing prior to restructuring. In interviews with teachers of eighth-grade teams in the spring of 1990, several said they had always tried to individualize their responses to students who were having trouble, but the teams made this easier. As one eighth-grade teacher put it, "Miss Hall may be successful with students that I don't know how to work with or vise versa. So we share ideas. The team really helps a lot, and you know you're not alone." Two teachers said they had rarely had discussions of this sort in the past, but with the collegiality of the teams they too were drawn into exchanges about "problem" students.

The focus on individuals was perhaps also supported by "individualized instruction," a relatively new idea at Gates, and one supported at the Restructuring Institute. It's thrust was to tailor teaching to a child's strengths and weaknesses. But because teachers constructed "at-risk" students as socially and economically disadvantaged, they focused particularly on individuals' social conditions. With the exception of Paulette, there was less discussion of individual students from an instructional perspective than from a psychological and social angle. This was reflected in the pervasive discussion of "individual needs." For example, after a long discussion about finding counseling for a student who had run away from home, Jim Meier said, "What is education if it's not meeting individual needs?"

Teachers also felt pressed by the immediacy and drama of individual students' problems. Once they began exploring family circumstances, they opened a Pandora's box of personal crises that seemingly overwhelmed questions of institutional reform and educational philosophy. The B Team's educational goals set at the beginning of the year received little attention. The urgency of immediate problems inevitably prevailed over topics that perhaps seemed more abstract and long range. And, taken one by one, individual problems seemed more amenable to action than the challenge of begetting academic success out of widespread student failure. Larissa, an African American teacher who was critical of her colleagues' narrow educational vision, explained: "Kids' problems are often so severe that they [teachers] have to deal with the immediate problems because, as teachers and educators, that's the part we think we can change, that's what's tangible."

However, this one-sided attention to the immediate and the individual obscured the fundamental problem school restructuring was to address—the school failure of African Americans as a group. A few Corys notwithstanding, the majority of African American students continued to achieve dramatically below their White classmates, were in lower-track classes, and faced significantly more disciplinary actions. Gates Junior High School continued to fail in its responsibility to educate its African American students. Personalized remedies, however beneficial in specific cases, obscured systemic and ideological roots of school failure.

Summary

The focus on individuals reinforced the deficit model and referring students to social services concretely made it the basis of action. Its efficacy was validated by individual success stories, negating the structural and cultural roots of African American students' alienation and marginalization. By concentrating on individual "problem" students, teams reproduced and echoed what Cornell West has named the dominant discourse about African Americans as "problem people" (1993).

Competitions and Incentives

A second major focus of the two teams was developing a system of competitions and material incentives as a way to motivate academic achievement and "reinforce positive behavior." This strategy was introduced to teachers at the Restructuring Institute and in visits to restructuring schools in other districts and was piloted by eighth-grade teams in 1989–90. Colleen, on the B Team, commented in the spring of 1990 that she was looking forward to restructuring: "A lot of teachers are skeptical about the teams, but it's got to be better than what we're doing now. The low kids have no motivation, but the eighth-grade teachers seem to be able to motivate their students with things like the popcorn parties and other incentives." Encouraged by the reported efficacy of this strategy, both teams made "planning incentives" one of their first tasks and, as reflected in team agendas, spent several meetings doing this at the beginning of the year. Before setting out on this path, they did not consult with parents or students or poll African

American teachers in their ranks. And as far as I know, the strategy was not weighed in light of the specific context of Gates with its bimodal pattern of achievement and discipline actions.

There were three kinds of incentives: individual competitions, team rewards and recognitions, and interteam contests. Teachers rewarded students for good behavior, completion of homework, improved grades, and correctly answering questions in class with specially designed tokens that could be redeemed for candy, pencils, a reprieve from homework, extra grade points, or used to buy items at an auction. Good behavior, parent participation, and other activities of the team as a whole were periodically compensated with outings, parties, films, or bulletin board recognition.

Especially in B Team regular classes, incentives were used heavily as an inducement to complete schoolwork and participate in class recitations. Indeed, in some classes these rewards seemed to govern class activity and serve as the principal vehicle through which teachers elicited what they considered to be good behavior and achievement. These fieldnotes from a B Team regular track English class are illustrative:

> The teacher says, "OK, let's get started. You have a chance to earn a lot of awards today. A lot of tokens." [She spends seven minutes checking homework and passing out tokens to students who have completed homework. They begin going over sentences orally and finding the adverbs. She gives out a token to every student who gives a correct answer.] "Ok, I know some of you know it, but I want to show you exactly how I want it so we can get lots of tokens out there." [There are four hands waving frantically, to answer questions and win tokens. For nearly every question several students shoot up their hands. Some are on the edge of their seats. . . . Before the end of class the teacher reminds them that as they walk by the office they will notice that the team has had fourteen days without a fight.] "When we get to 30 days, we can take a field day."

Although the incentives were used in all classes, they were clearly thought to be particularly beneficial for "at-risk" students. Indeed, one of the assumptions that seemed to govern the use of these inducements was that while high-achieving students were to some extent intrinsically motivated, low-achieving students needed extrinsic rewards. Jim Meier: "It takes special attractions to keep these kids' [his sixth-period regular class] attention. That's what we're using the tokens for. With the high-risk kids especially, it's important to make them feel important. They'll do it if they see that they'll get rewards for it."

Most of the team teachers also believed that the incentive of time off from school for team parties, field trips, and other outings was a constructive approach to improve behavior. As with the focus on individual students, there were two dissenting voices on the B Team. Stanley was opposed to detracting from academic tasks, although he was agreeable to outings that were clearly educational, such as a trip he proposed to a museum. On the other hand, Paulette saw outings and social activities chiefly as opportunities for teachers to get to know students rather than as extrinsic motivators.

Behavior Competitions—Privileging Gates's Dominant Student Culture

Competition was not new to Gates. It was integral to the school's culture and emphasized by several ninth-grade teachers. Jim Meier had institutionalized his own classroom incentive system. Gerrie organized her students into squads in an elaborate system of class competitions. Elaine posted grades and held competitions in her class. She was also the coach of the school's Academic Challenge Bowl team, which competed with other junior high schools. However, the teams created a new dimension of competitiveness and a new dynamic among students. Prior to restructuring, students had vied individually for grades or positions on the honor roll and Gates students had competed academically and athletically with other schools. With restructuring, there was an effort to forge a team identity in part through contests for team rewards and recognition. These activities were also meant to improve achievement and behavior.

In this context, rewards for achievement, "good" behavior, and parent involvement greatly favored the "honors team"—the B Team. Predictably, the B Team won handily in contests for bringing more parents to Parent Night, and having fewer suspensions and fewer fights. The results of all these competitions were displayed on oversized posters in the school entrance, broadcast over the public address system, and talked about among teachers.

The high-profile defeats of the A Team served to publicly highlight its subordinate status. When queried about the differences between the teams, several A Team students laughed and said, "We're the dummies." By mid-year, teachers had begun to refer to the "smart team/dumb team syndrome." The A Team teachers also began to doubt the wisdom of team competitions. After his team was embarrassed in the 30-day no-suspension contest, Jim Meier said the odds were against them. Reflecting resentment that had begun to simmer between the teachers on the two teams over the unequal distribution of honors students, he claimed that the rules had been bent for the B Team. After the A Team was again embarrassed in the No Fight Challenge, he said, "You and I know they [B Team] don't have the poor kids. So we have more suspensions. Kids in this team have to feel bad when they are up against losing situations. They know they are going to lose anyway." Gerrie insisted that she didn't want any more competitions. "We have sweet, quiet at-risk kids. Look at Cory. He has changed dramatically because of the team. But these kids don't get rewarded." Moreover, because of the close correlation between race and academic track, the failures of the A Team became a public display of the marginality of African Americans at Gates.

Competitions rewarded behaviors that were closely aligned with the cultural norms of the school's White, upper-class students, norms which were one reason for the disproportionate disciplining of African American students. They validated a world in which disputes were handled and conflicts acted out in ways very different from the realities of many of the African American students at Gates. What was called misbehavior was often teachers' interpretation of African American interactive styles and cultural nuances, such as loud, animated verbal contests, play fighting, and specific dress styles, for example, wearing hats indoors, as threatening. The role that these interpretations play in the disciplining of African American students, especially males, has been discussed elsewhere (Irvine, 1991; Majors & Billson, 1992). Doris, a White teacher on the A Team, described the problem, relating an incident in which she mistakenly thought two African American female students were fighting:

> They were yelling and ... I thought it was a fight. But they were just fooling around. But teachers don't understand these things and the kids get in trouble. . . . [But well-off White kids] talk back and act catty and get away with it. That's OK. But let the Black kids say something, the way they do it, it's another story.

Paulette and Doris were the only ninth-grade teachers who identified this issue. However, their insights seem not to have been shared, or did not register with their colleagues. When interviewed at the end of the school year, neither team mentioned this issue as one that had been discussed.

Sanctioning certain behaviors and punishing others through a system of public rewards underscored the "correctness" of White middle-class student behaviors and stamped some common African

American behaviors as deviant. To play successfully by the rules seemed to require that African American students act "White" as Fordham (1988) has argued; "Good behavior" contests became a display of the cultural inferiority of African American students. One African American student's resistance to the No Fight Contest reveals the conflict perhaps experienced by many African American students as the dominant ethos of the school was enacted and verified through these behavioral competitions.

> Elaine's second period regular class (B Team). Elaine reminds the students that as they walk by the office they will notice that their team has had fourteen days without a fight.

Elaine: When we get to 30 days we get to take a field day. . . . If you see a fight about to begin or if somebody is getting ready to fight, you should report it to a teacher.
Misty: (a Black female in the back row) But Miss Ross, why should you snitch? You're only going to get in trouble anyway.
Elaine: What we need to do is get kids involved and get teachers involved.
Misty: But Miss Ross, say for instance me and Rochelle get into it . . ,
Elaine: [interrupts] Rochelle and I.
Misty: Right. Rochelle and me. She's going to get me regardless. So why should I snitch?
Elaine: She's going to get you for snitching? Nobody is saying snitch.
Misty: But it is snitching. If you do that to somebody bad, they're not going to put up with it. And, if somebody hit me, I ain't going to put up with it either. Miss Ross, when you were little where you grew up, you went to the principal. Today you do that and they're going to beat you up. Besides, it goes against what your parents say. Your parents tell you to hit somebody back if they hit you.

In this exchange, the teacher's approach to conflict privileged actions that negated African American students' group loyalty and strategies that historically have been essential to survival under conditions of physical intimidation and danger, racial hostility, and conflict (King & Mitchell, 1990). The deep cultural divide over the question of self-defense was rooted in the fundamentally different historical and present-day realities of affluent White students and low-income African Americans. Without recognizing and addressing these different perspectives and their bases, the No Fight Contest was doomed. Importantly, this approach was chosen without consultation with African American families about appropriate ways to reduce fighting.

Because of the opposition of the A Team teachers, in the second semester, these contests for good behavior were eliminated, except for one No Suspension contest. Jim Meier explained that the reason for the change was that the contests were undercutting the self-esteem of the students on the A Team. But several related subjects teachers and one B Team teacher said it was because "at-risk kids don't know how to behave so there's no point in having these contests." These comments suggest that the contests had confirmed beliefs in the deficiency of African Americans, and to some this suggested the futility of a campaign to improve their behavior.

Incentives: Displays of African American Students'
Low-Achievement and Marginality

Team incentives for academic success had a similar effect. Because regular students could not hope to compete against honors students in this arena, teachers devised different standards for the two tracks. An "A" on a test in an honors class was worth one token, while regular students only had to get a "B" to get one token. Similarly, an "A" for the 9-week grading period in an honors class counted for five tokens, while a student in a regular class had only to earn a "B" to receive five tokens. This double standard publicly confirmed what most students already knew—less was expected of regular students, meaning most African Americans.

Moreover, despite this double standard, it was well known that the B Team students consistently piled up a disproportionate share of the tokens. In a debate among B Team teachers over allowing students to cash in tokens to see a movie, Elaine commented, "The honors kids will fuss if they don't get a movie because they have all the tokens and they know it too. But the other team [A Team] won't be able to because their kids don't have them [tokens]." Colleen added, "That reminds me, I need some. The honors kids have cleaned me out, again."

Some African American students resisted these humiliations, openly denigrating the contests or simply refusing to go along. For example, a challenge game pit the top squads from regular and honors science classes against each other. The squad that provided the most correct answers would be excused from the semester exam. This section of field notes reflects the oppositional behavior of some African American students to these competitions and compares it with the response of mainly White honors students.

Gerrie's fourth period regular class, A Team. There are 14 students, 12 Black and 2 White. It is about 12 minutes into the class. Students are quizzing each other on science facts. If they get the right answer, they keep the card the question is written on and get one point. The class is getting really rowdy. For the fourth time several kids ask how to play the game.

Jamilla, a Black student at a table in the middle of the room, is getting angry because she hasn't gotten a single right answer. Jamilla says loudly, "I don't care. I'm not playing." She throws down her cards. Another Black student, Karen, is yelling at Charles in a dispute over the rules. Jamilla gets up and dramatically stalks out of the room. "I'm going to the office," she announces loudly to no one in particular. Gerrie just watches her go and shakes her head. Jamilla is just visible lurking outside the door. Occasionally she bends her neck around the door frame and peeks inside. This goes on until the end of class when she walks back in, grinning. . . .

Several other students have gotten into a loud fight over the rules. "I'm not doing this," a Black male in a Levi jacket yells. . . . At least half the students are milling around. Cedric, a Black male in the front row, is into the game, an intense, serious look on his face. He knows almost every answer. Belinda, a Black student who's playing with him, makes a face every time he gets the right answer. He has the second highest score in the class.

A Black male in the back row had been playing until he got two in a row wrong. "This is stupid. Why are we doing this?" he says.

Each student's points are listed on a poster board and each squad's score is compared with those in other classes, and across A Team and B Team. Most of the kids have only 3 to 10 points compared to the next class (honors) where the first three kids have 42, 51, 39. . . .

At the end of the class Gerrie invites them to check their scores. Only Cedric and two girls (one White, one Black) go to check. A student who had been at Belinda's table gives Gerrie a dirty look. "You know your fifth-period class is going to win anyway," she shoots back over her shoulder on her way out the door.

Afterwards, the teacher commented that Jamilla's behavior was a reflection of some personal crisis. An alternate interpretation, that the student quite rationally avoided the humiliating situation by removing herself from it, did not occur to her.

The next class, an honors class. There are 21 students, 14 White and 7 Black. They go through the same procedures as the previous class, breaking down into work stations and playing the challenge game. There's no fighting or disagreement and no disputes over rules. One student has his hands over his eyes, groaning, "Boyles' Law. I know it. I know it. Oh, I just can't remember." Another group at the front table quickly flips through the questions. They have lost only a couple cards. . . . When all the teams finish they crowd around Gerrie to see their scores and where they stand with the other classes.

In this class, there was no fighting, just the ongoing effort to compete for the right answer. High-achieving, mainly White students clearly thrived on these academic competitions. This was their world, and they got validation from it. Although meant to motivate students perceived as "at-risk," contests like this one rewarded the dispositions and achievements characteristic of the dominant, White, upper-middle-class culture of Gates and forced African American students to compete publicly in a world that was not their own. By organizing students into racially identifiable teams (because of academic tracking), and establishing team competitions, the two worlds of Gates were made highly visible. The inability of teams with a large percentage of African Americans to compete successfully publicly displayed African American students' subordinate status and thus reinforced their lack of power in Gates's terms. The posters recording team scores in these challenges served as markers of African American students' outsider status. Jim Meier summed it up:

> These competitions are discouraging to the kids and to us. Ninety-five percent of our kids are not an ounce of trouble, but the few that are skew the results. The problem is that the kids feel inferior. It's not so much the reward for good behavior but broadcasting it.

Despite this recognition, there was no process to unpack the sources of academic and behavioral marginality of African Americans at Gates or to accelerate their academic achievement.

Because of differences between the teams, even joint team activities sometimes heightened race and class differences. Children from the Hills/Palisades had very different life experiences, opportunities, and financial resources than those from southwest Riverton. Although teachers were cognizant of these differences and eschewed expensive outings that might exclude low-income students, they seemed not to appreciate the ways in which their choices publicly marginalized these students and their cultural resources. This was illustrated by a ninth-grade spring trip to a theater outside of Riverton. In the first place, some White students complained vociferously because they had been to the theater "millions of times." Yet many African American students had never been there, as exhibited by a show of hands in several classes. The same contrast was evident in a trip to a museum earlier in the year. One teacher put the differences starkly: "Some of the rich White kids have traveled all over the world. I mean you wouldn't believe their vacations—to Africa, Europe, cruises. But some of the at-risk kids haven't even been out of the state." This comparison was made all too obvious in class discussions prior to the outings. Conversely, no outings were planned that might have built on African American students' cultural experiences and the resources of their community, for example, African American theater and music events or community institutions, and that would have benefited all students.

There was also a conflict over lunch on the theater trip. The B Team teachers had planned pizza at a restaurant, but the A Team teachers worried that many of their students couldn't afford it. In the new spirit of student participation, the issue was taken to the students. A teacher in an honors class (about three-fourths White) explained that they probably would not be able to go out for pizza "because some students can't afford it." This elicited a chorus of grumbling from most of the class. In the next period, a regular class with just two White students, the teacher again brought up the issue. Should they go out for pizza or bring cafeteria sack lunches? She explained that "somebody's mother agreed to pay for those who can't afford to eat out." The responses dramatized African American students' contempt for being publicly humiliated as "free lunch kids" and their disdain for, and resistance to, an activity about which they were not consulted and which they felt was an affront to them (as several explained afterwards in their critique of a play which they believed denigrated African Americans):

Student 1:   (sarcastically) I'll bring my food stamps, my ration book.
Student 2:   Let's go boogaloo instead.
Student 3:   What's it about?
Student 4:   A Black man driving a White woman.
Student 3:   I'll drive her. (loud laughter) For free too.

[They all crack up, refusing to make any serious decisions or to participate in this discussion about lunch.]

The teachers' insensitivity in this situation illustrates a more generalized lack of consciousness about how their own discourse and practice reinforced African American students' marginality. Plans arrived at in a new environment of teacher collaboration and meant to expand student opportunities, nevertheless reproduced old messages of African American inferiority and continued to distance both White and African American students from potentially enriching educational experiences based on African American community resources and culture.

Social Support and Academic Success

Riverton's *Second Year Plan for Restructuring* (Project Documents, 1990) projected that teams would "ease the transition from elementary to junior high school" and would result in closer adult/student relationships and a more supportive environment for young adolescents. Departing from the traditional notion of junior high as preparation for the anonymity of large high schools, schools would be reorganized into teams that would provided personalized relationships and guidance to students. This called for many teachers who had defined their professional duties more narrowly to take on new roles. The principal, a strong advocate of change, defined the new direction this way: "We've got to get away from treating these kids like college students. Come in, give them the material, if they get it fine, if they don't, too bad. We've got to see our role as providing support." The teams' interpretations of this notion was another defining theme of their collaboration.

Improving Relationships With Students

A number of White teachers, who said they had previously been intimidated by African American students, claimed that team activities and the collective support they received from their colleagues helped improve their relationships with these students. Teachers reported feeling friendlier, more empathetic, and more relaxed with "at-risk" students. A veteran teacher said the team had given her a new incentive to continue teaching: "I feel closer to the students. I feel now that I can be their friend. And I have less discipline problems. . . . Their behavior is better because, partly because my own attitude toward them is different." As restructuring progressed, one of the most consistent responses to the question, "What, if anything, has changed with restructuring?" was "My relations with my students" or "Students' attachment to the school." A typical comment was: "I've gotten a lot closer to students this year than ever before. I never really knew them before, I mean, personally, or what their family situations were. It's been a big adjustment for me, and extra work, but I've really enjoyed it."

Most teachers said they believed students liked school more and felt more a part of it as a result of the organizational changes. And several teachers described a de-escalation of student/teacher conflicts. The staff was encouraged to be more lenient about minor infractions of the rules. "We don't want big conflicts or suspensions over petty things like chewing gum," Elaine, the B Team leader, reported back from the steering committee. There was a new effort to resolve disputes with students by talking, giving time outs, taking them out of the room, and so on, rather than writing up official behavior complaints or sending them to an administrator as had been the practice. These changes reflected one goal of restructuring—"creating a positive school climate."

The team's mutual responsibility for a common set of students was central to fostering these changes. In the ninth-grade team meetings, teachers often shared strategies for handling behavior problems in more sensitive ways, including making allowances for personal difficulties that might cause students to overreact. They frequently reminded each other that they needed to be more supportive of their "at-risk" kids. In this respect, teachers, such as Elaine, whose personal style and philosophy already reflected this orientation, were validated and became mentors for others.

Of course, there were some teachers who had always been caring adults students could turn to. The Mentoring and Counseling Program, begun the year before restructuring, had institutionalized this relationship for a few designated students and teachers. However, the philosophy underpinning restructuring made connections between adults and students a schoolwide goal, and this became a formal aspect of teachers' professional responsibilities. This fit well with the belief shared by many teachers that students would do better in school if they had a stronger attachment to the institution and the adults in it (cf. Wehlage et al., 1989).

But, filtered through a deficit framework, the new roles were often interpreted as rescuing children from, or substituting for, their families and communities. Teachers began to see themselves as surrogate parents, compensating for the lapses of putatively dysfunctional and deficient homes. This was an aspect of what Delpit describes as the "messiah complex," "the view that schools must save low-income children of color from their communities rather than work with their communities toward excellence" (1992b, p. 238). Bob on the B Team and Jim on the A Team were strong advocates of this idea:

Bob: The main point of it is making a big school small, isn't it? I think it's helping a lot. Especially the at-risk kids. We're giving them parenting when their parents aren't there. At least they know they have five teachers who care. It's like a family. And they like going to school more because of it.

Double Standard of Nurture and High Academic Standards

"Nurturing at-risk students" became central to teaching at Gates. This included developing personal relationships with students, counseling, making school more fun, giving positive reinforcement, showing that one cared. The teachers on the 2 ninth-grade teams embraced these new behaviors to varying degrees. Some, like Colleen, Elaine, and Bob on the B Team and Marie, Jim, and Connie on the A Team, were enthusiastic. On the other hand, Stan, on the B Team, believed that teachers were giving students too much slack and were undermining academic work and high standards. He wanted to hold all students accountable to academic standards and levels of competence without "coddling" them and opposed "feel-good" activities that took away from instructional time. While he insisted on the importance of academic competencies, he did not entertain school-related explanations for why so many students did not acquire them, nor did he consider alternatives to help them meet high standards. In his view, if students failed, he bore little responsibility. The disagreement between Stan and the others was reflected in the grades for the first marking period when teachers were pressured by the administration to have a relatively equitable grade distribution between African American and White students. Stan gave significantly lower grades than did the other team teachers in general, and lower grades to African Americans in particular.

The conflict was rehashed in team meetings as Stan refused to go along with what he argued was "making excuses for students" and lowering academic standards. By the end of the first semester, the debate surfaced in nearly every B Team meeting and spilled over to the administration. The principal accused Stan of being "out of line with the rest of his team." The other team members urged Stan to be more supportive of students, and the principal insisted that he conform to the philosophy of "success for all." But Stan doggedly held that he would be violating his professional duty by giving away grades and coddling students. By the end of the year, the contradiction seemed irreconcilable.

On one hand, the argument was refreshingly candid. It was one of the few cases in which substantive differences were openly discussed and debated in team meetings. But there was no resolution. Each side tenaciously held to its position, and neither side acknowledged the kernel of truth in the other. The discussion did not get to the underlying issues—deficit models of African American students, the need to develop a strategy to accelerate the academic work of students who had been held to lower standards, and the roots of the alienation of many African American students at Gates. High academic standards continued to be pitted against personal support.

Underlying the differences were conflicting views of what it meant for "at-risk" students to be successful at Gates. While nurturing students and maintaining high academic standards were posed as opposites in the B Team, both were upheld as school goals. Despite the argument others threw up to Stan, all of the teachers were quite exacting in their honors classes. Colleen, for example, had a list of skills and operations each student in her honors algebra class had to master before advancing to the next unit. Indeed, Gates's reputation for rigorous academics was its central attraction for the children of professionals who might otherwise attend private schools. The apparent contradiction between nurture and standards was only reconcilable because teachers maintained quite different academic and behavioral standards for different groups of students, that is, high-achieving and "at-risk." Bob described one of his "low" classes:

> [S]eventy-five percent of the kids in here will be lucky if they finish high school. We just want to give them a family-type experience so they know at least there are teachers who care about them. Maybe then they'll want to come to school and at least not get into trouble.

Constructing school success differently for "at-risk" low-achieving students and high-achieving students meant, in the context of Gates's racial disparities, different definitions of success for many African American and White students. With the intent of being supportive, nurturing was focussed on "at-risk" African American students and divorced from, or sometimes even posed in contradiction to, challenging academics. Constructing some students as "at risk" and setting them apart became a basis for treating them differently. For students who were assumed to lack a positive home environment, "success" was feeling good about school, adjusting to rules and expectations, having positive interactions with adults, and attaining a sense of belonging. This definition was quite different from the high academic achievement for which the school was known. In their study of urban schools, Massey, Scott, and Dornbusch argue:

under the pressures of teaching, and with all intentions of "being nice," teachers had essentially stopped attempting to teach Black children. . . . We [the study's authors] have shown that oppression can arise out of warmth, friendliness, and concern. Paternalism and a lack of challenging standards are creating a distorted system of evaluation in the schools. (quoted in Delpit, 1988, p. 296)

The social support/academic challenge dichotomy was reflected in expectations for the two teams. Characteristically, when the teams had a half-day field trip, the B Team (more honors) returned to school to continue its academic schedule. The A Team (mainly regular) had a popcorn party, dance, or movie because, teachers said, "our kids need a break." These distinctions were not lost on the students. According to A Team teachers, B Team students "put out the message that our kids aren't as smart." When the A Team had a high number of students on the honor role at the end of the first 9 weeks, this was widely explained by students as "they have all the easy teachers." To combat these negative stereotypes, teachers in the A Team said they "did a reality check with our students. We showed the kids that they are doing more socially, that they are providing a lot of leadership in the school in extracurricular activities." Given Gates's strong academic culture and reputation, athletics and other extracurricular activities were clearly understood to be subordinate. So it is likely this "reality check" was precisely that, confirmation of the marginality of African American students.

Paulette was the only teacher on either team who, in my observations, transcended this dichotomy. She was repeatedly identified by African American students as someone they "could talk to if they had a personal or school problem." At the same time, in class, she urged students to prepare for college, to have high goals. "Even if you work at MacDonald's, don't just work there. Plan to be the manager. Prepare yourself," she told them. Paulette might have reframed the contradiction between Elaine and Stan, but by the time their debate came to a head (December), Paulette had begun to disengage from the team because she felt it was not dealing with serious issues.

Summary

The twofold construction of nurturing emerged as a central, though unrecognized, theme of the ninth-grade teams. For high-achieving Whites and a few, primarily middle-class, African Americans, social support, academic mentorship, and high academic standards were interrelated to promote intellectual development and academic success (as these were constructed at Gates). The dichotomization of social support and challenging academic work applied to low-achieving, primarily working-class African American students. Independent of the intentions of individual educators, this was essentially a way of keeping African American students down.

Team Responses to Tracking and Differentiated Curriculum

The overrepresentation of African American students in lower-track classes was a significant aspect of their unequal educational experience at Gates. Thus, teachers' response to this issue was an important indicator of the potential of restructuring to improve educational opportunities of African American students. Unlike the focus on individuals, competitions and incentives, and interpretations of social support that were salient in team discussions and activities, the teams' responses to tracking became significant by virtue of their absence.

Salience of Tracking and the Dominance of the Honors Track

A student's academic track assignment was her/his most significant educational marker at Gates. To be an "honors" or a "regular" student carried a world of meanings both overt and subtle, explicit and implied. Although regular students were not barred from any elective classes, ninth-grade teachers commonly understood that they were on a general education path, as opposed to the college-preparatory path of the honors students. Typically, they did not take foreign languages, comparative literature, or other special classes that were known to be college preparatory. On paper, the district curriculum guides were the same for both tracks, although honors students were expected to receive additional "enrichment," but practice varied. However, it was in the culture and expectations surrounding the two levels, and in teachers' application of the curriculum, that the differences came to life.

Talk about regular and honors tracks peppered the conversations of students and teachers alike. Nearly all the ninth-grade teachers openly described disparate expectations for the two groups of students. This was true after restructuring had begun as well as before. This is exemplified by an incident involving Bob, on the B Team, recorded in field notes at mid-year:

[At the end of the second period, Bob strides out of his classroom, obviously excited. He has just finished an honors class.]

Bob: (loudly) I'm really high right now. I had a great class. I mean, it was one of those classes that just really took off. We had a discussion about why people get into drugs. It was a great discussion, I mean really great in terms of critical thinking. It wasn't really on the curriculum guide, but I don't care. If they give me a hard time, I can just relate it to social issues. They're learning to think and that's what's important. . . .

PL: Did you do the same thing with your regular class?

Bob: Not really. The regulars just can't stay on the topic in the same way. They aren't focused enough. They start going off into stories about their sister or brother and laughing and carrying on.

Bob's distinctions between regular and honors students were common, a series of polarities familiar to anyone with experience in stratified schools: closed versus open-ended assignments; rigidity versus flexibility; repetition versus depth of study of material; emphasis on basic skills versus critical thinking; and especially, the need for more control over regular students (Oakes, 1985). Even Connie, on the A Team, who consistently demonstrated confidence in the abilities of even the least successful students in her classes, defined educational practice with the two groups along these dimensions. In the middle of a regular class, she whispered, "You'll see the difference with the [honors] kids. You don't have to stay on them. I can let them talk. I couldn't do that in here." From her comments and practice, it was clear that many of her distinctions between the two sets of students were behavioral. Yet these were translated through tracking and educational opportunities into academic and intellectual ranks.

Most teachers openly conveyed value judgments about the tracks to their students, and the talk of both teachers and students reflected a shared understanding of disparate expectations. For example, in an honors class, Elaine tells students several times: "You're honors kids. This will be easy for you." And in a regular class she says, "Adverbs, they're hard for you. But that's OK. You can learn it, but you have to be patient." Student comments in class showed that they understood that honors classes had a higher standing and teachers expected them to do better. For example, at the beginning of a regular class, Bob tells the students:

"I haven't had a chance to write down who's honors and who isn't [referring to the standings of different classes in an interclass competition he's conducting]. OK, the losing team is _____."

[A student in front laughs loudly.] "Ha, ha. That's in your honors class. And they're supposed to be smarter. Ha."

Doris and Paulette were the only two ninth-grade teachers who opposed tracking, and both of them taught the only untracked classes (SRM). Doris argued that the differences between the two tracks were more behavioral and cultural than ability-related. She found that in her Study and Research Methods class (the only heterogeneously grouped core class), a lot of the honors students did not do as well with analogies as the regular students. "They're used to just giving the right answers. . . . What the honors kids have are a lot of social skills. They're teacher pleasers. One reason they don't like SRM is that they're not doing well in it." Paulette found ways to respond to a range of skills in her SRM class. In a typical class, her students were arranged in three or four groups. Some students were writing research papers, others reading, others doing a writing exercise, and so on. She had students with greater mastery of skills help others. On another day, the entire class was engaged in a serious discussion of a powerful and sophisticated novel about an African American family in the South during the Depression.

Talk about regular and honors with their implicit values continued unabated throughout the year. There was no evidence that teachers changed how they thought about this issue or that they reassessed its impact on students, particularly those who were stigmatized as "regulars." In fact, as with the nurture/academic standards dichotomy, labeling some students "at-risk" seemed to reify the distinctions. By setting some students apart as "at-risk," a new dimension was added to the identity of these regular track students. Making them different from other students created an additional rationale for different expectations. This is reflected in Jim Meier's comment after a rote, lower-level skills lesson in his regular class: "Wasn't that good for an at-risk class?"

The Implicit Connection Between Race and Academic Track

The correlation between race and track was implicit in the conversations of both students and teachers. An incident involving the B Team is illustrative. For weeks the students could not agree on a design for the team T-shirt because, as teachers reported, "the honors kids like them plain and the regulars like stuff all over them." Of course, the preferences, which were ascribed to tracks, actually corresponded to White students' more conservative styles and African Americans' bolder choices. (Eventually they decided on two designs because no consensus could be reached.) Students at Gates were also highly self-segregated by race, and in the ninth grade, peer groups mainly coincided with academic tracks. Although there were exceptions, for the most part, White high-achieving students and African American low-achieving students stuck to their own groups. This became a sore point for the few White honors students assigned to the A Team. They formed a subgroup within the team, keeping to themselves and complaining bitterly all year about teams and everything associated with restructuring. Their attitude is reflected in this exchange captured in December 1990 field notes:

[During the class, Gerrie suggested I interview a group of five White students at the front table who had finished their work.... At first they wanted to know if I worked for Louis Dixon, the restructuring director, whom they knew by name.]

Donna: If you do, I have a message for him.
PL: What's the message?
Donna: We want to go back to the way it was last year. We're all the smart kids in our team. With teams you don't get to see your friends if they ended up in the other team.
Al: Which they probably did [laugh]. They have most of the smart kids.
Ilene: Yeah, you're in with all the same kids all the time. Like for example Charles [African American student]. He sits in front of me in every period and he's so stupid.
Others: Yeah.
Ilene: I just can't stand him. [They talk about one African American student who skipped school and then came back during the day.] He's so stupid. I mean, I can't believe how stupid he is.
Donna: SRM is the worst. We don't do anything. We can't ask questions. And we're gifted. And our teacher has been a remedial teacher for 10 years. And when we ask questions she tells us to put our hands down. And we're gifted.

On the other hand, some African American students resisted the efforts of well-intentioned teachers to transfer them to honors classes because they defined these classes as "White." Jim Meier described two African American males whom he wanted to promote to honors: "William Jackson and Shawn Taylor are really smart. We want to transfer them to honors but they won't go into it because they say it isn't cool. Those who can't succeed make a virtue of failure so others get caught in it."

Shawn and William's judgment about the honors track seemed to be confirmed by the characteristics of African American honors students. Like the high-achieving Black students studied by Fordham (1988), many appeared to express a less clearly defined African American identity. When I asked teachers to name a typical high-achieving African American student whom I could shadow for a day, most of the B Team teachers suggested Gaye, who they said was "different" from most Black students. Gaye was the president of several student clubs, on the honor roll, a cheerleader, and in all honors classes. She lived in the Palisades and was driven to school by her parents, as were many of her White peers from that neighborhood. Gaye sat in the front row in all her classes, and was a model student. When the honors club went on a weekend trip, teachers reported that although Gaye chose to room with African Americans, she spent her days with Whites. Because academic success was so narrowly defined by White middle-class norms, students like Gaye seemed to reinforce the belief that honors was "a White thing." And although her social class seemed to give Gaye a way in at Gates, it was her difference from the majority of African Americans—her similarity with Whites—that distinguished her in teachers' eyes. The association of school success with Whiteness as a potential barrier to African American students, was never discussed, as far as I could determine, although privately, two African American teachers, Larissa and Paulette, said African American students did not see African American models of success at Gates. Nor did teachers seem to recognize what Fordham (1988, 1991) has identified as the potential psychic cost for students like Gaye caught between two worlds and potentially competing loyalties.

Teacher "Empowerment" and the Issue of Tracking

With restructuring, teachers had the power to transfer students between honors and regular classes. They also could modify the curriculum and theoretically make regular classes as enriched as honors classes were thought to be. This was significant because it positioned them as change agents with the power to reverse policies and practices that contributed to unequal educational experiences for African American students. It is therefore important to dissect what the ninth-grade teachers did with this opportunity.

In the first place, the salience of tracking and its centrality in the construction of students' educational identities appeared neither to change with restructuring nor to be the subject of much reflection. Teachers continued to identify their expectations for their classes according to academic track. Apart from a couple of interdisciplinary units, there was little change in curriculum and instruction generally, and no attention to the enrichment of regular classes. Notes from observation of Gerrie's classes near the end of the school year illustrate the lack of change in beliefs and practice regarding tracking:

> It is fourth-period regular class. Gerrie whispers to me (loud enough for several students in the back to hear), "As you can tell, this is a very low class. But they're sweet." Working in groups, students are going through work sheets. She moves from table to table offering a few comments, smiling, generally doing little instruction. To me she says, "I have my honors class next period, if you want to see that. They [this regular class] do the same chapter and the first page of the test is the same. But they don't do the discussion and thought questions. The honors does the discussion and thought questions which the regular class doesn't." [She shakes her head.] "No. The regular class can't do that. . . . " After the class she says she has four "resource" [special education] students here and she thinks "their IQs are pretty low."

Tracking was not questioned in any team meetings I observed, nor did the topic appear on the agendas of steering committees or team meetings. The principal was himself strongly opposed to any revision in the policy, so it is unlikely that he would have initiated a reevaluation. The SRM class was an attempt, at the district level, to introduce a class that was expressly heterogeneous, but, as I discuss in the next chapter, this class was ill-fated, largely because of parent opposition to untracking. There were a few teachers who seemed to treat honors and regular classes the same, but their experience was isolated behind their classroom doors, as alternative practices often are in conventional settings. (I return to this issue in chapter 9.)

Teachers had their own reasons to maintain the status quo. They may well have found it easier, pedagogically, to separate students by "ability" or achievement. Certainly it would have required more work and thought to revise a system already in place. Indeed, several teachers alluded to these factors when questioned about untracking. Larissa, an African American teacher who advocated enriched curricula for all students, said SRM wasn't working because it was untracked and "the gaps are too wide" and there was not the curricular materials to support a heterogeneous class. This pointed to the fallacy of piecemeal changes in a systemically and historically stratified system.

The principal flatly rejected my query about moving to more heterogeneous grouping of students, "Ending tracking will never work for a school like this. It would be the worst thing that could happen. It's not open for discussion." Instead, he proposed to reduce inequalities by promoting more African Americans to honors classes. The fact that there were some African American students (mainly middle class) in honors classes—as both the principal and some teachers were quick to point out—legitimated tracking as nonracial despite the fact that the masses of African Americans were in low-track classes. In the ninth grade, there was more promotion of regular students into honors than in the past. This was particularly true on the A Team, where teachers seemed more focused on achievement for "at-risk" students than the B Team, which emphasized social factors: A Team teachers promoted at least nine students during the first semester. However, although they considered students' grades, the criteria were frequently arbitrary, even capricious. These notes from an A Team meeting describe their process:

[The next item is a discussion of moving kids from honors to regular or vice versa. They discuss the first student.]

Doris: I don't want her in my third period class. She'll ruin my third period class.

[They discuss the second student, Andre. Andre was moved from regular to honors math at the beginning of the year.]

Jim: He's gotten suspended and he's gotten too far behind. He failed the first 9 weeks because of suspensions. You can tell from his interactions that he's very bright. Behavior is the problem. So he needs to be moved back. . . . Well then, that takes care of that. . . .
Marie: What should I do with Latoya?
Gerrie: Oh, she's wonderful. Ability wise, she's excellent.
Marie: But can she fit in with honors?
Gerrie: I can't see her fitting in with honors. That would put her way up there. She's a C student. She may not be able to do it. . . .

[They go on to the next student, Alvin.]

Jim: He's creative. He's very deep. [He gives an example of an insight Alvin had when they discussed a novel.] He had the best insight in the class. Of course, he can't read, but he's got a brain.

Marie: He's coming along on writing though.
Jim: Well, we can't do much. Let's leave him. . . .

[They move on to yet another student, Belinda.]

Marie: Belinda. Should I put Belinda in honors? [There is a short
          discussion and everyone says she should be promoted.]
Gerrie: The problem is she has a baby.
Marie: Oh, well then, I won't do it because of all the homework. If
          she has a baby, she'll never be able to do all the homework.
          Honors requires so much homework and so many projects.
Gerrie: If there's a lot of homework, then I wouldn't do it. [They all
          agree not to move her to honors.]

Despite some awareness of students' talents, the teachers were
locked into the existing framework of allowing behavioral and dispo-
sitional qualities to guide academic placement. For example, teachers
assumed, without investigation, that Belinda's personal situation was
an obstacle to her academic work, and with little deliberation they
withheld an opportunity for her to advance. Furthermore, no one
supported an alternative to the load of homework in Marie's class in
order to provide greater educational prospects for Belinda and numerous other young women juggling the responsibilities of school and
parenting. One can also extrapolate from this meeting the ways in
which the behavioral norms at Gates and the disproportionate disciplining of African American students affected their educational opportunities, as in the case of Andre. In general, students were assessed
with little exploration of their strengths and no fresh approaches to
building on their talents and accelerating their educational progress,
particularly when there were behavior issues.

In spite of the superficiality of the above team discussion, decisions were made with potentially grave and far-reaching consequences
for the individuals involved. Advancing a student to the honors track
could change teachers' intellectual and behavioral expectations for the
student, the student's own self-concept, advice of counselors, and
ultimately the student's educational path in high school and beyond
(Vanfossen, Jones, & Spade, 1987). (See Metz [1978] and Page [1991], for
ethnographic accounts of tracking that lend credence to this projection.)
The ease with which dedicated and well-meaning teachers dispensed
with the educational destinies of students in their charge is remarkable.
They were newly empowered to reassess students' placement and to

find ways to advance them. But their process is an indication that teacher empowerment by itself may have little effect on the education of African American and other marginalized students, if the ways teachers think about them, the means they use to support their success, and the school's behavioral norms are not reassessed. Most important, while a few children were advanced, all students continued to be locked into a rigid tracking system.

Teams were intended to empower teachers and support students. But, in combination with academic tracking, they highlighted the subordinate status of African American students. This coexistence of two organizational structures—teams and academic tracks, which were essentially contradictory in Gates's context—reflected the desire to "do something for at-risk students" without tampering with the school's elite academic refuge for high-achieving students, most of whom were middle class and White. These contradictory goals persisted and solidified in tracking and teams.

Conclusion

An assumption of school-based reform is that change occurs, in part, through a process of teachers collectively examining and critiquing the regularities of their schools (Sarason, 1982; Sizer, 1984). Given the variations in perspective, culture, and experience among the ninth-grade teachers, there was some basis for a substantive dialogue. Despite the dominance of the deficit model and predilections for a social relations approach, there were teachers with other perspectives on both teams, for example, Doris on the A Team and Paulette on the B Team. Although most teachers were comfortable with a conventional lecture and recitation format, Connie and Paulette used cooperative learning, peer teaching, and other less traditional pedagogies that could support untracking. And despite the commitment of most team members to academic tracking, both teachers demonstrated high expectations and offered challenging content to low-achieving students. As I discuss in chapter 9, Paulette, as well as teachers in other teams, had investigated new curriculum frameworks and had an analysis of the racial disparities, effects of tracking, and cultural differences between White and African American students that might have prompted a broader critique of the assumptions underlying taken-for-granted regularities at Gates.

Yet dissident views were very rarely heard in any of the formal meetings observed, and they were not reflected in meeting agendas. The one exception was the ongoing debate between Stan and the others on the B Team regarding academic standards. Although candidly discussed, that issue remained unresolved, its polarities unchanged at year's end. By mid-year, both teams seemed to settle in to a routine of planning extracurricular activities and incentives, reviewing a succession of students in distress, and referring them to social services or counseling. There was little disagreement about the importance of concentrating on individuals or about the roots of racial disparities and little critical inquiry about these issues. As discussions of students' reputed psychological and social problems came to dominate a substantial portion of team meetings and the work focused on strategizing about individual students, the teams forfeited the potential to examine institutional and ideological roots of the school's failure of African Americans. Far from school reform, personalized interventions—filtered through the deficit model—became simply another vehicle to reform deficient individuals.

Gates's culture of individual competition encouraged the use of incentives. Since competitions were generally on high-achieving, largely middle-class, White terms, it is hardly surprising that they reinforced the subordinate status of African American students. Indeed, in the ninth grade, the intersection of teams, tracks, and race and class polarities, on the one hand, and team competitions, on the other, accentuated the marginality of working-class African American students. Despite an evolving recognition that incentives were problematic, teachers were unable to get to the bottom of the issue.

There is evidence that, as a result of trying to improve relationships with students, in some 9th grade classrooms there was a change in the dynamics that alienated African American students. Several teachers maintained they had become more empathetic toward these students. However, in the context of the school's competitive academic culture and deficit model of African American students, and without a plan for academic acceleration, teachers' evolved a double standard of success—feeling good about school for low-achieving students and academic achievement for high-achieving students. Labeling some children (virtually all of whom were African American) "at risk," and therefore needing support, rationalized this dichotomy. Moreover, one could argue that the philosophy of social support cloaked the real contradictions and unequal power relations at the root of African American students' alienation at Gates. The goal was to ameliorate student behavior, not confront social inequalities.

Although there were new arenas for collaboration, there was little substantive dialogue about the cultures, norms and structures that reinforced the low achievement of African Americans. Indeed, collaboration seemed to corroborate assumptions of student deficits, suggesting the limitations of collaboration alone to stimulate reflection and change in thinking and practice. Teachers gave little consideration to the meaning of their decisions in the context of Gates's race and class polarization and differentiated educational experiences. In fact, in a context in which African American students were outsiders, the activities and ideologies which coalesced through the teams may have actually heightened their marginalization.

6

RESTRUCTURING AT GATES: THE ROLE OF UPPER-MIDDLE-CLASS WHITE INTERESTS*

The problem in this community is that it's a very difficult context in which to make reforms. No matter what, you always have to deal with this opposition and they try to wear you down.

—District administrator, Riverton Public Schools

This chapter explores restructuring schoolwide at Gates and the relationship of school and community contexts and educational reform. I begin by briefly summarizing schoolwide team processes and then go on to examine a number of significant issues in depth. The first is the ways Gates used the teams for social control, particularly the disciplining of African American males. Underlying this focus on discipline was the relationship of race and behavior. The second is the political and cultural context for a double standard of success for high achieving and "at-risk" students. The third is the intersection of the culture of academic achievement at Gates with the restructuring agenda and implications for White and African American students. The fourth is the role that upper-middle-class White interests played in shaping the dimensions and direction of educational change. And, finally, I return to the theme of dialogue among teachers.

Schoolwide Team Processes

Based on schoolwide observations of classes, team meetings and steering committee meetings, and interviews with teachers and students, it appeared that the general patterns of the focus teams were repeated with some modifications across grade levels. All the teams

---

*Portions of this chapter appeared in Lipman, P. (1997). Restructuring in context: A case study of the dynamics of ideology, power, and teacher participation. *American Educational Research Journal*, 34(1), 3–37.

seemed to focus on individual students and their social problems and on competitions and incentives.

In interviews, teachers invariably listed discussions of individual students as a major part of their team's activity. Interviews with counselors confirmed that this was an emphasis of the core teams. Corliss, a seventh-grade counselor, said:

> The team identifies students to the counselor and we advise the team on particular problems. . . . Some students say they don't like the teams because they feel that the teachers are ganging up on them and talking about them all the time. It's too early to see the influence that teaming will have on the at-risk kids. But they do see the teachers and counselors keeping up with their progress, you know, individually.

My observations and team documents verified these reports. The minutes of the seventh-grade A Team, for example, show that the team met at least twice a week throughout the year. During the first semester, individual students were discussed in about one in three meetings. After January, the topic not only appeared on every meeting agenda, but took over more and more of the agenda. As in the ninth-grade teams, teachers in other teams generally presented student difficulties as individual and often assumed that home conditions and cultural and educational backgrounds were the problem. In my observations, teams did not generally discuss institutional factors (practices, policies, educational philosophies) or the need for educational reform. And, as in the ninth-grade A and B Teams, there was an absence of dialogue about the low achievement of African Americans as a group.

The steering committee (composed of all team leaders and administrators) also reinforced the focus on individuals. The committee developed a Student Profile Packet for identifying educational problems of at-risk students. The Profile Packet reviewed a student's academic difficulties, including an assessment of learning style, grades, and test scores. The profile was to be the basis of a remediation plan worked out with the Study and Research Methods teacher. (I never observed these assessments being used or discussed in team meetings or educators using the aggregate data from the profiles to consider wider patterns or causes.) The steering committee also validated the focus on individuals by promoting at nearly every meeting individual success stories without consideration of the progress of low-achieving students as a group. In the three steering committee meetings I observed, the narratives of individual success were not discussed as cases from which generalizations about educational practices could be deduced but as evidence that teams were on the right path.

Although the emphasis on extrinsic rewards varied from one team to another, all teams seemed to use incentives to some extent to reinforce "positive behavior" and achievement. Several teams even used a portion of their $500 restructuring money for incentives. As the principal put it at a faculty meeting in February, "A large part of our new direction involves incentives and activities." A review of the minutes of steering committee meetings for the year suggests how extensively incentives were used schoolwide. The committee planned a team contest for no suspensions, student recognition awards, a penny drive, rewards for attendance at the afterschool homework program, a party for every team with 100% attendance at the PTO meeting, a dance for the team that sold the most tickets to the PTO sock hop, and at least six other major contests throughout the year. These were in addition to separate team incentives.

Some teachers argued this was a step forward from the punitive climate that had characterized the school in previous years. However, it grew out of the assumption that students' academic problems, disengagement from school, and resistance were rooted in the students themselves and reinforced a behaviorist paradigm of extrinsic motivation. Although teachers did make changes in their practices, they were changes that continued to lay the responsibility for school failure largely on the students. Moreover, many of the contests, such attendance at PTO meetings, were clearly weighted in favor of neighborhood students. Under the mantle of creating a positive climate and using rewards rather than punishments, teachers were essentially opening up another avenue to reform delinquent and deficient individuals.

Effects of Restructuring Activities on Teachers

One result of all the new activities and attention to students' personal and social problems was teacher burn-out. Signs of stress began to surface early in the first semester. In October, Louis Dixon, the district restructuring director, commented that teachers were really tired and "meeting-ed out." There was extra work for all teachers, but some put in many additional hours each week planning incentives and organizing extracurricular activities, meeting with counselors, and conferring with each other by phone at night about individual students. By spring, some teachers were retreating from these demands, and, ironically, team leaders began talking about incentives for teachers (e.g., award dinners) to keep them motivated. Ron Walters commented that he was "spending more time counseling teachers this year because the stress level is very high."

Perhaps this was simply the inevitable pressure associated with the initial stages of any educational reform. However, the emphasis on success in nonacademic realms meant that teachers had to focus additional energies outside the classroom. Paradoxically, deficit explanations, which partly accounted for their strategy, were reinforced when teachers became frustrated with the ineffectiveness of what they were doing. An eighth-grade teacher explained:

> We need to meet everyday because we have so many problem kids. It's a hell of a lot more work for teachers and we're not getting paid anything. . . . We're making a big school small. We know more about kids. I love it, but where do we have the time? The problem is the kids are low-achieving anyway. The problem is at home.

Influence of the Principal

Gates was really a microcosm of the interplay of competing interests in the district, and the principal's position was a highly political one. Satisfying neighborhood parents was crucial because of their personal connections with several school board members and because Gates's ability to retain these powerful White families was important, both symbolically and practically, in demonstrating that Riverton Public Schools could provide quality education. At the same time, there were pressures from the district Desegregation Office; restructuring was intended to reduce failure, drop-outs, truancy, and reduce racial achievement gaps. Thus, Ron Walter's performance had districtwide implications.

Ron was a vocal proponent of restructuring. He played a leading role in the Restructuring Institute and gave presentations to civic and business groups on the philosophy and management of school-based reform and restructuring. On the one hand, Ron had an informal, collegial leadership style. He was on a first-name basis with all of the staff, including custodial and kitchen workers and professed to be a believer in participatory management. On the other hand, he ran a tight ship and set the school's direction. However, the need to balance what had been constructed as competing interests and tensions at Gates may well have influenced how he viewed the limits and possibilities of restructuring, as well as contributed to his obvious need to maintain control in a situation bursting with potentially explosive contradictions. For example, he conveyed tight limits on discussing politically volatile issues such as race and tracking.

Ron also conveyed different expectations for regular and honors students. At a fall 1990 Steering Committee meeting, he talked about finding a way for every child to be successful at something. At the same time, he reiterated the importance of Gates's strong academic reputation. When the parents of 11 White eighth-grade honors students complained that their children's English class was unchallenging, Ron called the teacher in to meet with the parents and insisted that he enrich the curriculum. Meanwhile, apart from incentives, his strategy for low-achieving students was, as he said at a faculty meeting in January, "constant remediation." Within this framework, it was predictable that success for low-achieving African American students would be interpreted in terms of adjustment to school and feeling good about themselves and according to lower academic standards.

In separate conversations, the principal made the different academic expectations for the two groups explicit: "What we want is some kind of success for every kid, with an adult, every day. I don't care if they give them all As." This was in marked contrast to his comments about the concerns of wealthy White parents: "What they want, and what we provide, are high academic standards." Thus, the foundation for a double standard of school success was laid.[1] Without leadership to link high academic standards with student support, without critical analysis of what success meant, and in the face of no apparent strategy for accelerated learning, particularly when a district goal was to reduce racial disparities in grades as well as test scores, a double standard may have been the path of least resistance at Gates.

Using Teams for Social Control

An aspect of restructuring that was not apparent in my observations of the ninth-grade teams was the use of teacher collaboration to intensify discipline. (Although the focus teams discussed discipline, it appeared to be less an issue in ninth grade.)[2] In some sense, student behavior was an aspect of the team agendas at the outset. Every team set as one of its goals developing a consistent set of rules—both out of a sense of fairness to students and to ensure that students were accountable to the teachers as a unit. However, a review of the agendas of some seventh- and eighth-grade teams, as well as observations of meetings, suggests that as the year progressed some teams increasingly became vehicles for controlling student behavior. This is reflected in notes from a December seventh-grade team meeting:

The first topic is discipline. The decision is to set up a ten minute detention hall at lunch. The teachers talk about how the students are misbehaving in class: excessive talking, don't bring materials to class, haven't done their homework, tardiness, chewing gum or candy. . . . "They are generally disrespectful," a teacher complains.

Another says, "It doesn't really matter what we do as long as it works." They discuss various alternatives for lunch detention. . . .

The team leader points out that students can't be sent home until they are officially documented: "We don't get to carry the big stick yet."

A teacher asks if she can assign 2 days for gum and talking. . . . They discuss the need to document misbehavior more frequently.

The Proliferation of Punishment

A goal of restructuring was to reduce out-of-school suspensions, which fell most heavily on African Americans, especially males. District leaders said some teachers wrote students up for minor infractions, and these led to a cycle of suspension, missed academic work, course failure, alienation, and dropping-out. To address this problem, several policy changes were made. First, with the advent of the first teams in 1989–90, restructuring schools began in-house suspension. Second, teachers and teams were authorized to handle discipline problems directly, rather than write up students and send them to an administrator. This was meant to reduce suspensions and other disciplinary actions. The Gates principal encouraged teachers to handle most discipline problems themselves while he continued to insist on the importance of controlling behavior.

With the mandate to reduce suspensions, new forms of teacher-directed punishments blossomed. These included the "hot seat," in which the team teachers talked with the student collectively about behavior; parent conferences; noon detention; cafeteria duty; a time-out room; and isolation within the classroom. The threat of punishment was omnipresent in many classrooms, and punishment was used liberally for minor "offenses" such as not following directions. Although the locus of control shifted to teachers, there was no accompanying reexamination of the roots of misbehavior. In particular, there was no discussion of the disproportionate suspension of African Americans. In essence, the problem was simply dropped into teachers' laps without the benefit of new thinking. Judging by the plethora of new punishments and the attention teams gave to discipline, it is plausible that the punitive environment of the school was not reduced but simply took new forms, and perhaps actually intensified. Comparing Gates's in-house suspension data provided by the school for the first semester of 1990–91 with comparable data for 1989–90, in-house suspensions declined, although the disproportionate disciplining of African American students did not (see Table 6.1).

African Americans continued to be disproportionately punished not only in the school but in the district as a whole. In 1990–91, 83% of out-of-school suspensions and expulsions in Riverton were of African American students compared with 81% in 1989–90.[3] (The district was 64% Black in 1990–91.)

Race and Behavior—The Not-So-Hidden Agenda

The significance of racial disparities in discipline is illustrated by a tragic incident involving Andrew, an African American student in the ninth grade. Andrew was categorized by his team's leader as "a typical at-risk, inner-city kid." He had been in trouble sporadically during his first 2 years at Gates and his attendance was poor. However, the team recognized him as a very talented student and resolved to promote Andrew to mainly honors classes in the second semester, an opportunity they had conveyed to him. However, in January Andrew received a 10 day in-house suspension for wearing his overall straps unsnapped and then saying something under his breath to a White assistant principal when told to snap them up. There was no specific sanction against unsnapped overalls in the district dress code, but Gates's administrators determined it was inappropriate. Two points

TABLE 6.1

Gates In-House Suspensions by Race: 1989–90, 1990–91:
First and Second Nine Weeks

	1989–90		
	Black	White	Total days assigned
First 9 weeks:	58	7	235
Second 9 weeks:	84	15	364
	1990–91		
	Black	White	Total days assigned
First 9 weeks:	35	6	144
Second 9 weeks:	66	11	269

are relevant. First, this was a popular African American style at the time. Second, at Franklin Junior High School, on the day after this incident, many students were observed with overall straps unsnapped in full view of administrators and office personnel. Thus the violation was clearly a matter of Gates's interpretation.

Although his team teachers tried to advocate for Andrew, there was nothing they could do to reverse the punishment. Their power did not extend this far. Andrew spent 10 days in in-house suspension under conditions painfully emblematic of Gates's punitive culture. The students (all African American males on each of my five visits to the room during 1990–91) were completely segregated in a room adjacent to the gymnasium and were not allowed to attend any afterschool functions during the period of their punishment. From the beginning to the end of the school day, they were required to work silently in separate, enclosed carrels. They were not allowed to talk with anyone other than the in-house supervisor throughout the day, including at lunch, which they ate separately in the cafeteria after the other students had finished. They were allowed two supervised, scheduled bathroom breaks a day.[4] After 10 days in an environment that seemed designed to break a child's will, Andrew returned to class sullen and resistant. He frequently pulled his head into his sweatshirt or rested face down on his desk. Obviously academically disengaged and demoralized, he failed to participate or turn in assignments and his grades plummeted. He was not promoted to honors and his teachers reported that by mid-March his attendance had become inconsistent again. Andrew's example suggests that although the ninth-grade teams did not seem to focus as much on discipline as did the others, ninth graders were very much affected by the punitive climate in the school.

The racial implications of Andrew's confinement in in-house suspension, his subjugation and dehumanization in this White-dominated school, are inescapable. The incident drew its meaning not only from the particular context of Gates, with its dominant White, upper-middle-class culture, but also from the historical and present-day subordination of African Americans in Riverton. Although his was an individual case, it confirmed that appropriate behavior was racially constructed and its interpretation could have disastrous consequences for African American students. While Andrew sat in in-house suspension, many White students sat in classes wearing jeans with holes fashionably cut into the knees and thighs. They were in fashion, but Andrew's violation was explained by one teacher as "insolence twice-over"—once for wearing his overalls unsnapped and twice for talking back.

At bottom, this incident, and the concentration on behavior more generally, were rooted in a powerful subtext at Gates—the connection between race, gender, social class, academic track, and behavior. There was a largely unspoken assumption that African American students, especially males in the regular track, were behavior problems and a threat. Occasionally this assumption surfaced, as when a teacher said, "You and I know they [another team] don't have the poor kids [read African American]. Therefore, we have more suspensions." The assumption was present when teachers speculated that a class of mainly African American males was "mostly gang members." It was palpable in an in-house suspension room populated with African American males as well as in the daily construction of what constituted appropriate behavior and dress. An administrator made these assumptions explicit, "You and I know, you can call it racist or whatever, that Black inner-city kids are going to be worst behaved. We have to get their behavior under control." This prevailing assumption did not escape students either. In a group interview of White honors students, one explained, "They can trust us more. We're in the accelerated classes. . . . [T]hey expect more out of you. . . . I think that between a honors student and a regular student and probably they put the blame on regular students." As reflected in these comments, it was clearly low-income African American students who bore the brunt of discipline. But some middle-class students also complained to us that, in their judgment, they were singled out for punishment unfairly because they were Black. Thus, although the public construction of urban Black youth marked this group as dangerous, the stigma extended to African Americans more broadly.

Gates was an orderly school by any standards. In 2 years of observations and numerous unannounced visits by three researchers, we never witnessed a fight or even a contentious verbal altercation, or heard of a student threatening or striking a teacher. There were the usual student/teacher conflicts, student resistance, and undoubtedly incidents we did not know of, but discipline was not an obvious problem. Yet the administration and many teachers were preoccupied with it. When asked at each interview how restructuring was going, the principal, almost without exception, began with an assessment of discipline. The orderly halls, reduced number of out-of-school suspensions, and infrequent fights and confrontations were frequently cited as evidence by some teachers and administrators that teaming was "working."

The connection between race and behavior, in a White school that had become majority African American was perhaps, for many

White teachers, a form of "dysconscious racism"—an uncritical accep-
tance of dominant White racial assumptions, attitudes, and beliefs and
the existing racial hierarchy. (King, 1992). This was precisely the interpretation echoed by some African American teachers. They believed
White teachers uncritically assumed that behaviors and interactive
styles of African Americans (males in particular) that they did not
understand were hostile and threatening (Irvine, 1991). And a broader
set of racial assumptions led them to conclude that a room full of
African American males was likely to be gang-oriented. They simply
accepted the disproportionate disciplining of African Americans. At
the same time, teachers, White and African American, complained
about colleagues who tolerated insolence from White students as simply "brattiness."

The concept of "dysconsciousness" is important here because it
was precisely the absence of critical dialogue about race in general
and the problem of discipline in particular that was a condition for
newly empowered teachers to simply reproduce existing patterns in
the disciplining of African American students. The overrepresentation
of African Americans in disciplinary actions was one of the two main
foci of reducing racial disparities. It was a problem that everyone from
the superintendent on down had acknowledged. Yet there was, to my
knowledge, no collective, cross-racial dialogue about it at Gates. Certainly the principal did not organize such a dialogue, nor were African
American educators and parents empowered to lead it. Despite excellent opportunities provided by new collaborative structures, and despite a mandate to reduce African American suspensions, educators
did not talk about beliefs and practices related to the behavior of
African American students. Instead, new punishments were devised.
Even if out-of-school suspensions were reduced through in-house
suspension, and in-house suspensions were reduced through alternate
punishments, the disciplining of African Americans continued.

For the principal, the connection between race and behavior was
also located in a broader political context. It was a question of balancing what were seen as competing interests. On the one hand, to satisfy
demands for fairness and to counter charges of racism, there was the
need to reduce racial disparities in discipline. On the other was the
need to satisfy the demands of upper-middle-class White parents.
Student behavior was not an obvious problem at Gates. It was the
numerical majority of African Americans, and the particular construction of African American males as a threat, that made behavior an
issue and controlling them an unarticulated restructuring agenda. Ron
Walters put it candidly:

The critical issue is student behavior. That's the issue for keeping White parents in the district. They're worried about their kids' safety. At Gates the parents' perception is that there is good behavior, that academically it's tracked and that there are academically challenging classes for their kids. That's what they care about. Race and academic challenge. Those are the issues. Their perception is that the Black kids act stupid and don't want to learn. That Black guys are putting their hands on White girls. The district has to deal with those issues.

Indeed, one way teachers and the principal chose to "deal" with this issue was to improve social relations with "at-risk" students in order to improve behavior while also creating a plethora of new punishments in lieu of suspension. In this way the school reduced out-of-school suspensions yet continued to focus on discipline. A widespread assessment of restructuring was that it was "helping" because "behavior is better." At the end of the year the principal said he considered his school a "model restructured school" because of improved behavior.

School Membership and Accommodation:
The Flip Side of Discipline

Developing "at-risk" students' sense of school membership seemed to many teachers to be a sign of the positive impact of restructuring. This was the flip side of discipline. At a Steering Committee meeting in December, I posed the question, "What is the effect of teaming?" Those present agreed with a team leader who said, "Kids feel more a part of the school; the climate is better than last year." Consistently, teachers said they believed that the teams and the team activities had improved social relations and "at-risk" students' sense of belonging to the school. These goals were also reflected in the Mentoring and Counseling Program (MCP), a mentorship program involving ten teachers, each responsible for a group of about 12 students who had been identified as "at-risk," which was "to provide every student with a sense of belonging and high self-esteem." The goals were also reflected in Lunch Crowd, small student discussion groups which met with a teacher over lunch once or twice a semester.

Nearly all the teachers interviewed said these programs were providing needed personal support and a greater sense of school membership. Some students confirmed that teachers "were nicer" than in the past and also that they felt a strong affiliation for their team. Several teachers contended that if it were not for their personal interactions with students through MCP and Lunch Crowd, they would have had very limited understanding of "at-risk" students, their backgrounds and barriers to education.

However, several African American teachers felt differently. William, who described himself as "an outspoken" member of Gates's Interracial Committee (a faculty group mandated at each school as part of desegregation) believed "at-risk kids are getting mixed messages." He argued that despite the benefits of teams and MCP, Gates continued to reinforce race and class differences and marginalize African American students through disparate behavioral and academic expectations and "dumping" Black students in special education classes. He thought that many of the team activities exacerbated these differences and was especially critical of the double standard for tokens and "unfair and insensitive competitions involving parent participation." Larissa, another African American teacher, appreciated the collegiality and support she received from her team and believed restructuring had generated less contentious relations between teachers and students. Yet, as I noted in chapter 3, she also saw African American students as fundamentally outsiders at Gates: "Black kids are not connected to school as White kids are. They see school as relevant, but not as Black people important in it."

These varied assessments suggest that school membership was multilayered and understood differently by different teachers. Although some students may have experienced an increased sense of belonging to teams, African American students continued to be structurally marginalized in lower-track classes, and outsiders in a Eurocentric school culture with a paucity of African American staff. The students' level of commitment to Gates was not independent of the relations of power in the school, and Gates was a White-dominated, upper-middle-class school. Genuine membership would have required inclusion of African Americans in the structures and cultural forms through which power was manifested at Gates. Although improving school membership appeared to the be the opposite of multiplying punishments, both served to make African American students accommodate to Gates as it was, an institution which largely negated their identities.

Political and Cultural Context for the Double Standard of Success

The developing dichotomy of academic standards and social support, which I described with the ninth-grade teams, was a schoolwide occurrence at Gates. So too was the district's prevailing framework of separating what were known as "equity issues" from quality education. This framework was a legacy of the implementation of

desegregation in Riverton. This section explores the influence of the
principal and the local political and cultural context on the construction of success for low-achieving African American students.

Balancing Competing Interests and Disparate Standards of Success

It was crucial that Ron Walters treated the demands of Hills/
Palisades parents to maintain the school's academic reputation and
the restructuring mandate to support at-risk students as claims of
competing interests that needed to be balanced. His response was a
condition for the developing schoolwide dichotomy between social
support and academic standards. This was consistent with the way
many teachers, administrators, and others posed what they saw as a
"dilemma": how to satisfy and retain White middle-class parents in
the district *yet* improve educational equity. This construction of the
problem was also a central theme of an authoritative 1988 foundation-
commissioned report on desegregation in Riverton, which stated that
the school board was committed to integration of schools, "as well as"
quality education. Indeed, it was precisely this framework of quality
education disconnected from racial equality and the privileging of
White interests (cf. Bell, 1980) that had guided Riverton's creation of
magnet and specialty schools to encourage White middle-class parents
to accept desegregation on the promise that in these special schools
quality would not be compromised.

In contrast, a major theme of the 1989 Desegregation Plan was
"the concept that school desegregation/integration and quality education are inseparable" (Project Document). Yet, in practice, most teachers narrowly constructed racial equality as racially integrated schools.
Significantly, although a principle goal of the 1989 plan was to reduce
racial disparities in achievement, it did not include an enriched education in predominantly Africa American schools. Academic excellence
in Riverton was implicitly linked to "Whiteness." Similarly, programs
or curricula that were considered multicultural or African American
culturally-centered were generally considered to be for the benefit of
African Americans only. They were not seen as inherently valuable
experiences for all students (see Shujaa, 1992, for similar findings).
This was particularly, but not exclusively, the perspective of Whites in
the district, and it surfaced at Gates in 1990 during a Black History
Day program produced by African American students. Throughout
the program there was noticeable and audible derision from numbers
of White students. Afterward, I overheard a group of these students
protesting to teachers, "Why do we have to attend these things? They
have nothing to do with us." Later, according to two teachers, several

White parents complained to the principal about the assembly and its questionable educational value.

In sum, the political context and the school and district culture implied that Whites and African Americans had different, even competing educational goals. It framed African American culturally-centered projects as satisfying special interests, disconnected from quality education in general. The African American educational agenda was often narrowly constructed as desegregation. At the same time, tracking literally divided Gates students, codifying differentiated expectations and validating a differentiated educational experience largely correlated with race. "Nurturing" African American students was accompanied by lowering the academic standards they were held to. Potentially countervailing factors (effective African American teachers, African American parents, African American advocates among the staff, a culture of African American educational values and school success at Gates) were not mobilized. In addition, the deficit model for African American students set these students up for a compensatory, remedial, behavior-oriented agenda. It was through these political and cultural lenses that the Gates staff interpreted "success for all" to mean quite different things for different students.

Student and Teacher Perceptions

In chapter 5, I suggested that because the two ninth-grade focus teams were held to different standards, the achievements of the "regular team" were devalued in the eyes of all students. Schoolwide data, although not as systematic, provide additional evidence of the negative consequences of this double standard. Most students interviewed, White and Black, honors and regular, indicated that different expectations implied unequal abilities. This is reflected in a group interview with three White eighth-grade honors students in March 1991:

Ellen: I mean like they [the "regular" team] don't have to learn
                as much as we do. I don't think they do. Because they're
                [teachers] like, "They're regular. We don't want them to
                fail. They don't have to do that."
Interviewer: Who says that?
Alex: They don't actually say it. They just, their actions show
                it, I mean.
Ellen: (inaudible) Does the regular have to do this? "No, they're
                regular."
Interviewer: You're talking about teachers' comments?
Alex: Teachers' comments and the material they give 'em. I
                mean, I, sure they could probably, they probably need

a little more time, but I think we should all have the
same material. (inaudible) They give 'em tests like "Who
was over here?" (laughter) Everybody knows. They're
just not challenged enough. . . .

Laura: I think I'm challenged in like everything but [SRM]. We
have to work a lot harder for what we get.

Candice, an African American student who was one of her team's
"at-risk" success stories, had very similar perceptions from the van-
tage point of a "regular" student. She believed the competitions were
unfair because the "smart" teams had inherent advantages:

[Team], you know, they just get the smart kids. You know where
all of 'em aren't smart, they got the average and the smart kids.
And, like we got the kids, like the kids that come to school when
they want to, you know, go fight when they want to, you know.
Seems like we got more of them students than we do the smart
students. . . . I'd just try to split 'em up even. . . . You know try to
play like a slow tag. You know, instead of having all the slow
kids on one side and all the smart kids on the other. You know,
mix 'em up so then when you mix the smart and the slower, the
smart or the average help the slow. Then you know, most likely,
then it's going to be some competition.

Teachers were also divided on the double standard of success
and the new emphasis on nurturing, with resistance especially from
teachers of high-status electives. A teacher who was a part of the Hills
social circle said:

I'm dismayed at the direction the school has taken away from
academics toward rewarding kids. That's the trend this year.
Everything is directed toward the kids with problems. All the
energy is going into getting those kids to pass the state test.
Lowering the standards.

This opposition was not new. In the previous year, electives teachers
resisted pressures from team teachers to reduce the number of "F"s
they gave. Even some core subject teachers were doubtful. As one put
it, "I think we're going too far. Bending over backwards with parties
and awards and rinky-dink activities for kids. Whatever happened to
teaching?"

In some instances, the new agenda fed an already existing frustration among the most veteran teachers, who believed that the school's

academic standards had been eroding for some time. With a more heterogeneous student body, the honors pool had been greatly expanded and, in their eyes, degraded. They believed this happened in order to retain White Hills/Palisades parents by tacitly assuring their children a place in honors classes, isolated from low-achieving African American students. This group of perhaps six to eight teachers clung to memories of "truly bright" students of the past. One of them said:

> I don't see that much difference between regular and honors classes anymore. There are too many honors students. They're not truly gifted. The honors curriculum has been watered down. There used to be a criteria, now a teacher can just recommend a student for honors. It's watered down, and I can't do the kinds of things I used to do in honors.

Nevertheless, tracking was a sort of buffer for these teachers, allowing them to conserve a way of life largely lost with desegregation. The honors students had the dispositions and offered the prestige that were traditionally associated with Gates. These teachers had an interest not only in maintaining tracking, but the invisibility of the low-achieving, African American student population at Gates. This was clearly reflected in prerestructuring interviews when several veteran teachers said they perceived "no problems" at the school because they had so many high-achieving students. Their status accrued from teaching high-track students and thus they had a stake in maintaining the preeminence of honors students at Gates (cf. Finley, 1984). One elective teacher commented at mid-year that most of her "at-risk students" had dropped and she "hoped" the rest would soon because "they simply aren't my focus."

For this group, "success for all" was an assault on their professional identity and ethos. As the year wore on, these teachers became increasingly negative about restructuring and resistant to the activities associated with it. The dual construction of "success" concretely confirmed fears that African American students would lower academic standards. In this way, the double standard could be said to have reinforced racist assumptions.

From an entirely opposite point of view, there were a few others who objected to lowering standards for any students. They believed that the focus on social activities and contests was further denying low-achieving students the opportunity to be academically challenged. William, the African American teacher who hated "the rinky-dink little projects and lowering the standards," complained that there were very few Gates students—regardless of academic track or race—who could think in original and critical ways or grapple with challenging problems. He contended that they were used to simply being fed information. But his concern was that the new emphasis on social relations and incentives directed to "at-risk" students would further diminish academic goals for African Americans in particular. He said, no matter what the administration called for, "I will not lower my standards." He continued to tutor students after school and pushed them to think more critically.

Summary

Although teachers met, talked, and collaborated, they did not challenge the paradigm of competing and different interests for African American and White children. Defining African American students in terms of deficits and evolving different and lower standards for them separated their interests from those of White students, fed racist assumptions that they would "drive down standards," and alienated teachers whose professional identity was bound up with high academic standards. Without reframing equity as part of a broader goal of challenging academics for all students, restructuring simply reinforced the politics that governed the district. This was an example of how the interplay of teachers' ideologies, the culture of the school, and community power relations influenced the shape of restructuring.

Academic Culture and Restructuring

In her study of African American high school students, Fordham (1988) describes students who reject an academic culture that implicitly defines academic success as "acting White." How academic achievement was constructed at Gates and whose knowledge was validated in the curriculum was central to the educational experiences of African American students. This section explores these issues and the influence of restructuring on Gates's construction of academic success.

The Culture of Achievement at Gates

The meaning of achievement at Gates was shaped by White, Hills/Palisades students. The salience of this fact cannot be overemphasized. It jumps out from the pages of the 1991 *Gateways*, Gates's 88-page, expensively produced, student yearbook. Between its covers are numerous glossy pictures of smiling young faces, White and African American. In 1991, a few highly successful African American students like Gaye, described in chapter 5, were featured on the "Most Talented,"

"Most Scholarly," "Most Likely to Succeed" pages and among the elected class officers. But more relevant were the photos of student activities reflecting the peer group organization of students by race. Group pictures representing 35 activities and clubs form a graphic illustration of the social location of African American and White students in the hierarchy of extracurricular activities and the academic culture of Gates at that time. The pictures show White students concentrated in scholastic and high-status academic activities, such as newspaper staff, language clubs, and National Honors Society, as well as in Teen Club, a social group akin to the elite Junior League with about 100 members. African American students were concentrated in athletics and music. The student government officers were all African Americans, perhaps because they were elected by Gates's majority African American student body. Racially mixed activities were mainly those in which the school showed its public face (pep club, cheerleaders, office monitors) or in which students were recruited by the administration (peer facilitators). Although sports were popular, and African American athletes enjoyed a high status among their peers, it was academics that really counted at Gates. These pictures clearly demonstrate the dominance of affluent White students in the academic sphere and the ghettoization of African Americans in activities of lower status (cf. Schwartz, 1981).

Further, observations of classrooms and extracurricular activities suggested that high-status academic activities were an extension of the social relations and neighborhood ties of affluent White students. The interweaving of social ties and academics was also apparent in high status academic activities outside of class. This is illustrated by field notes from a practice session of the Academic Challenge Bowl team (9 white students—6 females, 3 males).

[The teacher introduces me before they begin.]

Student 1:   I know her. I talked to her before. I asked her if she was in charge of restructuring. I thought she was Barbara Ellis [a district official]. My mother talked to her [Ellis] (laugh). She sat down on her desk and told her a thing or two (more laughter). [The student's mother was one of the vocal Hills opponents of the SRM class.]

Student 1:   If we go to the finals we're going to be on TV. I've known kids who were on TV before.

Student 2:   I have too.

Student 3:   I've been on TV before.

[There is general banter about having been on TV. They're divided into two teams, each with a captain. They choose a category (e.g., names from history, famous explorers, geography, literature, etc.) and are asked a factual, memory question.]

Teacher: Explorers. The name given to an important lake in up-state New York. Name the explorer. Miss Emerson should give you this from French history. How many of you take French?

[About two thirds of the hands go up. The others say, "I take Spanish."]

Student 3:   Lately it's been mainly Russian history (laugh). We went to see Chekhov at the Arts Center. She's trying to make us culturally current.

Teacher: Ancient Greek cities, prime numbers, rocks, Mein Kampf. . . . If you miss it, put it out of your mind. Those of you who play tennis, how many of you play tennis? [Almost all hands go up.] You know that when you miss a ball, you just have to go on. . . . It's the same thing here.

[At the end of the hour the teacher says, "Tomorrow after school. We'll work until 5:00 with Miss Kelly. We need to figure out who are the math stars in here. We'll meet tomorrow at noon also." Several of the girls walk out arm-in-arm. They are all dressed in similar styles: loafers, long plain wool sweaters, jeans, or nice pants. As they go out, the teacher says, "Aren't they cute? They love competition."]

   Field notes from classrooms and academic clubs like this one demonstrate the powerful culture that infused academic success at Gates. There was a strong sense of a close-knit, long-term social group, a kind of overlapping of school and neighborhood community that academically successful students were nurtured in. Many of them had grown up together in a tight community, and they shared an elite, Eurocentric background knowledge that was the essential cultural capital (Bourdieu, 1977) they brought to academic activities.
   This closed, upper-middle-class world was not completely exclusive of African American students. However, to be a part of it, African Americans had to be able to swim in this environment. Perhaps, the fact that some students like Gaye could be part of this world demonstrated that its essence was based on class as well as race. But at Gates these two social categories were so intertwined, and race was so salient in the

school and in the community, that academic success was generally equated with being White (Fordham, 1988). Students like Gaye were, as one teacher put it, "different" from other African Americans, and perhaps bore the "burden of acting White" (Fordham & Ogbu, 1986).

What was missing was an inclusive definition of academic excellence that incorporated the experiences and values of African American students, including working class students, and that allowed them to choose academic success without sacrificing their identity (Ladson-Billings, 1990b). Despite goals of improving African American achievement, restructuring did not provoke an examination of the culture supporting academic achievement at Gates, yet the exclusivity of this culture was central to one's success or failure at Gates.

Classroom Knowledge

Classroom knowledge was similarly exclusive. For restructuring to make a real difference in the academic experiences of low-achieving African American students, it would have needed to spark an examination of the curriculum, including whose knowledge it legitimated. Yet classroom observations, conversations with teachers, and reviews of texts made it very clear that the curriculum, both explicit and hidden, validated the cultural capital of middle-class White students and marginalized the knowledge, norms, and experiences of most African Americans (cf. Keddie, 1971). There was no evidence that teachers explored this issue. In its most extreme and overt form, this was reflected in high-status electives and honors classes. The French teacher did French cuisine with her classes. She wanted to make *mousse au chocolat*, she said, but doubted this would work with her more heterogeneous first-year classes. "Some of the kids are so deprived they don't even know what quiche is," she said.

In more subtle ways, regular classes also excluded the knowledge and experiences of most African Americans, negated their language and silenced their voices. This is illustrated by my observation of a heterogeneously grouped SRM class (12 students: 4 White, 8 Black; 5 males, 7 females):

> They are learning about inferences. Gaye, a high-achieving Black student . . . is in the front row (as in her other classes). She answers the first two questions with exact definitions from the book. . . .

Teacher: If a woman were to walk into the room right now dressed all in black silk, with lots of diamonds around her neck, wearing a fur coat, what would be your inference?

Black regular track student in the back:	She's crazy. It's hot outside to be wearing a fur coat.
Teacher:	(laughs) Well, that would be one possibility. Anyone else?
Another Black regular track student:	She might be selling something illegal.
Teacher:	(laughs) She might be selling something illegal (laughs). OK. Anyone else?
White honors track student in front:	She's rich?
Teacher:	(voice elevated) Right. She's rich. OK. What part of the newspaper gets away from the facts?
Same Black student in the back:	Dear Abby?
Teacher:	Oh, Dear Abby. OK. Anyone else?
Black student on opposite side of room:	The comics?
Teacher:	Hmmm. The comics. OK. Anybody else?
Gaye, black student in honors:	The editorials?
Teacher:	(voice elevated) The editorials. OK, so that's an example of opinion, isn't it?

On the face of it, this teacher might simply be noted for his unimaginative and overly directive pedagogy. More to the point here are the biases embedded in his responses. Certainly the inferences that the woman in the fur coat is crazy or selling something illegal were as plausible as, and not contradictory to, the "right" answer. The same was true of his analysis of the newspaper. Indeed, comics and "Dear Abby" are as much opinion pieces as are editorials. In both instances, some students' logic was negated, denying both the validity of their thinking and their knowledge. Repeated in class after class, these students experienced a curriculum of exclusion and a message that school was not their world, that as Larissa put it, "They are in school but not of it." Regardless of intent, the cultural subtext of classes such as this one negatively influenced some students' opportunities for academic success and inclusion and provided the context for finding other ways in which many African Americans could "succeed" at Gates.

An even more basic question was whether schooling at Gates was meaningful to most students—African American or White. Although an analysis of curriculum and pedagogy at Gates is not the focus of this book, my observations of classes—honors and regular at all grade levels—revealed little connection between the curriculum and students' lives and little opportunity for students to wrestle with issues they cared about. The curriculum was much like that criticized by Sizer (1984) in his study of U.S. high schools—lacking in intrinsic interest, superficial, dedicated to coverage, disengaging. Larissa made this point: "The kids don't perceive school in a personal way. They see it as a set of things. But they have to see school as a part of their lives." If she was right, then this must have been doubly the case for African American students, who not only experienced the structural inequality of tracking but also faced a curriculum even more distant from their own experiences and ways of being than the upper-middle-class White students whose culture the school mirrored.

Nurturing High-Achieving Students

Although social support for "at-risk" students was a new thrust with restructuring, the academic culture of Gates was already very supportive for high-achieving, college-bound students. Mentoring and counseling, both formally and informally, were nothing new for the teachers of high-powered and advanced classes, who coached and encouraged high-achieving students to academic success. For example, with restructuring, Colleen continued to tutor her advanced math students every lunch hour and before and after school. In this sense, nurturing was very much a part of what some teachers did at Gates— with some students—long before the onset of restructuring. Indeed, Gates, with its college-prep culture, its location in the heart of the Hills neighborhood, its high-status academic clubs, and its commitment to honors classes was a very nurturing place for college-bound students.

Honors-track classes provided their own kind of nurturing. It was not necessarily more challenging academics that made the difference. In fact, the curriculum in some classes was virtually identical for both tracks, although in the majority there was a marked simplification of the curriculum and much more rote learning in regular classes. There were even a few teachers who made regular classes richer and more intellectually stimulating than some honors classes. If a generalization were to be made, it would be that most classes, regardless of track, were teacher-centered, textbook-oriented, centered on discrete facts and skills, dedicated to coverage, and not very evocative of students' or teachers' creativity (cf. Goodlad, 1984). Indeed, there seemed to be a willingness, on the part of Gates White parents, to settle for very limited notions of academic success as reflected in standardized test scores, in part because of their favorable comparison with African American test scores. Rather than the content of curriculum across the school, it was the culture surrounding honors and advanced classes that was distinctive—a culture of high expectations, of assumptions of superior ability, of certain success.

Improving the academic achievement of African American students was a goal that the principal articulated. He told students, "We want you all to go on to college." However, as I have demonstrated with the focus teams, in practice, "success" for low-achieving African American students often meant social promotion, relaxed standards, and a one-sided emphasis on behavior. To "be supportive" was to be compensatory and lenient in response to perceived deficits. As a result of restructuring, the culture of academic and intellectual support that enfolded honors students was made no more accessible to most African American students.

Regardless of intentions, the objective implications of the double standards were that African American students were being prepared for lower academic trajectories and subordinate social/economic positions. Kevin, a White teacher of noncore academic subjects, complained (informally) about this issue all year, emphasizing that the double standard of success signified to most Black students their exclusion from the high-powered academic world of Gates and rendered an explicit judgment that they could not make it in that world. To be sure, this situation existed before restructuring in the school's comprehensive academic tracking and in some teachers' lower expectations for, and deficit assumptions about, African American students. However, activities stemming from restructuring formalized the dualism of academic achievement and social success and generated a compensatory and patronizing emphasis on the affective needs of African American students. By constructing a separate definition of "nurture" for low-achieving, "at-risk," African American students, and a new set of behaviors and practices directed to those students, the differential worlds of Gates were extended, evolving two distinct sets of teacher behaviors. Thus, the dialectic of the culture of the school and the restructuring process both fostered and intensified a double standard of school success and nurturing. This is consistent with other research on the influence of faculty cultures on the implementation of education reforms (Metz, 1986; Popkewitz et al., 1982).

An African American Culture of Academic Success

A few African American teachers tried to create an African American–centered culture of academic success to support the intellectual aspirations and collective identity of African American students. Like Colleen, William worked with students everyday after school. Although he was known by students and colleagues as strict and academically demanding, unlike Stan he tried to find new ways to help students meet these standards. He was surrounded every night by African American students. Larissa tried to create a bridge between the students' home culture and school. Building on a strong, multidisciplinary background and postgraduate education, her classes were among the most creative I observed at Gates. For example, she devised oral history projects and poetry units that compared rap with traditional African American and European poetic traditions. Paulette also relied heavily on African American literature, history, and political writings because most of the students in her reading classes were African American, and she based writing and reading exercises on students' real-life situations and concerns.

These teachers tended to promote a broader definition of success, one that emphasized not only academic skills and knowledge and individual achievement, but also education as part of one's responsibility to family and community (Ladson-Billings & Henry, 1990). For example, Paulette's classes were often values-driven, requiring students to examine their own values and stressing the inherent values in the materials they read and discussed. She often talked with students about the personal qualities required for success in school and linked them with similar qualities for work and participation in society. Paulette also initiated the AfroNotions Club to encourage African American–centered cultural expressions.

But Paulette, Larissa, William, and a few others were working in a marginal space. A small, isolated circle within the larger motion at Gates, they were few numerically, and they had little institutional support or recognition. For example, the yearbook shows just 8 students in the AfroNotions Club, compared with 40 in French club, over 100 in Teen Club, and 22 in Future Homemakers. Nor did they receive any additional institutional support with restructuring. If anything, their agenda may have become more peripheral as the emphasis on nurturing low-achieving students began to gel.

The Power of Affluent White Parents: The SRM Controversy

The power of affluent White parents was forcefully illustrated by a mid-year controversy over the new Study and Research Methods class. In the fall of 1990, a group of White Hills/Palisades parents, including a school board member/Gates parent, complained to the principal that SRM was not challenging and would pull down high-achievers such as the board member's child. Subsequently, the board member took these objections to the restructuring director and to the superintendent. As the first semester progressed, the controversy spilled into the media and became a hot topic in faculty lounges. Finally, in December, a special school board meeting was called. The board threatened the superintendent with "insubordination" for instituting the class without board approval and threatened the jobs of top district leaders and principals as well.

Throughout, the SRM issue was cast publicly as a question of academic quality. Critics claimed the class was "fluff" and "a waste of time." In fact, the class was experimental, conceived to facilitate scheduling as well as to fill a perceived need in the curriculum, and opinions of SRM teachers themselves were mixed. Some were enthusiastic about expanded opportunities for students to write and to develop study, research, and analytical skills lacking in other classes. Others were more skeptical. Larissa, for example, thought the class was uneven and its implementation premature because of the lack of professional development in curriculum and in teaching heterogeneous classes. At the board meeting, a second issue surfaced. The chief critic said she was concerned with two issues: that the class was not providing remediation to "our at-risk population" and that it would "pull down the high-achievers."

However, beneath all these concerns, it was quite clear to many people that I spoke with that the real issue was race and class—particularly at Gates. This recognition was shared by a broad spectrum of the community. An African American principal of a predominantly African American school said:

> When you really get right down to it, it's about race. We haven't had any problem here. The problem is more at the other schools where they have a higher socioeconomic group of students. Here we talked about it at registration and at orientation. We sent out letters. The classes are heterogeneously grouped. I told the parents most honors students also needed study skills. So even high-achieving students can benefit from this class.

SRM was the only core class that was explicitly and purposefully heterogeneous—a clear counter to tracking. Most school people who would talk about the SRM controversy contended that the Hills/Palisades parents felt the class threatened their children's privileged position within Riverton's largely segregated tracking system.

Administrators and community members I interviewed and letters to the editor in the local newspaper charged that affluent White parents simply did not want their children in classes with African American children. While admitting that the class was "uneven," a top district administrator, who was White, said privately:

> Some board members have kids in these classes. They're complaining that they aren't intellectually challenging. . . . But the real issue when you strip away all the rhetoric, is that these classes are heterogeneously grouped. Some parents think that when their kids get to junior high school, they will be able to say that they are supporters of the public schools, and they'll put their children into the public schools, but that their kids can be isolated and tracked. The real bottom line is that they don't want their kids going to school with Black kids. That's what we're fighting.

Among teachers, African American and White, there was a shared, widely accepted "knowledge" that this group of parents and board members acted out of concern to protect their race and class privileges. This belief was bolstered by the fact that the same board members had shown little concern for low achievers when they had been segregated in remedial classes. For example, ironically, when Franklin's principal requested an additional reading teacher at the beginning of the year, she was told there was no money. (These were the same board members who had spearheaded a $1 million increase in the budget for honors classes.) However, when concerns about the SRM class were raised, the board's solution was to pull out students who needed help with reading and hire additional reading teachers.

The outcome of a bitterly fought four-to-three school board vote was that SRM would be "modified": It would be optional in eighth and ninth grades where it would receive no credit; the lowest quartile would be reassigned to a reading class; and those in the next lowest quartile would be pulled out for reading two days a week. These changes undermined the class's heterogeneity and legitimacy. One principal said, "They killed it." Pulling out the lower quartile was presented as a response to reading deficiencies. Three Gates SRM teachers were transferred to reading, including Larissa and Paulette—the two African American SRM teachers, and Ron Walters hired replacements for them to teach the modified SRM. The teachers were disheartened. Not only had their hard work in developing and teaching the class been undercut, but they were cynical about the possibility of any innovation that challenged the political status quo. Thoroughly demoralized, a Gates teacher who was personally criticized by the school board member left at the end of the year. He said he was going to "get out of teaching."

The incident demonstrated the centrality of the political context and the relations of power to educational change at Gates, and in Riverton in general. The fact that SRM was instituted without the knowledge of the board also reflected the political weakness of those who dared to tamper with tracking and the privileges of middle-class White students. It suggested that some upper-middle-class parents were only willing to send their children to public schools as long as they were insulated from low-income African American children. The incident revealed that they held the levers of power at Gates and had great influence in the district. It also demonstrated that they had the power to check restructuring when it infringed on their interests, as they perceived them.

Obstacles to Dialogue Among Teachers

At Gates there were a number of obstacles to inquiry about substantive issues. In the first place, as in most schools (Sizer, 1984), there was no precedent for dialogue and reflection among the faculty. Although a structure was in place to facilitate discussion and reciprocal learning, there was no school or district leadership to take on difficult issues (Conley, 1993). On the most controversial topics—race, tracking, discipline policies and discrepancies in their implementation, substantive reform of curriculum—there was a culture of silence. (See Muncey and McQuillan, 1992, for related discussion.) Nor was there leadership within the teams to support critical self-examination.

A review of minutes of Steering Committee meetings for the year is one indication of this problem. Regular topics were reports on programs such as the afterschool program, administrative details, planning extracurricular activities, reports of individual/team successes, and team process issues. According to the minutes, the most meaty discussions were directed to solving immediate problems, such as why so few students were attending the afterschool program or the need for staff development on interdisciplinary teaching. Certainly these problems might have been the basis for inquiry about underlying issues of achievement, alienation, and marginalization, but my observations of several Steering Committee meetings, analysis of the minutes, and reports from teachers indicated otherwise. For example, the Steering Committee handled the problem of poor attendance at the afterschool program by devising administrative procedures to shepherd students to the appropriate room and to monitor their participation. There was no examination of why so few students wanted to attend, despite the fact that the program might have helped them pass classes they were currently failing.

There was little apparent dialogue in faculty meetings either. A 1-hour faculty meeting in January had 17 items on the agenda. Not surprisingly, my notes reveal little discussion:

> Walters passes out the agenda. There are coffee and donuts. He jokes with a teacher in the front row. Then he passes out a diagram called "Ladder of Learning" that Larissa had prepared for a discussion of instructional approaches to encourage critical thinking and analysis. This is passed out without comment. Announcement about SRM; it's to be reorganized to focus on reading. They'll hire two new teachers. There is no discussion about this issue that has had the restructuring schools in an uproar for a month. A visiting Atlanta principal reported that the Gates students are better behaved than those in restructured schools in Memphis and the racial balance at Gates is more Black. Academic skill development plan—they need to do "constant remediation" for kids who fail the state test. Students are ineligible for extracurriculars if they get 2's in citizenship. Some teachers want to go back to bells but he's "not going to do it."

When asked whether the issues they felt were very important were discussed in their team, teachers generally said they were not. A related arts teacher struggling with large numbers of African American failures in her classes sought advice from the researchers. When asked if she had taken the problem to her team, she said, "No. We don't discuss things like that."

Yet there were counterexamples to suggest that teachers mulled over substantive issues with their colleagues. As an example, I interviewed Larissa and Daniel, two African American teachers who usually ate lunch together and often discussed curriculum. Larissa: "There's no real communication in the team. The real communication I have is just with Daniel, like this. Last year I felt like the people in our team really connected. This year it's totally different." Also, Elaine and Kevin frequently discussed school policies at lunch. There is evidence that the ninth-grade A Team discussed at length ways to encourage students to prepare for college. However, generally, this dialogue was not a product of the organizational and governance changes associated with restructuring. It tended to take place mainly in the normal ebb and flow of professional conversations among personally or professionally compatible colleagues.

In the second place, teachers were not encouraged to grapple with ideas about educational change. Shapers of the reform within the district leadership saw teachers as implementers, and teachers tended to agree. When polled at the beginning of the school year, few of the team members said that rethinking curriculum was a central feature of their work in a restructured school. Instead, they were activity-oriented. They planned events, outings, contests, and occasional curricular units. These were concrete tasks with which they were more comfortable than the difficult and conflictual business of reassessing values, beliefs, and educational practice. Thus restructuring seemed to be seen as a process external to teachers. This is in contrast with Muncey and McQuillan's (1996) findings that faculty involved in the Coalition of Essential Schools became more reflective when the Coalition got them talking about educational goals and the need to transform their teaching and curriculum.

Perhaps, also, teachers had not grasped that restructuring meant a paradigm shift, even though the August Restructuring Institute made that point explicitly. They tended to see restructuring as a collection of programs and discrete interventions (cf. Wehlage, Smith, & Lipman, 1991) focused on the immediate and the tangible. In March, Gerrie said, "I really like my team. It's a lot easier to connect with the other teachers and there's a lot more support now. But it hasn't changed anything about the way I teach." Except for a few techniques (e.g., student peer coaching, classroom organization) and the few interdisciplinary units developed, all of the teachers reported that teaming had not significantly affected their thinking or practice related to curriculum and instruction. In February 1991, Larissa had this insight in her summary of what restructuring was accomplishing at the school:

> The teams are so busy dealing with the particular behavior of a particular student that they don't deal with these kinds of issues [curriculum, pedagogy, race relations, changes in policy]. . . . We're missing the bigger picture with restructuring. We're chipping away but only a little bit on established patterns. . . . I think in general we haven't processed what this change is about yet. What we need to do is to get educators now not into the act of teaching but into the process of educating. We've got to reprocess. It's a regrouping for teachers. But I believe that change is imminent.

We're restructuring for the long haul. But then, you don't change
140 years of education in 5 years.

Obstacles to substantive inquiry are perhaps predictable, particularly in the early stages of restructuring. Muncey and McQuillan's
(1996) study of the Coalition of Essential Schools identifies similar
difficulties in fostering productive dialogues of change. Also these
difficulties are not surprising given the traditional hierarchical organization that gives teachers a degree of individual autonomy (as
opposed to collective empowerment) yet often governs autocrati-
cally (Freedman, Jackson & Boles, 1983). Promoting dialogue and
encouraging debate among professionals socialized in such institutions is therefore likely to be difficult (although efforts have been
reported in some restructuring schools: Barth, 1988; Lieberman, Saxl,
& Miles, 1988). Connie, for example, recognized that her approach to
teaching was different from her teammates, but she never raised this
in team meetings. In conversations she conveyed that she saw this as
a personal matter, a question of style rather than a substantive team
issue.

Third, dialogue was stifled by an unwritten, powerful taboo
against discussing race. Under the weight of several hundred years of
racism and racial oppression, the general silence about racial issues
and unwillingness to discuss race (West, 1992) is apparent in schools.
In desegregated schools, racial issues may be hidden under a "veneer
of racial harmony" (Clement, Eisenhart, & Harding, 1979) or behind a
raceless "colorblind philosophy," in which to identify children racially
is said to negate equality (Schofield, 1982). Just as Tatum (1992) notes
that race is not discussed in college classes in part because it is a taboo
subject, this taboo coupled with a deep-seated defensiveness about
racial issues was significant at Gates.

This was brought home by an incident that occurred at the beginning of my research at the school in fall 1989. My colleagues and
I were attending meetings of the two experimental teams. The first
team, composed of three African American and two White teachers
(including a reading teacher), had been assigned all regular classes,
which in some instances were almost entirely African American. We
asked why the students had been divided this way. They were obviously disturbed and said, "That's the way [Ron] did it. Now you
figure it out." The next team, composed of four White teachers, had all
of the honors classes and a majority of White students. (The distinction between these two teams was so blatant that a teacher in another
grade said that the eighth grade was "divided up like South Africa.")
Notes from the second team meeting:

When we ask about the tracking between the two clusters, they become really defensive. They say all the teachers were offered training in teaching honors but the other teachers didn't take it. It's more work; maybe they don't want the extra work. Two teachers roll their eyes. One becomes quite angry and asks why we are asking that question and what we intend to do with our information. We repeat our explanation of our role and research agenda.

Later we learned that the teachers had complained angrily to the principal about our questions. He in turn complained to district leaders that we were making race into an issue at Gates. Later, reporting on initial findings to a group of district administrators, community leaders, principals, and foundation representatives, I identified academic tracking and the racial polarization that resulted as one problematic issue. This report, coupled with the incident at Gates, was so controversial that it brought the research to a halt for 3 months while access was renegotiated. The concern that was reiterated by some school leaders was that race had been made an issue (despite the fact that the stated intent of restructuring was to improve the school success of "at-risk" students who were acknowledged to be overwhelmingly African American) and that the restructuring project had to move slowly on this issue. This incident at Gates was so significant that it resurfaced periodically through the remaining year and a half of research. A year later, at a Steering Committee meeting in the fall of 1990, the principal alluded to it, reminding the teachers, "You don't have to answer any questions you don't know about or are not comfortable with. Last year we had a problem because teachers were asked questions they didn't know anything about or couldn't address."

The mélange of personal relationships, strong authority of the principal, and habit of not discussing substantive issues *as a faculty* prevailed over the need for collective critical inquiry. Indeed, there was little apparent recognition of this need and little leadership to instigate it. It was this culture of suppressed collective dialogue, coupled with taboos about discussions of race, that crippled opportunities for critical inquiry. As a result, the deep cultural and structural issues at Gates—its blatant subordination of African Americans; its ideologies, culture, pedagogies, and curricula; its silences and omissions—went unexamined and unchallenged.

Conclusion

Ideological and political factors in and outside Gates had a profound effect on teachers' conceptions of the kind of change that would

benefit African American students. The consistency of findings across
the teams and the school steering committee is an indication of the
power of these factors to shape the direction of restructuring. The
principal influenced the course of restructuring through his social and
behavioral interpretations of success for all, his lack of curricular leadership, and his selection of team leaders with a social relations approach. The confluence of the social relations approach, concerns about
student behavior, and race led to a potent subtext of restructuring for
social control.

This was coupled with Gates's entrenched culture of academic
success that validated the knowledge and cultural capital of upper-
middle-class students and intellectually and culturally marginalized
most African Americans. Across teams, teachers used the conditions of
restructuring to exacerbate the double standard of school success. In
the absence of a self-critical stance toward the school's narrow and
exclusive academic culture, teachers looked for nonacademic avenues
for low-achieving students to experience success. Instead of provoking critical examination of the culture of academic achievement at
Gates, restructuring was shaped by, and reproduced, this culture.

The direction of restructuring was also influenced by a school
district and community context in which equality and educational
excellence were framed as competing and separate interests. A flagship
junior high that served constituencies associated with these separate
goals, Gates became a focal point in the contest for power. Race and
class were at the root of competing agendas and contending political
demands on the school. Shaped by politics that divided the interests
of students along race and class lines, the African American educational agenda was detached from the school's vision of academic
excellence.

Riverton's White, upper-middle-class interests demonstrated their
power to limit and define restructuring through their opposition to
the heterogeneously grouped Study and Research Methods class and
their ability to reinstate their children's separation from low-achieving
African American students. This one heterogeneously grouped class
represented a relatively small change in the Gates environment, but it
was contested because it was perceived as a move against existing
relations of power and privilege. The web of race and class in these
power relations was difficult to untangle. Although Whites were a
minority at Gates, they maintained dominance in the school through
their hold on the honors classes, which not only assured their privileges but set the tone for the school. On the one hand, it seemed that
this was very much about social class. Elite White parents did not

seem to object to high-achieving, mainly middle-class African Americans in honors classes. In any case, they had no choice, since even honors programs in Riverton could not be all White. It was the incorporation of the majority of African American students who were low-income and who they perceived as a threat to academic excellence that they objected to. But the racial dimensions of this struggle were also salient. The majority African American population were not only low-income but also demonstrated distinct ways of being (language, styles, mannerisms) that were clearly identified as African American. It was these African American cultural forms that the honors classes were largely insulated from. Untracking was threatening because White elites might lose their hold on the honors classes and with it their cultural dominance of a school where they were a minority. Without the anchor of the White honors classes, Gates could become "a Black school."

Constructions of race at Gates also underpinned views of behavior, achievement, and tracking, yet race was a taboo subject. As a result, the new opportunities for teachers to share their understandings and use their colleagues' perspectives to help broaden their own were largely squandered. In part, the silence regarding race was simply an element of the overall absence of critical dialogue. But it was also a way of maintaining control over a potentially volatile political situation in which African Americans were the majority but were marginalized. Part of what was missing was a reconstruction of academic excellence that incorporated the experiences and values of African American students, especially low-income students, and that allowed them to choose academic success without sacrificing their identity.

7

FOCUS TEAMS AT FRANKLIN—
PROBLEMS OF COLLABORATION AND CHANGE

When the majority is Black and the minority is White, they [White teachers] feel they're being picked on. This happens in the team too. It's hard to say what you really think because people feel they're being attacked on racial lines. Usually, it gets interpreted as a racial thing. You know, "They're teaming up against me."

—African American teacher

In this chapter I describe the dialogue and activities of two teams at Franklin Junior High School. I begin with a summary of activities of the two teams and how they interpreted these activities. Then I discuss four central issues: (a) differing interpretations of student support and the problem of collaboration and change, (b) racial divisions and the absence of trust, (c) unrealized possibilities for reflection on teaching and learning, and (d) teachers' frustration and demoralization. Most of the students in the two teams were African American, and most team discussions and interactions were related to African American students. Thus, my analysis is mainly pertinent to these students. In the next chapter, I discuss the role of the principal and contextualize the teams within the school and its broader context.

The Focus Teams

As I described in chapter 3, the Franklin faculty was divided into various, somewhat overlapping informal groups. The principal, in consultation with the director of restructuring, drew up the teams to intermix teachers from these groups in an attempt to break down faculty divisions. Two teams in particular, the seventh-grade Eagles and the eighth-grade Stars, seemed to offer opportunities to explore the interactions of teachers with different perspectives as well as to observe the enculturation of new teachers in collaborative contexts. As it turned out, both teams had a high rate of turn-over. One teacher left the Eagles in mid-year and two teachers left the Stars. On both teams were teachers who planned to leave at the end of the year. This instability was characteristic of the poorest and least successful schools in the Riverton district. It affected the faculty's ability to plan a long-term, common agenda and limited teachers' commitment to change and to each other.

The Eagles

The seventh-grade Eagles teachers were an active group. They met frequently and planned student activities such as bowling parties, field trips, speakers, and talent shows. They also organized a number of incentives and awards and two lunch-time student discussion groups. They were diverse in experiences, ideologies, and classroom practices. Their interactions suggested both the possibilities and the limitations of restructuring to support dialogue and teacher change.

The defining core was three African Americans (Marion, Gloria, Juanita), part of a group of African American women teachers at Franklin whom I call the *Othermothers* (Hill Collins, 1991), a term that captures the essence of teachers who were community mothers to Franklin students. These three were involved in the first restructuring teams at Franklin in 1988-89. Their perspectives on low-achieving African American students were complex and contradictory, incorporating elements of a social relations approach and a critique of racism, and increasingly, as the 1990–91 school year wore on, deficit models. On the one hand, they stressed building self-esteem and identifying strengths in students where others saw weaknesses. They worked more closely with families than any other group of teachers, and were quick to point to racism against African American teachers and students in Riverton. On the other hand, they sometimes branded the students deficient, lazy, and "bad," and by the end of the year some were saying the families "just don't care." The complexity of their views is one of the topics of this chapter.

Gloria, a teacher for 12 years, was the team leader. The strongest proponent on the team of improving social relations, Gloria favored activities to build team membership (parties, T-shirts, logos) and was the strongest advocate of using incentives to improve behavior and achievement. Although she said she "agreed with Goodlad" (Goodlad, 1984) on the need for educational reform, her classes were conventional, teacher-centered, and frequently a struggle against student disruptions.

The other two Othermothers, Juanita and Marian, had both been teaching for about 14 years. They worked together on various projects, were in regular contact throughout the day and by phone in the evening, and often oversaw each other's classes while one of them attended to an individual student. They contacted parents, made home visits, took students on outings, and always had a story to tell about some student's predicament and how they planned to address it.

Juanita was a strong advocate of teacher empowerment and was critical of racism at Franklin and in the Riverton district. A member of Franklin's Interracial Committee, her outspokenness got her in trouble, especially when she demanded more authority for teachers and challenged the school administration for overlooking African American teachers. A team leader in 1989–90, she was replaced in 1990–91 because some administrators said she was "opinionated" and "uncooperative." Juanita also initiated numerous student-oriented projects. Marian was immersed in mentoring and assisting students. She pushed students to stay in school and live up to the same high standards she held for her own children, but her classes seemed to be dominated by work sheets and little teaching and punctuated by her shouts to "sit down, be quiet, and get to work"—without much instructional follow-up.

Chris, an innovative young White teacher in her 5th year, was part of the district core that developed the new Study and Research Methods course over the summer of 1990. She sometimes explained low achievement with references to family problems, but she also had a quite elaborate critique of the standard curriculum. In her own classes, she employed a wide variety of instructional approaches, including cooperative learning, creative writing, thematic multidisciplinary projects, and extensive use of a language arts computer lab for which she had written a grant proposal. She talked a lot about developing analytical skills and using an experiential approach to learning. Chris seemed to get along well with the African American members of the team and said she was comfortable at Franklin.

Adele, a new White teacher on the team, had recently moved from an affluent Midwestern suburban school where she had taught for nearly 20 years. She expressed frustration and "shock" at student "deficiencies." Adele was constantly tested by students (she said she even received a death threat) and could not maintain order in her classroom. Finally, they drove her out at mid-year. After a frantic search, the principal found a replacement, an older White man, Mr. Murphy (no one ever used his first name), who had not taught in years. He seemed bewildered by the students, the curriculum, daily administrative routines, and his inability to get students' attention. Mr. Murphy never seemed to grasp the purpose of the teams or to be aware that an educational reform was underway. During team meetings he often corrected papers, if he showed up at all.

At Franklin, counselors were much more closely integrated into core teams than at Gates and frequently attended team meetings. However, the seventh-grade counselor, Marissa, a White woman in her first year at Franklin, was clearly an outsider on the team. In interviews, she was quite candid about her belief that African American families were pathological and that African American students were prone to violent and deviant behaviors. In meetings, she consistently advanced psychological and behavior modification approaches for "problem" students.

The Stars

The Stars team was also diverse, although most agreed that students' low achievement was rooted in their own personal and family problems. On this team, pessimism and a series of disruptive circumstances thwarted substantive interaction. By December, team meetings were irregular. (Nearly every team meeting I scheduled to attend from November through April was rescheduled or canceled, and I frequently had to catch up with the teachers individually or in pairs.) The Stars had two teacher replacements during the year and became increasingly disconnected and inactive as a team.

Elizabeth, the team leader, was a 20-year veteran African American teacher. She had been at Franklin 8 years. Although less proactive than the Othermothers on the Eagles, I considered her part of this informal group. I frequently observed her talking with students about personal and social problems, and she worked with their families. Her classes were devoted to repetitive seatwork, and, in the second semester, drills for the eighth-grade state competency test. In November, serious family problems took her attention, and she became increasingly distracted until the spring.

The other two African American teachers on the team, Erline and Belinda, were part of the group who seemed to be just putting in their time. They both blamed student failure on individual deficiencies and families. Both often related to their students with exasperation and indifference, and Belinda seemed to have numerous conflicts with students. At mid-year, she took a medical leave, and Erline made plans to move out of state at the end of the school year.

The principal replaced Belinda with a long-term substitute, Katrina, an African American woman in her late twenties who was completing courses for teaching certification. In contrast to her team colleagues, Katrina was energetic and upbeat about her students and about teaching. She blamed low achievement on schooling that was neither stimulating nor relevant to students. She challenged her students to apply themselves and simply ruled out disruptive behavior "because we have so much important work to do." Her classes were creative, engaging, and frequently included serious discussions about strategies for learning, the importance of education, and life choices. Unfortunately, she arrived at a time when the team was already beginning to fall apart.

The two remaining Stars teachers, were both White, novice teachers. Heidi commuted from a White suburb in the county. Early on, she attributed school failure to students' backgrounds, reputed gang affiliation, and negative (by her definition) character. Her views were similar to Adele's on the Eagles, but she was more confident of her position with the students and brooked no nonsense in her classroom. Mark, who taught SRM, also drew on cultural models of deprivation to explain the lack of school success of African American students. He always seemed to be ready with a story about some student's "bad home life." In December, he was recalled to active duty in the army and left Franklin. He was replaced by an African American woman, Denise, a reading teacher, who was uninvolved in the team.

The new African American eighth-grade counselor, Jonetta, was a militant critic of institutional and individual racism in the school and the district. Her outspokenness quickly alienated her from many teachers and administrators, African American and White. At the end of the year she left under clouded circumstances. (District administrators said Jonetta's credentials were not in order. She told me she was forced out on a technicality for political reasons.)

Summary of Team Activities

Team meetings at Franklin were generally informal and not always organized around a fixed agenda nor documented by official minutes. Occasionally, meeting times were used to work with individual students. At first this informality seemed adapted to teachers' needs but gradually it led to a breakdown in communication between teachers who did not have strong ties prior to restructuring. Teachers' rooms had been reorganized so that those in a particular team were all located near each other. This created the opportunity for daily informal interactions, but teachers who had not established relationships did not necessarily avail themselves of this opportunity to discuss substantive educational issues. In some cases, teachers did not attend meetings for weeks. By January, the Stars, as a formal entity, was barely functioning beyond routine administrative details and occasional student activities such as a pizza party.

Through signs, bulletin boards, team logos, T-shirts, slogans, and activities the Franklin teams tried to create a team identity among students. Although they concentrated on some standard activities introduced at the Restructuring Institute (positive personal interactions with students, incentives, team rules and monitoring of academic achievement), the content of these activities was shaped by the teachers and the particularities of Franklin and its student body.

Incentives

Incentives played a relatively small part in teachers' interactions with students. Both teams offered various prizes for individual improvement (candy, discounts at fast-food restaurants, pencils, stickers) and some team rewards for good behavior (movies, pizza or popcorn parties, field trips). Eagles teachers also obtained donated radios, jackets, and hats from local businesses and awarded them to students for "good behavior and improved citizenship" and they organized several out-of-town field trips and visits to local businesses. Gloria, the Eagles leader, said, "You have to do something to keep the kids' interest. I have stickers for the kids and we're getting an Eagle stamp and they can compete for the most stamps. Lack of interest is what leads to these behavior problems. You have to make learning into a game." Marian said students were really trying because they "don't want to get written up. They beg us not to because they want to win."

However, the teachers generally downplayed individual and team academic achievement contests that they believed were inherently unfair. Although they had visited restructuring schools where the contests were used to motivate students, they saw them as potentially harmful to Franklin's low-achieving students. In fact, individual competition was not a visible part of the school culture. Incentives were used at Franklin primarily to reward good conduct, over which students presumably had more control than they did grades. At one Eagles meeting, a teacher pointed out that "incentive coupons aren't for regular activities like homework or tests," but for good deeds, "like a good neighbor award." Juanita, relating an incident in which a new student couldn't open her locker, said "Doris [a student] said, 'That's okay. I'll help you with it.' These are the things kids should get awards for." Franklin also had no interteam competitions. In one Stars meeting, an academic quiz show–style tournament with the other eighth grade was suggested but quickly rejected because the teachers were afraid the team with more "slow" students would be humiliated at their inevitable defeat.

Focus on Individual Students

Team discussions often focused on individual students with teachers searching for personal and family-related causes for school problems. This approach of the Stars teachers was outlined by Erline and Elizabeth in a joint interview in January 1991 in which they asserted that their rapport with students had improved with the establishment of teams. They listed individual cases in which they had learned something about a child on the team and had used the knowledge to respond to the child's special needs. They claimed that because of restructuring, they had been able to keep one child from being sent to the alternative school. On the Eagles, it was the practice of Marian, Juanita, and Gloria that defined the team. They took it upon themselves to identify students who were in trouble, search out the causes, and intervene personally. Conversations about individual students, contacts with social service agencies, shopping trips, and counseling sessions spilled over from team meetings to the hallways outside their classrooms, to evening phone calls, and back to team meetings.

The teams' focus on individuals seemed to facilitate some teachers' ongoing involvement with students. However, it confirmed for others that the students themselves were the problem. Heidi, Adele, and Mark remarked that team discussions had convinced them that the problems were "with the students." Their new awareness of social and family problems beyond their control also left them cynical about the efficacy of their own actions. Mark summarized this feeling: "There are problems I can't solve. I've laid awake lots of nights thinking about it and crying about it, but there're problems that I can't solve. I feel like I'm on a merry-go-round that I can't get off. There are a lot of their needs that I can't fill."

Most of the Stars teachers, regardless of race, were quite negative about students to begin with, and their meetings seemed to feed this negativity as each damning story about a student was topped off by another seemingly more hopeless one. By the spring, even Eagles meetings had become complaining sessions about individual students and forums to share deficit models for failure and feelings of powerlessness. Perhaps this was because teachers had become overwhelmed by the urgency of some students' situations. Their negativity was also fed by the lack of academic progress despite new team activities. Meanwhile, as I describe below, there was a growing frustration with the deterioration of discipline.

What was missing was a multifaceted analysis of students' strengths and resilience in the face of challenging circumstances (Winfield, 1991). Despite incredible difficulties, students came to school and some were relatively successful, even though many worked and some were effectively the mainstays of their households. Their ability to carry out these tasks and responsibilities reflected personal qualities and competencies on which to build educational practice. Moreover, in specific contexts, as I describe below and in chapter 9, students demonstrated engagement in challenging academic work. Yet even the Othermothers focussed on student problems. Discussions of individual students were the arena for this.

Young Men and Young Women With Dignity

The African American Eagles teachers understood that "high-risk" (their term) African American students faced a common set of social and personal challenges and shared a collective experience. They also believed that there was an absence of institutional support for African American cultural identity. To meet these needs, they organized *Young Men With Dignity* and *Young Women With Dignity*—or simply *Dignity*, two informal student groups for "high-risk" students. Dignity's mission statement said:

> We will use self-esteem activities and ideas to help students get to know themselves better and to appreciate how their likes, dislikes, and family heritage combine to make them special. With this insight, they can begin to recognize the same uniqueness in others.

The Statement of Objectives included: reducing suspensions (especially of males), improving achievement, building pride and a positive self-image, and clarifying personal value systems in relationships. The teachers hoped Dignity would counteract drugs, gangs, sexual irresponsibility and teen pregnancy, and strengthen students' commitment to school. Each Dignity group of about 20 students met twice a week, on alternate days, over lunch in Juanita or Marian's classroom. They talked informally about personal and social issues or heard speakers who were chosen as African American adult role models. Occasionally the teachers organized an after school activity such as bowling or a visit to a local social service agency.

Although carefully cloaked, the goal of supporting African American solidarity was implicit in Dignity's mission statement and in its almost exclusively African American participation (one White male occasionally attended the male group's meetings). As a teacher confided, "Everybody knows it's for Blacks, even though we can't say it." Dignity created a link between supporting individual African American students and the affirmation of their shared identity, culture, and heritage. The Dignity teachers believed this affirmation was central to educational achievement and to productive decision making. Their message was clear in these notes from a typical meeting of Young Men With Dignity:

> There are seventeen Black male students, Juanita, and Gloria in Juanita's room. The kids and teachers have carried in their hot lunch trays. The guest speaker is an African American parole officer. . . . He tells them they need to "buckle down on [their] studies." When he grew up he had to respect his elders. "I appreciate that now, because I made it. I appreciate the value of hard work and where it gets you in the world. Cool ain't about nothin. . . . If you are Black you have even more against you, so it takes more to succeed." He tells them 92% of the people on his probation caseload are Black males. "We won't make it as a people if we go on like this. You young brothers have to take responsibility." He offers to mentor any student who is interested.

Dignity filled a void at Franklin. Because of sensitivities about being labeled a "Black school," there were strict, unspoken taboos against racially identifiable activities. Desegregation mandates did not include African American cultural centeredness except within superficial "multicultural guidelines," that is, multiracial pictures on the walls, a smattering of multicultural literature, and racially mixed classes. As a result, connections between learning and African American values and experiences were tacitly proscribed as "too racial." To the extent teachers included African American perspectives in the curriculum, it was on their own initiative. Juanita, for example, brought in books on African American history and read them to her students and directed an African American history play.

Dignity was one of the few organized activities at Franklin that attempted to help African American students develop perspective on their place within an African American community context (cf. Henry, 1992; Ladson-Billings, 1992b). All of the teachers involved had been educated in Black schools and said the communitarian ethos of those schools had been central to their development and to the survival and advancement of African American communities. Juanita said, "We lost something when we went to integration because Black schools were a community and we don't have that anymore" (cf. Siddle Walker, 1996; hooks, 1994). Dignity was an attempt to recapture this experience, to extend the African American community of values to Franklin and to create an African American identity that would draw in African American students, bind them to one another and to school (Foster, 1992). Dignity did not challenge curricular, pedagogical, or policy issues that might be found to marginalize African American students, nor did it confront prevailing practices, but coexisted with them. Nevertheless, it was a forum through which African American students could build group identity and solidarity within a legitimated school context.

In some sense, Dignity was a product of the teams and was facilitated by the joint planning time that was part of restructuring. However, there was nothing inherent in the ethos of the restructuring project that spawned this group. Restructuring created the conditions, but it was the Othermothers who molded the conditions to their own purposes. Dignity grew out of the team but transcended it, inviting students to participate in activities that directly related to their common situation as young African American males and females. This connection was in contrast with the teams that were created to foster a sense of student membership but were largely artificial groupings devoid of unifying values or culture and with no glue other than a core group of teachers.

However, the group did not seem to draw in teachers beyond an initial core of the like-minded. The Othermothers saw no need to work with others with whom they had little in common and whose values were quite different. (See Foster, 1992, for similar findings regarding African American teachers in restructuring schools who eschew collegial relations with colleagues whose commitments and values differ from their own.) The Othermothers planned the group almost in secret at the beginning of the year and informed their team colleagues later. Teachers in other teams said they only heard about it through the grapevine. The Othermothers shielded Dignity in its infancy by keeping it informal and semiprivate to protect it against charges of racial exclusion. ("Racism" was a term used privately by some White teachers to cover African American-centered activities that they felt excluded Whites.) Later, at a team meeting in December, one of the founders officially described the group to the whole team, and told them: "It's open regardless of race, color, or creed. A few White guys have come but they haven't stayed. So you all are welcome to participate [directed to Adele and Chris particularly], to come in and help." (As far as I know, they did not.) In this way, Dignity, despite its potential, was much like other small, prerestructuring initiatives—isolated and additive without much influence on schoolwide practices or on those with different perspectives.

Student Support, Othermothering, and the Problem of Collaboration

Within the two teams, there were various interpretations of how best to provide support to students. The delineation of these interpretations and the problem of developing shared meanings illustrate the limitations of collaboration to engender reflection and change and shared vision.

Othermothering

Juanita, Gloria, Marian, Elizabeth, and later, Katrina, gave the restructuring goal of increased student support expanded meaning. They provided support that reached beyond the school doors into students' families, cultivating student leadership and shared values, and, for African Americans, nurturing pride in their identity as a People (e.g., Dignity). Unlike some of their colleagues who were prodded by teaming to strengthen relations with students, for this group the heart of teaching was caring for the whole child. Othermothering framed how some of these teachers envisioned restructuring. In May 1990, Marion, Juanita, and Gloria shared their hopes for the expansion of restructuring:

> Marian says, The issues they [restructuring office] need to address? Well, teen pregnancy, before and after. They need to have a class. We also need a caseworker. We wanted to request one from downtown but [the restructuring director] vetoed it. Our kids have so many serious problems. [She describes a series of incidents and a litany of social and personal problems faced by individual students.] ... We need help. We're trying to do this for the kids, not [for] ourselves, but we're doing two jobs.

These teachers embraced the emphasis on social support for "at-risk" students and reorganizing teachers into teams because these changes legitimated, facilitated, and provided a formal structure for what they were already doing informally for both African American and White youth. This group of teachers was similar to the teachers Foster (1992) calls "coincidental cooperators," who participate in educational reforms that correspond to their own orientations. A conversation with Elizabeth on the Stars illustrates this point:

PL: Is this kind of social support new?
Elizabeth: No. We've always done this, as long as I've been at this
             school [eight years]. The only difference is, it's easier with
             the teams. Our rooms are right next to each other and we
             can meet every day if we need to, so that way we can
             keep up with these kids better. Maybe Miss Cole will know
             something about a student that I don't know and that way
             we can help them more.

These teachers worried together about "our kids" and regularly
reached into their own pockets to provide everything from lunch money,
car fare, and treats, to shoes and coats. Home visits and calls to parents
were routine. Every day, before and after school, and during class
changes, they were surrounded by several students wanting to discuss
a problem, or just checking in. During the year, Marian literally became
a temporary substitute mother to several students in crisis whom she
took into her own family. Excerpt from February field notes:

[Marian launches immediately, without questions from me, into
an account of various students.] My little MCP girl, the one whose
father neglects her, I told her when she's 18 she can leave home.
She can come and live with me if she wants to. I mean it. . . . My
little girl in the front [a White student], the one we took to the
beauty parlor, she's withdrawn again. He father says she's like
that at home. She just goes in her room and plays her instru-
ment. I don't know what's going on with her and she doesn't
talk to us. After we took her to the beauty parlor she looked so
nice, even the other kids said so. "Ooh, your hair looks so nice,"
they said. And she really seemed to be happier. She smiled and
gave me a big hug. But now I don't know what's going on
again. . . . Another one of my little girls who just had her baby,
came back to school. She tried to jump in front of a teacher's car.
She was saying, "I don't care if I live or die." I told her, "You
have to care. You're responsible for two people now. You had
that baby and now you're responsible." I told her, "You know,
we have something in common—we're both mothers." She smiled
and hugged me. She didn't want to talk at first because she
didn't want to talk to the Black teachers, but I talk to all colors.
I care about all of them.

Dignity, an African American history play, and other afterschool
activities were all aspects of Othermothers' extended roles. These ac-

tivities primarily involved Eagles students identified as "at-risk" but included others as well. Juanita's formal mentoring group (MCP) of 12 mushroomed well beyond official limits. She explained, "They hang around in my room. 'Well, come on then,' I say. I just can't exclude anybody."

The Othermothers also tried to help African American students, in particular, acquire the attitudes and behaviors that would support their success in a middle-class White world while maintaining pride in their own cultural identity (Delpit, 1992a). During class changes and before and after school, Juanita, Gloria, and Marian patrolled their corridor like mother hens. They checked up on students, passed out advice and hugs, and sternly corrected inappropriate behavior. They described how they talked to students about "what is expected and how they can make things better for themselves". Their knowledge of students was clearly based on personal connections. Notes from an observation of Marian's class in May (20 students, 6 White, 14 Black):

> To a student who has come up to her desk at the beginning of class Marian asks, "What is it baby? What is it sugar?" She puts her arm around him. He asks for a pen. She admonishes, "Now baby, you have those nice cloths on and don't even have a pen?" He looks down embarrassed; she hands him a pen from her desk drawer, grins. . . . The students do work sheets throughout the class. Meanwhile, Marian interacts with them individually. About half of her interactions involve behavior reprimands: "Slide over and get to work, Rachel"; questions and comments about a personal problem: "Did you talk that problem over with your father, Mandy?"; or an academic problem in another class. After class she scolds a Black female she calls "Wilson" who is repeating the class. Marian says sternly, "Wilson, you're supposed to be a leader, a model for others. I count on you to be a leader and look at the way you act. You have to set an example for these seventh graders. This is how eighth graders act."

Collaboration and the Problem of Forging Shared Meanings

Team meetings at Franklin provided a context to initiate other teachers into the Othermothers' framework. Because othermothering was so central to their day-to-day work and because there were clear differences among teachers on the two teams regarding social support, the dialogue around this issue is an illustration of the processes of collaboration and change in the two teams.

At the outset there was wide variation within the focus teams on the meaning of social support. The principal had chosen Elizabeth as the leader of the Stars team in part because she was a committed student mentor. At the beginning of the year, Elizabeth set this tone for the team and drew in Erline and even Belinda, who seemed to have given up on students. In team meetings, she suggested teachers make home visits, buy things for needy students, try to understand their school and family problems, and make them feel good about school. Heidi and Mark tried to accomplish this last goal by rewarding students for small accomplishments. In my observations, they valued improved behavior over academics. Meanwhile, Jonetta, the eighth-grade counselor, pointed to these kinds of goals as evidence of low expectations for African American students. She was more concerned with racism and discrimination against African American students within the school than with either nurturing or improving social relations in ways she saw as patronizing. Although she agreed with giving students material and emotional support, Jonetta was first an advocate. She tended to see behavior issues as products of African American student resistance to racism.

Although I observed one open, heated debate over these issues, from my observations and interviews, Stars teachers engaged in little collective reflection on their different interpretations of social support. The team meetings I observed were generally scattered and inconclusive; occasionally teachers sniped at each other but there was little engagement of the issues. Elizabeth, as team leader, primarily moved the agenda and made administrative announcements. The teachers reported that their unresolved conflicts spilled over into conferences with students and parents, and some felt the team meetings were a waste of time. Heidi expressed this problem in a November interview, in which she said that the team sometimes called the kids into a meeting, but this didn't always work because different teachers had different experiences with the kids, and their differences were expressed in the meeting. According to her, there were a lot of "inconsistencies" in the team, but they "[weren't] getting anywhere on that." Belinda and Erline lacked strong commitment to the team at the outset, and by January, the Stars had become quasi-inoperative due to teacher turnover and lack of leadership. Beyond planning a few student activities and administrative matters, their work as a collective seemed to be suspended.

In contrast, differences among Eagles teachers were played out during the year in discussions related to individual students. Adele and Marissa (both White) were shocked by what they perceived to be serious cultural, intellectual, and social deficits in Franklin's low-income "at-risk" students. From the beginning, Marissa (a counselor) touted her professional credentials and knowledge about youth and unabashedly offered deficit analyses, as in this interview: "These type of students have to have some help. For a school like this, with kids who come from a lower socioeconomic base who are culturally deprived, kids who are going to be abused, kids whose parents need help as much as they do. These kids need counseling." Marissa's posture as an expert was an affront to Juanita, Gloria, and Marian, who had been functioning as informal counselors for years and felt they knew their students much better than a new, young White counselor could. This conflict was an undercurrent in nearly every meeting Marissa attended. Meanwhile, initially Adele embraced the forms of support provided by the Othermothers and began calling parents on her own. Chris was more interested in curricular issues than in social relations and was only peripherally involved in the activities and debates that surrounded this topic.

The Eagles agendas appeared to offer an opportunity to sort out some of these disagreements. In addition to the usual team activities and administrative details, in meetings I observed, they dealt with more substantive topics such as: reports from educational workshops, creating a parent network, disputes with the administration over limits on the teams' decisionmaking, and a debate over a discipline policy that excluded students from extracurricular activities. Different points of view also surfaced in discussions about individual students.

Early on, there were potentially fruitful exchanges about how to support students. Juanita, Gloria, and Marian were coaches in these meetings, sharing their experiences and knowledge to enculturate the other teachers. Gloria usually acted as a facilitator to help orient the new teachers. These exchanges are illustrated by excerpts of an October meeting in which Juanita tried to help Adele see a situation through a student's eyes, examining the roots of behavior rather than simply adopting a technical solution to manage it. Juanita identified school-related factors as well as family problems and proposed a program of action:

[Adele brings up the problems she is having with a student, Andre.]

Adele: I need help, y'all.
Gloria: We need to work together on this problem and try to help Miss Strong [Adele] out. [Adele relates that the student continues to disrupt her class and she can't stop him.]
Gloria: Maybe you should set up a conference with him and his mother.

Adele: We already did that, but it didn't do any good. The way he
           talked to his mother was just impossible. I've tried isolating
           him and ignoring him, but nothing works. [Marissa suggests
           using techniques of rewarding positive behavior and ignor-
           ing negative behavior that she learned in a behavior
           modification class. Others share their approaches with Andre.
           Adele is doubtful any of this will work with this student
           who "is really bad."]

Juanita: (interrupts) I want to share with you some information about
           Andre. I've talked with him. He feels that he's had a raw
           deal. We need to understand why he's acting the way he's
           acting. (To Adele) We need to have high expectations for him
           if he's going to change. . . . He has a stepparent who he doesn't
           get along with, and he was kept back a year and that's led
           to a lot of frustration. He's a smart boy. He could do well.
           [She goes on to describe his previous school and family cir-
           cumstances and how smart he is.] (To Adele again) We need
           to build him up, not tear him down. Support him and his
           self-confidence and self-esteem. [She describes ways she pro-
           motes his leadership in her class.]

Adele: I'll try that."

Despite promising interactions of this sort, divisions within the
team gradually widened. Instead of the new collaborative working relationship promoting dialogue and fresh perspectives, the gaps between
Marissa and Adele, on the one hand, and the Othermothers, on the
other, seemed to grow, and their oppositions hardened. A striking thing
at the meetings was the lack of communication between Marissa and
her colleagues. Her eagerness to offer advice and to interject professional counseling approaches in situations the teachers were accustomed
to dealing with in their own ways became a major source of contention.
This dynamic was demonstrated in a November team meeting:

First topic is students coming to class late. The teachers complain about the disruptions. Marissa says, "Why don't you just
go right on?"
     Several teachers roll their eyes. "We can't just go on," etc. . . .
     Marissa reports on a job fair being planned by the guidance
department. The proposal is greeted with little response. A few
minutes later, Marissa enthusiastically (and at length) describes
a peer facilitating program she wants to initiate. Again she is met
with icy silence. . . .

Marian reports on Claude who was acting out because he was ashamed that he had only one set of clothes and second-hand shoes that did not fit. She took him to K-Mart and got him new clothes and shoes, "Now he has a whole new attitude."

Adele offers, "Somehow we need to chip in together and see if we can't find him a coat. I have some old coats at home that I could bring in."

Marian cuts Adele off, "We'll get him a *new* coat" [her emphasis].

Perhaps the emerging rift in the team, exemplified in the above exchange, was in part because Marissa and Adele failed to perceive that they imposed their own meanings on situations with which they had little real experience. For example, in not recognizing the significance of buying Claude *new* clothes, Adele proposed to repeat the insult that he had clearly resisted and that the African American teachers were attempting to reverse. The racial overtones of White charity to an African American youth who was fighting to retrieve his dignity and the tone of Marian's rejoinder to this affront were the unspoken subtext of this exchange. Marissa's and, increasingly, Adele's disregard for the wisdom of the African American teachers provoked them to withhold the coaching witnessed in previous meetings and to objectively exclude Marissa and Adele from the conversation. Marian's glances at Gloria and Juanita made it clear that the "we" at the end of the conversation was the African Americans as distinct from the team as a whole.

This estrangement was exemplified by a subsequent meeting in which Marissa failed to investigate work the experienced teachers were already doing and tried to impose her professional authority in an area where the Othermothers were actually the experts:

Marissa: We need to think about what kids need.
Marian: We know what to do because we work with them in MCP. We're already doing it. . . .
Marissa: I have an idea. We should all take one of the bus routes the kids go on so we can see where they live. [Again, the others look blankly at her.]
Juanita: Oh, we do that anyway. . . . [Marissa complains that she doesn't know what's going on.]
Marissa: I'm not informed. MCP? I don't know anything about MCP. What's MCP? I should be included if it involves the counselors.

Juanita: It was in the bulletin. Don't you get the announcements?

[Marissa requests that they set up a special communication so she can be kept abreast of the teachers' activities. The others ignore her.]

The African American teachers seemed to resent what they perceived as the racism of an arrogant "White counselor who doesn't know what's going on but thinks she's an expert" (their words). Meanwhile, Marissa complained privately that "the Black teachers don't tell me what's going on. The teachers are not recognizing the expertise that the counselors have." This conflict between othermothering and Marissa's professional social work orientation, with its racial subtext and issues of power, recurred in other Eagles meetings I attended and was a significant impediment to emergent dialogue.

Racial Divisions and the Absence of Trust

Disagreements about school policies and student problems were rooted in conflicting ideologies, different life experiences, and racial antagonisms among teachers expected to collaborate on improving the education of a primarily African American student body. Distances were real and profound and resulted in very different constructions of African American student identities. The African American teachers' othermothering was rooted in shared cultural knowledge, experience, values, and their connectedness to the larger African American community that included their students. They supported African American culturally-centered activities. On the other hand, Marissa's perspective was that of an outsider whose negative cultural models of African Americans shaped her interpretations of student behaviors. Furthermore, she had the leverage of a White professional with the authority to broker social services for low-income, African American families. The tension in this dynamic was palpable.

Different Constructions of African American Student Identities

The tension in the Eagles team was dramatized by responses to a 14-year-old African American student who became pregnant. She and the future father, also an African American student in the Eagles team, decided to keep the baby. The young man ran away from home, and, after a frantic search, his mother was relieved to learn he was living with the young woman, albeit in an abandoned building. The Othermothers worked with the students and their families throughout this ordeal. In the midst of negotiations to get the young people to return to school, Marissa had a talk with the young man's mother. Differing interpretations of events and teachers' private judgments of each other revealed the underlying racial tensions in the team. Notes from my interview with Marissa:

> She attributes racial disparities to students' home life and the way they are being raised. She gives the example of a 14-year-old boy [Carlton] who ran away from home and is living with his pregnant girlfriend. "The mother thought it was okay as long as she knew where he was. I was shocked that the Black teachers backed her up. They said because I'm White I don't understand the situation." Marissa seems very resentful about this because she's the school counselor.

Adele related that she didn't get along with some of the African Americans on her team: "I'm very frustrated with the team. I came from a very wealthy district in Ohio and a lot of teachers [on the Eagles] don't trust me because of that. They think I don't know how to relate to these kinds of kids, but I do." She said they told her that she did not understand some of the situations, like the one with Carlton, because she is White. But she was shocked that the student would move out and live with his girlfriend and that the teachers went along with it. She shared with me her own views of African American teenage pregnancy:

Adele: It's a conscious decision they make to get pregnant. They pick the father. . . because they want something that belongs to them. We're dealing with a culture here. They love babies. But then, when they get to be 2 years old the problems start. And that's when you get abused kids. . . . Teenage pregnancy is a cultural thing. It's different for White kids. It's okay and it's accepted in their culture.

On their part, the African American teachers believed that Adele did not understand the student, and privately they called Marissa "an obstruction" to their relations with the family. One said:

> The counselor, she has absolutely no idea what she's doing. This situation with Carlton is an example. His mother said he ran away to stay with Latoya who is having his baby. They're staying in an abandoned building with no windows. His mother is very worried about him, but at least she knows where he is.

> She's relieved about that. She knows where he is and he hasn't done anything crazy. . . . But the White counselor gave the mother a lecture and told her she had to tell him to come home, that he couldn't live like that. Gave her a lecture! They decided to give it up [the baby] and I know that's weighing on all of them.

Later the families decided to raise the baby together. When it was born, Juanita, Marian, and Gloria were there with gifts, congratulations, and support for the families and the young parents. While the others continued to criticize, the Othermothers took a different tack, using the students' decision to keep the baby as a basis to urge the young parents to stay in school and "make something of themselves."

As the year wore on, race and racism were the subtext underlying many team disagreements. These topics never surfaced in team conversations, although privately, the African American and White teachers criticized each other. In team meetings, the teachers tolerated each other but maintained their distance, avoiding controversial issues. There was an essential lack of trust that precluded any serious dialogue about differences. Their dissolving commitment to each other was also reflected in the sporadic attendance of Adele, Marissa, and even Chris.

Although specific incidents brought it to the surface, the lack of trust was rooted in fundamental differences: some White teachers' blatant stereotypes of African Americans and African American teachers' charges of White domination at Franklin. Adele made no secret of her derogatory judgments of African American students and the deficiencies of their families: "They're developmentally delayed, speech delayed . . . they have no background. . . . These parents just don't know any of these things. They need life skills. The kids are left alone. They get pregnant at an early age." In an interview, Marissa was equally blunt:

> Teachers have too many social expectations for these kids. You can't expect such good behavior out of these kids. The statistics back it up. You know as well as I do, if a Black person and a White person were walking through an alley at night, you'd fear the Black person more. They just commit more crimes. . . . Black kids are getting too many breaks. Everything is done for them. Maybe we've made it too hard for them to drop out. School just isn't the place for some kids.

On the other hand, Juanita, Marian, and Gloria believed African American teachers and students were marginalized at Franklin, despite being a numerical majority. Juanita said, "They [Black students] don't know about their own history. They've never even heard of Harriet Tubman or Sojourner Truth. Black students are in this school but they aren't a part of it." The Othermothers also contended that the administration was favoring White teachers and had been trying to get rid of Black teachers. They also said White teachers were extremely defensive because African Americans were in the majority.

There were some of the same differences in the Stars team. As with the seventh-grade team, there was virtually no substantive dialogue about diametrically opposed views about the central problem of African American students' educational experiences at Franklin. Jonetta believed racism was pervasive at Franklin. "There's discrimination based on socioeconomic status and on race, definitely. A lot of teachers say, if the parents don't seem to care, why should we? That's the attitude." Jonetta criticized the disconnection of Franklin's educational program from African American students' lives:

> The curriculum precludes Black kids' experiences. The history books, for example, exclude the positive contributions of Blacks. For Black students, school is not interwoven into their life. They see their parents work their whole life, but they don't get ahead. Their life experience suggests that school doesn't do any good. . . . We need a program that makes [Black] kids feel their self-worth from kindergarten on. It has to be in the curriculum, and we have to get teachers to implement it.

Meanwhile, Heidi described the students as "street kids. They live in the slums, in projects. Their parents aren't there. The kids are on their own. The only stability that they have is in school." Her interactions with African American students were patronizing. Those she did not group with the "tough inner-city kids who won't do anything [academically]," she referred to as "just so sweet." In contrast, Katrina described the straightforward approach she took to cultivate the same students' commitment to school:

> I talk to them about negativity and positivity. I divide them in groups and tell them "You can learn from your colleagues." I tell them about college. I'm very open with them. I tell them I'm working on my certification. I tell them about my tests. . . . I tell them they're young adults and that's the way I treat them. This class is very sincere and if I want them to do something they try to do it. I work with them on discipline. I told them our time is very valuable. There is not enough time for fooling around.

In addition to the Stars' organizational difficulties, Jonetta claimed there was a lack of trust. In January she said the teams were not taking on "the hard issues":

> They're just going along with the program. The teams would have to be more like a family, like your sister or brother, where you can tell them exactly what you think, yell, scream, criticize, and you'll still be accepted. There's not that level of trust on the teams, and that's one reason they don't deal with really serious issues.

In my observations, when Jonetta or Juanita interjected the topic of race into their team's discussions, they were met with a wall of silence. In one team meeting, Juanita offered her colleagues a book that critiqued Eurocentric perspectives of U.S. history. There was no discussion, only nervous glances, and she did not push it further. These issues seemed to be thrown out, like a challenge, without any expectation or realization of discussion. Any allusion to racism seemed outside the bounds of approved discourse. Jonetta's unwillingness to mince words or moderate her views clashed sharply with these norms for muting racial issues, thus ostracizing her from the group. Moreover, the Stars team was too irregular to sustain serious examination of any topic, had they been so inclined. By February Jonetta had stopped attending eighth-grade team meetings because, she said: "There's no real Black/White dialogue. It doesn't happen in the teams. They mainly talk about behavior. It gets old after a while so I don't even go anymore."

The Centrality of Beliefs and Values in Educational Change

The experience of these teams adds another dimension to discussion in the literature about the importance of values consensus in teacher collaboration (Conley, 1993; Sarason, 1982; Sirotnik, 1987). Even though the teachers had the organizational arrangements, time, and authorization to collaborate, their starting points were so different that it was extremely difficult to develop common meanings. It would be naive, at best, to assume that collaborative arrangements would necessarily provoke dialogue across ideological and cultural chasms or that deep-seated mistrust reflective of the racial polarization and disempowerment of African Americans in U.S. society would be changed through dialogue alone. Perhaps the differences between Marissa and her African American colleagues on the Eagles and between Heidi, Jonetta, and Katrina on the Stars represent extremes. For example, Adele's relationship with African American teachers was initially more open and then changed. Yet these divisions are a reminder of the influence cultural and social contexts have on dialogue and change.

Furthermore, many of the teachers did not have the inclination for a dialogue. For the Othermothers, it did not seem necessary. Their activity was organized through an underlying informal, effective network through which, for example, they created Dignity and worked with students Carlton and Latoya. Collaboration and teacher empowerment simply afforded their own informal collaborative a wider field of action to pursue its agenda. Their experience suggests that even dramatic organizational restructuring may have little impact on deep, informal organizational patterns formed around shared cultural experiences and beliefs.

Jonetta was too pessimistic about some of her colleagues to consider dialogue worthwhile: "We need to clean house. We need to get a building of people who will be beneficial to kids, who are positive about these kids." Her outspokenness also isolated her. At the same time, Marissa declined to pursue a relationship with the Othermothers, whose views did not seem to alter her professional judgments. A cycle of insult, rejection, and exclusivity had been initiated. Facilitating a dialogue among these disparate and conflicting voices required leadership that neither Gloria nor Elizabeth, the team leaders, could provide. As the schism in the team widened, Gloria seemed to become increasingly passive as team leader. The experience of these teams challenges assumptions about the efficacy of teacher dialogue in contexts in which there are not only deep divisions, but some educators see no evidence that their colleagues are committed to educating African American and other marginalized students.

Unrealized Possibilities for Reflection on Teaching and Learning

Both the problems and the possibilities of teaching at Franklin were reflected in the focus teams. In each team there were teachers who exemplified the need to reexamine teaching and learning and others who demonstrated the possibility of meaningful learning communities. The teams and other forms of collaboration presented an opportunity for teachers to critically examine education at Franklin, to learn from each other, and to entertain alternative ways of teaching. In this section, I examine the difficulties teachers found in making use of this opportunity as well.

The Need to Transform Curriculum

At the beginning of the year, there were some preliminary indications that the Eagles teachers might work together on new directions in teaching and learning. The team had at least one seminar, led by the principal, on learning styles and several teachers attended workshops related to curriculum and pedagogy. They developed three "teaching across the curriculum" units with the SRM class at the center, reflecting initial steps toward interdisciplinary work. (The Stars were unable to create even one interdisciplinary unit.) Meanwhile, the rhetoric of "higher-order thinking" was prevalent, and Juanita and Chris both began developing curricular activities organized around problem solving. They felt these were marginally successful, although Juanita was generally frustrated that she "couldn't get students to think."

However, in my observations of both teams, dispirited teaching was the norm. Notes from a Stars teacher's class in December are representative (28 students, 24 Black, 4 White, 21 males, 7 females):

> The same posters and cut-outs that were on the bulletin boards in September are still up. A few are peeling off. A bulletin board that said "Reach for the Stars" has lost some of its letters, and some of the student pictures have fallen down. In one corner is a series of posters of Black scientists; two are askew.
>
> Without greeting students the teacher orders, "Sit down and take out paper." The objective (written on the board, as in all classes) is "to learn about layers of the earth and the effect of seismic waves."
>
> Without introduction, she begins a spelling test of 50 science terms: "Mountain, lithosphere, globe, relief. . . . " Two males—one White, one Black—come in about a minute late.
>
> The teacher barks, "Sign those tardy slips." Neither student begins the test. The White student has taken his seat in the back of the room and puts his head on the desk. She says nothing to them as she goes on with the list of words.
>
> After the test . . . the teacher reads notes on seismic activity: "Take these down, every word. Now I want you to underline some of the phrases. Those are the ones that'll be on my test." One student gets up to get his notebook, but she tells him to sit down. As he has nothing to write on, he doodles on his desk. This goes on for the 20 minute remainder of the period. . . . When the class is over they burst out of the room.

One would never guess from this class that the topic (seismic activity) was actually very timely. An earthquake had been predicted for the state the previous week. There were quake drills, and some students stayed home from school, but no connection was made in class between the recent events and the material in the text. The pattern observed here of mechanical, watered-down teaching with little apparent relevance for students was quite common, as were teachers' disrespect for students and student apathy and resistance. Even with the rich personal relationships Marian and her colleagues on the Eagles had with students, their students also frequently appeared bored and unchallenged and, predictably, countered the monotony with disruptive behavior or inattention. In turn, in too many instances, aggravated teachers exploded in blatant degradation of their students. This spiral of confrontation is illustrated by an African American focus team teacher's frustration with her inattentive class:

> The teacher says to the whole class, "I'm sick of it, of this snickering. I'm going to write you up. . . . (To a Black girl) Sit still or I'll write your tail up too. (To me in the middle of the class) See what I was talking about. This is just what I was telling the lady in the meeting. This room has so many failures. You don't know how to sit and be taught. You'll never have it."

The repetitive and unchallenging curriculum that contributed to this destructive spiral was itself partially a product of teachers' low assessment of student potential. Low academic expectations were common in the two teams. Adele said she had had to "lower [her] expectations" since she came to Franklin and couldn't do the activities she had planned because students "didn't have the background." Heidi's negative assessment of her students, particularly African American males, was reflected in her interactions with them, as in this "regular" class (16 students, 13 Black, 3 White, 13 males, 3 females):

> Heidi says to the class in a singsong voice, "If we understand what our problem is, and why we always have so much trouble on tests, it will help us. . . . If you don't come in here and be quiet and listen to me and do your work you will not pass." While they are filling in a worksheet, she comes over to the researchers and whispers and gestures. "Warren Cross. This is his third time in the eighth grade. He's almost 17. He will fail the state test again. Cooper Hale. He's just back from suspension. He's rebellious to authority. Sometimes he can have a filthy mouth. But sometimes he's wonderful. It's the inner city type outlook. . . . Tremaine is supposed to be in resource. He's a precious child, so cute."

This class spent 8 weeks reading aloud a 200-page novel because Heidi was convinced the students could not or would not read it on their own. This was also a class she said was incapable of creating analogies, doing independent projects, or working cooperatively—activities she saved for her one honors class. The problem of low intellectual expectations crossed racial lines. Some African American teachers, especially Erline and Belinda, and even the Othermothers, were pessimistic about students' potential at times. Frequently, teaching seemed secondary to the latter's work with students outside the classroom.

Both Marian and Gloria relied heavily on worksheets and other forms of repetitive individual seatwork; Juanita was more interested in experimenting with curriculum. She tried to design lessons that would encourage analytical thinking and used cooperative learning and peer teaching in her classes, but the results often failed to meet her expectations. As the year progressed, even her students became more unruly, seemingly reflecting a dynamic of boredom, confrontation, and student resistance that undermined academic work. In her frustration, Juanita repeatedly commented that she needed help, and said everybody in the team did also.

The Potential of Alternative Educational Models

The Eagles presented an interesting paradox. They invested little in examining curriculum and instruction, yet at least Chris, Juanita, and Gloria were convinced of the need for change, and Juanita and Gloria expressed frustration at not knowing "how to change." Teachers were met with unresponsive and resistant students who had endured too many classes of the sort described above, and the school failure and academic disengagement of so many students made the need for change unmistakable. Although most teachers readily said they lacked the knowledge of how to reach students and engage them in serious intellectual work, there were some beginning steps toward rethinking curriculum and instruction. Several teachers, sponsored by the restructuring project, attended national conferences and workshops on multicultural education, multiple learning styles, and middle school reform. Some also visited nearby schools affiliated with the Coalition of Essential Schools and were introduced to the Coalition's framework. Among Franklin teachers, the desire "to do something different" was palpable. Moreover, there were innovative teachers on the focus teams (Chris and Katrina) whose own practice might have been the seeds of more far-ranging reforms in teaching.

Both the problems and possibilities are illustrated by a class and an afterschool activity led by Juanita. The class typified disengaging and repetitive classroom activities, concentration on controlling students, and student resistance (24 students, 22 Black, 2 White, 12 females, 12 males):

> They are working on defining a topic sentence. Juanita asks, "What's a topic sentence, David?" He doesn't answer. Juanita says, "The main idea of a paragraph. What's a topic sentence, Derrick?" She calls on different people to give the definition and then repeats it. This goes on for almost 15 minutes interrupted by constant reprimands to students who are talking or fooling around. They read a paragraph on insulation, another on dolphins, a third on the Taj Mahal, picking out topic sentences. At any one time only about half, at best, are paying attention. There are constant interruptions from students asking for a pass, sharpening their pencils, walking around the room, etc. Juanita teaches the entire period from the open doorway so she can keep an eye on the hall. When someone gives the wrong answer she asks why but then supplies the answer. She frequently stops in mid-sentence to talk to a student in the hall or to reprimand a student in the class. At each interruption students begin talking with each other, turning around in their seats, running to the windows, etc. . . . Three girls seize the opportunity to pull their desks into a circle and one starts to apply nail polish. About five boys are literally running around the room. . . . After order has been restored, half-way through a student's explanation of his answer to a question in the text, Juanita drowns him out with reprimands to another boy. The student gives up in evident disgust and lays his head on his desk. . . . After class Juanita comments, "I don't know what's happening with these kids. They'll watch movies or a video but they won't read, or write or do any other kind of work. There has to be a different way and I wish somebody would tell me what it is."

As if in response to her own request, after school she is working with a group of 10 students (2 White, 8 Black) on a reading of an African American history play. From my field notes:

> They are reading through the parts with feeling and convincing gestures, completely engrossed. There are no "behavior problems" or interruptions here although I recognize about six of the worst offenders from the previous class. The play is sophisticated and includes very challenging vocabulary and ideas. The section they're working on is about slave rebellions.

The students are helping each other, correcting each others' mistakes. One student, Maya, is leaning over the shoulder of a student who was recently placed in special education. He's reading the lead part quite effectively; occasionally Maya helps him with a word. Periodically, they interrupt to ask Juanita what something means—"What is chattel?" And she occasionally interjects a bit of historical information.

At one point, they break into a discussion about the role of "house Negroes" during slavery. Maya says, "That's just like [a local Black political figure]."

Another student asks, "Why you say that?" There's a discussion of what motivates collaborators of this sort.

Juanita also points out that some Whites supported runaway slaves and a Black student grins and puts his arm around one of the two White students joking, "You're okay, Robert."

This was one of the most intellectually engaged and thoughtful learning experiences I observed at Franklin, and it contrasted dramatically with the previous class. Some of the most disruptive students in the previous class were the intellectual leaders here. It was a project they chose to participate in, with meaningful and challenging content and a valued purpose—they would perform the play for a school assembly in February. Although this sort of activity was rarely a part of the ongoing curriculum, it demonstrated Juanita's ability to create meaningful educational experiences in a humane and respectful context.[1]

A second example was Chris who brought her hands-on elementary school experience and constructivist approach to her junior high students. When she assigned Maya Angelou's *I Know Why the Caged Bird Sings*, Chris asked students to bring in family reminiscences and objects from the Depression. Through this project they made personal connections with the novel and narrated their own family stories, crossing boundaries of race to trade experiences. In her computer lab, I observed students, who seemed completely bored in other classes, so engrossed that they had to be pried away from the computers when the bell rang.

Despite the potential the team created for Chris to share her knowledge or for teachers to consider how to make classes more like successful afterschool activities, very little seemed to be shared other than joint planning with the SRM units. When Chris reported on the Maya Angelou project in a team meeting, everyone was interested and excited, but there were no questions about how she did it, what else she had done, or how they might build on their own students' experiences. I infer from this and other examples that models of curriculum and instruction were viewed more as a case of personal style than sources of pedagogical knowledge. All in all, there seemed to be little talk about teaching and learning in the Eagles team. This was surprising, given Chris's innovative stance and the fact that Juanita was on the district multicultural curriculum committee. Katrina's teaching was also fresh and challenging, but she arrived at mid-year, too late to invigorate other Stars teachers, even if they had been receptive.

Teachers said conversations about teaching and curriculum occurred informally between individual teachers, much as they had before the teams, and were not substantially broadened as a result of teams. When Chris wrote a large grant proposal for an expanded language arts computer lab, it was done with another teacher outside the team and with little input from her team colleagues who described it, again, as "Chris' project." As with student social support, informal networks among like-minded teachers superseded formal, collaborative structures.

Why Curriculum Was Not on the Agenda

Although the restructuring project emphasized "nurturing at-risk students," its goals also included changes in curriculum and instruction. Furthermore, flexible schedules were meant to encourage curricular reforms such as cross disciplinary teaching, in-depth lessons, and small and large group work. Still, the teams gravitated almost exclusively toward personal support and social relations. When asked what was being accomplished through restructuring, as at Gates, the usual response was something like, "the kids like school more," or that teachers were able to respond to social needs.

One plausible explanation for this direction is that providing social support was what some teachers on both teams were most comfortable with—in terms of their knowledge and their ideological dispositions—especially given the lack of self-critical dialogue. As Elizabeth said, "This is what we want to do." Mentoring and social support were the forte of the Othermothers. Even for teachers like Adele and Heidi, strengthening personal support and students' sense of belonging were more feasible than struggling with how to educate youth whom they believed to be so flawed and troubled as to be virtually ineducable. Some teachers may have created a more caring and personalized climate, but the intellectual development of African American students was neglected. In turn, teachers' limited effectiveness in the classroom fueled their pessimism about students' capabilities and reinforced deficit models.

Another possible explanation is, regardless of restructuring rhetoric, teachers had little sense of efficacy regarding curriculum. I came to see this as both real and imagined. It was real in the sense that teachers were expected to follow district curriculum guidelines, select from district book lists, and use required texts, and there was no consistent support for curriculum development.[2] But there were also individuals who went around and beyond the prescribed curriculum. And a curriculum audit conducted by outside evaluators in 1991 found such a plethora of unaligned curriculum guides that there was little uniformity across grade levels, schools, and the district. The tightest control was in the eighth grade, where the State Competency Test drove the curriculum. But even some eighth-grade teachers found ways to do what they thought best and still prepare for the state test. (Samuel, a teacher I describe in chapter 9, was an example.) Few teachers, including well-intentioned ones in this chapter, had tested the limits. Those who did, like Chris, were able to go in their own directions, especially since the principal did not object. My guess is that the most powerful limitation was a sense of powerlessness stemming from the district's history of capricious authoritarianism and the instability of teacher assignments in the past. There was a continued, though perceptibly fading, sense of vulnerability.

Finally, and perhaps most significant, despite many new opportunities for teachers' professional development, there was no powerful curricular vision driving the reforms. Although outside consultants talked about a paradigm shift in teaching and learning, the restructuring project did not concentrate leadership on the concrete meaning of this. Teachers on both teams said repeatedly they knew change was necessary but had no real sense of alternatives.

The Failure to Address Tracking

Academic tracking was also not a part of the discussion about educational change. On the surface, tracking did not seem to be much of an issue at Franklin. Only math and English were tracked, and a small percentage of students was assigned to honors and advanced classes. Compared with Gates, where every core subject teacher had two or three honors classes out of five, at Franklin five teachers of math and English had one and seven had two honors classes. Only eight students took advanced algebra, compared with two full classes at Gates, and there were fewer academic electives. Nonetheless, tracking was a sensitive issue. A number of teachers, including Juanita and Chris on the Eagles, were opposed to it on several counts. They believed: (a) "honors methods" were equally appropriate with regular students, (b) low-achieving students benefited from working with high-achieving students, and (c) honors students could also learn from working with regular students. In the second year of restructuring, a teacher, who had since retired, petitioned the central administration to experiment with untracking at Franklin. He had used what he (and several others, including Juanita) saw as the prerogative of teams to accelerate regular classes and to transfer regular students into honors classes. There was quite a political furor surrounding this petition. A district administrator came to Franklin to meet with the teachers involved and the principal, rejected their petition unequivocally, and warned them not to pursue this issue further. Juanita and the teacher who initiated the untracking were described by some central administrators as radicals and troublemakers for opening a Pandora's box of potentially perilous political consequences for the district.[3] Indeed, there were rumors that this incident was why Juanita had been replaced as a team leader in 1989–90. Regardless of its veracity, the rumor indicated an atmosphere of intimidation and fear of reprisal if one overstepped sacrosanct boundaries. With this recent history, talk of abandoning or revising tracking was out of the question. To my knowledge it was not discussed in team meetings, nor were teams used as a means of transferring students between tracks.

Differences between regular and honors classes varied. In some instances there was virtually no difference; in others, honors classes simply did more work with a few more opportunities for creativity; and in others the curriculum differed substantially. However, honors classes did not have the significance they had at Gates, where tracking was more salient. At Franklin, honors classes were not as dramatically linked with race, although the ones I observed had a disproportionate percentage of Whites, and honors classes did not shape the culture of the school. Nevertheless, there was a disparity in teachers' expectations for student performance in the two tracks, and this had important consequences for students.

This disparity was open and taken-for-granted and reflected assumptions about intellect and behavior of "regular" students. In interviews, Heidi, Mark, Erline, and Belinda, on the Stars, and Adele on the Eagles said regular-track students were less capable, needed more drill and practice, and were less able to manage work that required critical thinking or creativity. Heidi's comparison of honors and regular track students was representative:

The honors kids can handle the freedom for individual projects. But the regular kids are not mature enough for unstructured activities. They're the type that have to have the teacher bearing down on them all of the time. Face it, honors kids are smarter. . . . Of course, the honors kids like to talk too, but they can talk and get their work done. But the regular kids can only do one thing at a time, which is why talking is so bad for them.

Juanita and Chris, on the Eagles, and Katrina, on the Stars, had a different perspective. Juanita periodically attempted what she saw as challenging analytical and problem-solving activities with all her classes regardless of academic track. Although she complained that these often did not succeed with her regular classes, she persisted in the belief that tracking unfairly labeled students. Chris taught the untracked Study and Research Methods. She said she was surprised to find many of the regular students to be "better with analytical thinking and reasoning than the honors students," who were mainly good at "regurgitation." Katrina did not consider track assignments to be important; she expected all students to be serious and to "aim high."

As with curriculum, I found no evidence of team discussions about this significant issue during the year. In a couple instances, tracking came up in meetings as an obstacle to scheduling groups of students for common activities, but teachers said, "Well, we can't do anything about that [tracking]." The silence surrounding tracking, although perhaps indicating that some teachers did not realize alternatives existed, also indicated the power of district norms and sanctions to limit teacher agency. The reality that tracking was a taboo issue for teams meant that lowered expectations for regular students went unquestioned and unchallenged, despite a rich mix of beliefs and practices.

Summary

The classes of most focus team teachers were marked by uninspired teaching and disengaged students. Although a number of the teachers said repeatedly that they needed help to change both curriculum and instruction, this was not part of the team agendas. The teams also did not make use of examples of intellectually engaging and creative teaching within their ranks as a basis for reflection on teaching and learning. Although there were several possible explanations, this was certainly symptomatic of the absence of a powerful curricular vision at the center of restructuring. But the fact that teams did not examine tracking also indicated that teachers' opportunities to redesign educational practice were bounded by a district status quo that preserved the privileges of upper middle class, primarily White, honors track students.

Teacher Frustration and Demoralization

Paradoxically, along with the emphasis on mentoring students and activities such as Dignity, both teams were increasingly preoccupied with controlling students. By spring, student behavior seemed to be the number one issue. As early as December, Heidi said that Stars teachers were becoming preoccupied with behavior problems. The Eagles followed the same pattern, although to a lesser extent. A few days before Christmas, Adele walked out of her class and called security because, she said, "the kids went wild." She resigned later, saying "It's just too much stress. It's too hard to teach kids like this. And I love teaching." By February most of the teachers were complaining about student behavior. There were some signs of greater disorder in the building, but the general trend was simply more teachers shouting at their classes in an effort to restore order, more students wandering the halls without passes, and more unruly classes. In May, the administration told all the faculty to teach from their open doorways so they could patrol the halls.

The Issue of Discipline

How serious were these problems? I did not know of any instances of students threatening teachers, although teachers were observed to verbally threaten students regularly. (At the beginning of the year Adele said she received a phoned death threat, but this seemed to be a prank.) Rather there was a general climate in some teachers' classes of confrontation and resistance. In a few instances, teachers simply could not relate to Franklin students, and the students tested them to the limit. This seemed to be the case with Adele and possibly with Belinda, who took a medical leave. In most cases, however, there was a spiral of teacher negativity, student boredom and resistance, and hostility on both sides (McDermott, 1974) that led to verbal confrontations and more subterranean forms of student opposition, of which Juanita's class (described above) was an example. Despite two weapons (knives) found in student lockers, and one or two fights, there did not seem to be serious issues of violence or violent threats. Rather, some teachers simply had lost control of their classes and the commotion seemed to seep through the school. As students carried their challenges to one teacher into another class, I observed that after a while, even the most interested students stopped paying attention. Perhaps this phenomenon was merely cyclical (classroom observations from 2 previous years tend to confirm that assessment), but, in any case, frustration levels were high and the problems immediate, so that teachers could not look beyond them to probe the roots of disruptive behavior. There was more derogatory talk about students in team meetings, hallways, and lounges, even by the Othermothers. In April, even though she continued to mentor students, Marian said, "These kids are so bad, I don't know how I'm going to get through the year."

The weapons incidents generated pressure from the central office to "crack down on behavior" (personal communication from school administrators), and teams were a convenient arena for doing this because teachers had been given more direct authority over discipline. Although suspensions were down, as at Gates, new forms of discipline took their place. The Stars isolated malefactors within the classroom and did not allow them to communicate with other students. The Eagles excluded students from team social events. They also initiated many parent conferences to address discipline issues. As student behavior became a central issue, the teams spent more of their time dealing with it.

This was an interesting case in which teacher empowerment led to increased frustration as teachers became saddled with responsibilities that in the past had been the province of administrators. They had new responsibilities, but no new framework for addressing them. By February, the exasperation of teachers and administrators was palpable. Everybody on the two teams had a story to tell. Teachers stopped me in the hall to talk, and several who at first said they had no time, searched me out to say, "I'll make time." An administrator took me out of the building for 2 hours to talk. They were all eager for an outsider's ear to vent their frustrations.

Demoralization and Burn-out

The faculty was further demoralized by a 33% eighth-grade failure rate on the State Competency Test, by far the highest in the district. However, a Stars teacher said, "The team is not taking responsibility for the test failures. We identified the ones projected to fail and we used flash cards, computers, drilling, everything to remediate. We've done everything possible." By their own testimony, teachers were working harder than they ever had before, mainly in generating new forms of personal support, yet they saw few results. The failures confirmed their belief that there was little they could do with these students.

Franklin was beleaguered by a negative reputation, and unlike the situation at Gates, teachers did not have the reassurance that a sizeable percentage of their students were succeeding (by conventional standards of success). Furthermore, the teams' new emphasis on social support was not accompanied by additional resources or institutional support. (When a caseworker was installed in late spring, teachers on both teams rushed to transfer their "high-risk" students to her caseload.) Projects like Dignity rested on a few teachers with little administrative backing and little involvement from teachers outside their circle. The most active mentors, and those like Chris struggling in isolation to develop curriculum, were exhausted and questioning the efficacy of their efforts. In the face of these difficulties, there was little initiative to uncover the roots of the educational problems at Franklin.

There was ample evidence of burn-out. Elizabeth said, "I'm thinking seriously of getting out of teaching. It's so depressing. The kids are coming to school with so many problems that we can't do anything about." The lunch hour gatherings of the Othermothers, which had initially been devoted to Dignity meetings, planning activities, or deciding how to proceed with individual students, became complaining sessions about students and parents. (Dignity continued to meet, although less frequently.) Despite their continuing mentorship and their connections with families, they began echoing the deficit notions of their colleagues. My notes from a lunchtime conversation, near the end of the school year, with Marian, Juanita, Gloria, and two other African American teachers who were part of the Othermothers group are illuminating:

> Most of the conversation is about how wild the kids are, "worse than ever" and how many disciplinary forms they've written up on them. They say they are "sick of teaching."
>
> Marian complains, "These kids must have drugs in their systems. The parents don't care. . . . A parent told me, 'He's getting C's. Isn't that good enough?' Good enough! I told her, I'm a parent and I won't accept any C's and you shouldn't either." There's a lot of complaining about parents.
>
> Another teacher says, "And then they expect us to do something with them when they get here."
>
> Marian responds, "And blame us when they fail."
>
> Juanita says, "Things aren't getting any better with teaming either."
>
> Two others agree, "Uh uh."

Team meetings became a forum to share frustrations and to complain about students, parents, and administrators. The Eagles teachers' summation of the year was pessimistic, confirming the apparent impossibility of educating many of their students. The progression of the team's agenda was symbolized by Marian and Juanita talking about "getting out of teaching" and becoming counselors. And Chris, one of the more effective teachers at Franklin, announced that she had gotten a job in another state.

How can the demoralization of these teams and the contradictory, and increasingly negative, views of the Othermothers among them be explained? One condition was the lack of a strong educational vision guiding restructuring, a vision with the potential to break the cycle of educational failure, intellectual disengagement, and resistance in which both educators and students were caught. Another was the failure of teams to break through long-standing divisions and generate serious reflection and fresh ideas. In the absence of alternatives and in the face of institutional failure, the tendency to blame students and the "at-risk" discourse provided a commonsense explanation, particularly when others in the school continually disparaged students. The Othermothers' contradictory perspectives illustrate the complexity of ideology and the influence of school context and culture in elevating a particular ideological position over others.

Conclusion

One striking difference with the Gates focus team teachers was the number of demoralized and disengaged teachers in the Eagles and Stars teams at Franklin. Not only did the restructuring activities fail to reengage them, but some caring teachers also seemed to grow frustrated and demoralized as the year progressed. Yet, at least superficially, the work of the focus teams in both schools was similar. The teams concentrated on individual students and developed incentives. As at Gates, the knowledge gleaned from discussions about students' lives outside school seemed to harden some Franklin teachers' beliefs that children designated "at risk" were damaged goods, to confirm their ineducability, and to deepen teachers' cynicism. However, unlike Gates, the two Franklin teams rejected contests that pitted students against each other, believing these would only serve to embarrass low-achieving students. Also, because tracking was less significant than at Gates, the problematic interaction between tracking and teams that produced the "smart team/dumb team" division at Gates was not an issue at Franklin.

While teams at both schools emphasized nurturing students, the caring of the teachers I call Othermothers was essentially different from efforts at student support I observed in the Gates ninth-grade teams. This group of Franklin teachers' connectedness with students and families was in sharp contrast with the Gates teams' reliance on school counselors and other professionals for information and judgments about students. Whereas the Gates teams tended to contract out student problems to social services and school counselors, the Othermothers provided personal friendship and material support to students in the context of caring relationships. These teachers tried to work with families rather than viewing them as obstacles. The quality of their conversation and the tone they set for others at the beginning of the year was different from that in Gates teams, where deficit models and lack of knowledge about and connection with African American families generally produced patronizing efforts to save African American children from their families and communities.

However, the Othermothers' orientation did not carry over to the Stars and Eagles teachers as a whole. Dignity was a case in point. The group's emphasis on identity and solidarity was a significant departure from the paradigm of individual success and personal culpability that prevailed among some Franklin teachers and was prominent at Gates. It is important that Dignity had so little influence on the teams. As at Gates, there was little progress toward productive dialogue and change on substantive issues. Although Dignity was facilitated by the Eagles teachers' joint planning time, it was conceived and nurtured through the long-term working relationships of a few teachers with similar outlooks and did not extend to teachers outside their circle whom they did not trust. Part of the reason was the unwritten prohibition against African American identified activities at Franklin, making it dangerous to promote Dignity as a team project. Without political support, the ideological leadership of the initiators of Dignity was limited.

In both Franklin teams, affective and social concerns overshadowed attention to students' academic and intellectual development. Perhaps, as at Gates, teachers saw personal and social problems as so severe and immediate that they eclipsed academic issues. In both cases, this view seemed grounded in a folk theory that teachers have to attend to personal problems before they can concentrate on educating students (Mary Metz, personal communication, February 1993). The opportunity to reflect on the character of teaching and learning, to learn from each other, and to work together on educational change was not realized in the teams. Even though there were perhaps some embryonic models of teaching among the Franklin focus team teachers as at Gates, in both instances there was not an educational vision to focus debate and inspire change. Moreover, the web of one-sided emphasis on social support and controlling student behavior, inattention to a tedious curriculum, and student alienation contributed to frustration in both Franklin teams and to teacher demoralization.

Prior to restructuring, differences among faculty at Franklin were contained by the mutual isolation of like-minded subgroups, but restructuring brought together teachers with very different outlooks and life experiences. The Eagles' early, promising conversations suggested possibilities for dialogue across differences, but these conversations degenerated into polarization, largely along racial lines. The team's experience suggests that physically breaking teachers' isolation is insufficient to prompt dialogue and shared practice across significant ideological and cultural distances. The divisions in the Eagles also have to be seen in the context of African American teachers' perceptions of their marginalization (even in a school that was majority African American and in which they were 50% of the staff) and in the context of White teachers' seeming failure to hear what African American teachers knew. Issues of race and power in the school were reproduced in the team. If relationships that support reciprocal learning and growth involve trust, mutual respect, the ability to share experiences and build intersubjectivity, then the Eagles team suggests the difficulty in fostering these relationships among teachers with very different life experiences, beliefs, and access to power and privilege. This was also present in the Gates B Team, but because of the interracial composition of the Franklin faculty, it surfaced much more sharply at Franklin.

8

RESTRUCTURING AT FRANKLIN:
"IT'S THROW THE ROCK AND HIDE YOUR HAND"

Issues like *this* [racism against Black students] are never discussed.
They're too hot. They're pushed under the rug; nobody wants to dance
to the music. It's throw the rock and hide your hand.

—African American teacher

In this chapter, I revisit several of the themes I introduced in the
last chapter, analyze their schoolwide implications, and develop other
issues related to restructuring at Franklin. The major topics of this chapter are: the role of the principal in restructuring and her influence on
teachers' beliefs and practices, educators' responses to ongoing conflicts
between students and teachers, the role of restructuring in silencing
racial issues, and restructuring and Franklin's leverage in the district.

Generally, most of the Franklin teams replicated activities and processes of the focus teams I described in the previous chapter. At least half
used incentives, but they played a minor role in teachers' interactions
with students. All the teams discussed individual students, but what it
meant to provide more personal support for students varied within and
between teams. As far as I could determine, none mirrored the seventh-
grade Eagles' sharp dualism of othermothering versus a professional social
work orientation, although both of these philosophies were expressed by
individuals in other teams. No team developed an African American–
centered project comparable to Dignity, nor was there any other team I
was aware of that had a core of teachers as energetically devoted to
providing support to students as were the Othermothers on the Eagles.
Others of their ilk were scattered among teams.

The Influence of the Principal

The principal, Delisa Johnson, was an African American woman
in her second year at Franklin, and her second year as a principal.

Delisa attempted to create a culture of student support and mentorship at Franklin, through both example and persuasion. She was quick to embrace restructuring because she saw the ethos of the reforms as a vehicle for this direction. With her energy, her visible commitment to the school, and her positive stance toward the students, she might have exerted considerable leverage on the faculty and the direction of restructuring. As the year progressed, however, her influence was uneven, illuminating the limitations of even a strong principal in the face of opposing ideologies, a limited educational vision, and a complex and sometimes antagonistic political context.

Ethos of Nurturing and Mentorship

Delisa was a hands-on leader. She nearly worked herself to death during the year of this study; at one point she was actually hospitalized with a stress-related illness. She was at the school from early morning into the night almost every day. On weekends, she tutored students in a community-based program that served Franklin, and she worked on various school-related projects. She said she would not ask anyone, including cafeteria staff and custodial workers, to do things she herself would not or did not do. During class breaks she patrolled the halls along with the teachers, stationing herself at the most central point in the building where she alternately hugged, touched base with, and admonished scores of students, all of whom she knew by name. Before the school opened in the fall, she organized the staff to come in on a Saturday and clean up the grounds. Delisa was there early with a rake. When the school provided a snack to students in an afterschool activity, I found her behind the lunch counter frying french fries. She frequently visited teachers' classes, sat in on team meetings, counseled students, and intervened with discipline problems. When she discovered that students lacked adequate shoes or coats, Delisa took them shopping. When students were having problems, she made home visits.

Her immediate, personal, and visible interventions set an example of building reciprocal relationships between the school and families. For example, Delisa learned that a White transfer student was living with her mother and sisters in a homeless shelter, and that she had no access to soap, toothbrush, or shampoo, and possessed only one set of clothes. Straightaway, in the middle of the school day, Delisa took the student to the shopping center where she purchased clothes and toiletries for her with her own money. Then she invited the mother to come in to school and advised her how to negotiate the network of social services in the city. (On several occasions after this,

I observed the mother waiting to see Delisa or a school counselor for advice on her family situation.) This incident prompted Delisa to instruct the nurse to purchase toiletries and to encourage teachers to identify students who might need them. "We can't have these kids coming to school who can't keep themselves clean. They have to have some dignity," she said.

Delisa's concern for the whole child carried over to her approach to discipline. She summarized her philosophy as "looking on the positive side" and turning "negatives into positives," as well as having confidence that "these kids have a lot of strengths." Her example seemed to help a few teachers think about students differently. This is illustrated by an incident involving a student suspended for fighting: As Delisa and I were walking down the hall, we observed William, a student, gently leading another boy by the hand back to the classroom for severely disabled students. From my field notes of this incident:

> Delisa explains, "I'm using kids who've been suspended to work during their free periods in the Resource Room. That way, they learn a sense of responsibility." . . . .
>
> Later in the school office, the Resource Teacher comes in and speaks to Delisa. "William is real good with these kids. He's doing real well. He's real helpful too. He's not the kind of kid I thought he was. . . . It's going to help me and him a real lot."

Characteristically, Delisa also intervened directly in disciplinary situations, modeling the behaviors she hoped to promote in the staff. She viewed discipline as an opportunity to strengthen a young person's character, requiring students to engage in activities that would be growing experiences, and that would build a sense of accountability to the school community. In a representative instance, I went with Delisa when a teacher notified the office of an impending fight. When we arrived at the classroom, two African American eighth-grade males were squared off. Delisa walked into the room, closed the door, stepped between the two students, spoke sharply to them (this exchange was inaudible from my location in the hall), and then sent them out into the hall to cool off. For about 5 minutes they stood 10 feet apart, glaring, fists and jaws clenched, while she spoke to the class. When she came out of the class, she told them she was disappointed in them both. After a lecture, and a reluctant handshake on their part, she sent the two outside to clean up the schoolyard—together. Out of their earshot she said: "I just want them to work together and in the process they'll work through this thing. Later I'll talk to the teacher about it."

An hour later, I observed the two students still hard at work, talking and laughing. Through examples such as these, she made her principles clear. Her approach could be seen as an embodiment of the restructuring project's emphasis on supportive relationships with students. Indeed, the restructuring director often held up Delisa as a model of this.

Delisa's clear philosophy and concrete, visible leadership were a potentially powerful influence on the teams' receptivity to, and interpretation of, the social support agenda associated with restructuring. Several young White teachers commented that she helped them to work with students more "positively." And several team leaders attributed their team's greater empathy for students to her leadership. There is also evidence that her philosophy permeated some of Franklin's programs and the direction of some of the activities associated with restructuring, or at least reinforced this ethos in others. For example, while Gates had a difficult time staffing its afterschool program, Franklin had no trouble at all. In my observations, on any day, there were more than the requisite number of staff. Many teachers simply dropped in to help. The program also branched out to drama and dance groups and art projects. While Delisa was out on medical leave for several weeks, the teacher in charge of the afterschool program said all the teachers involved pitched in to keep the program running as "Miss Johnson wanted it to."

The Principal's Philosophy Reflected in In-House Suspension

The staffing and funding for in-house suspension, which were a part of the district's restructuring agenda, gave Delisa an opportunity to institutionalize her philosophy. Delisa hired Mr. Tatum, a health teacher, to run in-house suspension because, she said, she believed he cared about kids and would provide them with the guidance they needed. Periodically, she dropped in to check on the program's progress, and I observed Mr. Tatum conferring informally with her on a number of occasions.

The physical space for the in-house program, worked out by Delisa and Tatum together, was itself a reflection of her philosophy. In-house was located in a small room that was strikingly different from the penal in-house suspension space at Gates with its enclosed carrels, scarcity of learning materials, and rule of silence. The Franklin room had been freshly painted and carpeted and was fitted with long tables at which students worked. There were antidrug, antismoking, and African American posters, a list of rules, book shelves with paperback novels, several health texts, and a few reference books. In my observations, there were usually 4 to 10 students present, generally African American males.

Mr. Tatum said he viewed a student's stint in in-house as an opportunity to provide some intensive personal guidance. His approach linked care and concern with strict discipline—which he saw as a demonstration that he cared enough about students to hold exacting standards for their behavior. Although disallowing disruptions of any kind, Mr. Tatum was cognizant of the consequences of some teachers' antagonism toward African American students, especially males. He said, "Junior high kids are going through a lot, and they respond the way they feel. They think teachers give them a bad deal and parents [do] too." He concentrated on helping students develop self-confidence as well as coping strategies. Key to this was establishing a personal relationship as a concerned adult. He required students to work in silence, but he also led daily rap sessions. Frequently, the students read and discussed a chapter in the health text on adolescent emotional needs and forming a philosophy of life. He explained his rationale:

I talk to them all the time about what they're going to be doing 5 years from now. I tell them, "You're building your life." I talk to them all the time. I try to make them take responsibility for their own lives. . . . You have to be able to tune into these kids. If you don't you're going to lose them. You have to establish a dialogue with them.

With the backing of the principal's office, in essence, Mr. Tatum's posture was a male corollary to the guidance and connectedness of the Othermothers. He was the embodiment of the adult mentorship advocated by the restructuring project, as Delisa interpreted it. Restructuring made it possible for him to work with students individually, and Delisa's leadership set the direction. His approach was also actively supported by a number of teachers who praised his work and assisted him with the academic work of students under his care.

Teacher Resistance

However, Delisa's interpretation of social relations was not embraced by the faculty as a whole. As the year progressed, divisions, demoralization, and the strength of an oppositional group outstripped her ability to build commitment to mentorship. In particular, a group of 12 to 15 cynical White teachers of both core and related subjects completely rejected Delisa's philosophy, which they often called "coddling" students. These teachers were negative about Franklin students and very critical of Delisa, whom they held responsible for what they said was a deterioration of discipline. Above all, they were frustrated by a daily ritual of facing students they found both hostile and apathetic. Their classes tended to be very confrontational, reproducing a cycle of teacher-student antagonism, student resistance, and heavy-handed disciplinary actions and verbal insults.

Tightening up discipline was the main issue for this group. They flatly rejected notions that negative relations between adults and students contributed to students' lack of motivation and resistance. They were critical of Delisa and intolerant of her nurturing approach. As one teacher put it, "I think we're being too nice to them. There's too much said about making them feel good and not enough discipline. . . . Discipline has gone down at this school [she gestures thumbs down]. There's gang activity but the administration is denying it."

Some indicated that the problems at Franklin began with African American principals. They rejected taking responsibility for the learning of seemingly recalcitrant and unmotivated students, insisting that students and their families were fully responsible for their own failure. According to one teacher, "The reason kids fail is that there is not a lot of home support. . . . We're not going to make much progress until we get help from home. . . . Teachers are the scapegoats. Kids with a mindset against education dare you to teach them. They don't want to learn." Karen, one of the most vocal of this group, and a related subjects team leader, claimed: "They [students] cannot be trusted. They lose things. Ruin equipment. They're very slow. . . . I'm pretty sure they can't transfer information at all." These teachers also said that academic standards were being sacrificed in favor of "coddling the at-risk students." In their view, the students who failed, deserved to fail. Karen said, "What bothers me is that everything is accepted. We're too nice to them. They aren't accountable. We're trying to make it interesting to them. I think we're trying too much. They don't appreciate it and it isn't helping them, in spite of what the administration says."

Another group of at least five African American teachers, including two on the Stars team discussed in the last chapter, were also quite negative about the students. Their demoralization seemed to increase as the year progressed, and their classes seemed as confrontational and dispirited as those taught by some of their White colleagues. Considered together, these two groups of teachers formed a sizeable resistance, significantly blunting the impact of Delisa's effort to change relationships between students and adults at Franklin. Her clear philosophy and personal example, even when bolstered by the general ethos of restructuring, could not overcome their negativity. She attempted to draw them into the process of school change by placing them on various committees and task forces. She made Karen, for example, a team leader. However, throughout the year, the stand-off between the group of very critical White teachers, in particular, and the principal intensified. I found no evidence that these sharply divergent views were hashed out in meetings of teams, steering committees, or the faculty as a whole.

Among the obstacles was the restructuring project's failure to take on the academic challenges these teachers raised: students' lack of motivation, lack of academic preparation, and low achievement. During the first semester, I observed students with no pencil, no book, students who were doing nothing, just getting Fs. Like the Othermothers, the principal's focus on nurturing was one-sided. She did not have a strong educational direction to match her standards of caring and mentoring. Like the Gates principal, her answer to weaknesses in students' literacy skills and low test scores was "remediation and more remediation." This one-sidedness left her without a meaningful counter to claims of some teachers that it was futile to try to educate such recalcitrant students. Without clear pedagogical alternatives, she simply insisted at a faculty meeting that teachers not submit so many Fs. A White teacher, part of the cynical group, challenged her, "They deserve what they get." Several others said, under their breath, "Yea, Ann."

The Principal's Weak Position in the District

Relative to other junior high school principals, Delisa Johnson was in a rather weak position. As the only African American female junior high principal, and newer and younger than most of her peers, she had neither support in the district nor strong ties to the network of powerful African American administrators in the central office. Although her natural support within the faculty might have been expected to lie with the school's African American teachers and although her views seemed aligned with some of these teachers, she kept a careful distance from them. In response, some African American teachers were dubious about her stance, so they held her at arm's length. Despite her relationships with individual parents, Delisa did not have a parental base of support as Ron Walters did at Gates. Although there was a Parent Teacher Organization, only 8 to 10 parents were active. Franklin parents were not organized and did not have the resources Gates's White upper-middle-class parents had, nor did they have a representative on the school board dedicated to their interests. Because Delisa had no strong base among teachers, or among parents, balancing the divisions among the faculty placed her in a delicate political position within the school. Moreover, with its low achievement scores and reputation for poor discipline, Franklin was vulnerable. Delisa was under pressure from central administrators to "turn Franklin around" and to retain or expand the proportion of White students. Hanging over her head was the reality that every school that became overwhelmingly African American was made into a magnet or specialty school and its administrators transferred—usually downward.

The fact that Franklin served low-income, mainly African American students made it a low priority for resources and quality staff. An outside audit of the district completed in December 1990 found wide disparities in building facilities, equipment, and maintenance throughout the district. It also found that these discrepancies were partially based on the relative political influence of parents and administrators in each school. The audit stated that building administrators acknowledged that "a squeaky wheel system is in place . . . if you squeak loud enough and long enough, you will get the grease." From all appearances, Delisa's "squeaking" fell on deaf ears in the central office. Franklin was desperately overcrowded; even portable classrooms were packed. The district's failure to pave Franklin's muddy, pot-holed parking lot came to represent for the staff a kind of public insult, symbolizing the school's second-class status in the district. One day in utter frustration, Delisa pulled out a bulging folder and flipped through a three-inch stack of unfilled work orders she had submitted to the central administration over the course of about 16 months for various repairs: "I don't have a decent typewriter. I need a secretary. I have no computer and no money to buy one. By the end of the year the teachers don't even have paper. There are no classroom sets of calculators. It goes on and on." It is notable that Delisa did not attempt to rally parents in support of these needs.

In her most candid moments, she (and some teachers as well) angrily attributed the district's neglect to outright racism. Delisa protested:

My school is 80% Black, the most Black kids of any junior high in the district, and I can't even get the pot holes fixed. . . . I can't even get gravel. This is my beg file, memos I've written just since September. [It was February at the time.] They're waterproofing the specialty and magnet schools, but I can't get my parking lot fixed. What message does this send to kids?

Also, several of Delisa's most promising young teachers were recruited by other principals, although this was formally against district policy. Meanwhile, she had an extremely difficult time finding qualified staff. In mid-year she had no alternative to hiring an uncertified math teacher in the eighth grade and an unprepared seventh-grade math teacher replacement. "I can't get people to come to this school," she complained.

Given her weak position, Delisa discouraged controversial topics because any sign of conflict was all too quickly interpreted in the district as a loss of control. This defensiveness had a dampening effect on dialogue despite new forms of collaboration. As an illustration, at one team meeting Delisa attended, the counselor described a new program in which students were to be selected as delegates to represent the school to the public and to show visitors around the building. From my field notes:

Counselor: Now, what we need is students who are articulate and well-poised. Of course, they have to have a high GPA. They don't have to be honors, but of course, most of the kids with high GPAs would be honors. And also, we want them to wear red blazers, so that means they also have to have enough money to be able to buy red blazers. So, that'll be a certain kind of kid.

Delisa: Wait a minute. Wait a minute. That's not the idea of the delegates. I want a cross-section, a cross-section of kids— some with high GPAs, some with low GPAs, kids who've been suspended, kids who are poor, kids who are clean, and kids who aren't so clean—a cross-section that really reflects what our school is like.

Counselor: That's not what she [another teacher] said. I got a different message about the delegates.

Teacher 1: I agree with Miss Johnson.

Teacher 2: But they do have to represent the school. . . .

Delisa: (To counselor) You need to get with me to work this out. Let's go on.

The disagreement over this program might have been a rich opportunity to discuss important differences, but Delisa said she planned to handle it in private: "I'll talk to the counselor in my office, privately, and straighten it out. There's no need to have any controversy about it." She said she wanted to prevent conflicts because "Any little incident, just one student fight, anything, and the media swoops down on us. That's the way it is with the [Riverton] schools, and then they [central office] say we're not doing our job."

The increased visibility that accompanied restructuring magnified Franklin's vulnerability, at least in Delisa's eyes. In the first 2 years of restructuring there were several newspaper articles about Franklin's incipient reforms, and there were three major stories in 1990–91. Foundation representatives, consultants, district personnel, and evaluators were a consistent presence in the school. And there was a subtle pressure from the restructuring director to demonstrate that steady progress was being made and Franklin was running smoothly. This heightened visibility and pressure to appear successful created an environment inimical to the inevitable conflict and disruption of routine that is a necessary part of educational change (Sarason, 1982).

Summary

Restructuring created both the mandate and the organization for a nurturing principal to make her ethos of student support programmatic. To some extent this was realized with individual teachers and in the character of in-house suspension at the school. But overall, although the teams also offered an opportunity to influence groups of teachers, the principal was unable to overcome resistance from some teachers, particularly a group of negative, veteran white teachers. Her relative lack of power in the district and in the school and the political vulnerability that came with being a restructuring school were important factors in her unwillingness to promote debate among the divided faculty on controversial issues.

Confrontational Classrooms, Student Resistance,
and Institutional Legitimacy

In this section, I explore in greater depth student/teacher conflicts and discipline issues. Even in the fall of 1990, there was an obsessive concern with discipline at Franklin, a concern that seemed to be rooted in a pattern of conflictual relations between students and teachers. This pattern was sharply at odds with the goal of restructuring to strengthen students' commitment to school. The most vociferous complaints came from veteran White teachers who lamented that students no longer manifested what they perceived as "good student" behaviors. For these teachers, confrontations with students were rooted in race and class differences.

Conflicts Between White Teachers and African American Students

On one level, conflictual relations between students and teachers transcended race at Franklin. As I described in chapter 7, there were African American teachers who regularly clashed with both White and African American students. And there were White teachers who seemed to treat White students as disparagingly as they did African Americans. As an example, a representative incident of this type occurred in the library where a White teacher confronted two White students sitting quietly at a table. From the very outset her approach to them was hostile and suspicious, ending with her throwing them out of the library for no apparent reason but that, as she explained to me, "They're probably up to no good."

However, clearly, there also was a racial dimension to disputes between White teachers and African American students. First, in the broader social context, the very fact that these were hostile confrontations between White teachers and African American students over whom they had power, made the interactions racially charged. Second, some White teachers categorized alleged deficiencies and insubordination as specifically African American problems. First teacher, "They look down on White teachers telling them what to do. They will have a difficult time in the workforce." Second teacher, "Discipline is worse, which is a reflection of society. The demographics have changed [i.e., Franklin had become more African American]."

Third, African American interactional styles were perceived by some White teachers as threatening. When I explored descriptions of students as "a class full of criminals," "typical inner-city kids," "out of control," "disrespectful," and so forth, teachers' explanations were that students were "loud," clumped up in noisy social groups in the hallways, acted tough, sulked, glared, and so forth. Above all, these teachers found the behavior of African American students alien and intimidating (cf. Majors & Billson, 1992). This was especially true for African American males, although most White students also did not fit the profile of the model student these teachers recalled from days when Franklin was more White working- and middle-class. "Acting Black" was treated negatively and feared by White teachers, provoking a counterreaction by students, and frequently ending in hostile confrontations and disciplinary actions. Irvine (1991) describes this process:

> The language, style of walking, glances, and dress of black children, particularly males, have engendered fear, apprehension,

and overreaction among many teachers and school administrators. The fear and trepidation that black youngsters are able to engender in adults have contributed to the exaggeration and continued use of these behaviors. (p. 27)

According to Mr. Tatum, this was a primary reason in-house suspension was filled with African American students, particularly males.

The crux of the discipline issue seemed to lie in these confrontational classroom interactions, which intensified as the year wore on. An extended excerpt from my field notes from a March business education class illustrates the pattern (18 students, 3 White, 1 Asian, 14 African American, 8 females, 10 males):

Two African American males arrive about 2 minutes late. The teacher asks in a challenging voice, "Why are you late?"

One student mumbles something about "we had a hard time . . . couldn't find gym shorts."

The teacher interrupts them, glaring at the rest of the class. "Hush up. Listen. All the typewriter requires to work is electricity, not your mouth."

A student demands, "What book are we in?"

The teacher points to the blackboard where the assignment is written. She is yelling at them, "It says workbook. By now you should know the difference between a workbook and a textbook." The class is conducted in a shout. She calls out the role, demanding, "Karen Jones. Were you at school yesterday? Were you here yesterday?"

"I was in the office."

"Can you verify that? I want verification. . . . Tonisha, were you here the last two days?"

"I was here!" she challenges. She gives the teacher a dirty look and puts her head on her desk. . . .

"The assignment is on the board, just begin it." Sarcastically she says: "And where is my friend Katrina?" (staring at a Black female who has her head down on the desk).

Katrina mumbles, "I don't feel well."

The teacher (bustling to her desk), "Well, then, you need to go to health." She shoves a pass at Katrina without looking at her. . . .

The teacher asks, "What are the dimensions of a sheet of typing paper?"

A White male answers, "Eight-and-a-half by eleven."

A Black male laughs, pointing, "He got it off the box right there." General laughter. "Well, at least he knew where to look for it. That's more than you did. Okay, Mr. Swinney [the student who made the last comment], since you know so much, which way is $8^1/_2$? Vertically or horizontally?"

The student shoots back, "Vertical."

"Now, Mr. Swinney, hold up your piece of paper. Which is vertical?"

The student elaborately clears his throat and acts as if he is about to make an important pronouncement: "Well, the way I see it . . . " He points top to bottom. There is general snickering.

In a sarcastic voice the teacher says, "Now, Mr. Swinney, if up and down is vertical, which way does the paper look larger?" General laughter and glares at teacher ensue. "Then why would you say $8^1/_2$ is vertical? And you wonder why we aren't in the computer room!" She looks around disgustedly and sighs. . . .

"Carla!" she shouts at a Black female. "Turn your machine off. Turn it off!" There is general laughter. "That's an F for the day!" There is more laughter. Carla was one of the students who seemed most engaged in the exercise. "You have 10 seconds to get your typewriters to the center point. If you don't, you're in trouble."

Everyone begins typing.

Carla asks, "Can I turn my typewriter back on?"

The teacher responds, "Listen. Just listen."

When she is no longer watching, Carla turns the machine on and joins in the exercise. . . .

The teacher yells at the class, "You're always three steps ahead and four back."

This class exemplified a dynamic of disrespect, academic disengagement, punitiveness, and student resistance that I witnessed repeatedly at Franklin. The teacher involved was a team leader, a member of the school steering committee, and quite active in restructuring activities. Yet her responses in an interview after the class did not hide her disdain for the students and apparent absence of reflection on her own role in the dynamic I witnessed: "Their attitude is the main problem. They are very disrespectful. My attitude is, 'You can be disrespectful—I can do better.' I cut them down. Act like them to get their attention."

It is my sense that many confrontational classes like this and ongoing antagonism between teachers and students, especially White teachers and African American students, poisoned the climate for everyone at Franklin and delegitimated the institution as a whole. Students' anger, resistance, and testing of the most negative teachers carried over to other classes and to the hallways. This analysis was also voiced by two counselors who said students were continually coming to them to complain about their treatment by certain teachers. My interpretation was also supported by teachers' comments that they hated to get students after Miss So-and-so's class because they were "all heated up" when they came out of there.

Classroom confrontations like the one described above were part of a complex web of interactions that produced student resistance and reflected an ongoing power struggle between, in particular, a group of White teachers and African American students. These interactions were anchored in what Erickson (1987) describes as a break in trust and the institutional legitimacy of the school:

> Assent to the exercise of authority [in classrooms] involves trust that its exercise will be benign. This involves a leap of faith— trust in the legitimacy of the authority and in the good intentions of those exercising it, trust that one's own identity will be maintained positively in relation to the authority, and trust that one's own interests will be advanced by compliance with the exercise of authority. . . . The institutional legitimacy of the school is affirmed existentially as trust in face-to-face encounters between school staff and students and their parents. (pp. 344–45)

Broken trust was spun out in cultural misunderstandings surrounding African American student behaviors, teachers' negative racial stereotypes and fear of African American males in particular, and a cycle of resistance and punishment. Student resistance in defense of identity and dignity often took the form not only of open hostility, but commonplace noncompliance with teachers' directives, failure to complete work, refusal to pay attention, sleeping in class, acting out so as to be put out of the room, fooling around, and so on (cf. McDermott & Gospodinoff, 1979; Metz, 1978). The casualty in this process was students' intellectual engagement in school.

Some African American students who were interviewed were very candid about the racial aspects of these dynamics. The following notes record part of a conference between an African American male student, Winston; Cheryl, an African American counselor; and myself:

Cheryl: Okay, Winston. You know what I want to talk to you about, right?

Winston: My grades?

Cheryl: Right. Why are they going down?

Winston: Well, Miss _____, she picks on me all the time. And then she sends me out of the room. And then I just don't want to do anything.

Cheryl: Why do you think she's doing this?

Winston: She just doesn't like me.

Cheryl: Why?

Winston: (glancing at me, in a low voice) Because, because I'm Black.

PL: So, she treats Black kids differently?

Winston: No, not really. We're all Black.

PL: So how do you know it's because you're Black?

Winston: (meeting Cheryl eye to eye) Well, [pause] you know, you just know she's prejudiced.

Cheryl: Winston, we may not be able to do anything about that situation. But if you're willing, we could meet again tomorrow and develop some strategies so that you could be successful in that class. Do you want to do that?

[Winston shows mild enthusiasm for this plan, and they agree to meet again the next day.]

Although no racial slurs occurred, and Winston could produce no tangible evidence, daily experiences such as his were "symbolic encounters" (Clement, Eisenhart, & Harding, 1979) in which the subordination of African American students was affirmed and recreated. These daily encounters occurred in the context of a project designed to improve the educational experiences of the very students subjected to them.

Conflicting Views of African American Students

Schoolwide, there were varied views of African American students among the faculty and very different attitudes toward them. After the conference with Winston, Cheryl said:

You see what I mean? This happens over and over again with this particular teacher. There's a whole group of them really. My goal is to find ways for them [students] to adapt. For example, there are different ways of responding to a teacher's request. Our kids don't know how to respond, and they end up getting in trouble. So they have to learn to comply, to adapt. This is not their world and they don't know how to be teacher pleasers. They need these survival strategies. You can't change the system. It will take decades to change people's attitudes. Until that happens, we—our Black students—need to learn how to survive in these schools. [Pause.] But then, that's denying themselves. I don't know how to solve it.

The reaction of teacher-advocates of African American students was either to develop their own independent and relatively isolated support systems, such as Dignity, or, like this counselor, try to help students survive within the existing culture of racial subordination. There were a few staff members (both African American counselors and some Othermothers) who criticized the institution for racism and advocated a more activist posture. Jonetta: "We need a more positive stance toward ourselves [African Americans] and toward all children. We need to build on kids' potential for growth. Kids need a greater sense of belonging, self-worth, and self-esteem." But Jonetta was frustrated by the failure of the teams to directly confront these issues: "We need to change more things in the school. We can't go to the homes and change them, but we need to establish rapport with the kids and feed them positives. People within the teams are just going along with the program. They're just following suit." Some teachers were known for their high academic expectations, challenging curricula, and responsiveness to African American students' cultural backgrounds. Among the latter were several highly respected veteran educators, but despite the team discussions and opportunities for team teaching, joint curriculum planning, and peer observations, their work was largely individual and insular, as it had been before restructuring. (I describe two of these teachers in the next chapter and explain why they had little impact on restructuring as a whole.)

Meanwhile, teachers with a deficit framework had a very different analysis and solution. As if in antithesis to Jonetta's comment, a White teacher said, "We need to tell them, 'You're not all going to college.' Some are not college material and we should tell them that. They should set lower goals and follow them." Still others simply seemed not to care. Certainly, there were committed White teachers, such as Chris on the Eagles Team, and negative African American teachers. However, problems of racism, racial divisions, and cultural differences were salient.

Summary

The widespread student/teacher conflict, especially between White teachers and African American students at Franklin, reflected a fundamental lack of trust and institutional legitimacy. The question here is what influence restructuring had on a staff so deeply divided in its beliefs and practices, and whether restructuring fostered dialogue across these differences to support more productive, schoolwide relations between teachers and African American students. As much as I could determine, despite the focus on improving social relations and achievement of "at-risk" students, the issues raised by Winston, the African American student quoted above, were not openly addressed. Perhaps they were so deeply entrenched and ideologies were so sharply opposed that it would have taken a very explicit and concerted effort to bring them into the open.

Restructuring and the Silencing of Racial Issues

Race was both the most, and the least, talked-about topic at Franklin. On the one hand, there was an almost obsessive concern with creating visible signs of racial balance. On the other, there was an unspoken taboo against discussing racial issues, for example, the deep racial divisions between teachers, cultural differences, relations of power, and racial tensions between teachers and African American students (see Tatum, 1992; West, 1992). What influence did restructuring have on racial dialogues schoolwide?

Race, the Most and Least Discussed Issue

Delisa went out of her way to put a racially integrated face on Franklin. In the fall of 1990, she told each teacher to display multiracial posters and to ensure that students were not seated in racially segregated groups in classrooms. In March, the faculty was even admonished for segregated seating at faculty meetings. A teacher said, "We were told to watch who we sit next to at faculty meetings and make sure we we're not in separate [racial] groups." These instructions belied the very real segregation of the staff in separate lounges and informal groupings and their lack of dialogue across racial differences. These measures were a way of publicly addressing race without really dealing with it.

While some African American teachers wanted a deeper engagement with questions of race—"We're not getting down to the real issues," for some White teachers, the shallowness of these displays gave credence to the logic of racelessness. A White teacher summarized this reaction: "They're only interested in dealing with superficialities like posting honors, an equal number of Black and White. You know, counting Black faces. There's no substance to it. Kids are kids. Why can't we just teach kids? There's too much emphasis on the [racial] disparities."[1] Others were resentful of what they perceived to be the special treatment accorded African American students. Marissa, the seventh-grade counselor, articulated this position,

> Black kids get a free ride in this school. For example, a White kid can live a mile away but they have to be bused [to another school]. But Black kids can go anywhere they want in the school system. That's reverse discrimination, [which] quite a bit has been written about. . . . I came from a district that is mostly Black so I have a right to talk. I know what I'm talking about. There we just said, "Okay, we've got Black kids, so let's just go about educating them." We didn't pay any attention to race.

There were several sources for the visible concern with racial balance and integration at Franklin. Although instructions to "count heads" and display multicultural posters originated in the principal's office, there was some evidence the district leadership and the restructuring director were involved also. In part, this was another manifestation of the district's fear of White flight and the pressure to meet desegregation guidelines by showing that Franklin was not a racially isolated school. Moreover, the principal also had a direct stake in demonstrating that her school was not "a Black school." This would have been a "failure" for Delisa, and the school might have been turned into a magnet or specialty school. This was not only a question of meeting desegregation guidelines, but, according to a leading district administrator, also a response to public perception that all-Black schools were the worst schools and appearing "Black" was viewed as jeopardizing the support of White parents. Without strong political support, Delisa could not risk being "too Black" in a district in which powerful White interests held sway.

Restructuring greatly increased Franklin's visibility, and thus its vulnerability as well. In this new environment the principal tried to demonstrate that although she was African American and the school predominantly African American, there was no racial favoritism or African American–centeredness. She chose an equal number of African American and White team leaders and selected several White team leaders to represent the school at district restructuring conferences. She sponsored White and African American parents as PTO co-chairs and insisting that Dignity was not an outgrowth of restructuring but a "project of those teachers."

African American cultural identity was conspicuously absent at Franklin. The school followed the district's standard, textbook-based, curriculum, and there was little reflection of the African American majority in the school's public exhibits and extracurricular activities. In February, the principal hung a banner proclaiming "Black Americans Woven Into the Fabric of American History" in the school's central hallway. This was the first visible declaration of African American identity I observed in 3 years at Franklin. However, the banner was removed when state and district dignitaries chose the school as the site to sign a state education bill.

When the education bill was signed at Franklin, she chose two students, one White and one Black to be on the dias with state officials. She sat next to the White vice principal, while the African American vice principal was assigned to hall duty. And despite her personal critique of the inequities of tracking, she publicly supported the policy as "fair to the gifted students" and personally took a hand in squashing the untracking initiative in 1989–90. A leader of that attempt said Delisa was afraid that publicity surrounding untracking would cause a political backlash against Franklin. One message was that Franklin was not only desegregated, but that Whites would get the same treatment as in schools with White principals. Her efforts reflected both the potency of the politics of race within which she operated and the influence of these politics on restructuring. It is significant that Delisa did not organize her own independent power base in support of the specific concerns of African American students.

Some African American teachers were angry about what they viewed as Delisa's submission to White interests, or "playing the game." By the end of the year, they came to believe that restructuring was a "plot" to eliminate African American teachers, possibly laying the groundwork to turn Franklin into a school with a much larger percentage of White teachers. Their evidence was that at the end of the previous year, six African American teachers had been replaced by White teachers and there was some talk of making Franklin into a lab school associated with a local university. As one said, "If it's turned into a lab school, we [Blacks] will be the first to go." They also claimed that some African American administrators at Franklin were "completely ignored in restructuring. They don't know what's going on. They aren't kept informed." They saw this as another aspect of eliminating any identification of Franklin as an African American school. In short, they felt abandoned, believing Delisa was essentially abrogating her responsibility to provide leadership as an African American advocate.

Although there were political pressures to silence racial issues, there were counterpressures, from desegregation mandates, to provide equal education to African American students. Moreover, decades of desegregation battles left the district acutely sensitive to charges of racism. Race relations in the Riverton district were highlighted at mid-year after a racial fight at Hamilton High School and charges of racism by that school's African American teachers. District leaders responded immediately with an in-service for teachers on prejudice reduction conducted by central administrators via television hook-ups in each of the schools. An African American counselor typified the reaction of many African American teachers I talked with at Franklin: "It [the multicultural workshop] wasn't straight. They didn't get down to the issues. A Black man led it but he was concerned with not offending anyone."

In many ways, the district's response was typical of its symbolic demonstrations of concern about race relations, without engaging either the community or teachers in the longstanding questions of power and privilege that surrounded race in Riverton. This response as well as Franklin's and the Riverton district's attention to visible signs of integration must be understood within the context of broader national public policy on racial integration. Framing the problem of inequality in education as one of integration rather than structural racism (Kohl, 1996/97) led to the kinds of remedies that Franklin adopted, for example, displays of racial integration in classrooms and district efforts at prejudice reduction. As a result, the structural and cultural manifestations of racism within the schools were not examined.

The resistance of many White teachers to talking about race was rationalized by their insistence that they "did not see color." Comments by a White teacher are typical:

> I don't even think about color. Let me give you an example. We had to stop our team meeting to fill out a form about students. We had to put down their characteristics, you know, Black/White, male/female. I had to think, to honestly think, is Latoya Black or White? I don't even think about it.

Others tended to attribute African American students' problems to class rather than race (see Clement, Eisenhart, & Harding, 1979, for similar findings). For example, one teacher said, "It's not race, it's economics." There was some evidence for this argument; African American and white students were both considered "at risk" at Franklin. However, the racial meanings associated with student/teacher conflicts also reflected just how salient race was at Franklin. Professions of colorblindness denied race as a factor in students' identities and educational experiences (Schofield, 1982; Ladson-Billings, 1994) and concealed the significance of race at Franklin.

White teachers, in particular, were reluctant to discuss racial disparities with me, even though I was gathering information on a project with the explicit goal of reducing those disparities. An example is this exchange with a White male teacher, which was followed by his refusal to continue our conversation:

PL: Can you explain the racial disparity in achievement?
Teacher: Well, not really. I have a large number of Black students and a large number of As for Black students.
PL: Do you see racial disparities in achievement at Franklin or in the district as an issue?
Teacher: I don't see color. I don't see White and Black. I just see kids, and I don't want to answer any questions about that. I don't think it's relevant.

Some African American teachers were also reluctant to discuss racial issues. I interviewed one highly respected, experienced African American teacher four times during the year. In our first two interviews, she talked around questions about racial disparities and contended that race was not a factor in the academic disengagement of so many African American students. Perhaps she was simply skeptical of a White researcher's questions, but, later in the year, she suggested that although "it isn't talked about," ignorance over "cultural differences" is partially responsible.

In my observations, attempts to put racism on the table were tentative and short-lived. The reactions to those who dared to raise racial issues illuminated the culture of silence that surrounded race at Franklin. For example, as one faculty meeting ended, Juanita, chair of Franklin's Interracial Committee, announced, "I have something for each of you, and I want you to think about it." As teachers filed out of the room, she handed each one a cartoon about racism. Most took it stiffly, without looking at Juanita or the cartoon. Jonetta, the eighth-grade counselor, received a similar response at a team meeting. When African American and White members of the team berated an African American female student for lying and being uncooperative, Jonetta said, "Look. We're acting like we're trying to lynch her. A lot of Blacks are having the same problems." This was met with stony silence, and one African American teacher rolled his eyes to the ceiling and began humming as if to underscore the collective refusal to touch this topic.

As reported in earlier studies of desegregated schools, not talking about race is a way to avoid conflict over power and privilege (Clement, Eisenhart, & Harding, 1979; Schofield, 1982; Scherer &

Slawski, 1979). In her study of dropouts, Fine (1991) describes the structural fear of naming: "Naming involves those practices that facilitate critical conversation about social and economic arrangements, particularly about inequitable distributions of power and resources by which these students and their kin suffer disproportionately" (p. 34). To have publicly named the racial issues at Franklin—issues that were most probably discussed privately in the meeting places of the various teacher factions—would have involved considerable personal risk. Not only was it a breach of an unspoken taboo, but there was little support from school or district administrators even though it was at the heart of what restructuring was supposed to be about. Publicly identifying racial issues would have called into question the relations of power between Whites and African Americans at Franklin, in the Riverton district, the city, and the broader society. The inability of restructuring to address this fundamental issue was a reason some teachers (especially those with a critique of racism) lost confidence in the reforms.

"Let Sleeping Dogs Lie": Teams and the Suppression of Dialogue on Race

From the outset, whole school restructuring increased racial isolation at Franklin. Most high-status related subjects teachers (those who taught foreign languages, computer science, and music) were White. Many were part of the oppositional group of veteran teachers who had worked at Franklin when its student population was more White and middle class. Because related subjects teachers were assigned to a separate team, restructuring further isolated them from core subject teachers, many of whom were African American. This added a new dimension to racial divisions within the faculty. A White, related subject teacher said, "There's a lot of disrespect between teachers . . . a lot of jealousy. . . . Restructuring hasn't led to collegiality but to a split in the faculty. We don't meet with the [core] subject teachers." Another White related subject teacher, who sharply disagreed with the direction of restructuring, said that it had increased her isolation:

> I'm on the support team and we've had no meetings. Restructuring has led to more isolation for me. I think the teachers on the other teams have pulled closer together. . . . There's no integration of my work with the classroom curriculum. Anything I do with a team is on a voluntary basis. It's not structured in.

But even in racially mixed teams, those teachers who were willing to talk about it confirmed that restructuring had evoked virtually no substantive dialogue on racial issues. Their explanations echoed the teachers in the focus teams in the last chapter. First, despite "teacher empowerment," many alluded to fears of recrimination for "rocking the boat" or speaking up. Second, the divisions among the faculty were also so intense, and so racially charged, that they could not be transcended simply by creating new forms for engagement. At least at this stage, a culture of silence was not altered by the official rhetoric of collective decision making. Third, the taboo against race-related topics seemed to hold because the issue was so highly personalized. There was no leadership to address it as a problem of institutional norms and ideologies. Juanita said:

> It's hard to have dialogue because people feel they're being attacked on racial lines. Generally it gets interpreted as a racial thing. You know, "They're teaming up against me." Dialogue? Developing dialogue is the toughest mountain we have to climb. There are the district policies, the union agreement, and people are afraid of losing their jobs.

Finally, an African American counselor said there was so little dialogue among the staff because "it would be too explosive if people said what they really thought. Let sleeping dogs lie. There is discussion within teams, but it's superficial. Nothing is ever really resolved. People don't want to confront."

To be vocal was to place oneself outside the norms of teacher behavior and to be vulnerable to personal attack. Samuel, an African American teacher, had a reputation for speaking his mind. Initially very active in restructuring workshops, he became discouraged by the inability of teams to engender a more frank discussion. He said, "There is no dialogue between those who are negative and those who are positive. It always gets personal. People are afraid. The teams should facilitate that but it hasn't worked." Teachers at the other end of the faculty spectrum, including those in the group of negative White teachers, confirmed the administration's failure to lead discussions of controversial issues. Irene said, "There is very little discussion in this school about difficult issues. The administration has its head in the sand about the kids' involvement in drugs, for example. . . . The team agenda is too full to deal with a lot of these issues."

There was little apparent progress on this front throughout the year. In an interview in April, the school caseworker (who had come on board in January) said, "There's a lot of pettiness, disputes among the teachers, and it hasn't been overcome by the teams." At an end-of-the-year, all-day faculty meeting to develop team agendas for the coming year, the faculty remained split and fragmented. When each team reported to the group as a whole, the teachers seated themselves in informal, largely single-race, subgroups, which continued to supplant the restructuring teams. During the team reports, at least half the teachers showed marked disinterest in what their colleagues had to say—turning their backs, whispering, walking out of the room, and so on. Throughout, there was the familiar undercurrent of disgruntled mumbling, side glances, and occasional sarcastic jibes, as at faculty meetings throughout the year.

The *Keepsake Book:* Squelching an African American Initiative

Racial divisions among the faculty and contradictions between restructuring and African American–centered activities came to a head in the early spring of 1991 in an episode involving the creation of Franklin's first yearbook. In the fall of 1990, Samuel, an African American teacher working with about 11 other faculty, including the Othermothers and several White teachers, began planning the yearbook and involving students in the project. Although the group of teachers working on the yearbook was not exclusively African American, it was initiated by some of the strongest advocates of African American students, who conceived the project as a form of parity with wealthier, White-dominated schools such as Gates, which had established yearbooks. These teachers put in many hours during and after school planning the publication and recruiting students to work on it. They decided to dedicate the first volume to three African American Riverton educators known for their support of African American students.

Initially, Samuel recruited a White journalism teacher to the project. After a few weeks, she withdrew and organized a group of White teachers to develop the *Franklin Keepsake Book*, essentially a duplicate of the yearbook, for which she obtained funds from the district restructuring project. While the yearbook was to be financed by sales to students, the *Keepsake Book* would be free because of this subsidy. Although begun after the yearbook, the *Keepsake Book* not only had the backing of the principal as an official restructuring project, but there were incentives for students to work on it (teachers were authorized to give credit for student writing and photography). In early spring, pictures collected by the yearbook staff mysteriously disappeared and were later found mutilated on the football field. This incident was never cleared up.

African American teachers involved were furious at what they considered a blatant attempt to undermine their initiative. In this conversation, Juanita uses "they" to refer to the school administration and the restructuring office:

> They started the *Keepsake Book* and that took away from the year-book. I don't know who started it, but restructuring came up with the money. They're giving the *Keepsake Books* away free. It's just a duplication. They didn't support the yearbook. It's a case of divide and conquer. Everybody working on the *Keepsake Book* is White. Ms. _____ had her students collecting pictures and information for credit, so naturally they were motivated, so it all went to them. . . . The Keepsake people never consulted with the teachers putting out the yearbook. They stole our pictures. We found them spread all over, on the football field, and all over the schoolyard. We had to go around and track them down. The yearbook was supposed to be a project for the whole school.

Teachers involved in the *Keepsake Book* were more reticent about these events. One insisted there was no intent to undermine the year-book and no competition between the two projects. They scoffed at the accusation of stealing pictures, ascribing the incident to a student prank. One said, "We just want to produce a nice book that the kids can keep to help them remember the teams. We got restructuring funding for it. Isn't that what the restructuring office is for, to support projects like this started by teachers?"

Regardless of interpretation, the episode not only dramatized, but probably intensified, sharp racial divisions among the staff. The fact that the Franklin principal supported the *Keepsake Book* further convinced African American teachers that she was capitulating to White interests. She (and perhaps the central office) also insisted on approving the yearbook dedications—again undermining the credibility of African American teachers. The fact that the authority of the district restructuring office and restructuring funds supported an initiative counter to that begun by African American teachers, confirmed for them that restructuring was being used to further disempower them. Indeed, regardless of intent, the restructuring project stifled an African American–initiated activity. This was quite significant in a district where African American students were subordinated and in a mainly African American school with little public African American identity.

As if to demonstrate the marginality of the African American teachers involved in the yearbook, when it came out in May, its quality was obviously inferior to the *Keepsake Book*. There were pasted-on pictures, blank spots where pictures were missing, incorrect captions, and typographical errors. An addendum by the publisher apologized for the errors. There were also interesting hints of the book's conflictual history. On the one hand, the photo of the African American vice-principal was substantially larger than that of the White vice-principal. On the other, although the dedication was originally written to three African Americans, the final version had a pasted-over picture with a dedication to a White administrator, reflecting a last-minute decision to overrule the yearbook staff.

In the end, the yearbook displayed the weakness of African American teachers at a predominantly African American school with 50% African American faculty. Some teachers cited the episode as verification of the wisdom of not pushing other African American–initiated innovations, such as Dignity, schoolwide. They also concluded that the role of restructuring was to drive African American initiatives further underground.

Summary

While there were demonstrations of racial integration, there was a fear of naming the racial issues so salient at Franklin. Restructuring seemed to do little to increase racial dialogue. Organizational changes actually increased racial isolation, and new collaborative arrangements could not penetrate the culture of silence surrounding race and relations of power at Franklin. By raising the school's visibility, restructuring seemed to heighten administrators' fear of public conflict and charges that the school was, in any sense, African American-centered. In this context, the restructuring project directly supported the suppression of the African American-initiated Franklin Yearbook, increasing the suspicion of African American teachers that the reform would result in their further exclusion.

Restructuring and Franklin's Leverage in the District

Franklin parents seemed to have little collective impact on the school. Certainly, they showed concern for their children's education. An open house at the beginning of the year was attended by over 400 parents, reportedly far exceeding the attendance of parents at any other junior high in the district. The African American teachers on the Eagles team, inspired by the huge turnout, developed a plan for a parent network so that families could contact each other for support on parenting issues and to exchange school information. However, the teachers were so overwhelmed by their other duties that the idea never got off the ground. Parents did not play a significant, organized role in the school during the year. Many of Franklin's working-class families did not have the flexibility to visit the school during the day, and many lacked transportation to participate in school activities. Moreover, conventional forms of middle-class parent involvement, such as volunteering in the school, were not necessarily seen as appropriate by Franklin's families, who may have felt the classroom was strictly the province of educators (see Lightfoot, 1978; Siddle Walker, 1996).

Franklin families were also not visible advocates for their children, reflecting the absence of strong organization by African American and working-class families and communities in Riverton generally. As a result, the most potent community leverage on Franklin was those interests with power in the district as a whole—upper-middle-class White parents and the school board members representing them. This was demonstrated by the way the Study and Research Methods controversy unfolded at Franklin.

The SRM Controversy

The dispute surrounding the new Study and Research Methods (SRM) class was the defining event of the first year of restructuring at Franklin. It became the focal point for the interplay of internal and external political influences—Franklin administrators, staff, and parents; the restructuring project; the district administration; the school board; and various community interests—revealing the power relations among these groups and their relative impact on Franklin.

There were no reported complaints about the class from Franklin parents, and many of the Franklin teachers I interviewed supported SRM. (The exceptions were some related subjects teachers.)[2] Many core teachers and the principal said the class was an opportunity for all students to develop study and "higher-order thinking" skills. When the principals of restructuring schools appeared before the school board to fight for the class, Delisa was a passionate defender. Staff and PTO of Franklin signed a statement of support, and some teachers vigorously lobbied the board to give the class a fair chance and evaluate it at the end of the year. Despite their pleas, because of the Gates parents' pressure, the board voted that the lower two quartiles of students would be pulled out for remedial reading, and SRM would become optional and noncredit in eighth and ninth grade.

From the point of view of many Franklin teachers and administrators, this decision to revise SRM, over their objections, sent a clear message that their destiny was in the hands of powerful interests with no stake in Franklin. Although questions were raised about the quality of the class, Delisa was certain the opposition was racially motivated.

"They're the higher socioeconomic parents who don't want their children in heterogeneously grouped classes with Black kids," she told me.

To the principal and some Franklin teachers, the revision of SRM clearly signified that, despite rhetoric to the contrary, the interests of low-achieving, primarily African American children were not a priority in the district and that the restructuring emphasis on improving "at-risk" students' achievement was secondary in the larger scheme of things. At the beginning of the year, Delisa had requested an additional reading teacher because of a high percentage of Franklin students with low reading scores. Her request was denied for lack of funds. However, the board authorized using compensatory education funds to hire the extra reading teachers needed to implement the revision of SRM. In short, there was no money for extra reading teachers when the request came from a principal advocating for students who needed additional assistance, but the money could be found to satisfy the demands of powerful parents of high-achieving students to separate their children from low-achieving students. The episode was a slap in the face to Delisa and other teacher-advocates of African American students. Bitterly, they complained that their hard work on behalf of these students seemed useless. Delisa, generally optimistic and undaunted, was more angry and frustrated than I had ever seen her:

> SRM was filling a need. They [the teachers] spent a lot of time training, worked night and day to put the program together. They did everything but tap dance. We've done our level best. Teachers gave up their time during the summer, but as soon as we go out on a limb, they cut it off. It's racial. That's what the whole thing is about. They try to cover it over by talking about the quality of the program but the real issue is heterogeneous grouping. It's going to take generations, lifetimes, for things to change. I've sacrificed a lot the last 3 years, my children, my family, my health. . . . I get up and make speeches about these issues and I tell it like it is and all the other administrators and people from the district clap and nod, but that's just for show. When it really comes down to it, they don't want to deal with it.

The board's decision concretely marginalized low-achieving students by pulling out the bottom two quartiles for remedial reading and stigmatizing these students by publicly displaying their reading difficulties. Moreover, by creating a two-tiered class with higher-versus lower-order skills, SRM actually increased the disparity in educational experiences for low- and high-achieving students. At Franklin, the group confined to basic skills was very large. Ironically, the one course initiated through restructuring that provided more intellectually challenging experiences for low-achieving students ended up becoming yet another arena in which these students would have significantly less challenging educational experiences than other students. Immediately after the board decision, Delisa predicted:

> Those groups [the lower quartiles] will be the dummy groups. They'll be stigmatized and that will show up in behavior. . . . These kids will get reading while the top kids get the higher-order skills. That's a big step backward and towards more definite tracking. It can only widen the disparities. At Franklin it will be devastating. They've killed it [SRM]. In some classes over half the kids will be pulled out. It's worse than at the other schools.

Two months later, Jonetta, outlined the student responses she was seeing to the changes in SRM. As a counselor, a front-line person for student complaints, she said:

> I'm overwhelmed with kids who feel they are stupid because they have been pulled out of SRM and placed in reading. A teacher told a group of students in the SRM class, "You'll be pulled out for reading because your reading abilities are so low." She said this right in front of the whole class. Several of the students have come to me. They say, "I'm not going. They can't force me to go. I am not stupid." That's what we're dealing with here at this school. Kids are refusing to go. This is just another labeling. Once again these kids are feeling like they are on the lower end of the totem pole.

The SRM incident also made a mockery of teacher empowerment and site-based management. SRM was designed by a district specialist and a core group of teachers—one from each of the four restructuring schools. The class was experimental with unprecedented opportunity in Riverton for teacher initiative. Despite whatever weaknesses SRM had, some Franklin teachers felt it was a step toward a more innovative, experiential, and "higher-order thinking" curriculum. The opportunity for teachers to design a class and to work collaboratively with other teachers to integrate it into their disciplines was new. As such, it represented the potential for teacher-led curriculum development. When the board essentially gutted the class, it also dashed hopes that the district could turn away from its bureaucratic traditions. When I visited Franklin shortly after the board's decision, I found team meetings rife with frustration and complaining. Chris, the white SRM teacher on the Eagles Team, was one of the most frustrated: "I'm so put out with this whole district. I'm just fed up. We get no credit. I didn't get a master's plus to be babysitting. How am I going to classroom manage when they aren't getting credit. . . . There is no teacher empowerment." Shortly after this incident, she announced she was taking a job out of state.

To other Franklin teachers also, the board's decision demonstrated the foolishness of investing oneself in initiatives that board members and Riverton's elite parents might oppose. Delisa's assessment was pessimistic: "It will be a long time before any teachers at this school will be willing to innovate, work night and day like the SRM teachers did and then see their work cut out from under them." As one teacher said, the SRM episode showed, "Why it doesn't pay to try anything new in the Riverton public schools." After the SRM episode, the Dignity teachers reminded their team, "That's why we need to keep Dignity close to home."

A Counterexample: Signing the Education Bill at Franklin

In the spring of 1991, the governor chose Franklin as the site to sign a state education bill providing college tuition for graduating seniors needing financial assistance. The signing was to have been at Gates, "the logical choice," as one district leader put it. However, Delisa and the restructuring director lobbied hard for Franklin, and they were supported by the superintendent and some other district officials (although the latter privately worried to me about Franklin students' "behavior" during the event). The fact that Franklin represented educational reform for "disadvantaged populations" made it particularly appropriate.

The bill was signed with great fanfare at an all-school assembly. The governor and state legislators arrived with their media entourage. The superintendent and restructuring officials were also present. The school had been scrubbed from top to bottom by teachers, administrators, students, and custodians over the weekend. Windows and floors sparkled. On the day of the signing, a dias was set up in the gym and furniture was moved in to create a dignified setting. Custodial workers began early in the morning making incessant passes through the hallways with push brooms, and teachers and students bent to pick up tiny scraps of paper. About a third of the students were dressed in suits and party dresses. For the Franklin administration, the bill signing was a real triumph. To Delisa it represented a potential turning point after the set-backs with SRM, the staff's demoralization, and the publicized incidents of weapons on campus. Beaming, at the end of the day she said, "Now maybe we can get some resources." In fact, Franklin was subsequently scheduled for construction of an additional wing to replace the trailers.

The decision to hold the signing at Franklin was significant because it reflected the district leadership's confidence in the school. And it meant a vote of confidence for Delisa, whose school won out over Gates. Moreover, it suggested to Delisa and other Franklin staff that restructuring could be a countervailing force to the politics of privilege in Riverton. Franklin's participation in restructuring, and its backing by the restructuring office, gave it leverage and visibility in a way that was productive for the school. Probably more than any of the other restructuring schools, Franklin symbolized the issues that restructuring was particularly to address. As manifested in the governor's visit, because of restructuring, Franklin was seen as a school on the move.

However, unlike the revision of SRM, the governor's visit was not a policy decision. On the policy issue, the superintendent and the restructuring director, as well as Franklin staff, were essentially defeated at the hands of more powerful community forces. Thus, although restructuring gave Franklin some leverage, district policies that affected the educational experiences of Franklin's African American and low-income students were still decided in a divisive political context that often placed the interests of privileged students first.

Conclusion

Restructuring at Franklin was influenced, in its own way, by the same factors at work at Gates: the principal's role, the socioeconomic and racial composition of the student body, the school's standing in the district, the philosophy and ethos of the staff, and the community context. At Franklin, however, there was a more sharply differentiated and contradictory mix of philosophies, values, experiences, and practices among the faculty. Rather than a dominant school culture, as at Gates, multiple and contending cultures were apparent at Franklin. This fractured school culture is perhaps one reason the early phases of restructuring seemed to have contradictory consequences for teachers and students.

One might have expected that Franklin, with its supportive African American principal (a hands-on leader, quite different from Ron

Walters who ran Gates largely from his office) and a group of committed African American teachers, would have bent restructuring to the
needs of the school's largely African American student body. In fact,
restructuring facilitated some promising changes in social relations,
for instance, the in-house suspension program, which was actively
supported by a core of teachers. However, the principal's philosophy
and personal example, bolstered by the official aims of restructuring,
were not strong enough to overcome resistance from some groups of
teachers who were opposed to her leadership, negative about students, and focused on social control. Even more fundamental, substantive change in social relations at Franklin implied the necessity to
break the cycle of teachers' disrespect for, and fear of, African American students and students' consequent resistance and lack of confidence
in the legitimacy of adult authority. There was no evidence that either
the principal's leadership, the ethos of restructuring, or new opportunities for collegial dialogue disrupted this cycle.

Gates, because of its high-income student body and flagship status, was frequently in the public eye, but Franklin found new visibility
as a restructuring school. This heightened visibility cut two ways. On
one hand, given the school's sharply divided staff and the district's
racial history, increased visibility intensified fears of public conflict
and of being identified as a "Black School." Thus restructuring set a
context for suppressing controversial issues, particularly related to race,
and African American identified initiatives. For some teachers, restructuring came to be directly associated with suppressing African American initiatives by undermining the Franklin yearbook. The overall
failure of restructuring to deal openly with racism and racial inequality stood in the way of any serious analysis of the roots of African
American students' low academic achievement and widespread resistance. To have seriously discussed the racial issues at Franklin would
have opened up fundamental questions about relations of power between Whites and African Americans—administrators, teachers, students, and parents—in the school and in the city. On the other hand,
as evidenced by the college tuition bill signing at Franklin, restructuring also provided some political leverage and additional resources.
However, the benefits came at the expense of stifling African American–
centered initiatives and experiments with untracking that might have
lead to real changes in students' educational experiences.

The reconstruction of SRM as a two-tiered class, over the objections of Franklin teachers, administrators, and parents demonstrated
their weakness in the Riverton district. The principal downplayed her
visibility as an African American school leader and chose not to create

an alliance with the active core of African American teachers or with African American parents. This lack of a power base maintained Franklin's weakness in the district. Without a base of support inside the school or in the community, Franklin was subject to the same powerful interests as Gates. At both schools, conflicts were shot through with the politics of race and class and resolved in favor of those with political power and resources.

9

Missing Voices: Three Exemplary Teachers*

I could be a leader in the whole school. But they don't see that.

—Paulette

I hate that! Bribing children that way instead of bringing out the best in them.

—Samuel

Black students don't know their history and they never see their own culture in school. That is why they act out, because they've been put down.

—Helen

Despite the need for schoolwide and systemic change, in most schools there are teachers who provide an empowering education to students who are failed by the institution as a whole. There were several such teachers in this study. They demonstrated through their practice the potential to transform students' educational experiences through meaningful curriculum and pedagogy, humane relationships, and advocacy on behalf of marginalized students. It is my argument that these teachers, and others like them, are a crucial bridge between what is and what might be in restructuring schools.

---

*This chapter is a revised and expanded version of previously published material appearing in Lipman, P. (1995). "Bringing out the best in them": The contribution of culturally relevant teachers to educational reform. *Theory Into Practice, 34*(4), 202–208 [a special issue devoted to Culturally Relevant Teaching] and Lipman, P. (1996). The missing voice of culturally relevant teachers in school restructuring. *Urban Review, 28*(1), 41–62.

Exemplary Teachers—A Resource for Change

There is a developing literature on exemplary teachers of African American students (Foster, 1995, 1997; King, 1991; Ladson-Billings, 1994). As Ladson-Billings (1991) and Murrell (1991) argue, the knowledge of these exemplary teachers needs to be incorporated in teacher education and in-service professional development so others can learn from their wisdom of practice (Shulman, 1987). Taking this argument one step further, I contend that successful teachers of students of color have a special role to play in educational change (cf. Foster, 1991).

Although exemplary teachers have been recognized as resources for the improvement of teaching, for example, in plans for master teachers and career professionals (Holmes Group, 1986) and in professional development schools, the standards by which these teachers are defined as "excellent" may not include their cultural connections with students. (The 1996 National Board for Professional Standards did not certify one teacher of color in a number of categories. This disparity was so evident that an adverse impact committe was formed to investigate.) (G. Ladson-Billings, personal communication, August 1997.) It is even less likely that a criterion of excellence will be teachers' stance in opposition to unequal relations of power and privilege in schools. However, emergent literature on exemplary teachers of students of color has helped to broaden notions of pedagogical excellence[1] by highlighting committed, culturally responsive teachers who actively work against the subordination of marginalized students and for social justice (e.g. Darder, 1995; Foster, 1995; Ladson-Billings, 1994). Here I argue that the leadership of these teachers must be a part of transforming schools in the interest of *all* children. (See also Lipman, 1996.)

In this chapter, I describe three exemplary teachers of African American students—Paulette at Gates and Samuel and Helen at Franklin—and examine their role in educational reform. I examine their perspectives and practices and situate them in the developing literature on culturally relevant pedagogy and on successful teachers of African American students. Examining the stance of these teachers is essential to understanding that there were alternative frameworks, pedagogies, and resources at Gates and Franklin. I also analyze how their voices were silenced, practices ignored, initiatives stifled, and their leadership overlooked in the restructuring process. Although I do not assume that successful teachers of students of color must be persons of color themselves (e.g., see Ladson-Billings 1994), the three teachers I discuss are African American.

Paulette Washington

Paulette was a strong advocate for African American students at Gates. She was also generally recognized by her colleagues as success-ful in engaging low-achieving students, and she had a rapport with students whom other teachers labeled troublemakers. She involved students in challenging academic work, mentored them, and consis-tently maintained respectful, humane relationships in her classroom. She built curriculum around students' lived experiences and created opportunities for them to examine their values and beliefs. Because of her cultural knowledge and connections with African American stu-dents, she and others with similar strengths might have been an influential force for change in a school with an overwhelmingly white faculty, many of whom were distanced from their majority African American students.

Advocacy and Reflection on Values

The first half of the 1990–91 school year, Paulette taught the new ninth-grade Study and Research Methods Class (SRM). Working in half a classroom, separated by a room divider, Paulette's room was cramped but organized. Literature and writing were everywhere. The walls were covered with broadsides on cooperative learning, aspects of analytical thinking, book posters, posters on writing essays, and vocabulary words. There were several tall, circular racks of paperback books—a mix of classic British and European-American novels and plays and a large selection of African American, Native American, and Latino literature. Within this space, Paulette frequently reorganized the desks to accommodate several simultaneous cooperative activities. In her untracked SRM class, those who were stronger in particular skills helped others who were weaker. My field notes from an SRM class in the fall illustrate a typical class:

There are 15 students, 4 black males, 10 black females, 1 White female. Students are clustered in several groups around specific activities, their desks pulled together, each cluster facing a differ-ent direction. The class seems relaxed but serious, without disrup-tions or distractions; the only conversations are students consulting with each other about the work they are doing together. A group of seven begins by writing in their journals. The class had written rap songs over the weekend, and they are recording their thoughts about the project. When they finish they work independently in the language foundations workbook [a whole language–oriented text], which includes sections on writing compositions, different kinds of writing, some grammar, and editing. A special education student is at a listening station, reading a book and following a tape. The remaining students are caught up in a lively discussion with Paulette about an essay they had read.

Typically, in Paulette's classes, academics were bound up with personal guidance and reflection on values. In one class the students had been reading biographies of "high-achieving role models," and the discussion was about setting personal goals. Paulette talks to the students about " persistence, responsibility, and appreciation for others." She's straightforward, direct: "You don't get anything done staying in bed until one in the afternoon. You don't get anything by day dreaming." She tells them they can all aspire to college if they work hard. "The main thing is to set goals in life." My field notes note that the students are attentive and serious, and there is a thoughtfulness and respectfulness toward each other that is often missing in other classes.

Paulette's relationships with students outside the classroom embodied this same sort of mentorship. Groups of African American students clustered with Paulette outside her classroom before and after school and between classes. Paulette said:

> Last year I did MCP [Mentoring and Counseling Program]. I did lots of things with them, took kids bowling, things like that. My husband even had the boys overnight. Some of my same MCP kids still cling to me. They come by and say, "Won't you still counsel me, Miss Washington?" "I'll counsel you," I say, and pat them on the shoulder (laughing). But they come up to me in the halls. Even though I'm not doing MCP any more, I can't reject them. They know I care about them. They know when you're not pretending. You don't turn off realness.

African American students, in particular, sought her out because she was one of the few adults who grasped their alienation at Gates. Yet, although she was an advocate for students, she had little power to influence their overall fate at Gates. This was illustrated by an incident involving a young African American male recorded in my field notes:

> In the middle of class, Edward comes to the door. "Excuse me, Miss Washington, may I speak with you." He's part of the AfroNotions program—they do the afternoon announcements.

He's dressed in sharp green and black checked baggy pants, matching shirt and sweater [dressed for his day to be the announcer]. He tells Paulette he was given a one-week out-of-school suspension for not apologizing to Miss [teacher]. Paulette talks to him for about 5 minutes.

She shakes her head after he leaves. She's visibly angry. "He never did that before. He was just in a bad mood. She's mean and the way she does it—'You will apologize to me!' [Paulette mimics a mean face.] That's unfair. It comes from not knowing your kids. He came to say he couldn't do the announcements. But I told him I need him today. But after today he won't be able to." She shakes her head.

To Paulette, there was a clear connection between the marginalization of African American faculty, including herself, and the subordination of African American students at Gates:

There are no black role models for these kids. I've been at Gates for 6 years and during that time they've lost three or four Black teachers. I'm coordinating a Black history project right now. There's a teacher who will not let a kid in the room a couple minutes late because he has to come from the auditorium where we are rehearsing. Every day it's the same thing. I think he's doing it on purpose to this kid just to harass him, and there's not much I can do.

Building on Students' Lived Experiences

Unlike some of her colleagues who emphasized nurturing for low-achieving students and academics for high-achievers, Paulette expected all of her students to perform well academically and conduct themselves appropriately. Above all, Paulette said, she was "about learning." She explained her philosophy: "At first kids give you a hard time, but when they see that you're solid, they're okay. When they see that you're serious about learning, they're okay." She believed that the poor academic performance of many African American students at Gates was due to teachers' low expectations and inability to recognize strengths.

These kids need recognition. In my class they get recognized every day. In bigger classes they might not get recognized for 3 or 4 days. One girl said to me, "Miss Washington, I want to be in with you. I had my hand up for 3 days in my SRM class and I never got called on. He only calls on the honors kids." These kids are intelligent. They know the material. They have good memories. They can remember a 20-minute rap song, but they don't have school skills. They aren't subject wise.

Her strategy with these students could be described along three dimensions. First, in her classes and before and after school, she explicitly taught academic skills and procedures and discourse styles to which many students had not been exposed (Delpit, 1988). For example, some students were asked to write an essay in a social studies class. They lost points because they didn't understand the essay format. The students came to Paulette, "I broke it down for them. . . . They said to me, 'Oh, Miss Washington, this is the first time anybody ever showed me that.' "

Second, she built bridges between students' lived experiences and culture and academic knowledge, linking home and community with school. She taught reading by assisting students with their life responsibilities. They studied the driver's test manual (which they were all motivated to read). They wrote letters to government agencies and employers for family and community members who needed help. They read tax manuals and completed family income-tax forms. Paulette explained, "Some have to fill them out for their mama or grandfather, so they have to know how." In general, she was critical of a curriculum with little relevance or meaning for most students and that did not recognize their intellectual resources:

Kids don't know why they should know what they are learning. It doesn't relate to them. The teacher says you need to know about isotopes or you'll never get a job. But that's not true. They will get a job. I don't know how isotopes relate to me and I'm out of school. How is this kid supposed to know? They don't relate what they're teaching to what the kids already know. What's in their own experience. Our teachers don't know how to do that. They don't understand their culture. They don't start with what the kids are equipped with. We're supposed to be intelligent enough to know what they know and work with that.

Third, relationships with students were humane and mutually respectful. Paulette commanded respect from all students, not only the African American students who other teachers thought were "wild," but impertinent White students as well. Paulette observed:

Certain behaviors that well-off White kids display are no problem [to other teachers]. They are cocky, have superior attitudes, disrespect for adults. They challenge you as though they were your equal. I'm the only one who recognizes that and puts them in a child's place. I demand respect from all the children. I don't care who they are.

Recognizing Strengths: The Example of Raymond

Paulette saw strengths in students where others saw only deficits. This was illustrated by a small case study I did of Raymond, an African American ninth-grader whom several teachers named an "at-risk" student. Raymond was doing poorly academically and was frequently in trouble with teachers and administrators. Teachers in his team described him as "very low," "probably a gang banger," and "your typical at-risk kid." Following Raymond for a day, I observed him to be bored and alternately acting out or sullen and withdrawn. Only in Paulette's class did he demonstrate respect and a measure of academic engagement.

His behavior in math, third period, was typical of most of his classes. While most students were solving problems in cooperative groups, Raymond was busy bothering others, snatching papers from two girls in his group, and repeatedly sharpening his pencil. When the class began working on problems in pairs, he just stared into space or engaged in side talk with other students. The teacher paid little attention to him, and he did virtually no work the entire period. Later she told me she had given up on him.

In Paulette's fifth-period class, although Raymond appeared tired and irritable, he contributed to the discussion and asked several questions. Later, he was engrossed in an article about contemporary African American leaders. He told Paulette he was disappointed because he didn't get to do his "last will and testament"—a class exercise he missed. After class he spent a few minutes chatting with Paulette about an upcoming field day.

His seventh-period science class evolved into an escalating power struggle with the teacher. At the outset, Raymond had the sullen look he displayed in most of his classes. Then, after receiving several tokens for correct answers, he was drawn into the discussion, almost in spite of himself. However, a small contentious verbal exchange with another student quickly escalated when the teacher reprimanded him in a particularly humiliating way. From my field notes:

The teacher tells Raymond he's writing him up, "You've done really well in here today but we cannot have any interaction like that. That will not be tolerated. You can't stay in here like this."

The boy next to Raymond warns him, under his breath, "Don't say nothing. Just be quiet."

Raymond is absolutely sullen and hostile.

Raymond put his head on his desk and refused to do any work the rest of the hour. At the end of class, he tried to assert himself and regain some lost dignity by contending with the teacher to get out a minute early. From my field notes: "Raymond: 'Can I get out a minute early? I need to go to my counselor. Can I get out a minute early? I need some psychological help.' Teacher ignores him. Raymond asks again. The teacher tells him to stay after class." The incident ended with Raymond receiving an in-house suspension. "I told him I wanted to talk to him after class and he walked out, so that's it. That's the bottom line. I can't tolerate that kind of behavior," the teacher later explained.

Judging by these interactions, it was not surprising that there were contradictory assessments of Raymond and that he was caught in a cycle of antagonistic encounters with adults, discipline actions, and more hostility. All of his teachers, except Paulette, were negative about his behavior and thought him to be very deficient in reading and math. Although Raymond was only marginally engaged in Paulette's class, she had won his respect and begun to tap his interests in a way others had not. The other teachers' portrayals of Raymond were diametrically opposed to hers, as well as contrary to my own observations of his reading and listening skills. One teacher said, " He can't keep a piece of paper from one day to the next. He doesn't listen. He can't read. He's a zero. I think he has a hearing disability because he never seems to hear what I say. But as far as mental processes he's not special [mentally disabled]. But he's just not there."

Paulette's reaction to a team meeting where Raymond was labeled "a typical at-risk kid":

Raymond *can* read. He tested average in reading. And he's good in math. If they say he can't read they haven't checked with the reading teachers. That's just superficial. They haven't really gone into it. He has a lot of strength, a lot of strength. He's a *good* listener. He likes strokes, immediate feedback. Not long term rewards but immediate. He's a good conversationalist. But they don't see that. He's totally turned off to school.

Her views were sharply at odds with her colleague's pessimistic, even antagonistic, appraisal, and she was frustrated that others did not draw upon her deeper knowledge of this student. This was a clear instance in which teachers did not utilize the opportunities of collaboration to learn from Paulette's relationship with a student they were failing. But the lack of attention to her perspective is not surprising in light of her peripheral role at Gates.

Paulette's Marginalization in the Restructuring Process

As a teacher of reading (a remedial subject devalued at Gates) and one of the few African American faculty at Gates, Paulette was marginalized before restructuring began. However, she was excited about the possibilities of educational change and interested in teaching the new SRM class. The process of her disengagement from her team was gradual, the relationship eroding throughout the first semester of 1990–91. At the beginning of that year, there was evidence that she participated actively in B Team discussions, drafted a parent letter signed by the team teachers, proposed various team activities, and appeared to be a fully present member of her team. But she began to be distanced from the life of the team by a combination of factors: lack of support from her colleagues, disenchantment with the superficiality of the team's agenda, the reorganization of Study and Research Methods and her transfer back to reading, and lack of support for her initiatives from the principal. The process of her disengagement is instructive of the ways in which the voices of relatively less powerful teachers, particularly teachers of color in White-dominated schools, may be muffled in spite of collaborative structures and "teacher empowerment."

A pivotal event that distanced Paulette from the team occurred in December when a prominent White Hills parent complained to the administration about her SRM class. In a team meeting the other teachers said they were "pulling for her," but no one was willing to go with her to a conference with the parent. One teacher said she played tennis with the parent and did not want to get involved. While White teachers, such as her teammate Colleen, were enthusiastic about the support they got from their team colleagues, Paulette was left to deal with this parent alone. This bitter incident was a turning point in her commitment to the team. "The whole team should have been there, but they didn't back me up. So I knew teaming wasn't really about anything. After that I lost interest," she said.

At Gates, one result of the mid-year reorganization of the SRM class was that one SRM teacher at each grade level was transferred to reading and was no longer officially part of the core teams, although the teacher was encouraged to continue to sit in on meetings. The reading teachers did not give a grade and became adjunct to both the English and SRM teachers who had replaced them. Paulette, a veteran teacher, was transferred to reading where she worked mainly with African American low-achieving students. Her SRM replacement was a White male who had just received his teaching certification. Paulette's transfer/demotion pushed her to the periphery of the ninth-grade teams, both literally and symbolically, undercutting whatever pedagogical authority and voice she had and distancing her from the dialogue of the core teams. (She was not a part of the core when they made a mid-year analysis of the school improvement plan, for example.) She described how her views were undermined in the process:

> They replaced experienced with inexperienced teachers. I had gotten kids to recognize teachers' teaching styles compared with their own learning styles. I structured the class so I could work with students at different levels of skills at the same time. Now they've undone everything that was done. Now the students see the English teacher as their principal instructor, as the motive. . . . I'm acting as the reading teacher and the ninth graders who are being pulled out for reading resent it. The new [SRM] teacher said in his class, "You don't have to go. You don't have a reading problem." So the kids pulled out are stigmatized. . . . But the reading teachers are external. We need to develop students' strengths but they don't listen to the reading teachers. I've just stopped trying. They don't listen to me.

Even before the SRM teachers were transferred to reading, the English teacher insisted that Paulette use SRM to reinforce that teacher's writing strategies, although Paulette had her own model for teaching writing. In part, this conflict stemmed from inadequately planned integration of the two classes, but it also reflected Paulette's inferior position in the pecking order at Gates. This dispute reinforced for Paulette that she and other African American teachers were not equal partners in a supposedly collaborative venture. Although she had equal formal status, race seemed to work as a "diffuse status characteristic" creating expectations that Whites were more competent and teachers of color were rendered invisible (cf. Cohen, 1975).

Paulette also became discouraged by the triviality of the teams' goals and activities. Her vision of educational reform transcended the compensatory focus on "at-risk" students. She found the team agendas, over which she had less and less influence, to be irrelevant to the central issues, as she defined them, that is, teachers' beliefs about students, representation of African Americans in the school, recognition of student strengths, fundamental change in curriculum and instruction:

> They only see the Black kids as "deprived." They don't see kids' strengths. . . . Teachers need to understand Black kids better. . . . These are issues we would be dealing with if we were serious about disparities . . . A major problem in the school is the lack of adult Black role models, especially Black males. In the way we hire people, we're not thinking about this. There are no Black role models for these kids. . . . That's another issue we should be dealing with. . . .
>
> For kids who aren't achieving we should know that they have some strengths and build on that. Instead, we say just "leave that to resource." If he's in science or she's in science and he or she can't read the science book it's someone else's fault. It's not our job. We deal so much with discipline that we don't get on with the real restructuring. We need time in the team for the larger issues, but we don't think about our strengths. If you look at the agenda, it's always about so and so student. Each teacher is doing their own thing. They've just taken the path of least resistance and each one is just going back to his or her own style or philosophy. We need an in-service for teams to get the teams on track. The teachers are still operating in isolation.

Her skepticism echoed African American teachers studied by Foster (1993, 1994), who perceived restructuring to be incompatible with their commitments, beliefs about students, cultural perspectives, and educational philosophies. Isolated and largely impotent, Paulette pulled back from the team. Minutes of team meetings show her to be present at only two meetings after February.

Nevertheless, in the second half of the year, she continued to describe herself as a teacher who used to just "do her job" but was revitalized by the opportunity to make change at Gates. Frustrated with her team, she struggled to play a broader, schoolwide role. As part of a small, district multicultural project not connected with restructuring, she traveled with seven other teachers to visit an innovative school in another part of the state. Her purpose was to investigate alternative examples of restructured schools. She returned very excited. The district was all-White and rural, but she felt that their ideas were applicable to Gates's student body. She was amazed that the students were identified as at-risk, yet there was a high level of academic engagement. She was excited that they seemed to rely on humane relationships with students rather than traditional discipline and punishment as at Gates. And she was impressed with the curriculum and the freedom teachers had to reshape instruction and assessment of student learning. "You can feel a cheerfulness. It's almost like a song. None of this, 'Line up the seats, we're on page three.' . . . They took Julius Caesar and rewrote it and developed their own situation. We could do that here."

When she returned from this visit, Paulette began promoting this example of curriculum and pedagogy. For her, these changes were what restructuring was about. Her critique reflected a more far-reaching curricular and pedagogical vision than restructuring offered or than most of her colleagues expressed:

> I wish I could get over to them [Gates teachers and administrators] what I saw in _____. The way the curriculum is designed and set up there, it almost alleviates those discipline problems. They teach to the different learning styles. Those are the strategies . . . somebody has to set the focus. In this school, discipline is the top priority. We may not be aware of it but it is. If five of you have the same student then you deal with that. That's what we've latched on to and it seemed like a utopia. We did a couple of interdisciplinary units . . . but the key is to see other schools and see what is going on there. There isn't enough planning for what we want to do with restructuring.

However, she was unable to interest the school administration. There was no support for her to disseminate what she had learned, no forum for discussion. She was not a team leader and not part of the inner circle of teachers who had the principal's ear. No one in the school administration seemed to see her visit as legitimately related to restructuring. Earlier in the year she had lobbied to attend a statewide workshop on reducing teen pregnancy but got no support from the principal for that either. Paulette did not teach a high-status academic subject; she had little authority in the realm of curriculum and little status within the staff or among parents. She was frustrated by her colleagues' lack of enthusiasm and the administration's lack of interest in her initiatives.

Nevertheless, as part of the district's multicultural education team, she continued to push for multicultural curriculum at Gates. She contended, "We have a Black history month but it needs to be the whole year as a part of the curriculum. We're ready now for a multicultural curriculum." The district multicultural education project offered her a

$500 scholarship to attend a summer institute in the Caribbean, but she had to pay another $500. The restructuring project was spending thousands of dollars for staff development and teachers were being sent to conferences across the United States and even Canada. It would have seemed that staff development money might have been found to support her attendance, particularly since the principal was very influential in the district. However, she got no support from Gates's administrators and had no influence with district personnel. Paulette said: " It's all on my back. I talked to Ron and the next day he told me he tried but no luck. He suggested I organize a dance to raise money. I wrote a letter to the school district, called twice. I'm making sacrifices, but I would be able to bring it back to the school. I could be a leader in the whole school, but they don't see that."

Although restructuring and the rhetoric of teacher empowerment inspired Paulette to explore educational alternatives and to imagine herself as a school leader, her initiative was disregarded. In terms of rethinking curriculum and instruction, cultural responsiveness, and commitment to the education of African American students, Paulette was potentially one of the key change agents at Gates. She was a sharp critic of the status quo and the most active in seeking out alternative educational models of all the teachers I knew at Gates. Silencing Paulette (and others like her, such as William discussed in chapter 6) partially explains the failure of Gates teachers to seriously examine these issues for all students. At the end of the school year, she was frustrated and pessimistic:

> I'm disgusted that [Ron] wants me to raise my own money for that trip. I'm not doing it for my benefit. It's for the school, the whole school, but he doesn't see that. It's not important to him. And for a teacher like me who used to just come in and do my job and go home it means a lot. I was at a point where I just wasn't interested. Now I'm really enthused. I want to be a leader. I want to do these things for the school but he doesn't seem to be interested in that. He asked for our ideas for next year and I suggested we have an international bazaar. We could begin in the fall and work toward it, develop a whole interdisciplinary curriculum around it, and have it in February. But I haven't heard anything about it—and I doubt I will.

To my knowledge, no faculty clique or interest group conspired to suppress alternative perspectives or set out to undermine Paulette specifically. Rather, satisfaction with Gates's traditional academic culture and the subordination of African American staff and students produced a disempowering political and cultural environment for change-minded teachers, particularly if they were African American. Her case reflects ways in which school culture and informal power relations can stifle dissident voices. As I argued earlier, teachers and Hills/Palisades parents were generally satisfied with Gates's traditional schooling at which most of the neighborhood children were successful. There seemed to be a consensus that "real school" (Metz, 1990) consisted of the textbook-oriented, teacher-centered, closed-ended academic work that characterizes most U.S. secondary schools (Sizer, 1984), and there was little impetus to change it. Yet it was conventional notions of teaching and learning as well as the Eurocentric curricula that Paulette called into question. Resistance to change at Gates was compounded by a district context in which, despite rhetoric of teacher empowerment, central administrators and the restructuring director provided little concrete support for original, building-level initiatives. There was no culture of genuine innovation to encourage teachers like Paulette.

Moreover, the school's colorblind perspective and a culture of silence about race created an environment in which Paulette's views were not only not on the agenda, but proscribed. Had the subordination of African American students been open for discussion, teachers and administrators might have seen Paulette and other exemplary teachers of African American students as more central. In fact, Paulette was marginalized in part *because of* her controversial ideas. Thus the silence about race both caused Paulette's marginalization and reinforced it.

Underlying this silence was a more overt racism. One Gates administrator contended, privately, that racial disparities could be attributed directly to African American teachers:

> If you look at it, where you have White principals and a high percentage of White teachers, you have higher performance. Where you have Black principals and more Black teachers, there is lower performance and lower behavior standards. That's just the way it is, but the district doesn't want to deal with that. . . . Black teachers and Black principals have lower standards. I know it sounds real racist, but that's the reality even though no one wants to talk about it. You show me schools where Black subgroups are improving and in every case, in _____ School, in our school, that's the case. . . . The problem with Black teachers is that their style is verbal interaction with students. They want to reason with them rather than using their authority. Black

teachers let kids run wild, they talk back. There's a lot of loose behavior.

This deficit model of African American teachers paralleled many teachers' views of African American students. Thus, discussions of racial issues were taboo, yet African American teachers were privately judged inferior, and there was no critical mass of support for teachers like Paulette. In this world, her limited role in restructuring was highly predictable.

Samuel Thompson

Samuel Thompson was both dignified and flamboyant. Franklin drama coach, literature teacher, and writer, his teaching and everyday conversation were imbued with a flair that fascinated students. Samuel was widely recognized by his colleagues to be a creative and challenging teacher, popular with students. His classes were very experiential and student-directed, yet he was at the nucleus, like a dramatic concert master, spurring students on, correcting, applauding. He was also extremely outspoken and walked about the school with an air of authority. It was not unusual for Samuel, on his way through the school office, to stop and inquire about the situation of a student waiting to see the principal and to offer advice to both the student and her or his parent.

"Bringing out the Best in Them"

Samuel's classroom was impeccably neat, the walls covered with book posters, samples of student writing, the vocabulary words for the week, student projects, and several prominently displayed posters of African American leaders and authors. Rows of textbooks were in perfect order on the shelves, and there was a broad assortment of paperback novels, poetry anthologies, and plays. In front of the door was a small, clean, braided rug on which all who entered were expected to wipe their feet. Several times each day, Samuel could be seen sweeping his room and the hallway outside his classroom door. Although some teachers smiled at this eccentricity, Samuel went right on, explaining that maintaining his room was one way of generating respect for what occurred there. "Our classroom is our home," he insisted. Marking off his classroom, making it his own, was one of the ways Samuel projected a sense of agency and control.

Samuel exuded confidence and commitment toward Franklin students. For him, as for the Othermothers and the principal, working at Franklin was a calling:

If you preach negativism, that's what you get. I call them segmental children. Segmental. Teachers have a stigma about these
children and so they do about enough to keep them in their seat
and away from their desk. They don't spend enough time to
find, to see where the deficiencies can be corrected. Of course we
have children with deficiencies. We're a feeder school. You understand what I mean. Some schools won't take these children.
But we don't feel that way toward these children. We believe
every child can learn.

Samuel was outspokenly opposed to the incentives some teachers
had begun using. He believed they were demeaning and demonstrated
a fundamental lack of confidence in students. He commented on teachers who said, "You behave and I'll let you do my bulletin board":

I hate that! Bribing children that way instead of bringing out the
best in them. A student is in charge of room decor in my room.
He designs all the bulletin boards. When I say I want to change
the board, Arthur stands back and looks at it. "Oh no. I had a
very different idea," he says. So that's the way it is. I believe in
giving the children a lot of autonomy. They're responsible for
their own learning. I tell them what they'll learn but they suggest
how. They have ownership.

Samuel made academic knowledge accessible and meaningful by
building bridges between students' lives and the subject matter being
taught. He also used class materials as a starting point from which to
examine personal values and social issues. As a result, students were
not only academically engaged but the discussions I observed were
thoughtful and reflective. In a representative class, Samuel turned the
discussion of a novel by African American author Virginia Hamilton
into an examination of how to solve personal conflicts. The conversation pivoted on ethical issues posed by the text, shifting back and forth
between the book and students' experiences, interweaving an analysis
of the novel with their own dilemmas (17 students, 8 White, 9 Black):

They are discussing *Dies Drear*. There's a knock on the door. A
student in the back row automatically gets up to answer it. [I
learn later this is his responsibility.]. . . .
    They discuss some of the issues posed by the novel. Samuel
asks, "Have you ever felt someone was trying to gain in on your

territory at home? How do you handle it? How do you keep a good relationship with that person and solve your problems at the same time?" There's a surprisingly frank, personal discussion on these issues.

While some teachers degraded the knowledge students brought to school, Samuel used it as a basis for classroom learning, conveying to students the value of their lives and experiences. This was clearly different from an academic environment in which many teachers saw the students as deprived and deficient. In a world where test scores, academic tracking, an alienating curriculum, and exasperated teachers communicated that students were inferior, Samuel consciously reinforced students' confidence in their own knowledge and the worth of their own life experience. He was impatient with a system that designated some children "gifted" and others "regular." "They all have gifts and talents," he said. High academic expectations and high standards for all students was a hallmark of his teaching. This was more than attitude or interactional style. Concretely, he helped students translate what they knew into academic knowledge:

> I tell my students every day, "You're the best I've had to work with—the *very* best." And it's true because they're the ones I'm working with now. "You can do this because you already know this." Then I go into the heart of the matter. Sometimes I turn on the soaps. I say, "Today we're going to watch the soaps." "The soaps?" they say. They can't believe it. But we do. Then we talk about it. We go from the soaps and then I tell them what educated people call this and that. I ask them who is telling the story. They know that. Then I tell them, "You already know point of view. You just described it." We do the same thing with character and plot. I find them where they are. I say, "You've told stories. When you say, 'The way I see it,' that's point of view." I just do it like that. When kids believe you think they can learn, they will. If they know you're sincere.

In my observations, the explicit connection between the competencies valued in school and students' personal knowledge infused whatever Samuel did with students. For example, in the library, the students were practicing an African American history play that they were to perform for a group of visitors:

A student forgets his lines. Samuel: "Just make it up. Use your sense. Act like a politician." He waves his arms dramatically. "How do politicians act on T.V.? You already know this. You know how they act. Yes, yes, make it up." He applauds enthusiastically as the student improvises.

Jacob, an 18-year-old White, ex-student at Franklin, testified to the impact Samuel had made on his life, suggesting that his *pedagogy*, in its broadest sense, benefited all students, regardless of race. I interviewed Jacob when he stopped to visit the school. He had been expelled by an assistant principal the previous year when he was 17 years old and in the eighth grade but had maintained ties with the principal and Samuel. He had also been expelled from elementary school and had been retained several years. Now he worked construction. Despite his unsuccessful school experience, he earned his high school equivalency diploma in 2 months after leaving Franklin, without ever attending high school. He was currently enrolling in a community college.

PL: Did you like school?
Jacob: Some of it.
PL: What did you like?
Jacob: English. Mr. Thompson. He let you do things. The rest of it was boring. I like science, the lab. Most kids like labs; they like to do things. When you get to get up and move around, when you get up and do more things in class it's more interesting. When the teacher is just sitting behind his desk talking to kids all day, the kids are going to ignore him. I do. I just ignore 'em.
PL: Why was Mr. Thompson different?
Jacob: He let us do different things. And he was the only one who told us that what we were learning was important in life. He'd tell us how it might not seem like it now, but we'd need this stuff later. I come by and see him all the time. I respect him for what he taught me. [He goes on to talk about how Samuel influenced his decision to continue his education.]

Mentoring and Constructing a Sense of Family

Unlike teachers who had newly grafted "nurturing" and "mentoring" onto their teaching, and unlike the Othermothers who sometimes subordinated teaching to counseling, mentoring and teaching were intertwined in Samuel's pedagogy. This was inherent in the values-orientation of his classes, as in the one described above. Samuel also established his room as a sort of informal student center, a place where students could work on special projects. He extended an open invitation to them, and (from my observations and his testimony) the respect implied in this invitation was reciprocated by their conduct in his room regardless of whether he was present or not. Before and after school and during lunch period students met there to rehearse a play, complete an assignment, or plan a project. Sometimes Samuel was available as an informal adviser, as in this incident recorded in my field notes:

> While I am waiting for Samuel, two African American students come in carrying an old record player. They are practicing for the talent show. The boy is a talented singer. He sings along with a recording while his friend critiques him. Samuel comes in smiling, sits down to listen. "Ooh yes!" he interjects. At one point he sings along. He obviously really enjoys it. It is also obvious that the students feel free to use his room for these activities. Samuel makes a few suggestions and encourages the singer, "You are so talented."

When Samuel said, "Our classroom is our home," he was projecting the sense of family that he created within this space and a sense of student ownership that was visible. Some students who were reputed to be troublemakers and whom I observed to be disrespectful of adults and their peers in other classes, conducted themselves with maturity in Samuel's classes.

Indeed, because of the rapport and mutual respect he established with students, he rarely encountered the discipline problems so many teachers complained about. "I never send students to the office. That's not necessary here," he claimed. Also his teaching, much more intellectually engaging than was typical at Franklin, gave students an opportunity to use their intellect and creativity productively. His approach acknowledged the temperament of lively and creative young adolescents:

> Discipline is something that is unique to each teacher. What may be a discipline problem to some is not to others. I encourage my students to express themselves. At the proper moment, of course. But for some teachers that may be a discipline problem. But you have to give them an opportunity to express their creativity. You can't be so rigid.

Samuel's Marginal Role in Restructuring

Samuel's potential contributions to restructuring reached beyond the quality of his interactions with students. In addition to creating bridges between students' home/cultural experience and academic learning, Samuel was an inventive and challenging teacher. His room was filled with the products of experiential, active learning—a rarity in most Franklin classrooms. He had a closet stocked with ingenious games using vocabulary words, literary terms, literature, and writing. These, he was quick to point out, were invented each year by "regular students, not honors, regular." He was the director of the school newspaper and dreamed of a truly professional publication that would be the product of interdisciplinary studies in collaboration with other teachers. His dream for restructuring was to support this kind of curriculum development:

> I'd like to have it be multigrade so the ninth graders could teach the eighth graders. That way students could apprentice with other students, teach each other. But the school doesn't have the resources, and it's so much work to design a whole curriculum. I would like restructuring to help with something like that.

He was also the director of a myriad of school activities and creative projects in addition to the school newspaper, including drama club and various performances. In short, Samuel was an indisputable resource for other teachers in a process of rethinking curriculum and instruction schoolwide.

Despite his exemplary practice and leading role in many projects at Franklin, Samuel was not chosen to be a team leader. Although I do not know administrators' reason for this, both school and district administrators described him as talented but too argumentative and independent. In a culture that suppressed disagreements and silenced talk about race, Samuel was a maverick. He was outspoken. These qualities placed him outside the bounds of leadership as it was conceived at Franklin. His boldness and individuality also made him seem quirky in a highly conformist environment, and without public support from school and district administrators he was often dismissed by other teachers as somewhat eccentric. In a context where some teachers still feared retribution for challenging the status quo, Samuel's boldness scared off his colleagues. An African American teacher explained, "Samuel does speak his mind but a lot of people just write him off as a troublemaker. 'That's just crazy Samuel. Don't say anything because he'll just get you in trouble.' No one takes him seriously."

Moreover, Samuel was blunt about racial injustice, putting him squarely in conflict with Franklin's colorblind ethos that censured those who dared to speak out on issues of race. School and district administrators took no visible steps to break through this ethos. Samuel's open advocacy of African American teachers, his public sponsorship of African American culturally centered activities, and his initiation of African American–led projects such as the Franklin yearbook, isolated him, even from some African American teachers. When he proposed that the African American staff have a potluck dinner, the staunchest African American teachers opposed it because it would "separate us out" and might cause trouble. In turn, Samuel accused them of pandering to Whites. This turned into a significant conflict, and the rift took months to heal.

Over the 3 years I talked with him, Samuel remained positive about restructuring, but he came to focus narrowly on the benefits of additional professional development. Restructuring, he said, "has caused us to blossom. I've learned so much. And that has filtered over to the students." But he thought the teams were unproductive because they were mired in "personal jealousies." And he did not see the teams, building steering committee, or other forms of teacher collaboration, as having much effect on the beliefs and practices of the "negative" teachers because people were afraid to speak their minds. He was extremely pessimistic about bridging the divisions among the faculty, especially along racial lines:

> The faculty is very divided. In faculty meetings it's snowy white on one side and charcoal black on the other. Really the teachers are just big children. Just big children. We are behind here. We have a lot of socialization to do. It's really ridiculous. The students are more mature than we are. There is no dialogue between those who are negative and those who are positive. It's really a hopeless situation.

Discouraged by the divisions among teachers and their silent toleration of fundamental disagreement, he chose to bury himself in his own activities. He simply got what he could from the staff development associated with restructuring: "Those of us who are positive, we are all so [pause] busy. I guess we're tolerant. We tolerate them [negative teachers]." Thus, Samuel was essentially marginalized by the same factors that stifled critical inquiry and teacher initiative generally at Franklin: a culture that suppressed debate, a colorblind philosophy, and deep divisions among the faculty. Whatever role he might have played as an agent of change was blunted by the school culture and political context in which racial issues and controversies were suppressed. Furthermore, for an innovative teacher interested in curriculum, restructuring, as it unfolded at Franklin, was far too narrow and uninteresting. It provided no support for the sorts of sweeping curricular reforms he envisioned. Although he undoubtedly expressed his views to his team colleagues, Samuel's pedagogical knowledge and positive orientation toward students had limited influence on the direction of restructuring schoolwide.

Helen McAllister

Helen McAllister was one of the most highly respected teachers at Franklin—by other teachers, administrators, and students alike. Students and parents requested her, even demanded they have her for a teacher. Helen was both humane and exacting. She was a gracious and dignified woman who had made her 30-plus years of teaching into a life purpose. In addition to teaching at Franklin, she taught Sunday school at her church, worked in a tutoring program before and after school, and helped to organize Saturday classes in African American history in Black churches. She was also a recognized teacher-leader. She headed one of the new grade level teams, sponsored the student honor society, and chaired the English department.

Her room, like Samuel's, was cleaner, more appealing, and somehow brighter than most. The walls were decorated with many posters and samples of student work, all very tastefully arranged. On a shelf were samples of student productions—a box of finely etched soap carvings of characters in *Romeo and Juliet*, a model of the Globe Theater. Bookshelves were lined with precisely ordered texts, and there were racks of paperback books, both European and Euro-American classics as well as African American literature. Plants were arranged on file cabinets set at angles in the corners of the room. The six window shades were all pulled to exactly the same height, and to each was affixed a neatly lettered sign reading, "Please do not touch." On each window sill was a small room freshener. The room projected some of the most salient aspects of Helen's teaching: She was highly structured yet creative, respectful, celebratory of student accomplishments, and above all, serious about learning.

Recognizing Potential and Setting High Standards

There were no wasted moments in Helen's classes. Students understood that "you worked in Miss McAllister's room." But, she also projected a profound confidence in students' capacities and patience in helping them meet goals. Her appreciation of their strengths, her sense of responsibility for their growth as persons, and her respect for them elicited these same qualities from the students. One student told me, "The kids don't want to disappoint Miss McAllister." Although she was very positive about the collegial aspects of restructuring, as well as team activities, her concern was that restructuring result in stronger academic performance for low-achieving students and a reduction of the racial disparities: "They like the rewards, the pizza parties, the motivational speakers. But I want students to compete academically."

Her belief in the students and her conviction that they wanted to learn permeated her interactions with them:

> At the beginning of a class she announces, "First we'll do spelling. I know you're ready for your spelling and I don't want to disappoint you. Do you want to look at them first for a minute?" . . . When she discusses a paper the students are writing, she says, "I would like you to write as much as you can. I don't want to limit you."
>
> A boy raises his hand and asks, "Is it okay if I alter some things for my project?"
>
> Helen answers, "Surely. Surely. Be creative. I don't want to limit your creativity."

This theme of not limiting students ran through her teaching. "I think it's important to expose ninth graders to as much as possible," she said. She contended that a cause of the achievement disparities was teachers' low expectations for low-income and African American students. She taught regular track students the same way as honors students.

> I have high expectations for all of my students. I don't water down anything for them. If some need extra help, I work with them individually. I also tutor [Franklin students] after school and two mornings a week at the University before school. . . . I'm frustrated that we can't teach high school books. We can't teach any books from the high school list in junior high school. So this holds a lot of junior high school students back. We have to challenge these students. When we don't give them an opportunity, we're taking something away from them.

She projected confidence that students could meet the standards she set and then provided concrete support in meeting them. She worked with students individually and tutored them outside school hours. At the beginning of the year she gave the students their standardized test scores and mapped out a plan with them for improvement. In the spring she told students she would be preparing work for them to do over the summer as well as lists of books they should read to prepare them for high school and "to keep your minds active." Conversations about choosing a high school, planning for college, and preparing for college entrance tests were woven into Helen's classes. She organized a program for 75 Franklin ninth graders to shadow Hamilton High School students for a day to get a taste of high school. (Hamilton was the top college preparatory high school and most Franklin students did not consider going there.)

She was both demanding and humane. As an example, when she informed one of her classes she would be absent the next day because she was attending a workshop, a boy expressed concern that the assignment she left them would be so huge they would not be able to complete it. Helen reassured him, "I'll be human. You don't need to worry about that. I won't leave an assignment that you can't do, young people." Although she stressed academics, her ultimate concern was for the student as a person. She was aware of the damage done by years of miseducation and teacher neglect, and cognizant of the personal and social obstacles many students faced. In a team meeting she proposed that each teacher give a student who had just had a baby only a little homework until she was able to resume her full academic schedule. "We want to be realistic and help her stay in school," Helen counseled. The others agreed and mapped out a plan for the student.

Helen consistently reinforced the knowledge and creativity that students brought to her classes, and she encouraged them to learn from and help each other. This is reflected in notes from two classes. The first is a regular ninth-grade English class (9 students: 5 Black, 4 White; 6 females, 3 males). (Like many other ninth-grade classes, this one had a low enrollment, but on this day there were also many absences.):

The students quietly take their seats. As the class begins Helen reminds them to check their calendars for assignment due dates. "Today we're going to review *Romeo and Juliet*. First, let's review what's in the prologue and then, what's in the climax."

She asks what a climax is, and one student says, "The best part."

Helen smiles, "Yes! Yes! The best part. What a good way of putting it, Jason."

As they review different parts of the play, one student disagrees with another's interpretation of the Prince. Helen asks the boy, "Why do you think so?" and the whole class gets into a lengthy and spirited discussion of the effectiveness of the Prince's actions, drawing comparisons with gangs and their own experience. She encourages them to present their own interpretations, to express their own ideas.

The second is an honors class on the same day (10 students: 8 Black, 2 White; 8 females, 2 males):

[They are doing spelling and grammar (verbals).]

Helen:	You can do the hard words. These are words you'll see on the ACT, PSAT. Liability. Where might you see that word? In which class?
Keisha:	Civics.
Natasha:	Science.
Diane:	Why?
Natasha:	Discussing medical malpractice.
Helen:	I've told this class about the vast amount of knowledge that they can share with students. A lot of times we can learn from students and they can learn from us. Very good Natasha.

Discipline was simply a nonissue. Helen declared, "In all my years of teaching, I sent two students to the office." With patience and humanity she held attentive and respectful students to uniformly high standards of academic performance and behavior. To the disbelief of other teachers, the most unruly students in other classes did not act up or show disrespect in Miss McAllister's room. Those considered by other teachers as too tough to handle, gathered their composure as they entered with a respectful, "Good afternoon, Miss McAllister." They sat down, took out their work, and bent themselves to her challenges. Notes from another class reflect how her respect for students' integrity and her encouragement of appropriate behavior contrasted with the deprecation and verbal abuse to which students were sometimes subjected at Franklin. At the beginning of the class (10 students: 8 Black, 2 White; 4 males, 6 females):

It's picture day and some students are missing. Most of the young women are dressed up and have their hair elaborately styled. There is some confusion over the picture taking and an assistant principal thunders over the loudspeaker that students who are in the hallway "won't have your pictures taken in the future."

Helen says, "I know you are not the ones doing this but some desks have some writing on them. I would appreciate it, please, do not write on the desk. Any of you who have an urge to doodle, I will be happy to give you a piece of paper." All of this is in a quiet smiling manner, devoid of sarcasm or blame. Anne, a White girl holding a rose in a vase on her desk, is trying to clean the writing off. "That's okay, Anne. I have something to clean it off with." Smiling, she comments, "Your flower is beautiful. . . . Okay, Let's go, young people."

They begin a spelling test. "Infringe. We do not want to infringe on another person's rights." A girl walks in late. Helen smiles and asks, "Were you at the picture taking? We're on spelling. You might want to begin with number two. Let's give her a minute." She waits calmly for the girl to get ready to take the test.

There's another blistering announcement from the assistant principal about students in the halls. Helen says, matter-of-factly, "I hope you all didn't abuse the privilege. Okay. I just want you to be good examples."

Connections With Family and Community

Learning was based on the quality of Helen's relationships with students and their families. She was convinced that children would learn if there was a relationship based on trust and concern, like family. "I love this school," she said. "We've got some good students here. These kids are neat. They're loveable, and they're teachable, if they find out that you're concerned about them." She believed that restructuring was making students more interested in school because the teams sent the students a message that the teachers are concerned, that "we're here for your education. It's a family-type atmosphere."

Knowing the child as a whole person and building on the child's family and social experience was integral to her pedagogy. She visited students' homes, knew them from church, and talked with them outside class:

You need to see the living conditions of the child to understand the child. You have to understand that child in total. We have to see how the students are outside of class, have to look at the total child, find out about their home. We need to go into the homes. A lot of our students have good potential. They have a whole lot of potential.

In addition to making home visits and contacting families by phone, she often invited parents to attend classes with their children to see what they were doing in school. (Apparently, they did attend occasionally, although I never observed this.) Families were listened to, and Helen worked in partnership with them. In several team meetings I observed, she reported proposals parents had made for their children or strategies she and the parents had jointly constructed. In short, Helen was part of a student's family and community support system.

Educated in Black schools and an historically Black college, she carried on the tradition of teaching as a community responsibility, a calling akin to clergy or community leadership (Siddle Walker, 1993). She was dismayed that some teachers were simply "teaching for the paycheck. There needs to be more accountability on the part of teachers." She was very critical of elementary schools that passed students "without mastery." She considered this an abrogation of the school district's responsibility to be accountable for the learning of the young people in their charge. Disagreeing with current educational theory (see Shepard & Smith, 1989), she advocated retention in the third grade when necessary because she believed students should not be passed on until they could perform at a high level. She claimed Riverton had low retention rates (3.5%) because teachers and principals were afraid that retentions reflected negatively on them.

Helen took her responsibility beyond the classroom and the demands of her job at Franklin. In addition to volunteering in early-morning and afterschool tutoring programs, she worked with students during her lunch hour. Although she did not phrase it this way, teaching for Helen was fulfilling a responsibility to the family and the community to help raise the next generation to its fullest potential.

An Expanding Curricular Vision

Although Helen's pedagogical style was quite traditional, she said that "the whole curriculum needs changing." An advocate of what she termed "multiculturalism," she was a member of a district committee that was developing a more diverse book list for English classes. Initially reticent about these issues in our conversations, over the course of the year I heard Helen begin to unfold a critique of the Eurocentrism of both curriculum and pedagogy at Franklin. She recognized that marginalizing African American students' discourse and interactional styles played a significant role in their school failure (Irvine, 1991; King, 1991). In an interview, she said:

> There are cultural differences. They need to get in different resources and speakers from different cultures to talk with the students and the teachers. Some students may use dialect. If a teacher doesn't understand the student, that student may not do well. We have to know when and how to correct students so as not to damage their self-esteem. Teachers need to be able to relate to each culture. They need to understand why a child rolls his eyes. Why a child responds to directions differently. They need to understand the various cultures. . . . It would be helpful if we had more field trips. We could go to the art center to view works by Black and White artists. The students need to be exposed to all cultures in the educational process.

In interviews at the end of the 1990–91 school year, Helen was candid about the role of racism in the alienation and academic failure of African American students. In her own stories and those she told about her friends, she described the racial oppression that connected her life with her African American students. Describing the fight she had waged for her own son to be placed in advanced classes in high school, his unequal treatment in these classes, and the way he was overlooked by school counselors in his preparations to apply to college, she said, "There are two standards for placement in advanced classes. . . . In counseling too the Black students aren't told of all the opportunities unless the head counselor is Black." As an African American teacher, she considered herself responsible to right the injustices African American students experienced in school:

> Black students don't know their history and they never see their own culture in school. That is why they act out, because they've been put down. Some people want to get away from February as Black history month. It's been used as a stigma. Black history needs to be taught all the way through. They are not aware of their own history. They don't know Carver, or DuBois, or Bethune. The churches are beginning to take responsibility for teaching this history because the schools aren't doing it.

Untapped Pedagogical Knowledge

Formally, Helen was a leader of restructuring at Franklin and widely recognized as an excellent, experienced teacher. The principal selected her as a team leader and Helen frequently represented the school in district workshops on restructuring. Helen was positive about the educational reform, "This is one of my best years teaching. There's more cooperation and initiative from students and they love the incentives." She also said restructuring, "has given me some hope" because it encouraged teachers to work together for the good of the students.

In my observations, as a team leader Helen set a tone for her team (which was not one of my focus teams). For example, I observed her encourage her team colleagues to examine their own actions when discipline problems arose. She said, "If a student is negative in one class we ask, 'Have you said anything that turned the student off? That may have been a little abusive?' " I also observed teachers seeking her guidance informally, but this was not new with restructuring. Juanita, on the Eagles Team, said that when she came to the school Miss McAllister was her mentor.

However, Helen's pedagogical knowledge and her orientation to students did not help shape dialogue on educational change at Franklin. There was no systematic effort to make the elements of Helen's pedagogical excellence accessible to other teachers through, for example, workshops, co-teaching, or peer reviews. Despite her formal leadership role in restructuring, her perspective was nearly as peripheral as Paulette's and Samuel's. This was largely because her success was viewed by her colleagues as personal, a unique talent. One teacher described her as "one in a million." Delisa, the principal, said, "Oh yes, Miss McAllister, she has a way with students. She's special. I don't think anyone can do what she can with kids." Although this gave credence to Helen's teaching as an art, it also devalued her pedagogical excellence as somehow innate and intangible, and therefore unable to be delineated and learned from (cf. Foster, 1991). Others did not see in her work with students a set of practices that were perhaps elusive but nevertheless grounded in identifiable values, relationships, and beliefs about students that might help the school as a whole reshape teaching and learning. Nor was Helen's analysis of the problems African American students faced at Franklin part of the conversation about restructuring. Once again, a context that shunned controversy, particularly about race, was hardly conducive to these views.

The failure systematically to utilize the expertise of Helen and others like her is certainly not specific to this setting. Until recently, the pedagogical knowledge and perspective of teachers of color has been largely unexplored by educational research (Foster, 1991). Nor is it generally part of academic discourse in programs of teacher education (Murrell, 1991). Although Helen was active in restructuring, her potential contribution to substantively changing the educational experiences of low-achieving African American students was unrealized.

Stifling Teacher Initiative—The District Context

The failure to capitalize on the pedagogical knowledge of building-level staff was a general phenomenon in Riverton, and the limited role of exemplary teachers of African American students should be considered in that light. To the extent that disrespect for teachers' ideas and initiatives continued under restructuring, the rhetoric of teacher empowerment diverged sharply from practice. The school board's order to revise the Study and Research Methods class, severely compromising an experiment largely devised by teachers, was just one example. Squelching tentative steps toward untracking at Franklin was another.

The district restructuring office's apparent need to control what happened in the restructuring schools perpetuated this problem, although more subtly. True, teachers were reminded repeatedly by the restructuring director that they were "empowered" through teams, steering committees, and district task forces. But professional development sessions for team leaders through the Restructuring Institute (discussed in chapter 3) concentrated on specific activities and emphasized participation in group processes rather than discussion of policy questions or critical inquiry about the central issues facing the schools. Although a curriculum consultant worked intensively for a few weeks with some of the SRM teachers, and there were workshops and presentations on paradigm shifts in teaching and learning, there was little concrete support for teacher-led curricular and pedagogical innovation. A presentation at Franklin on the philosophy of the Coalition of Essential Schools (Coalition of Essential Schools, 1989) inspired little response by teachers. The restructuring director did not specifically encourage critical reflection on beliefs and practices and did not promote or facilitate learning from exemplary teachers. Thus, teacher participation was less spontaneous and bottom-up than mandated and administratively regulated (Hargreaves, 1991). The restructuring agenda itself was clearly bounded by what was politically safe and noncontroversial and did not promote much real teacher initiative.

The control emanating from both the restructuring office and other branches of district leadership was a limitation on the leadership of all teachers. However, even if this had not been the case, at both schools and in the district, there were political and cultural barriers to the leadership of teachers who were advocates for African American students. The politics of race and class in the district subordinated not only African American students but teachers as well. And professions of colorblindness and the tacit prohibition against discussing race created a culture that silenced these teachers.

Culturally Relevant Pedagogy—A Resource for Change

The developing literature on culturally relevant teaching (Foster, 1995) provides a theoretical lens through which to view exemplary teachers of African American studetns. Working within a critical paradigm, Ladson-Billings proposes a theory of culturally relevant teaching based on three broad propositions: (1) conceptions of self and others that reflect belief in and commitment to students and their communities, (2) classroom social relations that are equitable, reciprocal, and foster community, (3) knowledge as shared and collectively constructed, viewed critically, multifaceted, and built on children's culture and experience (Ladson-Billings, 1995). Culturally relevant teachers help students view knowledge and society critically and work for social change. Ladson-Billings (1990a) argues that "the real difference" between teachers who are successful with African American students and those who fail "is that [successful teachers] are engaged in . . . culturally relevant teaching. It is the kind of teaching that uses the students' culture to help them achieve success." Central to this kind of teaching is that "[it] allows black students to 'choose' academic excellence without losing a sense of personal and cultural identity. The ability to foster the choice of academic excellence and maintenance of cultural integrity represents what is meant by pedagogical excellence" (Ladson-Billings, 1990b, p. 337). Foster (1991) describes successful African American teachers who hold students to stringent standards of behavior and "at the same time they give students unconditional support to achieve academic success by actively engaging them in learning and challenging them . . . to critical thinking" (p. 298). They develop relationships with students that extend beyond the classroom and "references to family and community experiences and values undergird classroom pedagogy." (p. 301).

The three exemplary teachers described in this chapter reflected characteristics of culturally relevant teachers described by Ladson-Billings and paralleled successful African American teachers described by Foster. Although Paulette, Samuel, and Helen had quite different pedagogical methods, they shared common commitments, values, expectations for their students, and connections with families and community. They succeeded where their colleagues often failed. Instead of deficit models or a paternalistic second-class standard of success, they had confidence in students, recognized their strengths, and—as Samuel put it—brought out "the best in them." Their teaching was characterized by:

- High academic and behavioral expectations
- Caring and respectful relationships with students
- Connecting academic content with values and ethics of justice
- Valuing students' culture and experiences
- Relationships that transcend the classroom to family and community
- Seeing teaching as a calling and a responsibility to family and community
- Advocacy for African American students
- A sense of agency

Building on Knowledge, Teaching Codes of Power

Delpit (1988) argues that "progressive educators" often fail to recognize that children of color are excluded from the codes of power in schools and in society. She contends that without negating the value of students' culture, and while critiquing the power relations embedded in the dominant codes, teachers must teach the interactional styles, spoken and written language forms that are the cultural codes of power. The goal is fluency in multiple discourses. Cognizant that African American students would have to be twice as good as Whites to succeed in white dominated institutions, Paulette, Samuel, and Helen deliberately taught "the codes of power" to children who did not have access to them, while reaffirming the children's own cultural forms. Samuel explicitly taught "what educated people" say, yet he made his room into a studio for students' own cultural productions, directed African American history plays, and affirmed the knowledge acquired through their own experiences. Helen prepared students for college entrance tests, introduced them to the best high schools, and gave them work over the summer in standard English grammar. At the same time, she advocated for the integral place of African American history and literature in the curriculum. Paulette tutored African American students to be "subject wise"; she also initiated AfroNotions, connected classroom knowledge with students' experiences, and fought for multiculturalism at Gates. In various ways these teachers worked toward reaffirming the richness of African American experience while explicitly teaching "the discourse of power." All three helped African American students "choose academic success in the face of competing pressures" (Ladson-Billings, 1992b, p. 313) without sacrificing cultural identity or group loyalty (Fordham, 1988). In short, these teachers attempted to provide the exacting but caring guidance that they believed African American students did not receive as a part of their daily life at Franklin and Gates, recreating communities of support reminiscent of historically Black schools (Delpit, 1992a).

They held high standards for academic performance, and then tried to find ways for children to meet them. By my observations, their students were certainly more engaged in learning. Unlike teachers who saw low-achieving African American students as deficient and simply refused to lower their standards, each of the three gave them access to classroom knowledge by building on the experiences students brought into the classroom. (See Ladson-Billings, 1991, p. 237, for the culturally relevant notion of "pulling knowledge out" rather than an assimilationist approach of "putting knowledge into" students.) Samuel's assurance to students that "you already know this" and using soap operas and their own narratives styles to teach aspects of literary discourse are examples. Paulette teaching reading based on the literacy needs of students' families is another.

Connectedness

For Paulette, Samuel, and Helen, teaching was based on relationships akin to family. They expressed all-round concern for the young people in their charge and adopted parenting or mentoring roles with them. Murrell (1991) argues that, for preservice teachers of color, human relationships are central to learning; the expert teacher is one who displays "connectedness with students." These qualities were evident in Samuel's attitude that every Franklin student was his responsibility. It was the nature of this relationship that explained why Jacob, a White student completely alienated from school, returned to the school he was expelled from to visit Samuel, the one teacher who helped him value learning. It was the sort of relationship captured in Paulette's term, "realness." Similarly, it was, above all, the quality of Helen's relationship with her students that explained why they "didn't want to disappoint Miss McAllister." This was qualitatively different from teachers such as Stan at Gates who had high standards but adopted an impersonal, drill sergeant approach to students. And it was qualitatively different from the paternalistic, double standard of nurturing at Gates. Even the Othermothers at Franklin did not use their deep connections with students to consistently challenge them intellectually as did the three teachers in this chapter.

Paulette, Samuel, and Helen extended relationships with students beyond the classroom, to families and into the community. Helen invited families tino her classroom and taught classes in African American history and literature in churches in the community. Paulette invited students to her home. Although all three regretted the erosion of African American community and family cohesiveness that had been a mainstay in their own development, they did not view families as deficient. Nor did they use family problems as an excuse for not teaching. While they all said it was important to know the child's family to better understand her/his potential, they wanted to work *with* the family, not substitute for them as did some Gates teachers with a "messiah complex" (Delpit, 1992b). Teaching for them was a calling, demonstrating their sense of responsibility not only to the children and their families, but to the community (cf. Ladson-Billings, 1990b). They were preparing leadership for the uplift of the race in the tradition of African American schools (Delpit, 1992a; hooks, 1994).

Liberatory Pedagogy

As distinct from the paradigm of individual success (as in honors classes at Gates), culturally relevant pedagogy is personally and collectively liberatory (Ladson-Billings, 1992a). Although the teachers in this study did not explicitly describe their teaching this way, it embodied liberatory aspects. They measured success not simply by test scores, but by students' ability to reason and to apply knowledge to personal and social questions. They made academic content a basis for an examination of personal and social values. To varying degrees, all three chose literature and activities that affirmed African American culture and history and the struggle for social justice. Both Samuel and Paulette were advocates for African American students and organized activities that affirmed African American identity in their schools. Helen led in developing Saturday schools for African American history. They also encouraged community and cooperation in their classes. Perhaps most important, in their classrooms and in their character, they modeled a sense of agency and resistance to racism. Their dignity, the worlds they created in their classrooms, their resistance to the disempowering norms of their schools stood in opposition to the structural inequalities and dominant cultural forms that subordinated African American students and denied their role as actors in their own lives and in society. In these ways, they were "not merely teaching for individual success, but teaching for survival of the person, the family, the community, and the people" (Ladson-Billings & Henry, 1990, p. 82).

Conclusion

The three African American teachers described in this chapter were among the few at Gates and Franklin with the ideological basis, the cultural knowledge, and the pedagogical orientation to offer a sharp alternative to dominant beliefs and practices. They were among the few to address the political and cultural alienation which was so central to the experience of African American students at both schools (cf. King, 1991). Nevertheless, they had little influence on the restructuring agenda. Their marginality was the product of a constellation of organizational, political, and cultural factors. Organizationally, the separation of core and related subjects teams and the assignment of some SRM teachers to reading marginalized some potential leaders at Gates (e.g., Paulette, William, and Larissa). More important, there was a general absence of support for the critical inquiry necessary to challenge existing regularities and dominant ideas. Formally, teachers were more empowered as a result of restructuring, but they were not charged with rethinking their work. Although exemplary teachers might have served as pedagogical models and leaders, there was also no legitimation of this role and there were no mechanisms to bring it forward. Their pedagogical excellence was generally regarded as idiosyncratic. Perhaps most significantly, Paulette, Samuel, and Helen were marginalized, both overtly and subtly, by existing relations of power in their schools and community and by a political culture that suppressed dialogue about race.

The cultural and political perspectives of these teachers and their commitment to the education of African American children was a crucial, missing component in Riverton and one largely absent from the literature on restructuring. Foster (1991, p. 304) warns: "Researchers, policy makers, educators, and parents concerned with improving the education of poor minority students ought to be skeptical about reforms that disregard the perspectives of those very communities whose children already constitute a majority in 25 of the nation's largest cities." And Delpit (1988, p. 296) argues,

> I am also suggesting that appropriate education for poor children and children of color can only be devised in consultation with adults who share their culture. Black parents, teachers of color, and members of poor communities must be allowed to participate fully in the discussion of what kind of instruction is in their children's best interest. . . . Educators must open themselves to, and allow themselves to be affected by, these alternative voices.

This is also where exemplary teachers, such as those described here, might begin to set a direction, serve as models, and take a leading role as mentors for pre- and in-service teachers who could be exposed to their thinking and practice (King, 1991, p. 266). The cultural knowledge, understanding of oppression, and commitment to African American students embodied in these teachers can be crucial to impelling and sustaining a critical examination of the regularities of policy and practice affecting children of color and other marginalized students. Particularly as restructured schools embrace collegial mentorships and teacher collaboration, these teachers must play a leading role if reforms are to truly reverse the ways schools marginalize and alienate students of color.

Furthermore, although the teachers highlighted in this chapter were specifically relevant to African American students, this study suggests the importance of the voices of such teachers in the transformation of education for all students. Their concern for the whole child, the connections they made between curriculum and lived experiences, and their confidence in students' abilities would benefit all children. The breadth of their educational vision, their advocacy and sense of fairness, and the commitment of both Helen and Paulette to multicultural education were in the interest of Whites as well as African Americans. Paulette, Samuel, and Helen created meaningful educational experiences for students both African American and White. For these reasons, Jacob, a White student whom the Riverton schools had utterly failed, respected Samuel above all his teachers.

10

CONCLUSION: RESTRUCTURING IN SOCIAL CONTEXT

I have explored in some depth how teachers used new organizational forms and opportunities for collaboration and initiative to improve the educational experiences, outcomes, and commitment to school of low-income, working-class African American students. As I have argued elsewhere (Lipman, 1997), my research confirms the importance of situating school restructuring in social and cultural context. I found that educators' cooperative efforts and opportunities to change policy were profoundly influenced by their ideological dispositions, the culture of the school and school district, and the structuring of race, class, and power in multiple contexts. On balance, I have concluded that, independent of their intent, educators at Gates and Franklin were engaged in a complex process of reproducing African American student failure and disempowement through educational reform. Yet, in the ideology and practice of some educators, there were also the seeds of a far more empowering education

Although this study is grounded in the particularities of Gates and Franklin and the Riverton district, I believe its lessons have broader applicability. The specific ideological, political, and structural factors that influenced restructuring at Gates and Franklin may be particular to these schools, but I believe the influence of ideology and power on education reform is generalizable. And inequality along dimensions of race and class, which was so compelling at Gates and Franklin, saturates U.S. schools and is pertinent to educational change in any urban context.

The Limits of Organizational and Teacher-Centered Change

Theories of school restructuring and school-based reform make several assumptions about the potential relationship between change in school organization and teachers' roles, on the one hand, and students' educational experiences, on the other. As I outlined in chapter 2, three underlying assumptions of restructuring are: (1) decentralized organizations will strengthen teachers' participation and initiative foster innovation; (2) collaboration may promote critical inquiry and dialogues of change; (3) smaller, more collective settings will nurture students, strengthen their commitment to school, and build trust between students and teachers. I posited that for teachers of marginalized students, it is plausible that a greater sense of efficacy and professional responsibility may lead them to tackle tough issues such as racism and entrenched inequality. And the collegiality and opportunities for dialogue in restructuring schools may be conditions for the critical examination of beliefs about and practices with marginalized students. Teacher collaboration may also provide an arena for advocates of African American students to challenge existing regularities. Finally, the student-teacher relationships engendered by reorganizing large schools may prompt teachers to question some of their assumptions about students from marginalzied groups. This book challenges these assumptions, particularly when applied to contexts which have not demonstrated a commitment to low-income students and students of color.

Teacher Participation and Initiative

In June 1991, teachers described the changes at Gates and Franklin with adjectives as diverse as: "invigorating, exhausting, hard, supportive, confusing, great, disappointing." But most agreed with those who said, "I could never go back to the way things were before." For many there was a sense that things were indeed changing in their schools and they were part of the change. Yet some saw little of real substance emerging from all the effort. Perhaps their differing perceptions stemmed from how they defined "change" as well as how they perceived changes in their own work life. Regardless of whatever sense of efficacy educators may have experienced, the important question is the relationship between changes in teachers' work and students' educational experiences.

I found that teachers' participation in teams promoted initiatives that were potentially both productive and detrimental for students. It could be argued that teachers' efforts to address the problems of individual students reflected an invigorated sense of responsibility for each student's welfare. At Franklin, Young Men and Young Women With Dignity gave African American students a place to discuss the challenges they faced collectively and, potentially, to develop solidarity. This was an example of a programmatic effort to respond to the academic and social marginalization of African American students. The Study and Research Methods class, although initiated by district

leaders, was constructed by teachers to provide an enriched, intellectually challenging academic experience for all students. It was a beginning step toward untracking as well.

However, in general, the activities, programs and strategies devised by teachers reproduced the inequalities which shaped African
American students' lives in school. The incentives and contests, which
figured so prominently in the work of teams at Gates, actually highlighted African American students' subordination. The pervasive focus on individual students at both Gates and Franklin tended to
reinforce deficit explanations and the belief that students were the
problem, thereby masking institutional and social causes and collective oppression. Even at Franklin, the most empathetic emphasis on
students' social situations, manifested in the work of the Othermothers
and the stance of the principal, tended to substitute social for academic goals for these students. As a result, educators became absorbed
by the areas over which they had the least control, the family situations and social conditions students faced outside school, rather than
the educational conditions in school, over which they had the most
control and presumably the greatest expertise.

Those teacher-initiated projects that did hold the potential to
challenge the inequalities and marginalization confronting African
American students were thwarted by the social and political context
in which restructuring unfolded. Dignity, which grew out of a small
group of African American teachers' own cultural experiences and
commitment to African American children, was one of the few examples of a teacher initiative that built solidarity among marginalized
students. Although the teams facilitated Dignity's development, the
group was not supported by the restructuring project and indeed
operated semi-clandestinely outside of it. The restructuring project
also undermined the Franklin Yearbook, another African American
initiative. When teacher collaboration did lead to projects that fostered
students' group solidarity and identity, as with Dignity, it was because
of the particular ideology of some of the teachers. The teams created
conditions for greater collaboration and initiative, but it was the ideologies of the teachers that shaped them to these ends.

The mid-year revision of the Study and Research Methods class
dramatized the power of dominant, upper-middle-class White interests in the district to squelch teacher initiatives that challenged their
race and class privileges. Tracking appeared to be immutable, particularly at Gates, where teachers also derived prestige and satisfaction
from teaching honors-track students. The failure to take any steps
against tracking, which concretely denied African American students

access to relatively more challenging academic content and which limited their future educational opportunities, demonstrated the role of teachers' ideologies and the limits of teacher initiatives in the context of relations of power both in the school and in the community. It also demonstrated the limitations of teacher initiatives in the absence of reflection on their implications in contexts of race and class differences.

Teacher Collaboration and Dialogues of Change

An assumption made by proponents of restructuring is that teacher collaboration will facilitate critical inquiry, reflection, and dialogue essential to educational change. As new opportunities for collaboration unfold, they will bring together educators with different life experiences, identities, and educational philosophies. In multiracial, multicultural contexts, this might be expected to spur cross-racial, cross-cultural dialogues and potentially promote reflection on those regularities of practice and policy that marginalize students of color. There is some evidence that in the early team meetings at Franklin, this dialogue was beginning. There is also some evidence that some Gates teachers experienced more empathy for low-achieving African American students.

Although these few examples may suggest the potential of collaboration and dialogue, in general, there was little reflective conversation about beliefs and practices or school policies. Issues at the core of many African American students' experiences in school—deficit models, misinterpretation of discourse (language, style, social interactions), academic tracking, negation of students' strengths, the exclusion of diverse students' experiences and histories in the curriculum, the problematic implications of an emphasis on individual competition—were not touched. Indeed, team meetings and steering committee meetings reflected little real engagement of substantive issues. Although there were a few educators with a more institutional and systemic critique of racism and of the content and character of education in their schools, their more critical perspectives were peripheral. In spite of a few promising encounters across differences, there was little real sharing of views.

At Gates, African American teachers remained essentially marginal in the life of the teams. At Franklin, it seemed that teachers' informal organization, formed around shared cultural experiences and beliefs, was not easily superseded by formal collaborative structures. In spite of teaming, the real collaboration went on in separate faculty lounges and among close, ideologically compatible groups such as the Othermothers. At both schools, the isolation of teachers with opposing

views and quite different life experiences was exacerbated by the organization of teachers into core-subject and related-subject teams. But
even when teams brought together differing view points, as in the
Franklin Eagles team and the Gates A Team, they did not begin to
bridge racial and ideological divisions. Despite some promising initial
dialogue, instead of moving toward new, shared meanings, teachers
seemed to become more entrenched in their differences.

Perhaps most significantly, this book demonstrates that dialogue
among teachers is mediated by relations of power in multiple contexts. At bottom, lack of communication between some African American and White teachers at both schools was based in racial divisions
and lack of trust rooted in unequal relations of power in the schools
and in society. As Fine suggests, there is a distinction between "getting
a voice" and "getting a hearing" (1993, p. 695). Although theoretically
all teachers had a greater voice, through their teams and steering committees, in fact not all were equally heard. At Gates, Paulette, a potential leader, was largely unsupported and silenced by her teammates
and her principal. Even at Franklin, outspoken African American staff
had little real voice in the educational reforms. With the exception of
Helen at Franklin, they were not chosen to be part of the formal leadership, and their voices were stifled by a culture that suppressed viewpoints that threatened to puncture the veneer of unanimity covering
deep ideological and racial differences. A concrete result was that,
despite alternative views and practices, there was little evidence that
teachers began to question deficit assumptions about African American students and families. In fact, at Gates in particular, team discussions tended to strengthen some teachers' convictions that the students
and their families were the problem and to confirm that there was
nothing wrong with their own practice.

Dialogue was undoubtedly also stifled by the city's history of racial
politics. Riverton schools were shaped by a history of White supremacy.
The struggles of African Americans for equal and quality education
were ongoing. Indeed, the battle over school desegregation was the
defining event of the past 35 years in the city. The outcome was a series
of desegregation remedies that satisfied the interests of Riverton's White
upper-middle-class business and professional elite (cf. Bell, 1980). The
privileges they had won and the parameters they had set on desegregation created tacit limits on what was open for debate. At Gates, where
elite parents had a personal stake, their influence was direct. But it also
extended to the school board and the superintendent's desk with potent
consequences for Franklin and other schools. As revealed by the SRM
controversy, hanging over the district was the ever-present threat that

these parents would withdraw their support, and their children, from the Riverton schools. For school and district officials, or any group of teachers, to have led a critical examination of race and class inequality in Riverton schools undoubtedly would have been perceived as a threat to these powerful interests. In this environment, the increased public visibility that accompanied restructuring was an additional obstacle to dialogue on potentially dangerous issues.

Although race was at the center of nearly every major educational issue, a culture of silence on racial issues pervaded not only Gates, but also Franklin, a school with an overwhelmingly African American student body and a staff that was 50% African American. Teachers' insistence that they "didn't see color" and the fear of naming race negated racism as a factor in students' educational experiences and obstructed inquiry about the collective educational experience of African Americans. The astonishing failure to engage in dialogue about racial inequality and foreground the schools' failure of African American students, although these were the central issues in the Riverton schools and the principal focus of restructuring, is partly a reflection of how deeply entrenched is the fear of putting racial issues on the table. It is also a reflection of the relative political weakness of African American communities, teachers, and parents and their allies in Riverton.

Smaller, More Supportive Organizational Structures

A third assumption is that smaller, more supportive structures within large schools help reduce anonymity and foster understanding and trust between students and teachers. This may be particularly important when teachers and students bring very different sociocultural experiences and meanings to the school setting. Teachers' accounts provided limited confirmation of this assumption, at least at Gates. Some teachers at Gates reported feeling more empathetic toward low-income, working-class African American students and enjoying their work more as a result. A few said that tensions between themselves and "at-risk" students had de-escalated as a result of teams. At Franklin, teams also facilitated mentorship by teachers who were already deeply connected with their students, and the teams provided better conditions to monitor students individually. In both schools the teams attempted to develop a "family atmosphere," reflecting a heightened sense of collective responsibility for students.

However, in the context of deficit assumptions and racism, the one-sided emphasis on supportive relations with students led to paternalism. At both schools, many teachers adopted the stance of saving students from their families and communities rather than working with them to devise solutions in the interest of children. Moreover, at Gates, academic tracks, race and "at-risk" status, and teams converged to create unequal expectations and unequal educational experiences for African American students. The emphasis on nurturing "at-risk" students, primarily African Americans—making them feel good about school and rewarding them for "good behavior"—while expecting superior academic performance from high-achieving, primarily White upper-middle-class students, reinforced deficit models and unequal educational opportunities. In this way, teams at Gates can be said to have intensified and reified the subordination of African American students. This suggests that the meaning of smaller, familylike structures is constructed in relation to larger structures of equality or inequality, the culture of schools, and educators' ideologies.

The goal of developing supportive relationships with students in the teams was layered over a punitive culture of social control at both schools. In some instances, teachers seemed to use teams, and their closer relations with students, primarily to tighten their control over students, and some students claimed that teachers used the teams to "gang up on them." Talk of punishment and controlling student behavior pervaded the conversations of teachers and administrators and increasingly the work of the teams themselves. A deeply troubling example was Gates's harsh, in-house suspension program instituted as part of restructuring to reduce out of school suspension, student alienation, and dropping out. Through this program, the prevailing punitive ideology was actually reinforced by isolating and essentially incarcerating students labeled deviant. Rather than support children, its severity seemed designed to humiliate them and break their will. On the other hand, Franklin's in-house suspension provided students with intensive personal guidance and encouraged them to develop self-respect and a sense of future. These different meanings teachers gave to teams and to in-house suspension illustrate the central role of culture and ideology in the meanings attached to organizational changes.

Superficial forms of membership created by teams did not respond to the distance between African American students' experiences and knowledge, on the one hand, and classroom knowledge and norms, on the other, nor did it address students' lack of power. How and why should students be expected to develop commitment to schools and an educational system in which they were so unequal and so marginalized? Fostering trust between students and school adults has to do with students seeing themselves in school and with the school valuing them on their own cultural and political terms (Erickson, 1987). Thus, school membership is not simply "feeling good" about school, but being able to choose academic success without giving up one's identity and group affiliation. At Gates, to gain membership in the culture of academic success, even high-achieving African American students had to acquiesce to dominant norms and relinquish their own. At Franklin, it was the very identities of African American students that many teachers found so offensive. Whether by trying to get students to "buy in" to school or punishing them to force them to conform, the dominant meaning of school membership at Gates and Franklin was compliance with an essentially unequal institution that had little legitimacy for African Americans. Fine (1991) describes the effects of these kinds of institutional pressures: "a moderate level of depression, an absence of political awareness, persistent self-blame, low assertiveness, and high conformity" constituted the "good" urban high school student (p. 37). A more culturally and socially situated idea of "membership" would involve repositioning low-income African American students in the center of the cultural and intellectual life of Gates and Franklin and energetically promoting their personal and collective efficacy. The seeds of this kind of "membership" existed within the Dignity group and in the advocacy embodied by a few teachers but not in the ideology of the restructuring project.

Overarching Themes

The issues that coalesced through my research in Riverton bring to the forefront the social and ideological context of educational change. Concretely, this study suggests that educational change that will benefit those students who have been most failed by U.S. schools will require a protracted encounter with the social ideologies and relations of power that shape school life. Running through my analysis of restructuring at Gates and Franklin, are three central themes: (a) the powerful, mediating role of social context—the historical and current relations of power that shape social life and frame the limits and possibilities of educational change; (b) the influence of ideology on educational practice—the ideologies of individuals, the culture of schools, and the broader cultural/ideological contexts that shape how educators and the public view students and the role of education; and (c) the essential role of marginalized groups, both in and out of schools, to change the equation of existing power relations and to provide alternative, critical perspectives.

The Social Context

School desegregation in Riverton left a dominant White culture and power structure intact, and its implementation was shaped to satisfy the interests and retain the privileges of upper-middle-class

Whites. Despite the formal desegregation of Gates, inside the school-house doors resegregation and African American marginalization were the reality. The honors track assured upper-middle-class Whites quality education within the framework of desegregated schools. This "right" to an honors track education (as well as magnet schools) was deeply ensconced as the price Riverton payed to desegregate its schools. The honors track (as well as the magnet schools) might be understood as the bargain Whites struck in return for their support for desegregation (as evidenced in their continued participation in the public school system). This "interest convergence principle" (Bell, 1980) was a pivotal context for restructuring aimed at improving African American education; upper-middle-class White support for restructuring was contingent on preserving their interests. Reforms such as detracking or the heterogeneously grouped SRM class were viewed by upper-middle-class Whites as against their interests and a violation of the tacit terms that governed desegregation in Riverton.

The persistent idea that quality education equaled White education was part of the legacy of White supremacy and resistance to school desegregation in Riverton. This framework had a very conservative influence on educational reform. Since racial equality and the school success of African American students were framed as exclusively "Black issues," rather than the concern of the whole community, untracking, the Study and Research Methods class, and African American cultural programs—each of which could benefit all students—were presumed to benefit only African Americans. The Gates principal's lack of support for multicultural initiatives and the districts' unwillingness to support African American–centered projects denied all students the opportunity for a richer, more multifaceted education. While this narrowness continued to marginalize the culture, knowledge, and experience of African Americans, it also disadvantaged White students and teachers whose experiences and literacies were narrowly Eurocentric. It was also a reason for the failure to capitalize on the leadership of exemplary African American teachers whose pedagogical direction might have improved the schools for all students.

At both schools, the concern was with formal and superficial signs of integration, not racism and inequality. At Franklin, educators directed their attention to visible signs of racial balance while critiques of racism and talk about race were silenced. I witnessed Franklin being viewed with alarm in the district because it was becoming overwhelming African American (segregated), rather than because of students' poor educational outcomes. On the other hand, at Gates, despite dramatic racial disparities in academic achievement and discipline, teachers voiced satisfaction with their school because excellence (as they saw it) was maintained for a sizeable portion of those students who were at the center of Gates. Physically, African Americans were in the building, although few were part of it. The restructuring project's response was typical of the district's failure to engage teachers, parents, and the broader community in the enduring issues of power and privilege that surrounded race in the Riverton schools.

For some White teachers and parents alike, the status quo became something to protect against encroachments of "special programs" for the "at-risk" (read African American and low income), which were seen as a threat to quality education. Seeing the school failure of African Americans as somehow separate from the quality of education overall led to a self-satisfied stance on the part of honors-track educators. Further, this politics perpetuated divisions among staff committed to one or another supposedly competing agendas. As a result, the community as a whole lost out. It did not face up to the need to reform schooling for all students. While the political climate was particularly inhibiting to discussions of race and the abolition of tracking, the impetus to conserve the status quo dampened experimentation and debate generally.

Such a fragmented and competitive conception of the educational agenda failed to capture the common ground for all students. What was needed instead was transformative leadership with an alternative vision based on shared interests and interconnectedness that would cast equality, diversity, and cultural relevance as valuable to all students. A glaring weakness of restructuring in Riverton was the absence of such leadership at all levels of schools, district and community.

Restructuring brought into sharp relief the influence of politics on educational reform, particularly as reforms tampered with existing relations of power and privilege which were presrved in Riverton's desegregation policies. Indeed, this study brings to the foreground the role of power in the process of school restructuring and the conclusion that educational change involves changing relations of power in schools, school systems, and society. The stakes in this political contest are high. Schools and classrooms are shaped by, and act upon, the larger social system. The difficulties of restructuring urban schools, like the current reversal of African American achievement gains, should be seen in the context of a social, economic, and political assault on African American people, that is, urban violence, drugs, gangs, class polarization, a political climate that fosters and legitimates racism, and reversals in social, economic, and political gains. As Cummins (1986) argues, empowering minority students requires changing relationships between dominant and subordinated groups in the society, as well as in schools.

The Role of Ideology in Educational Change

The general direction of restructuring in Riverton—the issues educators addressed and their responses to those issues—was shaped by prevailing discourses about African American students and by dominant educational ideologies. The discourse surrounding African American and "at-risk" students exerted a particularly potent influence on how educators defined the problem of African American low-achievement and disengagement from school and on the actions that made sense to them. In the restructuring project and in the voices of many teachers and administrators, African American students were the problem, not racism or inequality, and remedies were directed to them. It is hardly surprising that much of the work teachers did focused on fixing, motivating, and controlling these students, who were described as deficient, unmotivated, dangerous, and deviant. This orientation resonated with the national discourse about African Americans as "problem people," directing attention away from the institutional norms and practices of schools and from social structures of inequality to focus on student characteristics.

From the outset, restructuring was constructed as an "at-risk" project. Operating as a scientifically determined trait, the "at risk" label concretized diffuse characteristics that were contrary to educators' conceptions of the "good student" (as exemplified by Hills and Palisades children at Gates, and by memories of Franklin's working- and middle-class White students of the past). Labeling children at risk allowed teachers to name African American students as deficient and different from the norm without referring to race. Once fixed by a label, students' "at risk" status rationalized different academic expectations and treatments than those reserved for "normal" students, for example, feeling good about school was an appropriate substitute for academic success for these students and a plethora of extrinsic rewards was necessary to compensate for lack of motivation. Conflictual student/teacher relationships were easily explained by reference to the behaviors of "at-risk" students. Once again, the focus of the problem and the range of possible solutions were directed away from the fundamental inequalities of schools. Despite organizational restructuring and new forms of teacher participation, much of the content of reform was shaped by an ideology that saw "faulty" children rather than failing institutions.

While low-achieving, low-income African American students were lumped together as "at risk," most educators treated each student in relation to her/his individual "problems," looked for individual solutions, and focused on the progress of individuals. It is not surprising that most of the teachers in this study took this individualistic approach to student success or failure and that it shaped the way they used the opportunities presented by restructuring. Individual achievement and the belief in meritocracy are the ideological backbone of U.S. education. At Gates, in particular, this ideology imbued educators' practice and was unquestioned. It was embodied in their concentration on the few students they believed they could "save," their preoccupation with the problems of individual students, the use of material incentives, and the individual success stories that validated restructuring. Like the "at-risk" label, placing the thrust of amelioration on the individual deflected a critique of institutional and social regularities in schools. In both Gates and Franklin, the work of restructuring turned more on remediating or, in the case of the Franklin Othermothers, supporting individuals, than on reconstructing curriculum and instruction, policies, and relationships with African American families and communities.

In general, the ideology of individual achievement and meritocracy serves to legitimate inequality, disrupt collectivity, sort students for unequal positions in the occupational and class structure, and cause students to internalize success and failure (Conforti, 1991; MacLeod, 1996). Moreover, some scholars argue that emphasis on individual achievement has a particularly devastating effect on African American students by pitting academic achievement against African American "group centeredness"and communitarian traditions (Fordham, 1988, 1991; Lee, Lomotey, & Shujaa, 1990). In the refusal of several students to be removed from their peers and promoted to honors classes, and in teachers' differentiation of high-achieving Black students from African American students as a whole, there was evidence to support the argument that individualistic notions of academic success may come at great psychic cost for African American students. The restructuring project's narrow, individualistic norms precluded broader conceptions of school success that may be highly valued by students, families, and communities and that are central to creating a more just society, that is, education that is personally and socially meaningful and culturally relevant.

Yet alternative notions of success were present. In Riverton, education for the development of the community as well as the individual had historical roots in the widespread struggles of African Americans for equal and quality education. This vision echoed in the community values of those teachers who harked back to the strengths of Black schools and who attempted to create community in the context of Gates and Franklin. The pedagogies of the exemplary teachers discussed in chapter 9 were moving in this direction. This illustrated that although dominant discourses shaped the direction of restructuring, there were competing perspectives with the potential to redefine that direction. Moreover, there were some significant variations in the actual content of initiatives as they were molded by educators. Different conceptions of the purpose and efficacy of incentives in the Gates and Franklin focus teams, contrasting philosophies of in-house suspension in the two schools, differences in the way social support was construed by Gates focus team teachers, the Franklin Othermothers, and the exemplary teachers described in chapter 9 all point to the role that individual educators play in shaping the meaning of educational reforms.

Thus, both the limitations and the potential of restructuring were forged by the complex intersection of ideological positions and discourses and inividual actors and by their relative influence in the district and the schools. This points to the powerful role of ideology at all levels in shaping the meaning of organizational and structural changes. Although restructuring schools and teachers' work may be necessary for fundamental change, it will take a profound and protracted engagement of ideas and values, and ultimately a significant challenge to the power of dominant ideologies, to transform education in the interest of all students.

The Role of Marginalized Groups in Educational Change

Although it is important to identify the factors that stifled critical dialogue, debate, and multiple perspectives in Riverton, there is a more fundamental issue: Even substantive and meaningful dialogue may not promote change in thinking and practice regarding disempowered groups. At Gates and Franklin, many teachers lacked the impetus for change. One of the assumptions of school leaders was that the will for change would be generated by educators. This assumption proved to be quite problematic. History demonstrates that cultural and political change and change in social policies vis à vis oppressed groups are grounded in the demands and the exercise of power by disempowered peoples themselves (Harding, 1990). This reality is central to understanding how the political will for educational change benefitting marginalized groups will be generated. My research suggests that those wanting to transform the school experiences of African American children cannot rely on the will or knowledge of educators alone. It may well be that the commitment to change and the direction of change must be pressed upon educators from without, by parents and communities of color, by working-class and other marginalized groups with the greatest stake in changing schooling for their children, and with the support of allies (Delpit, 1988). (This was part of the rationale advanced by some for the decision-making role of parents in Chicago school reform, for example [Fine, 1993].)

The inclusive public was not a constituency for Gates and Franklin. Only the most powerful parents had a voice in their own interests. The views of these parents shaped restructuring in a number of ways, while the perspectives of low-income working-class African American families did not. Yet the experiences, knowledge, hopes and dreams of African American families were sorely needed. They were holders of a knowledge base and commitment essential to reshaping schooling in ways that were meaningful for their children. The absence of working-class African American families significantly weakened the dialogue about the means and ends of restructuring. For example, one can speculate that their involvement might have fortified the Franklin principal, providing the base of support she lacked, might have reinforced the voices of exemplary teachers of African American students at both schools, and might have offered a challenge to the inequality of tracking, the double standard of success, and the disproportionate disciplining of African American students. However, there was no effort by the restructuring project to open up educational reform to engage their participation.

The central role of both marginalized families and successful educators of children of color has not been adequately recognized in discussions of educational reform. What is needed is their voices— viewpoints growing out common experiences in a society deeply shaped by racial oppression and exploitation (Ladson-Billings & Tate, 1995). Ensuring the voices of people of color would mean that they have a platform to name their own educational reality and that they propose and assess policies, plans, and solutions based on their lived experiences. The stories and perspectives of persons of color could help other educators see schooling from alternate cultural and historical perspectives and support changes defined by persons of color themselves (King & Mitchell, 1990). Furthermore, the pedagogies of exemplary teachers of color could provide leadership for educational change. I am not suggesting that all African American teachers and parents are exemplary or possess knowledge to reform schools, or that they share the same views, or that no other teachers possess this knowledge. There are both effective and ineffective teachers of all races and ethnicities, including some discussed in this study, and there are multiple perspectives within all social groups. What I *am* arguing is that the absence of the "voice" of African American educators and parents—and all that "voice" entails (the power to name one's reality and determine one's destiny)—was one of the most glaring weaknesses of restructuring in Riverton. As Foster (1991) argues:

> Efforts to improve the schooling of children can no longer ignore the voices of minority scholars, teachers, parents and students, even if they sound off-key. Without the combined experiences and wisdom of minority communities—its researchers, teacher-educators, teachers, and scholars—we will not substantially alter the schooling experiences of all students. (p. 304)

Despite the urgency of the problems of urban education and the plethora of studies of "minority" student failure and "at-risk" students, there is relatively little attention to the meaningful educational experiences of minority parents, students, and teachers. For example, one of the legacies of desegregation and of historical and present-day racism is that Black schools prior to integration are generally considered to have been academically inferior to White schools. Although there's abundant evidence of the injustice of Jim Crow education, as scholars have begun to retrieve the histories of historically Black schools and analyze their constructions of academic excellence and responsibility to the community (e.g., Anderson, 1988; Siddle Walker, 1996), they are also providing important lessons for how to reconstruct schools in new contexts. A number of teachers in Riverton drew upon the strengths of the Black schools in which they had been educated as they tried to carve out more supportive educational spaces for students within Gates and Franklin. Black independent schools may also serve as models. Still, there are relatively few scholars working on this topic. An important development is the research on culturally relevant pedagogy (Foster, 1995; Ladson-Billings, 1994) and on life histories of African American teachers (Foster, 1997) as well as histories of African American education. Following the leadership of these scholars, a much broader effort will be required to bring the wisdom of practice of African American education (as well as the educational models of other marginalized groups) into the center of conversations about restructuring U.S. education.

At the school level, there are teachers who, through their daily practice, refute the lie of student failure and deficiency and who cut against the grain of marginalizing, labeling, and disempowering students. I have described several such teachers in this study. Their humanizing pedagogy (Bartolome, 1994) exemplified the possibility of actualizing an alternative vision of education. One lesson from my research is that exemplary teachers of students of color need to be at the nucleus of restructuring in individual schools. Their pedagogical knowledge and educational vision is a concrete source of leadership to reshape the meaning and practice of education for all students.

Educational and Social Change

Reliance on organizational and governance changes, without giving full weight to ideological and political aspects of schools, may lead reformers to substitute the conditions of reform for the goals. Teacher empowerment, shared governance, collaboration, professional development and more time for reflection may become ends in themselves, divorced from the goals of transforming students' educational experiences. The organizational opportunities for teacher collaboration and dialogue at Gates and Franklin were excellent, but the cultural and political climate did not favor substantive change. By narrowly focusing on enabling organizational conditions, reformers negated the centrality of cultural change. Restructuring schools is deeply about educator change, yet restructuring did not engage teachers in examining their beliefs. As a result, some well-intentioned, hardworking teachers unwittingly reproduced, perhaps even intensified, the marginalization of African American students. Certainly, changes in organization and the roles of teachers and the character of their professional lives are necessary conditions to transform schools. However, difficult though it may be, what is also needed is a more tortuous, but profoundly more rooted, cultural and political process of resocialization and the reformation of shared meanings and reconfiguration of existing relations of power in and out of schools.

Educators—in partnership with parents, students, and community members—need to reflect on the values and relations of power in which practice is embedded. Sirotnik (1987) makes this point succinctly in a proposal for "critical inquiry" in schools:

> Critical inquiry requires that participants, as individuals and groups, maintain a self-conscious stance with respect to all types of knowledge. . . . First, the participants . . . must continually remind themselves that the problems they face have a current and historical context and that the problem . . . must be situated in those contexts in order to be understood. . . . Second, to be critical, the

inquiry must demand of participants that they confront the political reality of significant educational issues, and that they recognize and contend with embedded values and human interests. *Whose interests are (and are not) being served by the ways things are?* is the question to be addressed here [emphasis original]. (p. 17)

Faith in the efficacy of professional collaboration and dialogue can obscure the importance of ensuring that the interests of disempowered people are in the forefront. The participation of working-class students and students of color and their families can help turn educators' discussions to the issues Sirotnik raises. People in marginalized communities can help educators see how to educate their children and make sure they examine whose interests are being served by schools. Furthermore, although fundamental school restructuring is a long-term transformative task, kernels of a more liberatory, culturally affirming, and intellectually empowering education exist within current practice. Policymakers, educational reformers, and educators at the school level commited to transforming education could take the knowledge of culturally relevant, emancipatory teachers as one departure point.

Finally, however, the roots of students' school experiences are not only in the educational system but in the social, economic, and political order. The profound failure of schools to educate African American students is not a fault in the system. It *is* the system—as restructuring in Riverton demonstrated in even a limited way. In the final analysis, school transformation is part of a much broader process of democratic social reconstruction and struggle for social justice.

METHODOLOGICAL APPENDIX

In this appendix I describe how I selected the focus teams at each school and how I followed their progress. I also describe the evaluation study in Riverton and the implications of my role in the study for the data and analysis presented in this book.

Selecting and Following Focus Teams

At Franklin the staff was fragmented, with differing views about African American students and what should be done about low achievement and perceived "behavior problems." I chose to focus on a seventh and an eighth grade team, each with a mix of views and each with one new teacher. This gave me an opportunity to study the teams' dialogue and their processes of enculturating new faculty under conditions of restructuring. At Gates, the principal division was between high-achieving, well-off White, and low-income, low-achieving African American students. To study these divisions, I chose two ninth-grade teams: one mainly regular track, the other with a preponderance of honors students. This provided an opportunity to compare how teachers used new forms of collaboration with differing groups of students. I was also interested in the dialogue within and between these two teams.

To track teachers' perspectives on key racial and educational issues, I recorded topics raised for discussion and debate and followed the course of these debates in team meetings. As an observer and occasional participant in classrooms and meetings, I followed the evolution of practices and behaviors over the course of the school year. The interviews I conducted were open-ended, but they were generally guided by the five topics I list in chapter 1. In my observations of classes and meetings, and in interviews, I probed for perspectives related to these topics.

However, as the year wore on, their relative importance altered, and new issues emerged. During the year, I continued to follow the evolution of explicit and implicit meanings associated with the initial set of themes while simultaneously pursuing a more open-ended ethnographic approach. Several incidents during the year catalyzed debate and brought to the surface previously guarded beliefs and attitudes, for example, a districtwide controversy over a new, untracked course and the reassignment of some teachers to remedial reading. Exploring perspectives on, and responses to, these incidents helped me sharpen existing questions, formulate new insights, and identify fresh avenues of investigation.

The Evaluation Study—The Issue of
Wearing Two Hats and a Self-Critique

The foundation that supported restructuring, in partnership with the community collaborative, commissioned a national research center to conduct a qualitative evaluation of restructuring. Its purpose was to provide ongoing feedback and support to educators and the collaborative. As a researcher at the center, I led this study in Riverton. The data for the districtwide evaluation came from interviews and observations at three junior high schools in 1988–89 and at four junior highs in 1989–90 and 1990–91 and from interviews with district officials and community leaders, and observations of policy and planning meetings. Franklin was a part of the study during all 3 years, Gates during the last 2 years. In the language of the project, the evaluation was concerned with the impact of school reform on "at-risk" youth. The issues the evaluation study addressed were: (a) the district plan for and progress toward restructuring; (b) efforts to improve academic achievement, students' sense of membership in school, and academic engagement; (c) discipline policies, curriculum and instruction, educators' perceptions of restructuring, and the role of leadership at all levels.

Because the evaluation study involved five junior highs over 3 years, it contributed to a broader view of the Riverton schools within which to situate what happened at Gates and Franklin. It also provided information on the history of the district and schools and background and baseline information for issues central to my research, disclosing policies, practices, and social interactions that appeared to be problematic for African American students. It gave me a sense of teachers' morale and attitudes, the general character of curriculum and instruction, and the organization of the schools at the beginning of the restructuring project. From January 1988 to the fall of 1990, I also developed relationships with people in and out of the schools, along with the knowledge to select schools and focus teams for my study. As part of the evaluation, an outside research organization also collected annual and longitudinal statistics on junior and senior high school enrollment, attendance, achievement, course failure, retention, suspension, and drop-out rates and social variables such as teen pregnancy and youth employment, all disaggregated by race, gender, and school. I used these statistics as a starting point in my conversations with teachers about racial disparities.

Functioning as both academic researcher and researcher for a commissioned evaluation creates potential conflicts in selection of schools, data, limits on one's analysis, sharing of findings, and so on. Some of these conflicts were alleviated by the fact that, within a broad framework established by my research center, I had great flexibility in the design of the evaluation in Riverton. The choice of restructuring schools that the evaluation concentrated on each year did not influence my focus schools for this book. I was free to collect whatever school and district data were appropriate. Although the questions and the framework of the evaluation study were not the same as for this book, there was certainly overlap. I use some of the interviews and observations I did for the evaluation (although not the evaluation reports) in the book. The research center's agreement with the foundation was that independent academic writing would also be a product of our research, with the goal of informing a broader audience about educational change. Thus, the evaluation study did not limit what I have said here.

However, wearing two hats did influence the ways in which various school and community people responded to me—as expert, representative of the foundation (mistakenly), academic, evaluator, confidant, colleague, or ally. For example, sometimes principals and some teachers seemed to put the best face on restructuring (for the evaluator). Notes of steering committee meetings shared with me by one teacher included comments that everyone should be "positive for the evaluators." My role for the foundation made some people suspicious and closed, and thus led me to question some of their claims. However, over time, relationships I developed with teachers and administrators generally punctured this facade. Moreover, few educators at the school level seemed compelled to defend, for my benefit, a reform project that had just begun and that many felt initially they had little stake in. On the other hand, because of my connection with a foundation supporting restructuring for "at-risk" students, I was seen by some as a potential ally in their advocacy for students. As a result, they took me into their confidence, sharing information about problematic policies and practices in their schools, racial disparities, and so on. I tried consistently to be alert to the ways in which responses to my roles influenced what people said and did. (These responses were a powerful source of data in its own right.) And I triangulated data whenever possible, including checking perceptions with those of local researchers.

The evaluation study also compounded ethical and political dilemmas created by the relationships I developed and the confidences that people in and out of the schools shared with me. I had access to information with potentially damaging consequences for some teachers and schools and potentially productive consequences for others and for students, and I was expected to share my findings publicly, in a prescribed format, with people in a wide range of positions of power within the city and schools. The evaluation study was sufficiently general to protect the anonymity of individuals yet pointed enough to raise straightforwardly the issues I considered to be important for students, teachers, and administrators. On several occasions, I shared quite publicly concerns about educational inequalities and punishment of African American males. In other cases, I had frank discussions with teachers and administrators. But I never resolved comfortably the ethical and political dilemmas posed by the knowledge I acquired as researcher and evaluator.

These problems were exacerbated by difficulties related to sharing findings with school-level educators. I was not empowered to determine how evolving issues in the study would be shared, but to support change, local school leaders were expected to promote discussion at all levels. Indeed, the evaluation was conceptualized as a catalyst for change. Because our research team was committed to democratic research methods and research as a tool for change, we consistently struggled for open exchanges about our observations. But some school officials were leery of information that they interpreted as "negative" and failed to circulate our findings or to facilitate discussion of them at the school level in a timely manner as we expected. Often this took place only informally, on our initiative, until the spring of 1991 when there were formal sessions with principals and some teachers. What is crucial is that, because the evaluation study analysis was sheltered from many teachers, it did not evoke much rethinking that I was aware of. An exception was our open questioning, in 1989, of the obvious racial identification of honors and regular track students and their segregation into separate and isolated teams. The controversy surrounding our questions lead to the teams being reconfigured in 1990 to be somewhat more heterogeneous, particularly in seventh and eighth grade, and much less isolated from each other. Some teachers said our prodding struck a chord in a context sensitive to desegregation mandates.

Thus, although the evaluation study provided significant data about restructuring, it made my own role messy and limited opportunities for a more collaborative, change-oriented research process. Because of my role in the evaluation, I was not at liberty to independently share what I was learning with teachers, undermining my own research as a catalyst for change. Over all, the absence of teacher and administrator participation in data analysis and the absence of opportunities for sustained discussion of the data are real limitations of the study. On balance, the evaluation did not evoke much change at the school level (at least during the time period I was involved with it) and the ethical and political dilemmas it posed continue to trouble me. This experience has led me to insist on a more democratic research strategy that includes teachers, administrators, parents, and students as researcher partners (see Gutstein, Lipman, & Hernandez, 1997). I also hope that publication here and elsewhere of what I learned in Riverton will inspire some rethinking among a broader audience of educators, policymakers, and others.

NOTES

Chapter 1

1. *Low-income working class* refers to working class people who work for low wages and those who cannot find work

2. These policies include disinvestment in productive industry and the neglect of the physical infrastructure, financial speculation, buy-outs and take-overs, corporate downsizing and export of jobs and capital to cheap labor markets, weakening trade unions, corporate tax breaks, and redistribution of wealth They are coupled with the failure of liberal social policies of the past 35 years and inflation and debt due to the militarization of the economy.

3. For additional discussion of these issues see: Bell (1980), Ladson-Billings and Tate (1995), Tate, Ladson-Billings, and Grant (1996).

4. Over the past 25 years, African American children have been called disadvantaged, culturally deprived, marginal, drop-outs, and now "at risk" (Cuban, 1989, p. 781).

5. In the 1988–1989 and 1989–1990 school years, I visited Riverton five times each year for about 4 days each visit In 1990–1991, I spent about 1 week a month in Riverton, dividing my time between the two schools. During all 3 years, two local researchers spent 2 to 3 days a week in schools and at district meetings. In 1990–1991, a local researcher and I interviewed 22 teachers at Gates and 21 at Franklin (about 40% of each faculty) and had informal conversations with others. Many teachers were interviewed multiple times. I also interviewed counselors, nurses, case managers, student teachers, all administrators, security guards, several parents, and principals (the latter at least once a month). Although teachers and administrators were the focus, we formally interviewed 10 Gates students and 2 Franklin students (7 of these were audiotaped) to get their perceptions of specific events and had informal conversations with others throughout the years. We observed classes in all 3 years (64 in 1990–1991) that were quite evenly distributed among all grades, subjects and tracks. Data from a third restructuring school, Magnolia Ridge, also informed the questions and perspectives I brought to my research at Gates and Franklin.

Chapter 2

1. I use racism here to mean "culturally sanctioned beliefs which, regardless of the intentions involved, defend the advantages whites have because

of the subordinated position of racial minorities" (Wellman quoted in King, 1991).

2. Rooted in scientific rationalism and the development of large-scale industry and the White supremacist eugenics movement, early intelligence tests (biased in favor of Whites) were used to classify African Americans, Jews, and southern Europeans as intellectually inferior (Karrier, 1972). See also, *Fair Test Examiner* (National Center for Fair and Open Testing) for an ongoing examination of bias in testing.

Chapter 4

1. These included: poverty, single parent homes, parents with little formal schooling, teenage parenthood, trouble with the juvenile justice system, gang and drug-related activities, low achievement, over-age for grade, course failure, multiple disciplinary infractions, general resistance to school.

2. Belief in the efficacy of retention was an orthodoxy held by many teachers interviewed. Its validity was frequently verified by reference to the specific traditions of African American schools in the South where teachers would have been remiss to allow students to advance without teaching them what they needed to know. Retention seemed to have a different meaning in these contexts than it may in present situations in which it is not accompanied by the support to accelerate student achievement. See Shepard and Smith (1989) for a summation of recent research on the effects of grade retention on student achievement.

Chapter 6

1. The definition of school success was a narrow one in any case, limited to grade point averages and scores on standardized tests, not inclusive of the acquisition of critical literacy, ethical and valuative perspectives, or social and cultural success. See, for example, Ladson-Billings (1992b), Ladson-Billings and Henry (1990), and McLaren (1989) for a broader, socially and culturally located definition of school success.

2. Some teachers claimed that Gates weeded out most disruptive students by ninth grade, suspending them and having the district transfer them to other schools. This was confirmed anecdotally by an administrator at another junior high school who received Gates transfer students.

3. Prior to 1990, the district reported total incidents of suspension; after 1990 the district reported numbers of students suspended. Thus this comparison is of percentage of incidents with percentage of students by race. Out of school suspension data by school were not available for 1990–91. However, school statistics and anecdotal data from the principal and

district administrators indicated that there were fewer total suspensions in the district and at Gates in 1990–91 than in the previous year. The Gates principal attributed this to restructuring, that is, teams and in-house suspension.

4. In the previous year, the in-house suspension teacher spent time building relationships with the students assigned to her. She saw the small group setting as an opportunity for group discussions and mentoring and supporting students. However, in 1990–91 the principal replaced her with a teacher whose priority was to isolate and punish the students assigned to in-house suspension.

Chapter 7

1. Juanita could not seem to make sense of this contradiction. Even when she developed more intellectually challenging activities in class, she struggled to retain the students' attention and cooperation, particularly in regular classes. She consistently said she needed help, and perhaps she did need professional support to use her own implicit framework for afterschool activities as a basis for transforming her pedagogy. Unpacking the content of these afterschool activities as a way to begin to reconceptualize teaching and learning might have been a fruitful collaborative activity for the teams.

2. There were occasional district workshops, foundation-sponsored consultants, and opportunities to attend national conferences, but there was no consistent professional development integrated with teachers' daily work.

3. During the same year, a teacher at Magnolia Ridge, another restructuring school, turned an eighth-grade general math class into an algebra class in order to learn if general math classes could be accelerated so all students could have the opportunity to take algebra in eighth grade. Although she judged this experiment a success (all the students except one earned As and Bs), the district curriculum director insisted she drop the experiment the next year.

Chapter 8

1. Although the district was under pressure to reduce racial disparities in achievement, retention, course, failures, and suspensions, in reality, Franklin's response was limited to intensified remediation for low-achieving students.

2. Some related subjects teachers were disgruntled because an extra period had been cut from the school day several years prior, eliminating some elective classes. Thus, they were resentful of the addition of an extra period in September 1990 to accommodate SRM but not electives.

Chapter 9

1. Here I use the term pedagogy to refer to social relationships; conceptions of knowledge; and beliefs about the role of teachers, teaching, and possibilities for students.

REFERENCES

Anderson, J. D. (1988). *The education of blacks in the South, 1860–1935*. Chapel Hill: University of North Carolina Press.

Apple, M. W. (1979). *Ideology and curriculum*. Boston: Routledge & Kegan Paul.

Apple, M. W. (1995). *Education and power (2nd ed.)*. Boston: Routledge & Kegan Paul.

Apple, M. W., & Weis, L. (1983). Ideology and practice in schooling: A political and conceptual introduction. In M. W. Apple & L. Weis (Eds.), *Ideology and practice in schooling* (pp. 3–33). Philadelphia: Temple University Press.

Au, K. H., & Jordan, C. (1981). Teaching reading to Hawaiian children: Finding a culturally appropriate solution. In H. H. Trueba, G. P. Guthrie, & K. H. Au (Eds.), *Culture in the bilingual classroom: Studies in classroom ethnography* (pp. 139–152). Rowley, MA: Newberry House.

Ball, S. (1981). *Beachside comprehensive*. Cambridge, UK: Cambridge University Press.

Banks, J. A. (1995). Historical development, dimensions, and practice. In J. A. Banks & C. A. M. Banks (Eds.), *Handbook of research on multicultural education*. New York: Macmillan.

Barth, R. S. (1988). School: A community of leaders. In A. Lieberman (Ed.), *Building a professional culture in schools* (pp. 129–147). New York: Teachers College Press.

Bartolome, L. I. (1994). Beyond the methods fetish: Toward a humanizing pedagogy. *Harvard Educational Review, 64*, 173–194.

Bell, D. (Ed.) (1980). *Brown* and the interest-convergence dilemma. In D. Bell (Ed.), *Shades of Brown: New perspectives on school desegregation* (pp. 90–107). New York: Teachers College Press.

Berman, R., & McLaughlin, M. (1978). *Federal programs supporting educational changes, Vol. 8. Implementing and sustaining innovation*. Santa Monica, CA: Rand Corporation.

Bolman, L. G., & Deal, T. E. (1988). *Modern approaches to understanding and managing organizations*. San Francisco: Jossey-Bass.

Bourdieu, P. (1977). Cultural reproduction and social reproduction. In J. Karabel & A. H. Halsey (Eds.), *Power and ideology in education* (pp. 487–511). New York: Oxford University Press.

Brandt, R. (1990). On restructuring schools: A conversation with Al Shanker. *Educational Leadership, 47*(7), 11–16.

Business Higher Education Forum. (1983). *America's competitive challenge: The need for a national response.* Washington, DC: Author.

Carnegie Council on Adolescent Development. (1989). *Turning points: Preparing American youth for the 21st century.* New York: Carnegie Corporation.

Carter, R. L. (1980). A Reassessment of *Brown v. Board.* In D. Bell, Ed., *Shades of Brown,* (pp. 20–28). New York, Teachers College Press.

Clement, D. C., Eisenhart, M., & Harding, J. R. (1979). The veneer of harmony: Social-race relations in a Southern desegregated school. In R. C. Rist (Ed.), *Desegregated schools* (pp. 15–64). New York: Academic Press.

Clune, W. H., & White, P. A. (1988). *School-based management: Institutional variation, implementation, and issues for further research* (CPRE Research Report Series RR-008). New Brunswick, NJ: Rutgers University, Center for Policy Research in Education.

Coalition of Essential Schools. (1989). *Prospectus.* Providence: Brown University, Coalition of Essential Schools.

Cohen, E. (1975). The effects of desegregation on race relations. *Law and Contemporary Problems, 39,* 271–299.

College Entrance Examination Board. (1985). *Equality and excellence: The educational status of Black Americans.* New York: Author.

Comer, J. P. (1988). Educating poor minority children. *Scientific American, 259*(5), 42–48.

Conforti, J. M. (1992). The legitimation of inequality in American education. *Urban Review, 24*(4), pp. 227–238.

Conley, D. T. (1993). *Managing change in restructuring schools: Culture, leadership, and readiness.* Eugene, OR: Oregon School Study Council.

Connell, R. W., Ashenden, D. J., Kessler, S., Dowsett, G. W. (1982). *Making the difference: Schools, families and social division.* Sydney: George Allen & Unwin.

Cuban, L. (1989). The "at-risk" label and the problem of urban school reform. *Phi Delta Kappan, 70*(10), 780–784, 799–801.

Cummins, J. (1986). Empowering minority students: A framework for intervention. *Harvard Educational Review, 56*(1), 18–36.

D'Andrade, R. (1986). *Cultural schemas as motives.* Paper prepared for Annual Meeting of the American Anthropological Association, Philadelphia, PA.

Darder, A. (1995). Buscando America: The contribution of critical Latino educators to the academic development and empowerment of Latino students in the U.S. In C. E. Sleeter & P. L. McLaren (Eds.), *Multicultural education, critical pedagogy, and the politics of difference* (pp. 319–348). Albany: SUNY Press.

David, J. L., Purkey, S., & White, P. (1989). *Restructuring in progress: Lessons from pioneering districts.* Washington, DC: National Governor's Association, Center for Policy Research.

Deal, T. E., & Kennedy, A. A. (1982). *Corporate cultures.* Reading, MA: Addison & Wesley.

Delpit, L. D. (1988). The silenced dialogue: Power and pedagogy in educating other people's children. *Harvard Educational Review, 58,* 280–298.

Delpit, L. D. (1992a). Acquisition of literate discourse: Bowing before the master? *Theory Into Practice, 31,* 296–302.

Delpit, L. D. (1992b). Education in a multicultural society: Our future's greatest challenge. *Journal of Negro Education, 61,* 237–249.

Edelman, M. (1964). *The symbolic uses of politics.* Urbana: University of Illinois Press.

Edelman, M. (1971). *Politics as symbolic action.* Chicago: Markham.

Elmore, R. F. & Associates. (1990). *Restructuring schools: The next generation of educational reform.* San Francisco: Jossey-Bass.

Epstein, J. L. (1986). Parents' reactions to teacher practices of parent involvement. *Elementary School Journal, 86,* 277–294.

Erickson, F. (1986). Qualitative methods in research on teaching. In M. C. Wittrock (Ed.), *Handbook of research on teaching* (3rd ed., pp. 119–161). New York: Macmillan.

Erickson, F. (1987). Transformation and school success: The politics and culture of educational achievement. *Anthropology and Education Quarterly, 18,* 335–356.

Erickson, F., & Mohatt, G. (1982). Cultural organization of paeticipation structures in two classrooms of Indian students. In G. Spindler, (Ed.), *Doing the ethnography of schooling* (pp. 132–175). New York: Holt, Rinehart & Winston.

Ernst, G., Statzner, E., & Trueba, H. T. (1994). Theme issue: Alternative visions of schooling: Success stories in minority settings. *Anthropology and Education Quarterly, 25*(3).

Feistritzer, C. E. (1996). *Profile of teachers in the U.S.* Washington, DC: National Center for Education Information.

Fine, M. (1991). *Framing dropouts: Notes on the politics of an urban high school.* Albany: SUNY Press.

Fine, M. (1993). [Ap]parent involvement: Reflections on parents, power, and urban public schools. *Teachers College Record, 94,* 682–709.

Finley, M. (1984, October). Teachers and tracking in a comprehensive high school. *Sociology of Education, 57,* 233–243.

Firestone, W. A., & Rosenblum, S. (1988). Building commitment in urban high schools. *Education Evaluation and Policy Analysis, 10,* 285–299.

Flores, B., Cousin, P. T., & Diaz, E. (1991). Critiquing and transforming the deficit myths about learning, language, and culture. *Language Arts, 68,* 369–379.

Fordham, S. (1988). Racelessness as a factor in black students' school success: Pragmatic strategy or pyrrhic victory? *Harvard Educational Review, 58,* 54–85.

Fordham, S. (1991). Peer-proofing academic competition among Black adolescents: "Acting white" Black American style. In C. Sleeter (Ed.), *Empowerment through multi-cultural education* (pp. 69–90). Albany: SUNY Press.

Fordham, S., & Ogbu, J. U. (1986). Black students' school success: Coping with the burden of acting White. *Urban Review, 18,* 176–206.

Foster, M. (1991). "Just got to find a way": Case studies of the lives and practice of exemplary Black high school teachers. In M. Foster (Ed.), *Readings in equal education: Qualitative investigations into schools and schooling* (vol. 11, pp. 273–309). New York: AMS Press.

Foster, M. (1992). *Urban African-American teachers' views of organizational change: Speculations on the experiences of exemplary teachers.* Center on Organization and Restructuring of Schools, Wisconsin Center for Education Research, University of Wisconsin–Madison.

Foster, M. (1993). Urban African American teachers' views of organizational change: Speculations on the experiences of exemplary teachers. *Equity and Excellence in Education, 26*(3), 16–24.

Foster, M. (1994). The role of community and culture in school reform efforts: Examining the views of African-American teachers. *Educational Foundations, 8*(2), 5–26.

Foster, M. (1995). African American teachers and culturally relevant pedagogy. In J. A. Banks & C. A. Banks (Eds.), *Handbook of research on multicultural education.* New York: Macmillan.

Foster, M. (1997). *Black teachers on teaching*. New York: The New Press.

Freedman, S., Jackson, J., & Boles, K. (1983). Teaching: An imperilled profession. In L. S. Shulman & G. Sykes (Eds.), *Handbook of teaching and policy* (pp. 261–299). New York: Longman.

Freire, P. (1993). *Pedagogy of the city*. New York: Criterium.

Fullan, M. (1982). *The meaning of educational change*. New York: Teachers' College Press.

Giroux, H. A. (1983). *Theories of reproduction and resistance in the new sociology of education: A critical analysis*. South Hadley, MA: Bergin and Garvey.

Giroux, H. A. (1985). Teachers as transformative intellectuals. *Social Education*, 49(5), 376–379.

Giroux, H. A. (1988). *Schooling and the struggle for public life*. Minneapolis: University of Minnesota Press.

Glaser, B. G., & Strauss, A. L. (1967). *The discovery of grounded theory: Strategies for qualitative research*. Chicago: Aldine.

Goodenough, W. (1971). *Culture, language and society: An Addison-Wesley module in anthropology* (vol. 7). Reading, MA: Addison-Wesley.

Goodlad, J. I. (1984). *A place called school: Prospects for the future*. New York: McGraw-Hill.

Grant, L. (1984). Black females "place" in desegregated classrooms. *Sociology of Education*, 57, 98–111.

Grant, L. (1985). *Uneasy alliances: Black males, teachers, and peers in desegregated classrooms*. Paper prepared for the Annual Meeting of the American Educational Research Association, Chicago, IL.

Gramsci, A. (1971). *Selections from the prison notebooks*. New York: International Publishers.

Gusfield, J. R. (1986). *Symbolic crusade* (2nd ed). Urbana: University of Illinois Press.

Gutstein, E., Lipman, P., & Hernandez, P. (1997). Culturally relevant mathematics teaching in a Mexican-American context. *Journal for Research in Mathematics Education*, 28, 710–738.

Hammersley, M., & Atkinson, P. (1983). *Ethnography: Principles in practice*. London: Tavistock.

Harding, V. (1990). Gifts of the black movement: Toward "A new birth of freedom." *Journal of Education*, 172(2), 28–44.

Hargreaves, A. (1991). Contrived collegiality: The micropolitics of teacher collaboration. In J. Blase (Ed.), *The politics of life in schools: Power, conflicts, and cooperation* (pp. 46–72). Newbury Park, CA: Sage.

Haymes, S. N. (1995). *Race, culture and the city: A pedagogy for black urban struggle.* Albany: SUNY Press.

Haynes, N. M., & Comer, J. P. (1990). Helping black children succeed: The significance of some social factors. In K. Lomotey (Ed.), *Going to school: The African-American experience* (pp. 103–112). Albany: SUNY Press.

Heath, S. B. (1983). *Ways with words: Language, life, and work in communities and classrooms.* Cambridge UK: Cambridge University Press.

Henderson, A. (1987). *The evidence contiues to grow: Parent involvement improves student achievement.* Columbia, MD: National Committee for Citizens in Education.

Henry, A. (1992). African Canadian women teachers' activism: Recreating communities of caring and resistance. *Journal of Negro Education, 62,* 392–404.

Hill Collins, P. (1991). *Black feminist thought: Knowledge, consciousness, and the politics of empowerment.* New York: Routledge & Kegan Paul.

Hollins, E. R., & Spencer, K. (1990). Restructuring schools for cultural inclusion: Changing the schooling process for African American youngsters. *Journal of Education, 172*(2), 89–100.

The Holmes Group. (1986). *Tomorrow's teachers: A report of the Holmes Group.* East Lansing, MI: Author. (ED 270 454)

hooks, b. (1994). *Teaching to transgress: Education as the practice of freedom.* New York: Routledge.

hooks, b. (1989). *Talking back: Talking feminist, talking black.* Boston: South End Press.

Hopfenberg, W. S. (1991, April). *The accelerated middle school: Moving from concept toward reality.* Paper presented at annual meeting of the American Education Research Association, Chicago, IL.

Irvine, J. J. (1991). *Black students and school failure: Policies, practices, and prescriptions.* New York: Praeger.

Jaynes, G. D., and Williams, R. M., Jr. (1989). *A common destiny: Blacks and American society.* Washington, DC: National Academy Press.

Joint Center for Political Studies. (1989). *Visions of a better way: A Black appraisal of public schooling.* Washington, DC: Author.

Karrier, C. (1972). Testing for order and control in the corporate state. *Educational Theory, 22,* 159–180.

Keddie, N. (1971). Classroom knowledge. In M. F. D. Young (Ed.), *Knowledge and control* (pp. 286–316). London: Collier-Macmillan.

King, J. E. (1991). Unfinished business: Black student alienation and Black teachers' emancipatory pedagogy. In M. Foster (Ed.), *Readings in equal education: Qualitative investigations into schools and schooling,* (vol. 11, pp. 245–271). New York: AMS Press.

King, J. E. (1992). Dysconscious racism: Ideology, identity, and the miseducation of teachers. *Journal of Negro Education, 60,* 133–146.

King, J. E., & Mitchell, C. A. (1990). *Black mothers to sons: Juxtaposing African American literature with social practice.* New York: Peter Lang.

King, J. E., & Wilson, T. L. (1990). Being the soul-freeing substance: A legacy of hope in Afro Humanity. *Journal of Education, 172*(2), 9–27.

Kohl, H. (1996/97). Tender warriors: The dilemma of "inherent" inequality and the personal toll of integration. *Rethinking Schools, 11*(2), 22–23.

Kohl, H. (1994). *I won't learn from you: And other thoughts on creative maladjustment.* New York: New Press.

Kozol, J. (1991). *Savage inequalities.* New York: Basic Books.

Ladson-Billings, G. (1990a). Culturally relevant teaching: Effective instruction for Black students. *The College Board Review,155,* 20–25.

Ladson-Billings, G. (1990b). Like lightening in a bottle: Attempting to capture the pedagogical excellence of successful teachers of Black students. *Qualitative Studies in Education, 3,* 335–344.

Ladson-Billings, G. (1991). Returning to the source: Implications for educating teachers of Black students. In M. Foster (Ed.), *Readings in equal education: Qualitative investigations into schools and schooling* (vol. 11, pp. 227–243). New York: AMS Press.

Ladson-Billings, G. (1992a). Liberatory consequences of literacy: A case of culturally relevant instruction for African American students. *Journal of Negro Education, 62,* 378–391.

Ladson-Billings, G. (1992b). Reading between the lines and beyond the pages: A culturally relevant approach to literacy teaching. *Theory Into Practice, 31,* 312–320.

Ladson-Billings, G. (1994). *Dreamkeepers: Successful teachers of African American children.* San Francisco: Jossey-Bass.

Ladson-Billings, G. (1995). Toward a theory of culturally relevant pedagogy. *American Educational Research Journal, 32*, 465–491.

Ladson-Billings, G., & Henry, A. (1990). Blurring the borders: Voices of African liberatory pedagogy in the United States and Canada. *Journal of Education, 172*(2), 72–88.

Ladson-Billings, G., & Tate, W. F. (1995). Toward a critical race theory of education. *Teachers College Record, 97*(1), 47–68.

Lareau, A. (1989). *Home advantage: Social class and parental intervention in elementary education.* London: Falmer Press.

Lee, C. D., Lomotey, K., & Shujaa, M. (1990). How shall we sing our sacred song in a strange land? The dilemma of double consciousness and the complexities of an African-centered pedagogy. *Journal of Education, 172*(2), 45–61.

Lee, V. E., & Smith, J. B. (1992). *Effects of school restructuring on the achievement and engagement of middle grade students.* Unpublished paper. University of Michigan.

Levin, H. (1988). *Accelerated schools for at-risk students.* New Brunswick, NJ: Rutgers University, Center for Policy Research in Education.

Levine, D. U., & Eubanks, E. E. (1986). The promise and limits of regional desegregation plans for central city school districts. *Metropolitan Education, 1* (1), 36–51.

Lieberman, A., Darling-Hammond, L., & Zuckerman, D. (1991). *Early lessons in restructuring schools.* New York: National Center for Restructuring, Education, Schools, and Teaching.

Lieberman, A., & Miller, L. (1990). Restructuring schools: What matters and what works. *Phi Delta Kappan, 71*, 759–764.

Lieberman, A., Saxl, E. R., & Miles, M. B. (1988). In A. Lieberman (Ed.), *Building a professional culture in schools* (pp. 148–166). New York: Teachers College Press.

Lightfoot, S. (1978). *Worlds apart: Relationships between families and schools.* New York: Basic Books.

Lipman, P. (1995). Bringing out the best in them: The contribution of culturally relevant teachers to educational reform. *Theory Into Practice, 34* (3), 202–208.

Lipman, P. (1996). The missing voice of culturally relevant teachers in school restructuring. *Urban Review, 28*(1), 41–62.

Lipman, P. (1997). Restructuring in context: A case study of teacher participation and the dynamics of ideology, race, and power. *American Educational Research Journal, 34*(1) 3–37.

Lipsitz, J. (1984). *Successful schools for young adolescents*. New Brunswick, NJ: Transaction Books.

MacLeod, J. (1991). Bridging street and school. *Journal of Negro Education, 60*(3), 260–275.

MacLeod, J. (1995). *Aint no makin' it* (2nd. ed). Boulder: Westview Press.

Majors, R., & Billson, J. (1992). *Cool pose: The dilemma of Black manhood in America*. New York: Lexington Books.

Marburger, C. L. (1985). *One school at a time: School based management a process for change*. Columbia, MD: National Committee for Citizens in Education.

Massachusetts Advocacy Center. (1988). *Before it's too late: Dropout prevention in the middle grades*. Boston: Author.

McCarthy, C. (1995). The problems with origins: Race and the contrapuntal nature of the educational experience. In C. E. Sleeter & P. L. McLaren (Eds.), *Multicultural education, critical pedagogy, and the politics of difference* (pp. 245–268). Albany: SUNY Press.

McCarthy, C. (1993). After the canon: Knowledge and ideological representation in the multicultural discourse on curriculum reform. In C. McCarthy & W. Crichlow (Eds). *Race, identity, and representation in education* (pp. 289–305). New York: Routledge.

McDermott, R. P. (1974). Achieving school failure: In G. Spindler (Ed.), *Education and cultural process: Toward an anthropology of education* (pp. 82–118). New York: Holt, Rinehart & Winston.

McDermott, R. P., & Gospodinoff, K. (1979). Social contexts for ethnic borders and school failures. In A. Wolfgang (Ed.), *Nonverbal behavior* (pp. 175–195). New York: Academic Press.

McLaren, P. (1989). *Life in schools: An introduction to critical pedagogy in the foundations of education*. New York; Longman.

McNeil, L. (1986). *Contradictions of control: School structure and school knowledge*. New York: Routledge & Kegan Paul.

Mehan, H., Hertweck, A., & Meihls, J. L. (1986). *Handicapping the handicapped: Decision making in students' educational careers*. Stanford, CA: Stanford University Press.

Metz, M. H. (1978). *Classrooms and corridors: The crisis of authority in desegregated secondary schools*. Berkeley: University of California Press.

Metz, M. H. (1983). What can be learned from educational ethnography? *Urban Education, 17*, 391–418.

Metz, M. H. (1986). *Different by design: The context and character of three magnet schools.* New York: Routledge & Kegan Paul.

Metz, M. H. (1990). Real school: A universal drama amid disparate experience. In D. Mitchell & M. Goertz (Eds.), *Education politics for the new century: The twentieth anniversary yearbook of the Politics of Education Association* (pp. 75–91). New York: Falmer Press.

Michaels, S. (1981). Sharing time: Children's narrative styles and differential access to literacy. *Language Socialization, 10,* 423–442.

Moore, D. R., & Davenport, S. (1989). Cheated again: School choice and students at risk. *The School Administrator,* 46(7), 12–15.

Muncey, D. E., & McQuillan, P. J. (1992). The dangers of assuming a consensus for change: Some examples from the Coalition of Essential Schools. In G. A. Hess Jr. (Ed.), *Empowering teachers and parents: School restructuring through the eyes of anthropologists* (pp. 47–69). Westport, CT: Bergin & Garvey.

Muncey, D. E., & McQuillan, P. J (1996). *Reform and resistance in schools and classrooms.* New Haven: Yale University Press.

Murphy, J., & Hallinger, (1993). *Restructuring schooling: Learning from ongoing efforts.* Newbury Park, CA: Corwin Press.

Murrell, P. (1991). Cultural politics in teacher education: What's missing in the preparation of minority teachers? In M. Foster (Ed.), *Readings in equal education: Qualitative investigations into schools and schooling* (vol. 11, pp. 205–226). New York: AMS Press.

National Center for Children in Poverty. (1992). *Child Poverty News & Issues* [On-line], 2 (3). Available: CPMnet.

National Center for Fair and Open Testing. (1986–1997). *Fair Test Examiner* (vols. 1–6). Cambridge, MA: Author

National Commission on Excellence in Education. (1983). *A nation at risk: The imperative for educational reform.* Washington, DC: U.S. Government Printing Office.

National Committee for Citizens in Education. (1988). *School based improvement and effective schools: A perfect match for bottom-up reform.* Columbia, MD: Author.

Newmann, F. M. (1990). *Proposal for center on organization and restructuring of schools.* Madison, WI: University of Wisconsin–Madison, Wisconsin Center for Educational Research.

Newmann, F. M. (1991). What is a "restructured" school? A framework to clarify means and ends. *Issues in Restructuring Schools (Issue Report No. 1).*

Madison, WI: University of Wisconsin–Madison, National Center on Organization and Restructuring of Schools.

Newmann, F. M., & Wehlage, G. G. (1995). *Successful school restructuring. A report to the public by the Center on Organization and Restructuring of Schools.* Madison, WI: University of Wisconsin, Board of Regents.

Oakes, J. (1985). *Keeping track: How schools structure inequality.* New Haven, CT: Yale University Press.

Ogbu, J. U. (1974). *The next generation.* New York: Academic Press.

Ogbu, J. U. (1978). *Minority education and caste: The American system in cross-cultural perspective.* New York: Academic Press.

Orfield, G. (1978). *Must we bus?* Washington, DC: Brookings Institute.

Page, R. J. (1991). *Lower track classrooms.* New York: Teachers College Press.

Perry, T., & Fraser, J. W. (1993). Reconstructing schools as multiracial/multicultural democracies: Toward a theoretical perspective. In T. Perry & J. W. Fraser (Eds.), *Freedom's plow: Teaching in the multicultural classroom.* New York: Routledge.

Peshkin, A. (1985).Virtuous subjectivity: In the participant-observer's I's. In D. N. Berg & K. K. Smith (Eds.), *Exploring clinical methods for social research* (pp. 267–281). Newbury Park, CA: Sage.

Peters, T. J., & Waterman, R. H. (1982). *In search of excellence.* New York: Harper & Row.

Popkewitz, T. S., Tabachnick, B. R., & Wehlage, G. (1982). *The myth of educational reform.* Madison: University of Wisconsin Press.

Project Data (1989, 1990, 1991). Unpublished data.

Project Documents (1988–1991). Documents of the Riverton School District and Restructuring Project. Unpublished raw data.

Quality Education for Minorities Project. (1990). *Education that works: An action plan for the education of minorities.* Cambridge, MA: Author, Massachusetts Institute of Technology.

Quinn, N., & Holland, D. (n.d.). *Culture and cognition.* Unpublished manuscript.

Ratzki, A., & Fisher, A. (1989/90). Life in a restructured school. *Educational Leadership, 47*(4), 46–51.

Reich, R. (1987). *Tales of a new America.* New York: Vintage.

Rist, R. (1970). Student social class and teacher expectations: The self-fulfilling prophesy in ghetto education. *Harvard Educational Review, 40,* 411–451.

Robinson, S. P. (1996). With numeracy for all: Uban schools and the reform of mathematics education. *Urban Education, 30,* 379–394.

Rosenholtz, S. J. (1989). *Teachers' workplace: The social organization of schools.* New York: Longman.

Rossell, C. H. (1979). Magnet schools as a desegregation tool. *Urban Education,* 14(3), 303–320.

Rubin, L. B. (1994). *Families on the fault line.* New York: HarperCollins.

Sarason, S. B. (1982). *The culture of the school and the problem of change* (2nd ed). Boston: Allyn and Bacon.

Scherer J., & Slawski, E. J. (1979). Color, class, and social control in an urban desegregated school. In R. C. Rist (Ed.), *Desegregated schools* (pp. 15–64). New York: Academic Press.

Schlechty, P. C. (1990). *Schools for the 21st century: Leadership imperatives for educational reform.* San Francisco: Jossey-Bass.

Schlechty, P. C., Ingwerson, D. W. & Brooks, T. I. (1988). Inventing professional development schools. *Educational Leadership,* 46(3), 28–31.

Schofield, J. W. (1982). *Black and white in schools: Trust, tension, or tolerance?* New York: Praeger.

Schofield, J. W. (1990). Increasing the generalizability of qualitative research. In E. W. Eisner & A. Peshkin (Eds.), *Qualitative inquiry in education: The continuing debate.* New York: Teachers College Press.

Schwartz, F. (1981). Supporting or subverting learning: Peer group patterns in four tracked schools. *Anthropology and Education Quarterly, 12,* 99–120.

Sharp, R., & Green, A. (1975). *Education and social control.* London and Boston: Routledge and Kegan Paul.

Shepard, L. A., & Smith, M. L. (Eds.). (1989). *Flunking grades: Research and policies on retention.* London: Falmer Press.

Shujaa, M. J. (1992, Summer). What teachers think they are doing when they think they are teaching African/African American curriculum content: Some observations. *Graduate School of Education Newsletter* (State University of New York at Buffalo).

Shulman, L. (1987). Knowledge and teaching: Foundations of the new reform. *Harvard Educational Review, 57,* 1–22.

Siddle Walker, E. V. (1996). *Their highest potential.* Chapel Hill: University of North Carolina Press.

Siddle Walker, E. V. (1993). Caswell County Training School, 1933–1969: Relationships between community and school. *Harvard Educational Review, 63,* 161–182.

Sirotnik, K. A. (1987). *The school as the center of change* (Occasional Paper No. 5). Seattle: University of Washington, Center for Educational Renewal.

Sizer, T. R. (1984). *Horace's compromise: The dilemma of the American High School.* Boston: Houghton Mifflin.

Sleeter, C. E. (1991). *Empowerment through multicultural education.* Albany: SUNY Press.

Smith, M. S., & O'Day, J. (1990). Systemic school reform. In S. H. Fuhrman & B. Malen (Eds.), *The politics of curriculum and testing: The 1990 yearbook of the Politics of Education Association* (pp. 233–267). London: Falmer Press.

Spradley, J. (1979). *The ethnographic interview.* New York: Holt, Rinehart & Winston.

Spring, J. (1994). *Deculturalization and the struggle for equality.* New York: McGraw-Hill.

Stack, C. (1974). *All our kin: Strategies for survival in a Black community.* New York: Harper & Row.

Strauss, C. (1986). *The indirect force of American cultural models of achievement and success.* Paper presented at the annual meeting of the American Anthropology Association, Philadelphia.

Takaki, R. (1993). *A different mirror: A history of multicultural Aemrica.* Boston: Little, Brown.

Task Force on Teaching as a Profession. (1986). *A nation prepared: Teachers for the 21st century.* New York: Carnegie Forum on Education and the Economy.

Tate, W. F., Ladson-Billings, G., & Grant, C. (1996). The Brown decision revisited: Mathematizing a soical problem. In M. Shujaa (Ed.), *Beyond desegregation:The politics of quality and African American schooling* (pp. 29–50). Thousand Oaks, CA: Corwin Press.

Tatum, B. D. (1992). Talking about race, learning about racism: The application of racial identity development theory in the classroom. *Harvard Educational Review, 62,* 1–24.

Therborn, G. (1980). *The ideology of power and the power of ideology.* London: Verso.

Trueba, H. T. (1989). Culture and literacy for minority student empowerment. In H. T. Trueba, G. Spindler, & L. Spindler (Eds.). *What do anthropologists have to say about dropouts?* (pp. 27–42). New York: Falmer Press.

U. S. Department of Education National Center for Educational Statistics. (1996). *The condition of education, 1996* (NCES 96-304). Washington, DC: Author.

Valdés, G. (1996). *Con respeto: Bridging the distances between culturally diverse families and schools.* New York: Teachers College Press.

Vanfossen, B., Jones, J., & Spade, J. (1987). Curriculum tracking and status maintenance. *Sociology of Education, 60,* 104–122.

Villegas, A. M. (1988). School failure and cultural mismatch: Another view. *The Urban Review, 20,* 253–265.

Wallis, J. (1994). *The soul of politics.* New York: The New Press.

Wasley, P. A. (1991). Stirring the chalkdust: Changing practices in essential schools. *Teachers College Record, 93,* 28–58.

Wehlage, G., Rutter, R. A., Smith, G. A., Lesko, N., & Fernandez, R. R. (1989). *Reducing the risk: Schools as communities of support.* London: Falmer Press.

Wehlage, G., & Rutter, R. A. (1986). Dropping out: How much do schools contribute to the problem? *Teachers College Record, 87,* 374–392.

Wehlage, G., Smith, G., & Lipman, P. (1992). Restructuring urban schools:The New Futures experience. *American Educational Research Journal, 29,* 51–93.

Weiler, K. (1988). *Women teaching for change: Gender, class & power.* New York: Bergin & Garvey.

West, C. (1993). *Race matters.* Boston: Beacon Press.

Wheelock, A. E. (1992). *Crossing the tracks: How untracking can save America's schools.* New York: The New Press.

Wilcox, K. (1982). Differential socialization in the classroom: Implications for equal opportunity. In G. Spindler (Ed.), *Doing the ethnography of schooling* (pp. 268–309). New York: Holt, Rinehart.

Wilson, W. J. (1987). *The truly disadvantaged: The inner city, the underclass, and public policy.* Chicago: University of Chicago Press.

Winfield, L. (1991). Resilience, schooling, and development in African-American youth. *Education and Urban Society, 24*(1).

Wolf, E. N. (1995). *Top heavy: A study of the increasing inequality of wealth in America.* New York: Twentieth Century Fund Press.

Zeichner, K. (1992). *Educating teachers for cultural diversity.* East Lansing: Michigan State University, National Center for Research on Teaching and Learning.

INDEX